CALIFORNIA 1850

⌇ A SNAPSHOT IN TIME ⌇

Janice Marschner

Library of Congress
Catalog Card Number:
99-98054

ISBN 0-9677069-3-9

First publication: February 2000
Copyright ©2000 by Coleman Ranch Press, Sacramento, CA
All rights reserved. Manufactured in the U.S.A.

Cover and text design & layout by Ghedeon Bere.

Quantity sales: For information on bulk purchases, corporate premium sales, academic sales
or textbook adoptions, contact: Special Programs, 1-877-7OLDCAL, Coleman Ranch Press,
P.O. Box 1496, Sacramento, CA 95812-1496 or www.CAL1850.com

CONTENTS

PREFACE

1850

Attempting to write a book of less than 300 pages about the history of the entire state of California—even if only one year of that history—was a challenge. My initial interest in the early history of California had started when I visited the Empire Mine State Historic Park in Grass Valley in 1995. Knowing that California would be commemorating its sesquicentennial of admission to the Union of the United States in the year 2000, it occurred to me that others interested in California history might enjoy having one concise, easy-to-read book that would give them a snapshot view of what California was like in 1850, two short years after the discovery of gold in Coloma in 1848.

The California Gold Discovery to Statehood Sesquicentennial Commission had recently been established by then-Governor Pete Wilson to plan for the three-year commemoration scheduled for January 24, 1998 through September 9, 2000. In line with one of the Commission's mission objectives, my desire was to "promote an appreciation of California and a greater understanding of its history." Unfortunately, California political skirmishes led to the abolishment of the Commission in 1999, but other state entities, as well as local historical organizations and chambers of commerce have continued with many of the original plans. My personal passion for providing a snapshot of California in 1850 continued unabated.

Historians will not find any new historical discoveries in this book. I combed through hundreds of books in the California History Room of the California State Library in Sacramento, the Sacramento Room of the Sacramento Public Library, and numerous local libraries throughout the state. I acquired recently published history books on individual counties and collected pamphlets available at historic sites. And, of course, I used the newest source of historical research—the Internet. My research often produced conflicting dates and facts; in those instances I always tried to locate additional sources and then used my own intuition as to which source appeared to be the most credible. The well-known *Historical Spots in California* by Mildred Brooke Hoover, Hero Eugene Rensch, Ethel Grace Rensch, and William N. Abeloe provided a useful roadmap for charting my course through each county's history. The *Historical Atlas of California* by Warren A. Beck and Ynez D. Haase was an invaluable resource I used throughout the project to identify the hundreds of land grants and the original county boundaries.

I also wanted to provide useful information for the reader desiring to visit existing 1850 historical sites in California. Therefore, a list of destinations where historical sites or museums relevant to the year 1850 may be visited is provided for each county. (A few counties have no 1850 sites to visit, either because no development had taken place by 1850 or because time, development, or natural disasters such as fire and earthquakes have obliterated them.) Entrance fees and days and hours of operation often change, so telephone numbers are provided to allow readers to obtain current information on their own. Most historical museums are free, but they do appreciate small donations, so always carry a few dollars with you. Also be sure to thank the museum personnel (many are volunteers) for the time they devote to making history come alive for their visitors. I am grateful for their assistance to me.

Over one thousand California State Historical Landmarks have been placed throughout the state, many of them for pre-1851 historical sites. I have chosen to note only two plaques not attached to existing structures. In general, I think it is preferable to just happen upon the landmarks in your travels rather than agonizing over searching for them. But if you wish to seek them out, the California State Parks Office of Historic Preservation has published the book *California Historical Landmarks*, which is available in most bookstores and libraries. (Several Internet sites list California's historical landmarks, as well.)

Between 1823 and 1846, more than 500 land grants were awarded to soldiers, friends, or relatives of the various Hispanic governors who ruled Alta California. It would have been too tedious and lengthy to provide narrative descriptions of all of the ranchos, but the names, owners, and general locations are provided in chart form. I hope the information provokes thoughtful consideration of California's Hispanic heritage–before the Euro-Americans became dominant. Narrative descriptions are provided of some of the more interesting ranchos.

Sidebars containing biographical sketches of some of the most influential and/or interesting 1850 Californians are featured throughout the book.

Finally, more than three hundred footnotes provide valuable information about people, places, or events not directly related to the year 1850. The footnotes appear at the end of each chapter. (These footnotes constitute a collection of some of the most interesting material discovered in my research. Enjoy them!)

It is my hope that *California 1850, A Snapshot in Time* will make a positive contribution to the commemoration of California's sesquicentennial in the year 2000 by enlisting new converts to the study and appreciation of California history. An enhanced understanding of California history can only improve the way Californians interact with one another in the midst of the most complex and culturally diverse population in the world.

Special appreciation is conveyed to all of the writers of local history books who have preserved the information that was a critical component of my research.

Hopefully what I have presented in this book will encourage those interested in exploring the history of their own county in more detail to seek out such books in their local bookstores and libraries.

Grateful acknowledgment of family members and several friends also is due. Gil Campbell drew the maps, which bring clarity to the printed word by delineating the 27 counties created in 1850, and outlining the present-day county lines of the 31 additional counties created between 1851 and 1907. Gil generously shared his time and talent.

To Jeff and Julie Marschner, my husband and daughter, go my eternal gratitude for the countless hours they expended formatting the maps and marking the place names. Jeff also edited the text, did most of the photography, and managed the production portion of the project. His patience with me throughout the final months of writing deserves a special measure of my gratitude.

Another faithful and meticulous editor was Jeff Boese–thank you very much. I also am grateful for the encouraging words from friends like Quentin Kopp, Julie Wright, Liz Magill, Michael Bastine, and Pat Macias-Najar and her parents. Those words always seemed to come when I needed them the most. And thank you to E. Jesus Arredondo for your assistance with the translations of the rancho names, Jennifer Thompson for taking the photograph I needed at the last minute, and Alice Seamans, for your wise advice to hire a professional to do all of the book design work. The professional selected, Ghedeon Bere, contributed immensely to the final presentation of this book through his cover design and text layout.

Janice Marschner
Sacramento, California
February 2000

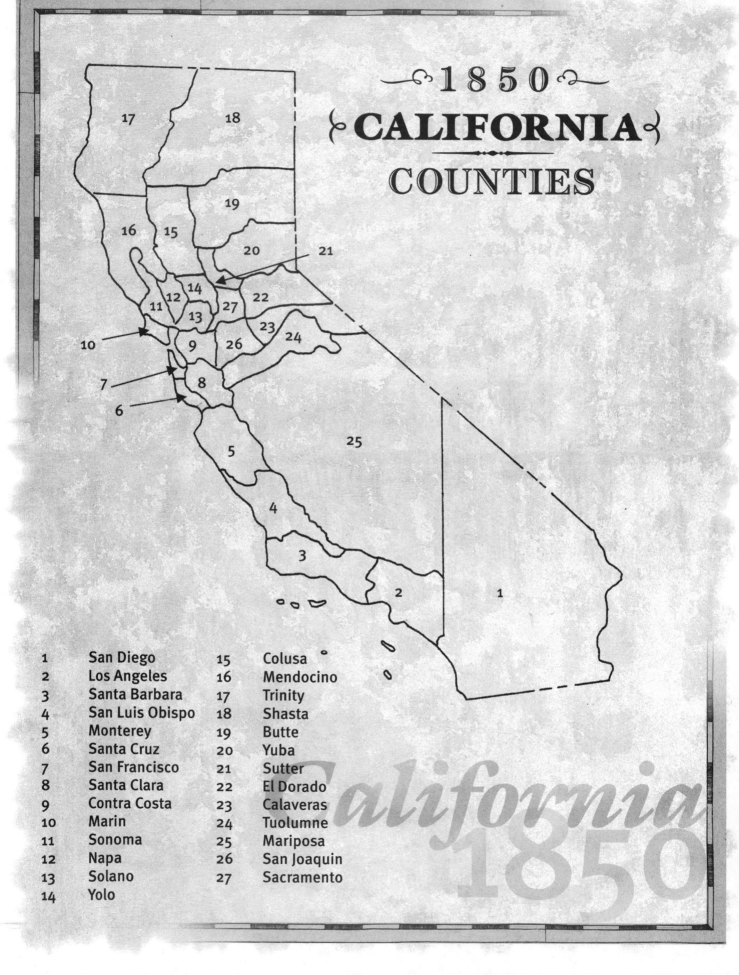

ᵜ1850ᵜ
ᵜCALIFORNIAᵜ
COUNTIES

1	San Diego	15	Colusa
2	Los Angeles	16	Mendocino
3	Santa Barbara	17	Trinity
4	San Luis Obispo	18	Shasta
5	Monterey	19	Butte
6	Santa Cruz	20	Yuba
7	San Francisco	21	Sutter
8	Santa Clara	22	El Dorado
9	Contra Costa	23	Calaveras
10	Marin	24	Tuolumne
11	Sonoma	25	Mariposa
12	Napa	26	San Joaquin
13	Solano	27	Sacramento
14	Yolo		

INTRODUCTION 1850

WHY THE 1850 SNAPSHOT IN TIME?

In 1850 California was in the midst of social, environmental, and economic change unparalleled in world history—before or since. For many years, geographic barriers had isolated California from much of the western world. Once its many attributes were discovered by early pioneers and later gold-seekers, the United States soon recognized the political and economic value of this unique area located between desert wastelands and the Pacific Ocean.

There had been a short initial settlement period of 79 years under the Spanish-Mexican mission and rancho systems before the U.S. acquired California in 1848, but the rapidly growing population and new found wealth, both products of the Gold Rush, brought California to statehood without undergoing the customary territorial process.[1] By some estimates, at least in the San Francisco Bay Area, Sacramento, and parts of the Gold Country, fifty years of normal growth were compressed into less than six months. On September 9, 1850, California became the 31st state of the Union, less than three years after gold was discovered and only 24 years after the first American arrived by land in search of furs.

California's American Indian and Spanish heritage is ever present today in the names of its cities, streets, parks, shopping centers, industrial complexes, sub-divisions, and natural geography, but it was the tidal wave of American and foreign immigration following the discovery of gold in January 1848 and the infusion of new ideas and spirit that created the unique mosaic that is California today. As California commemorates its sesquicentennial—150 years of statehood—and moves into a new era of changing ethnic and racial balance, it is critical that the past—both the good and the bad—be understood so that California can confront the challenges and benefit from the opportunities presented by the diversity that has been its hallmark and is a certain part of its future.

PRE-1850 CALIFORNIA HISTORY

TIMELINE

8000 B.C.	First American Indians—Pomos in Clear Lake area—inhabit California
1542	Juan Cabrillo discovers Cape Mendocino
1602	Sebastián Vizcaino charts California coast
1769	Expeditions set out from New Spain to colonize Alta California

1812	Russians establish Fort Ross
1821	Mexico gains independence from Spain
1823	First Mexican land grant made
1826	Jedediah Strong Smith becomes the first American to arrive in California by land
1839	John A. Sutter arrives in California
1842	First discovery of gold in California east of Newhall in Los Angeles County
1845	Doctrine of "Manifest Destiny"
1846	U.S. declares war on Mexico in May; Bear Flag Revolt in June; American flag raised at Monterey and Yerba Buena in July; Battle of San Pasqual in December
1847	Capitulation treaty to end the fighting in California was signed at Campo de Cahuenga in Los Angeles in January
1848	Gold is discovered by James Marshall at Sutter's Mill in Coloma in January; Treaty of Guadalupe Hidalgo ends war with Mexico in February; word of Marshall's discovery reaches U.S. in June; *New York Herald* publishes news world-wide in August; President Polk's message to Congress confirms reports of discovery
1849	First steamer arrives in San Francisco in February; hundreds of wagons leave Missouri in April; State Constitution drafted in Monterey in October and approved by voters in November
1850	California admitted to the Union as 31st state on September 9th

Native Americans

California's earliest social and cultural history consists of the chronicles of its diverse Native American population. California Indian history is not the subject of this book, but a brief overview is essential to understanding California history. When the first Europeans arrived in California in the 16th century, between 100,000 and 300,000 American Indians were residing in *rancherias* (villages). More than 100 tribes speaking more than 80 languages and maintaining diverse lifestyles were living in relative peace in every part of California except the inhospitable climes of the High Sierra. After the conquest of the Native Americans' lands by the Spanish, with no acknowledgment or consideration of their rights, thousands died of imported diseases and others subsequently were exterminated during regional wars and vigilante movements. By the middle of the 19th century, the California Indian population had dwindled to less than 50,000.

The Native Americans' experiences during the Spanish and Mexican periods of California history are described in those sections of this introduction. Following the discovery of gold in 1848 and the sudden, massive invasion of foreigners, the Native Americans were overwhelmed and perplexed by the culture, economic ambitions, and values of these newcomers. In the early days of the Gold Rush, the natives tried to be accepting, agreeing to work for the miners and later, for settlers who established farms. But the invasion of their property, decimation of their natural sources of food, and the climate of persecution and terror that developed, prompted California's Native Americans to either relocate to less desirable areas or react with violence against the new settlers. Following numerous regional Indian wars, the federal government established treaties with the Native Americans who "agreed" to give up their claims to California land in return for eight and one-half million acres of reservation land and such things as food, clothing, tools, and schools. In the 1850s land was set aside for these reservations; the federal government was to have control of this land, its sale, and its use.

Spanish Period

Alta California (Upper California) had been the site of numerous Spanish exploration expeditions since the 16th century, when the strongest military and naval power of Western Europe was seeking to expand its holdings and find new sources of gold. These explorers included Juan Rodriguez Cabrillo, Hernando de Alarcón, Sebastian Vizcaíno, Gaspar de Portolá, Pedro Fages, Juan Bautista de Anza, and Fathers Juan Crespí and Francisco Garcés.[2] Spain remained unchallenged in her claim to the Pacific Coast of North America until the middle of the 18th century when Britain, France, and Russia began seeking a territorial presence in North America. In order to protect their title to Alta California, the Spanish began overland exploration and occupation in 1769.[3]

Three institutions were typically established to achieve Spain's goals of colonization—missions, presidios, and pueblos. *Misións* (missions) were designed to be an inexpensive way to establish outposts that would transform the Native Americans into productive Christian citizens of the Spanish Empire. The mission system had been used in other Spanish territories, including Mexico and Baja (Lower) California. The Franciscans, under the leadership of Father Junipero Serra, established a chain of 21 missions along the coast of Alta California usually within a day's travel of each other. The missions were sited strategically, based on three factors: close to a sizeable population of Native Americans, close to a source of fresh water and fertile land for crops and grazing, and close enough to the ocean to receive and ship goods and materials. The missions eventually stretched from San Diego to Sonoma, and were established between 1769 and 1823.

The original intent of the mission system was to have the priests Christianize and educate the Native Americans for a period of ten years, and then turn the mission and all of its improvements over to the self-governing natives as Spanish subjects. The 21 missions were successful in working towards this goal for a time, but eventually their native populations were decimated by foreign diseases from which they had no immunity and by the ultimate failure of transition from a hunter-digger culture to the mission agrarian system.

In addition, Mexico won independence from Spain in 1822 and the new Mexican Constitution emancipated the mission Indians, allowing them to leave the missions, which many of them did. The new government had many compelling challenges, and dealing with the mission outposts that were failing to meet their original goals was a low priority. The Mexican government soon passed the Secularization Act of 1833, which converted the missions into ordinary parish churches, released the Native Americans from complete supervision by the friars, and opened up the vast mission territory to individual ownership. Under the Act, the mission properties were to be transferred primarily to the mission Indians, but a change in the administration following the death of Governor Figueroa in 1835 resulted in the mission properties instead being parceled out to soldiers in lieu of wages and also to Mexican citizens in return for political favors. The Native Americans who remained were assimilated into the local society as an underclass of laborers, household servants, and *vaqueros*

California Missions

Basilica San Diego de Alcalá (1769)

San Carlos Borroméo Del Rio Carmelo (1770)

San Antonio de Padua (1771)

San Gabriel Arcángel (1771)

San Luís Obispo de Tolosa (1772)

San Francisco de Asís (Dolores) (1776)

San Juan Capistrano (1776)

Santa Clara de Asís (1777)

San Buenaventura (1782)

Santa Barbara (1786)

La Purísima Concepción (1787)

La Exaltación de la Santa Cruz (1791)

Nuestra Señora Dolorosíma de la Soledad (1791)

San José (1797)

San Juan Bautista (1797)

San Miguel Arcángel (1797)

San Fernando Rey de España (1797)

San Luís Rey de Francia (1798)

Santa Inés (1802)

San Rafael Arcángel (1817)

San Francisco Solano (1823)

(cowboys). Many lived in clusters of huts built near the main adobes of the *rancheros* (ranchers), while others lived in nearby *rancherias*. The Native Americans were completely subservient to the *rancheros*, but generally were well-treated. The mission structures began to fall into ruin due to neglect and the pilfering of building materials by nearby homebuilders, so the Mexican government decided to sell the missions to prevent their total ruin and pay some of the missions' debts.[4]

The *presidio* (fort) system was the second institution of Spanish colonization. Presidios were military posts established to provide coastal defense from foreign invasion and to provide protection and support for the missions and towns. Four presidios were established by the end of the 18th century at San Diego, Santa Barbara, Monterey, and San Francisco. By the end of the Spanish/Mexican period in 1848, the presidios were in ruins due to disuse and the theft of building materials.

Finally, *pueblos* (towns) were secular settlements composed largely of families recruited in Baja California to settle in Alta California. Several incentives were offered settlers willing to relocate, including house lots (*solares*) situated around a plaza, farm lots (*suertes*) on which to grow crops and raise the pairs of livestock loaned to the heads of the families, necessary farm implements, and a five-year grace period from taxation. In return, the settlers were required to sell their surplus products exclusively to the presidios and to be prepared to engage in military service in the event of invasion. When formal transfer of the land was completed, each settler received title to his land and a branding iron to mark his cattle.

Three pueblos were established, one in San Jose (*San José de Guadalupe*) in 1777, one in Los Angeles (*El Pueblo de Nuestra Señora la Reina de Los Angeles del Rio de Porciúncula*) in 1781, and one in Branciforte (present-day Santa Cruz) (*Pueblo de Branciforte*) in 1797. Other settlements later qualified to become pueblos by virtue of their size, but the same benefits and obligations were not attached to these subsequent designations.

Mexican Period

There never was any real Mexican period of California history, but Mexico did win independence from Spain in 1822. The Spanish-speaking Californians, especially the oldest families such as the Castros, Bandinis, Alvarados, Vallejos, and Sepúlvedas, had continued to regard themselves as Spanish. These families were greatly outnumbered by the Mexican Californians of Spanish descent, as well as the Californians of Spanish and Indian or Spanish, Indian, and African American descent, but they remained at the top of the social hierarchy. Added to the mix of Spaniards and Mexicans were the American, British, Scottish, German, French, and Russian newcomers. Most of these men became citizens of Mexico, joined the Catholic church, and married into the Spanish families. They were then treated as equals by the Spanish hierarchy and took on the language, style, and customs of the bride's family. In some cases, the men even changed their names to Hispanic translations, like Benito (Benjamin Davis) Wilson, Juan (John) Forster, and others.

Over twenty Spanish concessions—essentially grazing permits—had been authorized before the Mexican independence of 1822. Most of the Spanish permits to settle and use specific tracts of land were rewards for military service. After Alta California became part of Mexico and secularization was instituted, more than 500 grants of previously unused land were awarded to soldiers, friends, or relatives of the various governors who ruled California between 1823 and 1846. Reputable Mexican citizens also petitioned for desired land by submitting a *diseño* (rough, simple descriptive map). Since land was so plentiful, the identification of specific boundaries was not important. Many of the Spanish concessions were patented under Mexican laws in 1824, 1828, and 1834, which provided the legal basis for them.

The grants were known as *ranchos*, which specifically meant cattle-raising ranches based upon land grants. Mexican law limited the ranchos to eleven square leagues (nearly 49,000 acres), but many were smaller and a few much larger.

The *ranchero* usually named his holdings for the patron saint of his family or the saint upon whose holy day the grant was made. Sometimes the previous American Indian name for the area was used or a name describing regional characteristics. Today many rancho names have survived as geographic place names.

Technically, the grantees were required to construct and occupy a permanent residence on the land within a year of the grant, but many ranchos were unimproved and used only for grazing. Some of the *rancheros* merely built rustic adobes for their *mayordomos* to occupy. But many other *rancheros* did establish self-sustaining ranchos that provided for nearly all of the needs of their large extended families.

Rancheros also were required to respect the rights of the Native Americans living on the land. Thus, in most cases, the natives were allowed to remain on their *rancherias* or were given a place in the household to live in exchange for their work for the *rancheros*.

The trade in hides and tallow was the major livelihood of the ranchos, especially after Mexican independence. The hides were scraped clean of the clinging meat and fat, then salted and stretched to dry. After drying they were folded once and stacked in bales ready for shipping. The tallow was rendered in large iron kettles and poured into skin pouches that held 25 pounds.[5] There had been no international market for beef because the trading ships had no way to keep beef from spoiling. Therefore, the rancho scavenger dogs, buzzards, bears, and coyotes got fat on the wasted meat left in the fields after the cattle were slaughtered. By 1849, with the arrival of the thousands of gold miners with appetites for red meat, the *rancheros* began shifting their focus to beef cattle. In 1850 most of the cattle were still sold for hides and tallow, but an ever-increasing number were being trail-herded north.

A year after California became a state, the U.S. Congress would establish the U.S. Land Commission to reconfirm the California land grants. This process violated the Treaty of Guadalupe Hidalgo that had been entered into between the U.S. and Mexico at the termination of the Mexican-American War. The treaty had guaranteed the property rights of the Mexican residents in California who had acquired their property prior to July 7, 1846, but the Land Act of 1851 virtually invalidated all titles to land unless the occupants could present proof of ownership. All claimants were required to present their petitions for verification within two years or forfeit their rights.

Unfortunately, the Mexican grants had been conditional, the boundaries were vague and overlapping, and the legal titles were faulty or did not exist. And some land claims were in fact falsified, which cast suspicion on the valid ones. The process of proving title to rancho lands was tedious—taking an average of 17 years, and

Characteristics of a Typical Rancho

More than 100 residents, few of whom could read or write

Don, the highly respected *ranchero*

Doña, wife who managed the household and rancho staff

Children, who rarely received any education beyond religious training; girls usually married in early teen years, with their duties extended to raising 10 or more children; many married Euro-Americans because there were few Hispanic bachelors

Mayordomo, ranch manager

American Indian servants and *vaqueros* (cowboys), who supplied bulk of labor force

Adobe *casas* could not be kept very clean because dust and dirt entered through the open windows and doors; food was prepared outdoors in kitchen areas under verandas; bee-hive-shaped ovens called *hornos* were used

Variety of crops and livestock raised to feed the residents; the hides (50 to 80,000 per year) and tallow were traded for cloth of all types, especially silk, as well as for clothes, dishes, hardware, furniture, chests, lumber, fine foods, and tools, mainly from China. Currency and debt were measured in terms of cow hides ("California banknotes" or "leather dollars") owned or owed

Annual gatherings for branding, counting of livestock, slaughtering, and preparation of hides and by-products of cattle, associated with rodeos and other festivities, especially *fandangos* (dances)

Women and children traveled by *carreta* or ox cart; men rode only their horses—their horses and saddles being their most prized possessions

Rancheros offered boundless friendly hospitality to travelers

(continued next page)

Characteristics of a Typical Rancho (continued)

Leisure activities were a priority

• Gambling—*Dons* gambled[6] day and night and borrowed from Euro-Americans to sustain their elaborate lifestyles, often pledging their vast landholdings as security

• Horse racing, cock-fighting, and bull and bear fighting

• Music, especially guitar, violin, and harp

sometimes went all the way to the U.S. Supreme Court, costing the claimants dearly in lawyers' fees that had to be paid in advance. The *dons* typically lived by credit, awaiting the day that their hides were picked up by a schooner. Consequently, they had to borrow money from the Euro-Americans at high interest rates. Although 75 percent of the cases resulted in the confirmation of grants to the original owners, many *rancheros* were forced to mortgage or sell most of their holdings in an effort to pay the costs of litigation.

The title confirmation process was also harmful to the newly arriving settlers,[7] who were unable to determine which land was private and which land was public and thus available for homesteading. Due to this confusion, many immigrants settled and paid taxes on lands they erroneously thought were public. The squatters' riots of the 1850s, 60s, and 70s arose partly because of this heritage of confused land ownership. California's flourishing title insurance companies of today had their origins during this time period.

After the boom in the gold mines subsided in the late 1850s, the demand and prices for beef would drop. This drop in the market, coupled with the debt and mortgages incurred defending land titles, resulted in the ownership of most of the ranchos passing from the *Californios*[8] to the Euro-Americans, ending California's romantic Mexican rancho days.[9]

Arrival of Euro-American Explorers and Settlers

A new wave of explorers had begun entering California in the 1820s. Most of these explorers were fur trappers, traders, scouts, and adventurers who became well-known for their role in opening up the west to migration and permanent settlement. Among these men were Jedediah Strong Smith in 1826, the first American to come by land to California; mountain men Ewing Young in 1832 and Joseph Walker in 1834; John Augustus Sutter (originally from Switzerland) in 1839; and John C. Frémont and the U.S. government-sponsored expedition parties of 1844 and 1845.

Reports from these early explorers and subsequent newspaper and magazine articles by men like Thomas O. Larkin and Dr. John Marsh, as well as books written by Richard Henry Dana, Alfred Robinson, Edwin Bryant, and others, spread the word about the temperate climate and fertile soil, as well as the abundant game and natural resources in California.[10] All of this appealed to a restless population in search of financial and social opportunity and spurred the organization of overland settler parties like the Bidwell-Bartleson and Workman-Rowland parties in 1841; the Lansford W. Hastings, Joseph B. Chiles, and Joseph R. Walker parties in 1843; the Stephens-Townsend-Murphy party in 1844-45; the Grigsby-Ide party in 1845; and the Donner party in 1846-47.[11]

Although many of the early fur trappers and settlers had become Mexican citizens, the later arrivals brought their families and skills to California and had no desire to become Mexican citizens. A number of actions taken by the Mexican government[12] in 1846 caused the Americans settled in the Sacramento and Napa valleys to become fearful that the Mexican government would evict them. In June 1846, a small group of rough frontiersmen captured Mexican General Mariano G. Vallejo in his home in Sonoma, occupied the Sonoma Barracks, and declared California an independent republic.[13] Three weeks later, this so-called "Bear Flag Revolt" ended quietly when the U.S. Navy under Commodore John Sloat landed at Monterey and raised the American flag, thus making California a territory of the United States without a single shot being fired.

At first the *Californios* accepted the Americans with resignation. The takeover was expected because Mexican rule had always seemed temporary and the likelihood of conquest by a foreign power inevitable. However, a change in the U.S. command of the occupation and the imposition of oppressive and arbitrary rules led to a four-month retaliatory revolt, which was waged between September 1846 and January 1847. A capitulation treaty ending the fighting in California between Mexico and the U.S. was signed at *Campo de Cahuenga* in Los Angeles on January 13, 1847; the Treaty of Guadalupe Hidalgo ending the Mexican-American War was ratified by both countries in mid-1848. (The U.S. agreed to pay a total of $15 million for New Mexico and California. The territory of New Mexico included the present states of Nevada, Utah, and Arizona, as well as portions of Wyoming and Colorado.)

The Americans' unofficial adoption of the so-called "Manifest Destiny" doctrine also contributed to the new interest in California. The term "manifest destiny" had first been used in January 1845 in connection with the U.S. annexation of the Republic of Texas to convey the idea that the rightful destiny of the U.S. included imperialistic expansion. Originally, manifest destiny was primarily promoted by agricultural interests in an attempt to acquire new lands for settlement and farming. In California, Americans begrudged the Native Americans[14] and Mexicans for not using the prime agricultural land to the best advantage. But eventually manifest destiny became entwined with Anglo-Saxon racial superiority, the notion of a specially ordained American mission in the world, and the need to prove American military superiority. The latter concept certainly contributed to the Mexican-American War.

When California became subject to the jurisdiction of the U.S., the *Californios* had a difficult time adjusting. They were socially and politically ill-equipped to cope with the greedy, enterprising, and often unprincipled newcomers.[15] The Euro-American *rancheros* who had become naturalized Mexican citizens, on the other hand, easily adapted to the new way of life. They and their newly arrived compatriots began asserting themselves and disparaging the Mexicans for their perceived idleness and lack of business skills. The white Anglo-Saxon Protestant ethic of hard work being a virtue and pleasure being a vice clashed with the customs of the *Californio* society that included a way of life based on trust and generosity, as well as customary time devoted to *siestas* and *fiestas*.[16] There also was an American Protestant condescension toward Catholicism and a generalized fear of racial mixing.

Out of the unavoidable cultural collision between the Euro-Americans and *Californios*, and the gradual acquisition of the lands by the former, came much ill feeling between the two races. Such derogatory terms as "greasers" for Mexicans and "gringos" for Americans and Englishmen had their origins in this era.[17] Following the discovery of gold in 1848, California's population suddenly increased from 15,000 in 1848 to 200,000 by 1852,[18] further contributing to chaos in the previously small, slow-paced California society.

California State Government in 1850

After California first became a territory of the United States in 1848, military governors appointed by the President provided official leadership for its affairs. The U.S. Congress should have established a civilian government, but it was struggling with the issue of slavery. (See below.) The military governors retained the existing Mexican *alcalde* system; *alcaldes*, who were mostly Euro-Americans, acted as the mayor, local magistrate, and judge. Without a central government authority there was no viable means by which to establish and enforce consistent laws, build roads and bridges, or empower local jurisdictions to establish schools, hospitals, police, or fire departments. "Gold Rush" California was in a state of near anarchy and it was obvious that there was no justification in law for the continuation of the military and *alcalde* system of governance. Without any authorization from the U.S. Congress, an election was called by Brigadier General Bennett Riley and was held on June 3, 1849 to choose delegates to a constitutional convention.

The 48 delegates assembled at Monterey on September 1, 1849 to frame a constitution.[19] They completed their task on October 13, 1849 and presented it to the voters for adoption on November 13th. The votes were 12,064 in favor of adoption and 811 against. The State Legislature began meeting in San José on December 15th, electing the first governor, lieutenant governor, and the first two U.S. senators. The U.S. senators subsequently presented certified copies of California's Constitution to Congress along with a resolution in the name of the state's citizens requesting admission to the Union.

Washington was in the midst of debating the slavery issue, and since California's Constitution prohibited slavery, the pro-slavery south was strongly opposed to admitting California, which would upset the balance in the number of free and slave states. In January 1850, Henry Clay proposed that California be admitted to the Union with no mention of the slavery issue, but it took a number of spirited debates and political maneuverings before the Compromise of 1850 was hammered out and approved. The compromise allowed slavery in the territories of New Mexico and Utah, with California being admitted to the Union as a free state. (To appease the pro-slavery southerners, the compromise also provided for stricter enforcement of the Fugitive Slave Act.) The President of the United States signed the legislation on September 9, 1850. The good news that California had become the 31st state reached San Francisco on October 18th.

In the meantime, in early 1850 the Legislature divided California into 27 counties—a difficult task due to the lack of knowledge about much of the geography of the state and the ever-changing population. Counties were governed by a panel consisting of the county judge and two justices of the peace, called the Court of Sessions, which served administrative, legislative, and judicial functions, all in one. (Legislation in 1852 would create boards of supervisors in each of the counties to assume all of the Court of Sessions' administrative and legislative functions.) Counties that failed to organize immediately were given a second chance in April 1850 when the Legislature passed a supplementary act allowing these counties to petition the county judge of any adjoining county to order an election.

The first session of the Legislature made provisions for public schools. Congress donated 500,000 acres of land to be sold to raise proceeds to create an education fund, but it would take several years to organize the fund and realize the benefits of the system. The first free school was organized in San Francisco on April 2, 1850, and small schools would be established in many of the mining towns later on.

Characteristics of the Prospectors and Society in the Mines

Among the first to arrive in the gold fields had been those who were already living and traveling in the area. These included the fur trappers, the Mexican and American *rancheros* and settlers, and ex-soldiers from Colonel Jonathan D. Stevenson's First Regiment of New York Volunteers[21] and the Mormon Battalion.[22] Oregonians were among the first non-residents to enter into California after the discovery of gold, using an existing trail blazed into California by fur trappers.[23] The Oregonians were soon followed by Americans from Missouri, Ohio, Michigan, Kentucky, Illinois, Georgia, Alabama, Massachusetts, Texas, New York, Maine, Louisiana, Iowa, Wisconsin, and Tennessee.

The non-Americans arriving were mainly from France, Germany, Spain, Italy, Chile, Hawaii ("Kanakas"), and China.[24] Many of the foreigners arriving in search of gold were trying to escape undesirable conditions in their homelands—revolutions in France, Germany, and Italy; the potato famine in Ireland; and the opium wars and Taiping Rebellion, as well as droughts, floods, and inflation in China.

Many of the prospectors were ambitious, optimistic young men, who had left their homes and families in the spirit of high adventure; they intended to strike it rich, either in gold mining or in business, agriculture, or land speculation. The long and arduous journey they endured en route to California had tempered them and developed their independence and determination. Most of the newcomers originally intended to work hard, become wealthy or make enough to get out of financial debt, and then return home. Many called themselves "Argonauts," after the mythical Greek heroes who sailed in the Argo with Jason in search of the Golden Fleece. But in the end, many would choose to stay or eventually return later with their families to become permanent residents of California.

African Americans were a presence in the gold fields; some had arrived in California before the discovery of gold and were farming or operating businesses in other parts of the state.[25] Even though California was created as a free state, African Americans were not always permitted many of the most basic civil rights. An 1850 law, for example, prevented African Americans, as well as Native Americans and mulattoes from giving evidence in any case involving an Anglo. However, any type of slave labor, including unpaid Native American labor, was strictly prohibited.

Men from every walk of life—professional and non-professional—were mining for gold and their common pursuit erased all of the usual class and status barriers. Family standing, social status, and financial worth were of little relevance in the midst of the struggle to find a bonanza. Hard physical labor was admired; slackers were disdained, regardless of race or national origin.

Those who supplied mining tools, provisions, and general merchandise benefited the most from the Gold Rush. They were able to charge whatever the market would bear. A simple wool shirt cost $50; sugar sold for $4 a pound; and boots and shoes ran from $25 to $150 a pair. The merchants' customers were the ill-equipped miners[26] and the local Native Americans who had no concept of fair rates of exchange for their gold dust that they gladly traded for beads, raisins, and other items that caught their fancy.[27] Gold dust served as the medium of exchange throughout the 1850s, and was not usually measured by any precise means. The miners resented the ever-present high prices; they frequently complained that they were doing all of the hard work and the merchants were the only ones profiting.

Blacksmiths also did quite well in the mining camps, usually finding that exercising their special skills was more profitable than mining. In his prime, the blacksmith was the master of all things mechanical, from making and repairing the equipment for mining, as well as the saws and axes for cutting and milling lumber, to shoeing horses. Later the blacksmith would design and make the metal hardware that held buildings together and enabled doors to swing.

Men generally came to California by themselves or in small groups in order to have the mobility necessary in the search for gold. The nearly all-male society[28] of the early mining period was generally law-abiding, honest, and generous, and there was little need for any type of justice system. By late 1849, however, with the tremendous surge in population, a new breed began to appear; armed robbery and theft, as well as assaults and murders became more commonplace. The mass hysteria created by the Gold Rush created a general tolerance of greed, disorder, and violence.

Before statehood, *alcaldes* or miners' courts meted out summary justice quickly in the form of whipping, hanging, banishment from the camp, or fines. Because the miners had little time to spare from their mining, justice was swift, but every effort was made to hear both sides of any controversy. After statehood and the formation of the counties and county courts, as well as the election of justices of the peace, miners' juries in the larger mining camps were replaced, the process of justice took longer, and jails became necessary to hold the accused until due process ran its course.

There was no federal mining law that applied to U.S. public lands. The earliest miners in 1848 had established an unofficial claim law that looked upon the Gold Country as government land and part of the public domain. Thus, miners moved in on the land freely without asking for anyone's permission. The basic claim law that everyone obeyed was that a man could claim and mark a reasonable square footage of workable ground as long as he continued to work it at least one day a week. When the number of prospectors began increasing and competition developed for mining sites, "codes" were adopted in each camp. The bottom line was respect and fair play.

Mining was hard work, and when the mining was done for the day the miner was ready to have some fun. Entertainment often took the form of non-laudable social activities, including drinking and gambling, or watching bull and bear fights,[29] knife duels, or hangings. The shortage of women also led to the establishment of houses of ill-repute, which served up temptation to otherwise virtuous men. There were few legal or social restraints curbing bad habits, so alcoholism was common and gambling was an addiction for many.

Suicide rates soared to a rate of 1,000 a year,[30] and others fell victim to the violent actions of their neighbors. Accidents, disease, malnutrition, and other forms of hardship contributed to a high mortality rate, as well. Diarrhea and cholera were prevalent in 1850 in many parts of California, and cholera proved fatal to about 50 percent of its victims, especially those already weakened by long sea voyages or trips across the plains.[31]

The residents of mining camps were exposed to extremely unhealthful living conditions. Their health was further endangered by days spent walking for miles carrying heavy loads to and from their claims, and standing knee-deep in the cold water of the river in all kinds of weather conditions. A plethora of insects, including lice, ticks, fleas,[32] and mosquitoes, not to mention deadly rattlesnakes, were common visitors to the miners' bedrolls. There were no medical facilities and few bona fide physicians. Infections were treated with medications containing such toxic substances as arsenic and mercury, and often proved disabling, if not fatal. Quacks seized the opportunity to make money by offering untried and ineffective treatments, as well as worthless advice—all for a fee of an ounce of gold.

When miners heard of a new strike they would often abandon well-paying claims to head out for the new diggings[33] in hopes of richer dirt. But more and more during 1850, the easily accessible gold was dwindling and it was becoming apparent that only a handful of miners would become rich.[34] The disappointed miners had to decide whether to return home and admit failure, continue to search for gold, or try to make a living in California using skills that had served them back home. Many of the prospectors had been farm boys before heading west, so they decided to stay and use their farming expertise in the valleys and alongside the many streams in northern California. Some of the former miners began moving onto property that was held by the land grantees of the Mexican-era, thus becoming involved in suits over property ownership. Others were able to purchase small portions of ranchos from the grant owners, and they, like the squatters, chose the land that lay alongside the streams because it seemed to be the best suited for farming.

Gold Mining Methods

The California Gold Rush was characterized by the expression "Seeing the Elephant," which was an expression commonly used in the U.S. in the 1800s. Originally, it meant to see the last and most exciting act in a circus, the elephant. The expression gradually evolved to mean gaining a measure of worldly experience and adventure. With the California Gold Rush, the expression came to refer to a trip to *El Dorado* ("the Land of the Gilded Man"), and mining for gold. Even unsuccessful prospectors were proud to be able to claim that they had "seen the elephant" and thus had the adventure of a lifetime.

During ancient geologic times, placer gold had been dislodged from its original location (typically as a vein within quartz) and was washed into the rivers or streambeds. Placer mining, which is mining for gold in streams and rivers, was the first form of gold mining in California. A mining pan was the basic tool employed, replacing the knives and spoons used initially. While standing in ice cold water, the pan was used to scoop up dirt, sand, gravel, and rock; the rocks were picked out; the pan was submerged in water with one lip of the pan lower than the other; and then the pan was swirled around until only the gold[35] and heavy black sands were left at the bottom. Mercury, or "quicksilver" as it was called, was used to separate the black sand from the gold.

The "rocker" was the first tool to replace the pan as a means to separate the gold. In appearance, it resembled a child's crib—a box several feet long with wooden or metal riffles (grooves) attached to a sloping bottom. It was open at one end and the other end had a hopper with a screen or a metal plate and holes punched in it at the bottom. Rockers worked most efficiently if three people functioned as a team—one shoveling the dirt into the hopper and picking the larger rocks out that did not fall through the screen; one pouring buckets of water down through the screen, which washed the finer material along the riffles and out the other end; and the third continually rocking the rocker. This continual motion agitated the material passing over the riffles and allowed the heavy gold pieces to drop behind the riffles and not be washed out. The team of men usually rotated jobs throughout the day.

The most notable improvement in early mining equipment was the introduction of the "long tom" in the spring of 1850. The long tom was an inclined stationary wooden trough or box, narrow at the upper end and widening at the lower end. Perforated sheets of iron were placed in the bottom and a shallow, flat riffle box, with cross bars to catch the gold, was placed under the bottom. Dirt was shoveled into the upper end by one or more men while a continuous stream of water, usually carried from a dammed stream through a flume, naturally flowed across the riffles, thus allowing the heavy gold to settle behind the riffles.

Soon the long tom would begin to be replaced by the "sluice," which either was a number of long toms attached together to form a sluice several hundred feet long, or simply a ditch or flume with a good pitch lined with rock instead of wooden riffles. The ground-sluice method of recovering gold involved first cutting a race (a channel for a current of water) to divert the river into a dammed area so that the river's bed could be mined.

Enlarged dams and more extensive fluming operations made it possible to have large-scale operations. Fluming companies formed, in which the members, particularly at first, had a working interest. The number of shares was limited to the amount of money required for the construction of the flume and for operating expenses until the recovery of gold produced income. The amount of overhead expense was small, and all of the members of the company were active participants. The greatest drawback to this type of mining was that any sudden rise in the river's water level due to an early storm, could interrupt the activity and/or wash a dam completely away after one to two months of hard labor.

By the end of 1849, most of the easily recoverable placer gold had been mined. Thus it became necessary to seek the gold locked in its original quartz below the surface of the ground. The early inexperienced miners began digging small shafts that were known as "coyote holes." These were short, unsupported shafts into the ground that often filled with water or caved in, suffocating the miners. (Later they would start lining the tunnels with timbers supported with strong beams to prevent cave-ins.)

Once the miners had pried the quartz from the ground, they used the Mexican *arrastré* to crush the quartz gold ore. The *arrastré* resembled a large circular tub, with a smaller one on the inside, and had been used by the Spanish in Latin America. After first breaking the quartz down as much as possible with hammers, the quartz was then dumped into the *arrastré* and a mule dragged a millstone around in a circle over smooth paving stones, crushing the quartz until it became a powder. Mercury was added to the powder to combine with the gold that had been freed from the quartz. The combination of mercury and gold was then placed in a retort (a vessel in which to heat the ore) so that the mercury could be boiled off, leaving the gold behind.

The miners found the *arrastré* process to be inadequate because of the large amount of time required. Late in 1850, the first stamp mill was brought around the Cape Horn to Mariposa. A stamp mill is a tall structure containing one or more stamps—large heavy metal shoes mounted on long vertical connecting rods, which are lifted up by rotating camshafts and then dropped. Wooden cylinders, drive belts, crescent-shaped cams, and metal plates at the bottom were all part of the mechanical process powered by gravity and a steam engine. At the end of the process, the stamp dropped the great distance to the bottom, crushing and grinding the ore that had already been physically broken up to a piece about the size of a fist. The crushed ore was then washed out into a large sloping table fitted with riffles and the mercury removal process was applied.

The era of large-scale hard rock mining would get under way in the early 1850s, necessitating a new kind of miner and large initial capital expenditures. Corporations and individual investors brought in thousands of miners with experience in hard rock techniques from the gold, tin, and copper mines of Mexico, Peru, Bolivia, and Cornwall, England. These miners knew how to reach the underground gold bearing quartz and how to deal with the water that often was a major hazard of underground mining. Hard rock mining would continue until the Job Ordinance Act of World War II limited mine output and resulted in the permanent closure of most mines.

The hydraulic mining process would be invented by two Nevada City miners in 1853. They crafted a canvas hose and a tapered nozzle of sheet iron through which to shoot water onto a hillside, exposing soil and rocks that in ancient times had been a riverbed. The sand and gravel left by that ancient river was washed away from the hillside and directed through long toms. Hydraulic mining also required large initial expenditures, and so by the end of the 1850s, access to capital became a prerequisite to mining for gold. The downside of hydraulic mining was that the muck and silt blasted away from the hillsides flowed into the streams and rivers, threatening agriculture and river shipping in the Sacramento Valley. Hydraulic mining would be halted by a federal court order in 1884.[36]

One other later method of mining was "dredge mining." Miners built large, floating gold factories called "bucket line dredges" that dug up entire river valleys. The dirt and rock left behind from this type of mining resulted in the huge piles of rock, or tailings, that can still be seen along rivers in Trinity County and the Sacramento Valley today.

Geography of the Gold Country

James Marshall discovered gold in the area that some have called the Central Mines. This area is more commonly included in the Northern Mines region, however, which stretches all the way to the Oregon border. The Southern Mines were located along the Sierra foothills between Amador County on the north and Merced County on the south. The principal gold quartz belt of the Sierra Nevada is known as the Mother

Lode, which is usually restricted to a series of gold quartz veins lying south of the Cosumnes River, and extending in a southeasterly direction into Mariposa County near the town of Coulterville.

Tributaries of the streams in the Gold Country were named in relation to the main stream, thus nearly every river has a north fork, middle fork, and south fork. Along each stream, mining camps were established on "river bars," one every few miles or several to the mile. River bars were ridges of gravel slightly above the surface of the river that contained gold. These bars might be extensive, but more commonly were fairly small and short-lived.

It was the rich "placers" (deposits of gravel or sand containing gold) scattered throughout the Gold Country that first attracted the 49ers, leading to the establishment of thousands of mining camps. These camps were able to survive the depletion of the placers if gold-bearing quartz veins were discovered nearby or if there was some other reason for a settlement to exist, such as serving as a supply center or an important crossroads or river crossing. The flavor of the Gold Rush can still be captured in the Gold Country today by visiting its rustic towns, state historic parks, and huge tracts of national forests and public lands.

California Architecture in 1850

The most common type of building in 1850 was the adobe,[37] which had its origin during the mission days when adobes were constructed by American Indians from the missions or neighboring villages. The adobe bricks were made from a mixture of water, earth, and clay found near the homesite. Straw or horsehair was added to the mix to hold the adobe together. The wet mud-like substance was then poured into rectangular wood frames, allowed to dry, and assembled layer upon layer with adobe mortar into two- to three-foot thick walls. The exterior surface was then plastered to protect it from the rain, and frequently whitewashed. Adobes were economical and could be built quickly.

Traditionally most early adobes were simple single-story buildings. In the mid-1800s larger, elaborate adobes and two-story adobes, known as Monterey-style adobes or Monterey Colonial, started to appear.[38] Early adobe houses had flat, thatched roofs made from tree branches or tules (swamp rushes) found near swamps, rivers, or streams. The roof materials were sealed by molten tar or *brea* found in natural tar pools. Later roofs were made from wood support beams and planks. The wood was usually obtained from local trees or transported down from the mountains by ox-driven carts. *Brea* was used to caulk the space between the planks. Some of the more elaborate adobes had tile roofs. Because of the unavailability of lumber, early adobes had compacted earth floors, which were swept out several times a day to remove loose dust. In later years, wood plank floors were added.

Building with adobe bricks became impractical in the mid-1850s when most Native Americans, who had previously provided cheap labor, retreated to the wilds, moved onto reservations, or died. Most of California's adobes have disappeared from the landscape due to neglect, vandalism, erosion, or intentional demolition. But some remodeled homes have incorporated the original thick walls of early adobes into new structures, and many adobes were saved by civic groups and historical societies in the 1920s and 30s, or incorporated into state parks.[39] The State of California began implementing a statewide preservation program in 1927 by establishing a State Park Commission and conducting a statewide survey to identify the most significant scenic, recreational, and historic resources.

During the Gold Rush any kind of labor was at a premium, so the practice of shipping pre-fabricated "Boston" houses around the Horn was begun. Most of the pre-cut frame houses were in the simple New England "salt box" style, but a few were in the Victorian Gothic style.[40] Over the course of the Gold Rush years, several thousand disassembled houses were shipped to San Francisco and redistributed among the nearby towns in the Bay Area.

The earliest structures in the mining towns and camps were canvas tents made from recycled sailcloth taken from the hundreds of abandoned ships in the San Francisco Bay. When more permanent structures were desired, most of the buildings were constructed of shakes (thinly split shingles) or pine lumber or a combination of wood and canvas. These materials were cheaper and more available than brick and much faster to assemble. Because these materials were very combustible, fires were a frequent occurrence. By the mid-1850s, the residents of the gold mining towns started constructing red brick buildings with iron doors and windows to prevent the spread of fire. Even though fires and the years have taken their toll, many of these historic buildings remain in the Gold Country today.

Travel to and Within California

Travel to and within California in 1850 was an ordeal. A 15,000-mile ship journey around the tip of South America—Cape Horn—could take five months. Cutting across the Isthmus of Panama could reduce the trip by several months, but travelers ran the risk of contracting cholera or malaria. By land, the 2,200-mile journey from trailheads in Missouri or Iowa took three or four months, assuming no major hardships occurred, such as a cholera epidemic within the party, flooded roads along rivers, or Native American hostility. The overland route was the most popular way to reach the mines, especially for those coming from the Midwest.

Once within the borders of California, there were only a few "roads" in California in 1850 and these were actually only trails. *El Camino Real* (the King's Highway) had stretched from San Diego north to the San Francisco Bay since the days of the missions. The present-day U.S. Hwy 101 between Petaluma and Los Angeles and Interstate 5 between Los Angeles and San Diego closely follow this route, which linked the missions and their settlements.

El Camino Viejo was the oldest north/south trail. It traversed the entire length of the San Joaquin Valley and beyond, from San Pedro in Los Angeles County to San Antonio, which today is East Oakland in Alameda County. It also was known as the Los Angeles Trail, and later the Stockton-Los Angeles Road.

An overland route from Santa Fe, New Mexico was known as the Old Spanish Trail or later, the old Emigrant Trail, and formed a part of the Southern Overland Trail, which was much traveled during the 1840s and 50s. Roads led out of the *Pueblo de Los Angeles* across the Santa Ana River to the ranchos of the San Diego area, and others led to the Santa Barbara region. The Pacheco Pass was the principal route between the coastal areas of Central California, the San Joaquin Valley, and the Sierras. A trail connected Sacramento with Shasta in northern California.

The major rivers of the Sacramento and San Joaquin valleys—the Sacramento, Yuba, American, San Joaquin, Stanislaus, and Tuolumne rivers—became natural highways during the Gold Rush. The earliest vessels to be put into service were scows (flat-bottomed boats with square ends) with detachable steam engines that were dismantled and stowed in the hold of sailing ships for the trip around the Horn. A few of the ships abandoned in the San Francisco Bay were used on the rivers, and soon shipwrights started building ships from simple plans sometimes even drawn on the ground with a sharp stick. The builder was often both the owner and the captain, and could usually recoup his costs in a few months.

Ferries also came into use during the Gold Rush. The ferries were fairly primitive vessels at first; they were propelled by the current of the river and controlled by ropes. All ferrymen were under the jurisdiction of the local county government, which levied personal property taxes and license fees. The license fee was based on the popularity or usage of the ferry. An annual fee for an established ferry might run as high as $300 per year and all ferrymen were required to post a bond, usually $5,000, indemnifying the county against damage or suit from any accidents. Local county governments also regulated the amount of fare charged.

Professional "freighters" were just beginning to operate in 1850. Their mule pack trains delivered staple foods like flour, coffee, and potatoes, as well as mail and small parcels. The freight rate was one dollar per pound, regardless of the commodity, and letters for delivery to the miners were carried for one and one-half dollars each.

The *Californios*—the men and some women—traveled primarily on horseback. The *carreta*, a two-wheeled wooden cart drawn by oxen, had been the only wheeled vehicle for transporting most women, children, and supplies until 1844 when the Stephens-Townsend-Murphy party introduced the wagon to California.

California Industry in 1850

In 1850 gold mining was the primary driver of California's economy, but cattle ranching was still very important and several other industries were developing as well. The demand for beef in the mines was sustaining the prosperity of the ranchos, and by a more gradual process, the other food demands of the diggings were stimulating the development of farming. Agriculture had initially declined after secularization, and most of the *Californios* relied on Hawaii and the Oregon Territory for their foodstuffs. But the demand created by the prospectors for flour, potatoes, turnips, onions, melons, grapes, berries, and other fruit provided the catalyst that started California on its way to becoming the state with the most diversified agriculture.

Lumber milling was in full swing in Santa Cruz, San Mateo, Santa Clara, Alameda, Contra Costa, Marin, and Napa counties. Several mills were also operating in Nevada and El Dorado counties. The demand for lumber was created by the building boom in San Francisco, the fluming operations in the gold fields, and towards the end of 1850, the stamp mills and structure needs in the Gold Country.

Merchandising was not only lucrative for the merchants operating in the mining camps and towns, but for the middlemen—commissioners—who boarded the ships in the San Francisco Bay to bid on the cargo arriving from China, Hawaii, Panama, and the East Coast. Merchandising had its drawbacks, however, because the commissioners were not able to place orders. Arriving goods were what the international merchants thought might be in demand, which did not always match reality. The California merchants never knew what was coming or when it would arrive. A whole cargo of stoves might arrive, for example, many of which were worthless because too many had arrived at one time. (The excess items would be thrown into the muddy streets of San Francisco and serve as stepping stones.)

Since the hide and tallow trade had used "leather dollars" as currency, there had been no reason for bankers in California. However, the onset of the Gold Rush created a necessity for banking. The first banking house on the Pacific Coast had opened in October 1849 in Sacramento. Another bank opened in San Francisco the following January, an East Coast express company was providing banking services to the miners in Coloma, and similar companies began forming throughout California. The chief requirement to become a banker was to own a strong safe, so some merchants accepted deposits, made loans, and performed some of the other normal banking functions. In 1850 there were fifteen different operations making privately minted coins in California. The Moffett, Grant and Company in San Francisco minted octagonal-shaped coins in ten-, twenty-, and fifty-dollar denominations. Another San Francisco firm, the Pacific Company, stamped the company name on its coins. The first western branch of the U.S. Mint would not be established in California until 1854, and privately minted coins remained legal tender for another two years.

The burgeoning population created a demand for many other new types of professions and services in California. This included the need for lawyers, physicians, hoteliers, restauranteurs, and newspaper publishers.[41] Letter sheets were also popular among gold miners and emigrants to California. California artists were producing pictorial "letter sheets," which were elaborately-illustrated pieces of stationery that usually consisted of a large single piece of paper folded in half, with one page for an illustration of local subjects and three blank pages for letter writing. They served a function similar to the picture postcards of today.

California Organizations in 1850

Euro-Protestantism had been making its way westward since the early part of the 19th century. Home mission boards were founded in the 1820s, and the interest in spreading Protestantism to the American West was increasing. California, especially when in the throes of the Gold Rush, however, required the ministers arriving in the state to depart from the traditional strategies of the home mission movement and improvise as they went along.

Few churches were established in 1850 because it was difficult to keep men in one place long enough to bring them into fellowship or to interest them in the long-term welfare of a local church. Small towns would arise quickly, but just as quickly, they were abandoned. Ministers preached on the streets or in tents; worship services often were well attended. Many worshipped out of conviction; others were homesick and merely sought the solace of the church as a traditional institution.

As soon as women started arriving in the 1850s, the task of organizing churches was greatly simplified for the missionaries. The women attended to visiting potential congregants and organized fund-raising activities. In December 1850, for example, the ladies of the First Presbyterian Church in San Francisco held a fair to raise money for the new church building, netting almost $4,000.

The Sabbath was an important ritual in California in 1850, even in the Gold Country, but the activities that took place on the "day of rest" did not strictly conform to the evangelical standards of the missionaries. Men living in mining communities washed their clothes and sluices, wrote letters, and gathered in the nearest town or camp to sell their gold dust, buy supplies and equipment for the coming week, and visit. They also sought ways to be entertained, such as gambling, drinking, and watching a horse race or a dogfight.[42] Some were decidedly uneasy about using Sunday to catch up on chores and activities that they had no time for during the workweek, but felt that the voluntary cessation from gold mining was a positive attempt to honor the fourth commandment. Religious and other customary holidays like the 4th of July were celebrated in the best way possible, given the means at hand.

Fraternal organizations began forming in the 1850s throughout northern California. Peter Lassen had brought a charter for the first Masonic lodge in California across the plains in 1848; the first recorded meeting of the Free and Accepted Masons in California had been held in San Francisco in 1849; and California's first Masonic lodge hall was built in Benicia (Solano County) in 1850.

The grand order of *E. Clampus Vitus*, originally a spoof of the fraternal organizations of the day, was organized in Mokelumne Hill (Calaveras County) by Joseph Zumwalt in 1850, and eventually spread to all the gold camps of the Mother Lode. It later came to have more serious aspects, such as the care of widows and orphans of unfortunate miners who lost their lives in the mines.[43]

The Society of California Pioneers was founded in August 1850 in San Francisco by pre-Gold Rush pioneers to preserve, promote, and enjoy California heritage. W. D. M. Howard, the owner of the Mellus and Howard warehouse where the Society first met, was the first president. The Society continues to this day and operates a museum in San Francisco (Society of California Pioneers Museum), thanks to the direct descendants of those who arrived in California before 1850.

California's Natural History

The abundance of bears, especially grizzlies all over California, was unique to the state; hence the logo on the state flag and the more than 500 geographical features and settlements in California designated by the "bear" place name. (The grizzly bear would be hunted to extinction in the state by 1924.)

California has over 6,000 kinds of native plants.[44] The loss of native vegetation in California is the most visible sign of the Euro-American invasion. Thick forests of live oak were cut for fuel for sailing ships and fuel for the stamp mills in the Gold Country. Trees were also cut for firewood for warmth and timber for cabins, dams, flumes, and sluices. The numerous large groves of redwood trees up and down the coast were destroyed by the lumber milling industry and eventually replaced by second growth redwoods or exotic imported trees. Although once widespread, giant sequoias now occur only in preserved groves in the Sierra Nevada.

The most common "exotic" tree imported to California, and one that can be seen in large stands throughout California today, is the eucalyptus tree. The very first eucalyptus trees came to California from Australia in clipper ships in 1849. Later, seeds were brought from Australia with the thought that this fast-growing tree would fill the need for wood in areas that lacked forests. Some claimed that eucalyptus trees would drive away malaria and provide useful oils and excellent wood for furniture and fuel, but they proved to be useless as a structural wood.[45]

Earthquakes have always been indigenous to California. As far back as the early 1800s, Spanish missionaries had recorded strong tremors. In 1846, the author of *Life in California*, Alfred Robinson, described an 1842 earthquake as being "the 25th shock experienced in the last two months." He presumed the cause to be the existence of "mineral formations in the earth." The San Andreas fault, the one that caused the 1906 and 1989 earthquakes in the San Francisco Bay Area, had caused no known fatalities before 1906. However, an earthquake on this fault in 1803 destroyed the church at Mission San Juan Bautista, and several strong shocks along this fault line were reported during the 1860s.

Notes ⌒ INTRODUCTION

1

For purposes of comparison, Colorado did not become a state until 18 years after gold seekers had arrived.

2

The English sea captain Sir Francis Drake also visited California in 1579, inconsequentially claiming land in present-day Marin County for the Queen of England.

3

The Spanish explorers never ventured into the Sierra Nevada and surprisingly never noticed bits of gold in the streambeds in the foothills as they traveled through the Central Valley. In Mexico and Peru, they had known about the presence of gold and silver because the Indians had discovered them. But the California Indians either had not discovered the gold or they had no appreciation of its value. The history of California could have been quite different if the discovery of gold had been made before the Mexican-American War. As it was, gold was discovered on January 24, 1848—nine days before Mexico ceded California to the U.S. by signing the Treaty of Hidalgo on February 2, 1848.

4

In the 1850s, 60s, and 70s, following decisions handed down by the U.S. Land Commission on a case-by-case basis, the U.S. government returned the missions to the Catholic church. Today 18 of the restored missions serve local parishes, maintain a museum and gift shop, and are open to the public. The other three missions are state historic parks. All of the missions are referenced in this book with addresses.

5

The hides were used to make leather goods and the tallow, derived from boiling down the fat, was used to make lard, candles, and soap. The hides and tallow were traded for merchandise supplied by foreign merchant vessels ("floating department stores") from around the world, as well as for goods supplied by the few *ranchero* and pueblo merchants. International trade was vital because there was very little manufacturing in California.

6

Monte, played with a special deck of 40 cards in which the players bet against a banker on the suit of cards to be turned up from the deck, was the favorite gambling game.

7

Many new arrivals to California refused to accept or believe that any single person could own as much land as most of the ranchos contained.

8

Californios were Hispanics born in California before California statehood.

9

There are charts throughout this book that indicate the 1850-ownership of each county's ranchos. Although tedious, the charts are intended to provide a complete picture of land ownership in 1850 and provoke thoughtful contemplation about California's Hispanic heritage.

10

Thomas O. Larkin was the American Consul to California; Dr. John Marsh was California's first physician; Richard Henry Dana was the author of the 1840 literary classic *Two Years Before the Mast*, which told the story of his voyage on a sailing ship from Boston; Alfred Robinson was a shipping clerk who wrote the 1846 book *Life in California*; and Edwin Bryant was the author of the 1848 book *What I Saw in California*. These books and articles also would become the first histories of California, though often more promotional than factual.

11

The Donner party, the most well-known because of its tragic misfortune, was composed of farmers and a high proportion of women, elderly, and children. About 100 persons left Independence, Missouri in May 1846 and the party was making steady progress. However, 87 members of the party decided to follow a supposed shortcut through Utah into Nevada. They lost precious time and suffered through severe desert conditions. Their "shortcut" trail finally intersected the California Trail on September 30th, where the smaller group of the original party had crossed 45 days earlier. By the time the second party reached the base of the Sierras, the physical condition of both humans and animals was deteriorating, as was the emotional stability of the humans. They mistakenly took five days to rest, which resulted in the party being snowed in for more than two and one-half months. As members died, they were cannibalized by the survivors, and in the end, after rescue by four relief expeditions, only 48 of the original 87 reached the Sacramento Valley.

12

The history of the Mexican period in California was not at all as simplistic as it appears in this brief introduction. During the 1840s there were many power struggles between the administration operating out of Mexico City and the influential *Californios*, and a number of "revolts" took place, as well. In fact, Alta California was on the verge of separating from Mexico to become an independent republic when the Mexican-American War broke out in 1846.

13

The "Bear Flaggers" were unaware that the U.S. had declared war on Mexico the month before. The group was called the Bear Flaggers because they crafted a flag with a depiction of a bear on it for their new republic. The State Legislature would adopt a version of the Bear Flag as the state flag in 1911. The current design is the result of several makeovers, the last in 1953.

14

Hindsight has allowed historians to appreciate the resourcefulness of the hundreds of Native American tribes in managing the vast lands of California and ensuring steady and adequate supplies of natural resources to meet their daily needs.

15

The majority of Euro-Americans arrived in California after 1848 and had no appreciation of the generosity that had been extended to all foreigners during Mexican days. By the end of the 1850s, the *Californios* would become the "strangers" in California and the Euro-Americans fully in control of the state.

16

Mexican women, however, were highly esteemed by foreigners. They were perceived to be more industrious than the men and also more humane and charitable.

17

Racism had been fomented in some of the articles and books written to lure American settlers to California; this racism manifested itself in various ways. Some of the *bandidos* (outlaws) of the West, who ruthlessly murdered and robbed Americans, began their anti-social practices in retaliation for the anti-Hispanic sentiment and land takeovers. The more well-known marauders included Salomon Pico, Joaquin Murieta, and Tiburcio Vásquez.

18

An accurate 1850 population count for California is unavailable because the official U.S. censuses for several jurisdictions were lost.

19

Eight of the 48 delegates elected to the convention were *Californios*, a notable figure since there were only 13,000 *Californios* in a total population of 100,000. The state constitution declared Spanish and English to be the official languages.

20

John McDougal became the governor in December of 1850, following the resignation of Governor Burnett.

21

Colonel Jonathan D. Stevenson's regiment arrived by sea in 1847 to take part in the American occupation of Alta California.

22

In 1846 the U.S. Army enlisted a battalion of 500 Mormons to assist it in the Mexican-American War. Five companies of 75 to 100 men each were recruited from the Mormon Camps in Iowa. Thirty-two women, 20 of them laundresses hired at private's pay, left for California with the Battalion. The group made the longest march in military history, consisting of 2,000 miles from Council Bluffs, Iowa to San Diego.

23

The name Oregon appears more frequently in California's mining regions as a place name than any other state.

24

Less than 800 Chinese were in California in 1850, but thousands would arrive the following year. Some were not interested in gold mining, but in operating restaurant, mercantile, or laundry establishments in San Francisco. Others had been brought to California as laborers by Charles V. Gillespie, who lived in China for a number of years.

Fully intending to return to China when conditions improved there, the Chinese rarely brought any women with them, and they adopted very few American customs, tending instead to live in separate communities. Few Japanese had joined the Gold Rush because leaving Japan was illegal until 1868.

25

The 1850 U.S. Census counted 962 African Americans, 90 of them women.

26

The basics for a miner usually consisted of a single suit of clothes, a revolver pistol, a Bowie or butcher knife, a roll of blankets for a bed, and a knapsack of provisions consisting of pork and beans, flour and salt, coffee or tea, a dish or two for cooking, a large iron or tin pan for washing gold, a shovel, and sometimes a pick. If he traveled with a mule or horse, his outfit was more extensive. If several miners traveled together and had pack animals, they ordinarily carried a tent.

27

One man purportedly obtained $6,000 worth of gold from a Native American for a small lot of beads that cost $2.50 in San Francisco.

28

There were American Indian, Mexican, and Chilean women in California in 1850, but less than four percent of the female population was Anglo. After 1850, a few Euro-American women started arriving to try their hand at mining or to work in the saloons or prostitution houses that were being established throughout the gold country. Others arrived to join their husbands or fiancés who had decided to settle in California. These women often contracted their services to perform domestic chores for the miners, and often earned more money than most men were making prospecting. Some operated boardinghouses or hotels.

29

Bull and bear fights would be banned in California in 1855.

30

Failure implied personal fault in the Euro-American culture. Disappointment and financial problems due to unsuccessful prospecting, gambling losses, and/or the high cost of living were common reasons for suicide.

31

Funerals were always held for deceased comrades. Although death became accepted as a part of Gold Rush life because it was so prevalent, nearly everyone was fearful about the thought of dying, far from friends and relatives, with no one to stand at the graveside.

32

From indications of those who wrote about any part of California in the early and mid-19th century, the whole state was infested with fleas, a product of the inferior hygiene habits of the time and the fact that most slept in a bedroll on the ground.

33

Many mines were referred to as "the diggings" because the first step in mining usually involved digging.

34

Xenophobia and racism reared their ugly heads with the disappearance of the easy gold. Americans considered any non-Anglos, even the *Californios*, to be "foreigners" with no right to own a mining claim. In an effort to drive out non-American miners, the Foreign Miners' Tax of $16 per month was imposed by the Legislature in 1850, mainly on the

Mexican and Chinese miners. Most of the non-American Anglos, even the Canadians, filed for American citizenship to escape taxation. But the Mexicans, especially the *Californios*, simply refused to pay the taxes and many simply left the state. The tax was a failure—producing more resentment, even by Anglos, than revenue. The tax was lowered to $20 for four months ($5 per month) and in 1851 it was repealed.

35

Gold is among the heaviest of elements and will quickly sink to the bottom in water.

36

The incredible impact of hydraulic mining may be seen at Malakoff Diggins State Historic Park. See the Nevada County list of sites to visit.

37

The word "adobe" can refer to a single brick, to a home or building, or to a type of soil found in California.

38

Thomas O. Larkin had built a house in Monterey in 1835 that combined the New England two-story wood-frame house with the California adobe.

39

These historic adobe buildings have been restored for the public's viewing and are referenced in this book with addresses.

40

One 1850 "salt box" house remains in San Diego and an 1850 and an 1851 Victorian Gothic style house remain in Benicia and Sonoma. All three of these houses are referenced in this book with addresses.

41

The miners were particularly hungry for news from the East, but it never was very timely; mail service was very slow. (There was no provision for overland mail shipments, and the steamship companies' contracts only required them to put in at most seaports "if practicable.") Since the miners had no official mailing address, families sent their letters care of the Post Office, San Francisco. The newspapers from New York sold for as much as a dollar, so the miners developed an interest in California newspapers, which led to a boom in the newspaper industry in the 1850s.

42

Soon after 1850, professional entertainers arrived in the Gold Country. The entertainers included promoters of bull and bear fights, vaudeville acts, and concert and theatrical artists such as the famous Lola Montez.

43

As the mining camps disappeared, the vigor of the *E. Clampus Vitus* brotherhood declined, but the order was revived in 1931 and a grand council of all 30 chapters was organized in 1950, with a new emphasis placed on preserving history and having fun. Since that time, over 200 historical plaques have been dedicated by different chapters of Clampers in California and Nevada.

44

The Rancho Santa Ana Botanic Garden is dedicated to the collection, cultivation, study and display of native California plants. See the Los Angeles County list of sites to visit.

45

There are 200 species of eucalyptus native to Australia, and the one chosen to import, the blue gum, was the wrong one because its wood was too soft.

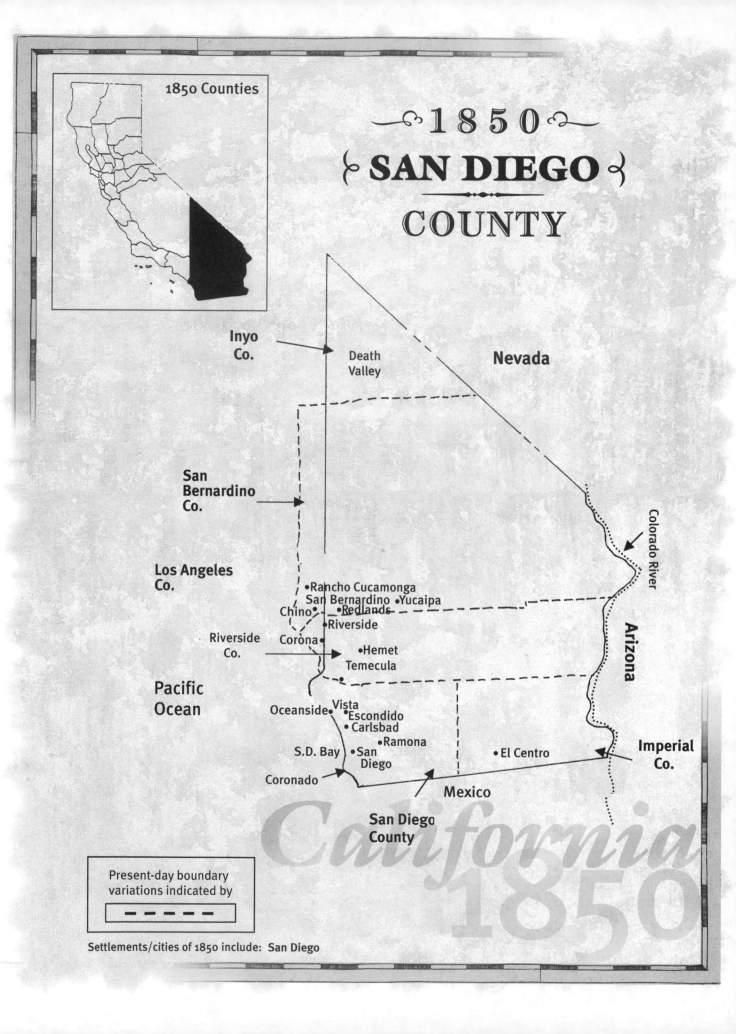

1850 Counties

∽ 1850 ∾
⸭ SAN DIEGO ⸭
COUNTY

Inyo Co.

Death Valley

Nevada

San Bernardino Co.

Colorado River

Los Angeles Co.

• Rancho Cucamonga
San Bernardino •Yucaipa
Chino •Redlands
•Riverside

Riverside Co.

Corona

Arizona

• Hemet
Temecula

Pacific Ocean

Vista
Oceanside• •Escondido
• Carlsbad
•Ramona

S.D. Bay •San Diego

Coronado

• El Centro

Imperial Co.

Mexico

San Diego County

California
1850

Present-day boundary variations indicated by

– – – – –

Settlements/cities of 1850 include: San Diego

SAN DIEGO COUNTY
1850

The geographical area of 1850-San Diego County included the areas that today make up San Diego, Imperial, Riverside, and San Bernardino counties, as well as half of Inyo County. Its 798 residents counted in the 1850 U.S. Census included Californios, Americans, and Europeans. The uncounted Native American inhabitants included members of the Kumeyaay, Yuma, Diegueño, Luiseño, Cupeño, Cahuilla, Halchidhoma, Mojave, Chemehuevi, Serrano, and Kawaiisu tribes. Spanish was still the area's common language.

AREA WITHIN PRESENT-DAY SAN DIEGO COUNTY

In 1850 the area within present-day San Diego County consisted of its port on San Diego Bay, a sleepy former mission/presidio town, and a vast expanse of ranchos on mostly barren, uncultivated land.

San Diego Bay

Juan Rodríguez Cabrillo landed on Ballast Point in 1542. His arrival to California is commemorated at the Cabrillo National Monument and Visitors' Center located on Point Loma.[1] Harbor and Shelter islands, two peninsulas reaching into the harbor today, did not exist in 1850. These popular tourist destinations and the center for San Diego's yachting industry would not be created from landfill until nearly a century later.

Coronado was considered an island, but even in 1850 it was the peninsula it is today connected to the mainland on the southern coast of the county by a narrow nine-mile isthmus of sand called the Silver Strand. Several different short-term owners grazed cattle on this land grant of brush and sand dunes known as *Rancho Península de San Diego*. These owners were regarded as crazy for owning a rancho where the grass was sparse, there was little water, and the only way to move the cattle to or from the rancho was on the narrow strip of sand separating the Pacific Ocean from the San Diego Bay. Quail and jackrabbits would roam freely on the barren land of Coronado until 1885; shortly thereafter, the famous Del Coronado Hotel was built and much later the U.S. Navy established major operations here. The "islanders" survived without the San Diego-Coronado Bridge across the bay until 1969.

At high tide, North Island was in fact an island, separated from Coronado by a narrow body of water called the Spanish Bight. The Navy filled in the bight in 1944.

Sites to Visit in San Diego County

Asistencia de San Antonio de Pala, Hwy 16 in Pala, east of I-15

Asistencia de Santa Isabel and Museum, Highway 79, 1.5 miles n. of Santa Ysabel

Cabrillo National Monument, 1800 Cabrillo Memorial Dr., San Diego 619.557.5450

Camp Pendleton, Vandegrift Bl., Oceanside

Junipero Serra Museum, 2727 Presidio Dr., Presidio Park, San Diego   619.297.3258

Mission San Diego Alcala, 10818 San Diego Mission Rd., San Diego 619.283.7319

Mission San Luis Rey, 4050 Mission Av., Oceanside 760.757.3651

Museum of San Diego History, 1649 El Prado, Balboa Park, San Diego   619.232.6203

Old Town San Diego State Historic Park, 3990 Old Town Av., San Diego   619.237.6772

Rancho Buena Vista Adobe, 651 East Vista Dr., Vista   760.639.6164

San Pasqual Battlefield State Historic Park, 15808 San Pasqual Valley Rd., Escondido 760.737.2201

William Heath Davis House Museum, 410 Island Av., San Diego   619.233.5227

San Diego International Visitors Information Center, 11 Horton Plaza, San Diego, CA 92101 619.236.1212

Old La Playa served as San Diego's port until 1870. A rustic trading and shipping village housed the "hide-houses" that were an integral part of the lucrative hide and tallow trade business. Richard Henry Dana, author of *Two Years Before the Mast*, found the San Diego port to be the best one in the 1830s for loading and unloading the hides. The site, now altered by land fill, was located on Point Loma near the current entrance to the Military Reserve on Rosecrans Street.

Even though the port of San Diego was hundreds of miles away from the gold fields, it was also a debarkation point for many gold-seekers arriving by ship from around Cape Horn or from Panama, Nicaragua, or Mexico. A few of these adventurers fell in love with San Diego's unrivaled climate, however, and never ventured north.

Presidio Hill and the San Diego Pueblo

The first California mission and fort were built on Presidio Hill in 1769. The *San Diego Royale Presidio* was situated a short distance from the river and the bay with an excellent view of the surrounding area. The old garrison was completely deserted and dismantled by 1837; in 1850 only the walls of the presidio chapel and portions of other buildings were still standing.

The original site of *Misión San Diego de Alcalá* was found to be unsatisfactory because of its proximity to the presidio (the soldiers at the presidio often abused the mission Indians) and lack of fertile soil and a dependable water supply; the mission was moved six miles away in 1774. Several of the date palms planted by Father Junipero Serra—the first non-native plants to be planted in California—remained atop the hill in 1850, but nothing remained of the original mission. Today the Junipero Serra Museum, the Serra Cross, and the sites of the various presidio buildings make up Presidio Park.

As soldiers stationed at the presidio retired, they began to cultivate plots of land below Presidio Hill. As the presidio declined in importance, a new settlement evolved and became large enough to qualify as a pueblo by the mid-1830s. The pueblo—the area known today as "Old Town"—sprang up at the height of the hide and tallow trade business.

San Diego was the first city to be incorporated by an act of the California State Legislature on March 27, 1850. Joshua Bean was elected the first mayor.

Visitors to San Diego in 1850 found the residents to be extremely hospitable, but were a little surprised by the primitiveness of the buildings and the general state of uncleanliness throughout the town. The San Diego River passed close to town; its water was muddied and contaminated because clothes were washed at the foot of every street and horses and livestock were watered there. The river polluted the harbor and several times came close to flooding and destroying the pueblo. Other times, water was in short supply and stone water filters were used to clear small pebbles out of the water. There were few trees and the open areas were sandy and overgrown by bushes and thickets.

Gambling and excessive consumption of alcohol were prevalent, which led to frequent occurrences of dueling, gun battles, and knifings. Visitors hitched their horses to the railing around the flagstaff on the plaza, and large numbers of cattle were allowed to run free, causing a nuisance and safety hazard, especially at night.

José Antonio Estudillo (1805-1852)

- Owned property in San Diego and Riverside counties
- First treasurer and assessor of San Diego County
- Father of 12 children

A public school was started in 1850, but an official schoolhouse would not be built for another 15 years. Catholics worshipped at the mission, but the first Protestant church (the First Baptist Church of San Diego) was not founded until 1869.

The Mormon Battalion made many improvements to the pueblo after their arrival in 1847. The soldiers arrived too late to participate in the Mexican-American War, so they hired themselves out to the townspeople—whitewashing the adobe buildings throughout the town to brighten it up, building log pumps, digging wells, blacksmithing, repairing carts, and building a kiln for firing bricks to repair and reinforce existing buildings. They also helped the residents build a fired-brick building, originally intended to be the schoolhouse and town hall, but which became the first courthouse of San Diego in March 1850.

U.S. Army Lieutenant Cave Johnson Couts had drawn the first subdivision map of the pueblo in 1849. Many structures were situated around the plaza, a number of which remain today, including the San Diego Courthouse, the San Diego House, which was a small adobe saloon operated by the first two African American men to live in San Diego, Richard Freeman and Allen B. Light; and the United States House, a two-story prefabricated wood frame building brought to San Diego from San Francisco in 1850 by Charles Noell. He and John Hayes operated a provisions store here. The Colorado House was under construction in 1850; Couts would begin operating San Diego's first two-story hotel the next year.

A number of residences were situated on the plaza, as well. José and María Silvas and their children lived in the *Casa de Machado y Silvas*, which was a nine-room, thatched-roof adobe, with a patio and garden. The American shoemaker, Thomas Wrightington, and his

The San Diego Courthouse in "Old Town."

The San Diego House was an adobe saloon operated by the first two African American men to live in San Diego, Richard Freeman and Allen B. Light.

The Colorado House was under construction in 1850 and would open as San Diego's first two-story hotel the next year.

family lived in the one-story *Casa de Machado-Wrightington* adobe, which had views of the plaza and the beach, which was only a short distance from the plaza then. Francisco Alvarado and his wife, Thomas Pico, sister of *Don* Pío Pico,[2] lived in the *Casa de Alvarado*, one of the earliest structures. The Frenchman Adolph Savin lived in the *Casa de Bandini*, a one-story building (at the time) with a portion of the house converted into a dry goods store. *Don* José Antonio Estudillo, son of the late *commandante* of the Presidio, lived in the *Casa de Estudillo* with his wife and 12 children. The house he inherited from his father had long been the social and political center of San Diego. The José Manuel Machado family, including their daughter and her husband Jack Stewart, a sailor and carpenter from Maine, lived in the *Casa de Machado y Stewart* adobe.

Other adobe homes were scattered around the town, including the *Casa de Lopez* and the *Casa de Carrillo*, which today stands on the Presidio Golf Course. Some of the adobes fell into disrepair when residents left town temporarily for the gold fields; other homes were available to rent until the rainy season when the owners were expected to return. (For the most part, however, San Diegans did not join the Gold Rush. Instead, their cattle were their "gold mines.")

San Diego would remain a sleepy village for many years to come—contrasting

The Casa de Bandini is a popular restaurant in "Old Town" today, but in 1850 it was a one-story residence and dry goods store.

The Casa de Estudillo had long been the social and political center of San Diego.

The Casa de Machado y Stewart housed the extended family of José Manuel Machado.

with its current ranking of second largest city in the state and the sixth largest city in the nation. The *San Diego Herald* began publication in 1851. It would be another 34 years (1884) before the transcontinental railroad provided San Diego with the needed transportation link to the rest of the country, finally allowing it to become competitive with other California cities that had already reaped the benefits of the "iron horse" since 1869.

A visit to Old Town today provides a vivid picture of San Diego's Spanish heritage, thanks to the restoration that began in 1968 in preparation for its 200th anniversary in 1969. A fire had destroyed much of Old Town in 1872, but a number of pre- and post-1850 structures have either been restored or reconstructed to make up the Old Town San Diego State Historic Park, which recreates the San Diego of 1872. The San Diego River no longer passes near town as it was engineered to turn into "the false bay" in 1853. The beach is no longer visible from Old Town as Interstate 5 and Mission Bay Park lie in between.

Mission Bay, America's largest aquatic park today, was created in 1960 by dredging, filling, and landscaping the area west of Old Town. This area was called "the false bay" by the early Spanish explorers because the body of water sometimes became a swampy marshland due to the irregular flow of the San Diego River.

Present-day La Jolla along the coast—the tenth most affluent community in the U.S. today—was part of pueblo land owned by the City of San Diego. It would remain so until 1869 when it was sold to Samuel Sizer for $1.25 an acre.

The area southeast of Old Town, developed into Balboa Park in 1868, was a rugged, uninhabited canyon in 1850. It would be 42 years before Kate O. Sessions began planting trees from all over the world, and many more years before the ornate exhibit halls and world-famous San Diego Zoo were built.

New Town

The new arrivals to San Diego who opted not to continue on to the gold fields concentrated instead on transforming the quiet Mexican community into a thriving commercial center. The town's location three miles from the natural shipping port seemed inappropriate to the ambitious financier, William Heath Davis. In 1850 he convinced the U.S. Army to build a sup-

The Casa de Carrillo stands on the Presidio Golf Course in "Old Town."

ply depot south of town in the vicinity of the current Pacific Highway and Market Street. It was called the New San Diego Post and was occupied by troops from December 1850 to May 1866. Davis set up a few prefabricated, wooden houses by the bay, but ran out of money before his city could become established. His 1850 "salt box" house (the William Heath Davis House), built in Maine and shipped around Cape Horn, stood at State and Market streets. Today it has been relocated to the Gaslamp Quarter, where it serves as a house museum and the offices of a historical foundation. It would be 1867 before Alonzo E. Horton transformed the mudflats and sagebrush of the area into "New Town," which in turn led to the general decline of "Old Town."

San Diego Mission

The second *Misión San Diego de Alcalá* was built in 1774, six miles northeast of the pueblo. In 1846 the mission was deeded to *Don* Santiago Argüello, a former Presidio *commandante*. The terms required him to pay the mission's debts, support the priests, and maintain religious services. In 1850, and until 1859, the U.S. Calvary occupied the mission. The troops cut down most of the trees in the orchard for firewood, but at least kept the mission in repair. The mission would fall into ruin in later years, however, and require complete restoration, which was done in 1931.

San Diego County Ranchos

Vast ranchos made up the rest of present-day San Diego County. Cattle, horses, and sheep roamed the unfenced rolling hills and quiet valleys beyond the pueblo and the former mission. Details about some of the more interesting ranchos follow.

One of the most desirable ranchos in the county, *Rancho El Cajon*, was owned by *Don* Miguel and *Doña* María Antonia Estudillo de Pedrorena.[3] *Doña* María was the daughter of *Don* José Antonio Estudillo. She was the original recipient of the land grant and also one of the few women to be fortunate enough to receive a land grant. The Pedrorenas built a large adobe home and smaller house on the rancho and continued to harvest grapes from the vines planted 50 years earlier by the mission padres.

Don Domingo Yorba purchased *Rancho Cañada de San Vicente* in 1850 from *Don* Juan Bautista López, the original grantee. The sales agreement for $2,000 included the requirement that Yorba feed, clothe, and provide a house for López and his wife for the rest of their lives.

Rancho Santa María and *Rancho Santa Ysabel* were owned by Captain Edward Stokes, an English merchant ship captain, and his father-in-law, *Don* José J. Ortega. The Stokes family lived on the *Santa Ysabel*, operating the two grants as one rancho.

Asistencia de Santa Ysabel, which had been an outpost of the San Diego Mission to serve the Native Americans living in the region, was located between the *Santa María* and *Santa Ysabel* ranchos. The chapel that continues today as a place of worship for American Indians from five area reservations was built in 1924. The original chapel lay in ruins in 1850 and was later completely destroyed by fire. A museum of history is maintained on the grounds today.

Don Juan (John) Forster[4] owned *Rancho San Felipe*, which was located at the foot of Banner Grade at Scissors Crossing on the road to Warner Springs. Thousands of cattle and horses grazed on the rolling hills and grassy valleys of this semi-desert rancho. Explorers, adventurers, and missionaries had passed through this area before Forster became the owner.

The restored chapel of the Asistencia de San Antonio de Pala near Pala is used for worship services today.

The Mormon Battalion had accomplished quite a feat in 1847 by using axes to cut a pass through the solid rock of Box Canyon near San Felipe Valley. Many settlers and stagecoaches would follow the Southern Emigrant Trail through this canyon for years to come.

Jonathan Trumbull Warner, a Connecticut fur trader, came to California in 1831. He learned Spanish, became friends with Pío Pico, and received a land grant for the entire valley lying between the Cleveland National Forest and the Anza-Borrego State Park. The land grant was composed of *Rancho San José del Valle* and *Rancho Valle de San José*. Warner built an adobe house and trading post four miles southwest of present-day Warner Springs.

Warner was a generous host and Warner Ranch became a popular place along the trail to San Diego that diverged from the main Southern Emigrant Trail to Los Angeles. Today an old adobe ranch house and barn are preserved as a National Historic Landmark on San Felipe Road, but questions have recently arisen as to whether this was Warner's or buildings built in 1857 by a subsequent owner. It is possible that Warner's ranch house was built on a nearby hill and destroyed by an American Indian uprising in 1851.

Asistencia de San Antonio de Pala lay in ruins just north of present-day Pala. This branch of *Misión San Luis Rey* had served the American Indians living on the nearby ranchos located 20 miles inland from the mission on the coast. The chapel has since been restored and is used for worship services today.

On the coast, *Misión San Luis Rey de Francia*, one of the largest of California's 21 missions, and *Las Flores Asistencia* lay in ruins. When the mission was sold in

1846, the property was divided up and its buildings stripped of all material goods. The "King of the Missions" would not be restored until the late 1800s. Today this structure serves as a Franciscan retreat center, but is open to the public, as well.

Rancho Santa Margarita y las Flores, considered the choicest grant in the area, was owned by the Pico brothers, Pío and Andrés. There were 35 miles of coastline, seven rivers and streams, seven small lakes, and three mountain ranges on this property. The Picos raised cattle, horses, and sheep; their barns and corrals covered many acres. Their adobe home on a knoll overlooking a small lake would become the residence of the commandant of Camp Pendleton[5] (with considerable modernization) and still stands today, as does a chapel built nearby by mission Indians in 1810, which the Pico brothers used as a winery. Many of the U.S. Marine Corps camp names on this base reflect the Spanish heritage of this former rancho.

The Misión San Luis Rey de Francia, located in Oceanside, is known as the "King of the Missions."

Two Native American brothers, Andrés and José Manuel, owned *Guajome Rancho*. Several ponds and lakes graced this rancho that was sold to *Don* Abel Stearns[6] for $550 in late 1850. Stearns would give it as a wedding gift to his sister-in-law, Ysidora Bandini, when she married the American Colonel Cave J. Couts in 1851. Today their 1852 adobe is located in the Guajome Regional Park in Oceanside.

The Rancho Buena Vista Adobe, located in the center of Vista, looks as it did following the remodeling done by its owners during the 1870s.

Rancho Buena Vista was a cattle ranch owned by a Native American, Félipe Subria. It was once part of the grazing lands of *Misión San Luis Rey*. Today the Rancho Buena Vista Adobe, built in the late 1840s, is located in the center of Vista and looks as it did following the remodeling done by its owners during the 1870s.

Don Juan María Marrón owned *Rancho Agua Hedionda*, but in 1850 he and his family no longer lived here. The Marróns nevertheless continued to gather salt from the lagoons located on the property, traveling from their home in San Diego. John Brown, an American sailing captain, leased a portion of the rancho from Marrón and raised cattle and horses here.

The widow of the late Joseph F. Snook, a British sea captain who had forsaken the sea to become a *ranchero*, lived on *Rancho San Bernardo*. She married Henry Clayton in 1850, who was the county's first surveyor.

The famous Battle of San Pasqual of the Mexican-American War had taken place a few miles from the Snook ranch house in 1846. Mule Hill was so-named because the weary, beaten American troops awaiting reinforcements from San Diego had to resort to eating their mules at this site to avoid starvation.[7]

Finally, *Rancho San Dieguito* was owned by *Don* Juan María Osuna, the first *alcalde* of San Diego. The excellent grazing land was stocked with cattle and horses.

SAN DIEGO COUNTY RANCHOS

NAME OF RANCHO	GRANTEE AND/OR 1850 OWNER	1850 AND/OR CURRENT SITES
Rancho Peninsula de San Diego	Various owners	Coronado
Rancho de la Misión San Diego de Alcalá	Santiago Argüello (leased to Philip Crosthwaite)	San Diego Mission, San Diego
Rancho El Cajon (The Box or The Pass Between Two Hills)	Miguel and María Antonia Estudillo de Pedrorena	La Mesa, El Cajon, Bostonia, Glenview, Santee
Rancho de la Cañada de los Coches (Glen of the Hogs)	Polinaria Lorenzana	28 acres within Rancho El Cajon (see above)
Rancho Jamacha (Wild Squash Vine or Gourd)	Polinaria Lorenzana	Sycamore Canyon County Park
Rancho de la Nación (National Ranch)	Juan (John) Forster	National City, Bonita, Sunnyside, Chula Vista
Otay (Brushy Place) and Janal (Spongy Ground) ranchos	A son and daughter of José Antonio Estudillo	Chula Vista, Otay
Rancho Jamul (Slimy Water)	Pío Pico	Jamul
Rancho Cuyamaca (Rain Above)	Agustín Olvera	Cuyamaca Rancho State Park
Rancho Cañada (Glen) de San Vicente	Domingo Yorba	San Vicente Reservoir
Rancho Santa María and Rancho Santa Ysabel	Captain Edward Stokes and José J. Ortega	Ramona, Julian
Rancho San Felipe	Juan (John) Forster	Foot of Banner Grade at Scissors Crossing
Rancho San José del Valle and Rancho Valle de San José	Jonathan Trumbull Warner	Warner Springs
Rancho Cuca	María Juana de Los Angeles	South of Mt. Palomar
Rancho Pauma	José Antonio Serrano	Pauma Valley
Rancho Guejito y Cañada de Palomino (Small Pebbles in the Glen of the Small Pigeon)	José María Orozco	Lake Wohlford
Rancho Monserrate	Ysidro María Alvarado	Pala Mesa
Rancho Santa Margarita y las Flores	Pío and Andrés Pico	Oceanside, Camp Pendleton, Fallbrook
Guajome Rancho (Home of the Big Frog)	Andrés and José Manuel; Abel Stearns	Guajome Regional Park, Oceanside
Rancho Buena Vista (Good View)	Félipe Subria	Vista
Rancho Agua Hedionda (Stinking Water)	Juan María Marrón	Carlsbad, Vista
Rancho Los Vallecitos de San Marcos (Little Valleys of St. Mark)	Luguarda Osuna Alvarado, widow of José María Alvarado	Vista, Escondido
Rancho El Rincón del Diablo (Devil's Corner or Nook of the Devil)	Juan Bautista Alvarado family	Escondido
Rancho San Bernardo	Widow of Joseph F. Snook	Rancho Bernardo, Lake Hodges
Rancho Las Encinitas (Little Live Oaks)	Heirs of Andrés Ybarra	Encinitas
Rancho San Dieguito	Juan María Osuna	Rancho Santa Fe
Rancho Los Peñasquitos (Little Cliffs or Small Rocks)	Francisco María Alvarado	Del Mar, Rancho Peñasquitos

An adobe ranch house and an adobe barn stood on the property. The Osuna house was restored and remodeled, and once was owned by the late Bing Crosby.

Today San Diego County is often called the "desert on the ocean" because its lack of natural sources of water requires 90 percent of its water supply to be imported from regions hundreds of miles away. The lakes and reservoirs of San Diego County would not be constructed until the 1880 to 1920 period—another cause of San Diego's slow growth.[8]

Area Within Present-Day Imperial County

There are no 1850 Sites to Visit in Imperial County

El Centro Chamber of Commerce & Visitors Bureau, 1095 S. 4th St., P. O. Box 3006, El Centro, CA 92244 760.352.3681

The part of 1850-San Diego County that would later become Imperial County in 1907 was a mere thoroughfare for the adventurers, gold miners, and settlers coming to California. Tracks of emigrant wagons can still be seen in several areas through which the historic trails passed. There were no ranchos and no towns. Only the Kumeyaay and Yuma Indians inhabited temporary villages during limited periods of the year when it was not too hot or the Colorado River was not flooding the valley.

Two missions—*Misión La Purísima Concepción* and *Misión San Pedro y San Pablo*—once were located in the southeastern corner of Imperial County on the Colorado River, but were destroyed by the Yuma Indians in 1781. The hostility of these American Indians led to the abandonment of several of the routes through Imperial County, and was the impetus behind the establishment of Fort Yuma in 1850, where *Misión La Purísima* once stood.

Several ferries were transporting gold-seekers across the Colorado River in 1850 below its junction with the Gila River. Lumber for at least one of the ferries was transported across the desert from San Diego by pack train.

Today, much of this barren desert has been transformed into the vast farm, pasture, and recreational lands of the Imperial Valley. Although water from the Colorado River would not flow into the first irrigation canal until 1901, the idea of the reclamation of the desert was the brainchild of an Ohio-born physician, Dr. Oliver Meredith Wozencraft,[9] who came to California during the Gold Rush. While on an expedition from San Francisco to the Colorado Desert in 1849, he developed the idea of reclamation and dedicated the rest of his life to pursuing his dream. (He died in 1887 and his work would need to be completed by Charles Robinson Rockwood and George Chaffey.)

It also should be noted that the Salton Sea, one of the world's largest inland bodies of saltwater today, did not exist in 1850. It would be created by floodwaters from the Colorado River in 1905.

Development of the cities of Imperial, Calexico, Brawley, Holtville, and El Centro would not take place until the early 1900s following reclamation and the construction of a branch line from the Southern Pacific railway. El Centro was not linked to San Diego by rail until 1919.

Sites to Visit in Riverside County

Agua Mansa Cemetery—See San Bernardino County Sites

Riverside Municipal Museum, 3580 Mission Inn Av., Riverside 909.782.5273

Visitors and Convention Bureau, 3443 Orange St., Riverside, CA 92501   909.787.7950

Juan Bandini (1800-1859)

- Well-educated Peruvian of Italian descent
- Builder and original owner of *La Casa de Bandini* in San Diego
- Large landowner in Riverside and San Bernardino counties
- Social and political leader in San Diego and Los Angeles, including *alcalde* of San Diego
- Father of Ysidora (wife of Col. Cave J. Couts) and Arcadia (wife of Abel Stearns), and one other daughter and two sons; five more children from second wife

AREA WITHIN PRESENT-DAY RIVERSIDE COUNTY

Most of present-day Riverside County was within 1850-San Diego County until 1893. A small northwestern portion was part of Los Angeles County until 1853 and a northern strip was in San Bernardino County between 1853 and 1893.[10]

The low desert and mountainous areas of the eastern and central parts of Riverside County remained Native American lands in 1850. Palm Springs and the surrounding area would not begin their development as recreational oases until the late 1880s, and non-natives did not even discover Indian Wells and Desert Hot Springs until 1906 and 1908, respectively.

Rocky hills, uplands with annual grasses and dry brush, and fertile river valleys that were occasionally flooded by the Santa Ana and San Jacinto rivers made up the rest of Riverside County. No pueblos, missions, or *asistencias* were located in the county, but the San Gabriel, San Juan Capistrano, and San Luis Rey missions had used some of the area for raising grain and cattle. Many early explorers and adventurers had passed through here, as well.

Riverside County Ranchos

Three clusters of ranchos and one isolated rancho occupied the western portion of Riverside County; the eastern portion of the county was in the public domain. Most of the 13 ranchos were undeveloped; settlement in Riverside County was off to a very slow start and would not really get under way until the citrus industry was established in the 1870s. Details about the more interesting ranchos follow.

Little Temecula Rancho was a two thousand-plus-acre land grant owned by *Don* Pablo Apis. John Magee operated a store on this property in 1850 at the crossroads of the Southern Emigrant Trail and the road to San Diego. His establishment provided a resting-place for settlers and gold-seekers traveling the southern route into California and would later become a stagecoach stop.

Rancho Pauba, *Rancho Temecula*, and *Rancho Santa Rosa* were located in an area that would remain a working cattle ranch—Vail Ranch—until the mid-1960s when it was sold to various partnerships and developed into Rancho California. What is known today as "Old Town Temecula" was not established until 1882 when the Santa Fe Railway came through the valley.

Don Julian Manríquez owned *Rancho La Laguna*, where the present-day community of Lake Elsinore is located. *Don* Abel Stearns acquired ownership of this rancho sometime during 1850. Underground springs and the unrestricted flow of the San Jacinto River fed the lake. The lake and the surrounding area would become a resort spot when the hot sulfur springs were discovered in the 1880s.

Don Juan Bandini raised sheep on his *Rancho Jurupa*, which lay south of Slover Mountain. Bandini, formerly of San Diego, was one of the first non-natives to settle in the area in 1838. His home on a bluff overlooking the Santa Ana River was the center of social life in the region.

Don Louis Rubidoux owned a portion of Bandini's *Rancho Jurupa* in 1850 and lived in an 1843 adobe house. Rubidoux built a two-story east wing soon after he purchased the property overlooking the Santa Ana River. He also enlarged the vineyard and built an irrigation ditch. He grew wheat and operated one of the first grist-mills in this part of California.

There also were two settlements of "New Mexicans" on the *Rancho Jurupa* in an area called the "Bandini Donation," which crossed the present-day Riverside/San Bernardino County line. Bandini had given an allotment of land to these Spanish-speaking Mexican-Indian settlers, who were led by Manuel Lorenzo Trujillo. They moved here from Politana, which was located on a rancho in present-day San Bernardino County, to establish a permanent settlement designed to deter the local Native Americans from attacking the region.

In two villages on the banks of the Santa Ana River—*Agua Mansa* (Gentle Water) and *San Salvador* or *La Placita* (The Little Place) *de los Trujillos*—they farmed, built schools and churches, and formed a community that reflected their traditional background. The settlers used the limestone from the Jurupa Mountains to make the whitewash for their adobe buildings. Their sheep, cattle, and horses grazed for miles in the river bottom.

A flood in 1862 would destroy these two settlements; both were rebuilt on higher ground, but the towns never returned to their original size and were eventually abandoned. The Agua Mansa Cemetery is the only remaining evidence of this settlement. The cemetery lies atop a bluff in San Bernardino County overlooking the Santa Ana River Valley.

Louis Rubidoux (1796-1868)

- Originally Robidoux
- French immigrant fur trapper from Missouri
- Served as a judge
- Namesake of several geographical features, including a mountain in the city of Riverside

RIVERSIDE COUNTY RANCHOS

NAME OF RANCHO	GRANTEE AND/OR 1850 OWNER	1850 AND/OR CURRENT SITES
Little Temecula (Sweat Lodge)	Pablo Apis	Temecula
Rancho Pauba	Luis Vignes	Temecula, Rancho California
Rancho Temecula (Sweat Lodge)	Luis Vignes	Temecula, Rancho California
Rancho Santa Rosa	Juan Moreno	Temecula, Rancho California
Rancho La Laguna (Lake)	Julian Manríquez, Abel Stearns	Lake Elsinore
Rancho San Jacinto Viejo	José Antonio Estudillo	San Jacinto, Hemet [11]
Rancho San Jacinto Nuevo y Potrero (Pasture Land)	Miguel Pedrorena	San Jacinto, Perris, and Moreno valleys
Rancho San Jacinto y San Gorgonio	Santiago Johnson	Beaumont, Banning, Cherry Valley
Rancho Jurupa (Water Place)	Juan Bandini, Louis Rubidoux, "New Mexicans"	Riverside, Rubidoux, extended into San Bernardino Co.
Rancho La Sierra Sepúlveda	Vicente Sepúlveda	Norco
Rancho La Sierra Yorba	Bernardo Yorba	Corona
Rancho El Sobrante (Surplus) de San Jacinto	José Antonio and María del Rosario Estudillo Aguirre	South of Riverside
Rancho Serrano or Rancho Temescal (Sweat Lodge)	Leandro Serrano	Temescal Valley near Glen Ivy Hot Springs

Finally, *Rancho Serrano* was owned by *Don* Leandro Serrano, the county's first permanent European resident. He and his family lived on this rancho in the first house built in Riverside County. Serrano taught the local Native Americans how to plant fruit trees and vineyards, and raise sheep and cattle. A small settlement would develop as his 13 children built their own homes on the rancho.

AREA WITHIN PRESENT-DAY SAN BERNARDINO COUNTY

Sites to Visit in San Bernardino County

Agua Mansa Cemetery, 2001 W. Agua Mansa Rd., Colton 909.370.2091

San Bernardino Asistencia, 26930 Barton Rd., Redlands 909.793.5402

San Bernardino County Museum, 2024 Orange Tree Ln., Redlands 909.307.2669

Yorba-Slaughter Adobe (1853), 17127 Pomona Rincon Rd., Chino 909.597.8332

Yucaipa Adobe, 32183 Kentucky St., Yucaipa 909.795.3485

San Bernardino County Convention and Visitors Bureau, 201 N. E St., Ste. 103, San Bernardino, CA 92401 909.889.3980

San Bernardino County would be organized in 1853 from part of Los Angeles County, but in 1850 it was part of San Diego County.[12] In terms of physical area, San Bernardino County is the largest county in the U.S. and larger than nine states. The huge Mojave Desert covers 90 percent of its area. The San Bernardino and San Gabriel mountains separate the desert from the San Bernardino Valley. In the 18th and early 19th centuries, many explorers had traveled through the Cajon Pass, which lies between these two mountain ranges.

In 1850 the San Bernardino Valley was a grassland, with native trees growing in the foothills and along the banks of the streams flowing out of the mountains and across the valley floor. Most of the trees would be logged off in the 1850s for timber or firewood as settlements arose in the valley, or died due to the dropping water table caused by the increased demands for water.

The Santa Ana River originates in the San Bernardino Mountains and is the major stream of the San Bernardino Valley. It was an all-year stream until 1860. The river flowed through the valley in a confined, tree-lined channel. Today most of the river is contained within a cement-lined canal. In low rainfall years, the canal is often completely dry.

Several small lakes filled natural basins within the boundaries of San Bernardino County, but Big Bear, Arrowhead, and Silverwood lakes would not be created until the late 1800s and early 1900s. However, the Big Bear area had been named by *Don* Benito (Benjamin Davis) Wilson[13] in 1845 when he discovered a valley crawling with grizzly bears.

San Bernardino County Ranchos

The greater part of what was to become San Bernardino County remained in the public domain; Mexican land grants had been awarded only in the valley area. From mission times on, raiding parties of outlaws seeking valuable livestock plagued the San Bernardino Valley in the southwestern corner of the county. Settlement was deliberately encouraged in the area to deter the raiders from attacking the ranchos.[14]

Rancho El Rincón was originally owned by *Don* Juan Bandini. *El Rincón* was adjacent to his *Rancho Jurupa* in Riverside County, crossing the present-day county line. Bandini had built an impressive, two-story home on the *El Rincón* property around 1840 or 1841, using lumber from the San Bernardino Mountains.

In 1850, however, *Don* Raimundo Yorba was the owner of *Rancho El Rincón*. In 1851 he built a house on the site where the Yorba-Slaughter Adobe stands today in Chino. His home burned and was replaced by the present structure in 1852-53.

The road at the foot of the hill on this site was part of the travel route from Fort Yuma to Los Angeles and the Yorba Adobe would become a stage stop.

Rancho Santa Ana del Chino, a former *Misión San Gabriel* rancho, was owned by Colonel Isaac Williams, the son-in-law of the wealthy and influential *Don* Antonio María Lugo. The rancho had orchards, vineyards, and wheat fields, as well as a grist-mill and soap factory. Scattered around the rancho were adobe huts for the many Native American and Mexican laborers that tended the crops and cared for the cattle, horses, and sheep. The adobe ranch house, with its roof of tule thatch water-proofed with asphalt brought from the La Brea tar pits in Los Angeles, stood just south of present-day Chino. It was the center of much activity, due to its proximity to the well-traveled Southern Emigrant Trail. Williams was especially generous, often hosting 10 to 20 guests at his dinner table, and frequently loaning supplies or money to the travelers passing through. In fact, his rancho was the southern California counterpart of Sutter's Fort in northern California—a stopover for rest and supplies.

Don Tiburcio Tapia, a prominent merchant and former *alcalde* in Los Angeles, owned *Rancho Cucamonga*, which lay where the city of the same name is located today. His huge adobe sat on the slope of Cucamonga's highest hill, Red Hill. Tapia, through the efforts of his *mayordomo* José María Valdez, established the first commercial winery in California in 1839—the Cucamonga Rancho Winery. The *Misión San Gabriel* provided the black mission grape cuttings used by Tapia to establish the mother vineyard; the winery's two 1400-gallon oak aging casks were brought around the Horn on a clipper ship. As early as 1845, there were 3,400 vines on Tapia's 15,000-acre spread.

Don Miguel (Michael White) Blanco, a former English sailor, owned *Rancho Muscupiabe*. The Lugo family that owned the adjacent rancho had persuaded him to build on his property to provide protection for the valley ranchos from the raids on livestock by the desert and mountain American Indians and traders from New Mexico. White built a fortress home of logs and earth overlooking both the lower Cajon Pass and the old Mojave Trail, but he was unsuccessful at warding off the raiders and even lost his own livestock. After only nine months, he abandoned the site and moved to a land grant in Los Angeles County that he had acquired in 1843.

SAN BERNARDINO COUNTY RANCHOS

NAME OF RANCHO	GRANTEE AND/OR 1850 OWNER	1850 AND/OR CURRENT SITES
Rancho El Rincón (Corner)	Raimundo Yorba	Chino, extended into Riverside Co.
Rancho Santa Ana del Chino (Curly Hair)	Isaac Williams	Ontario
Rancho Cucamonga	Tiburcio Tapia	Rancho Cucamonga
Rancho Muscupiabe	Michael White	North of San Bernardino
Rancho San Bernardino	Lugo brothers	San Bernardino, Fontana, Colton, Redlands, Yucaipa

Three Lugo brothers and a cousin of the Lugo family owned the former *Misión San Gabriel* rancho, *Rancho San Bernardino*. Livestock raising was the principal activity here.

Don José del Carmen Lugo repaired the former mission rancho structures and lived in the old buildings of the former *Asistencia San Bernardino*. A gristmill and a tile and limekiln stood on the property. An irrigation ditch, which the mission Indians had built in 1820 to bring water from mountain streams to this mission outpost 12 miles away, was still in operation. Lugo had his own *Plaza de Toros* for bull and bear fights.

The *Asistencia* and other adobes on the property were abandoned in later years and fell to ruin. The reconstructed, six-room *Asistencia* standing today was completed in 1937; it is much more beautiful than the original building and serves as a museum, with a historic 1840s dining room and a wedding chapel.

Don José María Lugo lived in an adobe located where the San Bernardino County Courthouse stands today, and *Don* José Diego Sepúlveda, cousin to the three Lugo brothers, lived in an adobe located in the Yucaipa Valley between Redlands and Yucaipa. Sepúlveda raised cattle as well as a number of swine that prospered on the acorns of the live oaks growing in what came to be known as *Cañon de Prierco* (Hog Canyon), the present-day Wildwood Canyon.

The reconstructed Asistencia San Bernardino serves as a museum, with an 1840s dining room and wedding chapel.

There are differences of opinion as to when the Yucaipa Adobe was built— 1842 or 1858.

Until recently, the Yucaipa Adobe was thought to be the oldest standing residential building in San Bernardino County and built by Sepúlveda in 1842. Now, however, some believe that his adobe was actually located a few hundred yards away and that the Yucaipa Adobe was not built until 1858 by James Waters. Others are of the opinion that the first floor of this adobe was built by Sepúlveda and the second floor added on by Waters.

The third brother, *Don* Vicente Lugo, built a home near Sienna Hot Springs on a ridge, which today leads from Bunker Hill to an area near the San Bernardino Valley College in San Bernardino.

A band of Cahuilla Indians from the Santa Rosa Mountains lived in an area of present-day Colton called Politana, where the New Mexican settlers had lived before they moved to *Agua Mansa* and *San Salvador* in Riverside County. The Lugos brought the Cahuilla Indians in to provide further protection for the valley from livestock raiders. The New Mexicans had built homes, dug irrigation ditches, and planted crops on this land. An adobe church was still standing in 1850.

On the side of Slover Mountain in Colton, Isaac Slover, an American hunter and trapper from Kentucky, and his New Mexican wife from *Agua Mansa* made their home. The mountain, a prominent valley landmark, was originally known to the Native Americans as Tahualtapa (Raven Hill), because it was the nesting place for large flocks of ravens. Slover frequently hunted in the mountains.

A colony of Mormons from Salt Lake City would purchase the *Rancho San Bernardino* from the Lugos in 1851. The Mormons are credited with starting the community of San Bernardino and establishing the valley's irrigation system, as well as the lumber and agriculture industries that made San Bernardino a vital force in the growth and development of southern California in later years.

Southern California's largest gold rush would occur in 1860 in the Holcomb and Bear valleys of the San Bernardino Mountains, and silver was discovered in the Calico region near present-day Barstow in the 1880s. Growth of the county also coincided with the construction of the railroad in 1875. Settlers were attracted to the San Bernardino Valley by the pleasant climate and inexpensive land.

AREA WITHIN HALF OF PRESENT-DAY INYO COUNTY

Finally, the San Diego County of 1850 included a triangular portion of present-day Inyo County, which consisted primarily of most of Death Valley on the eastern border of California.[15] The long, sunken desert basin, surrounded by high mountains, had received its grim name following the William Lewis Manly and Jayhawker gold-seeking parties' attempt to cross the valley into California in 1849-50. Legend has it that one member of the party turned back and said, "Goodbye, Death Valley!" In truth, only one man in the entire group of lost forty-niners died within the modern day boundaries of Death Valley. However, the ascribed name stuck.

Chemehuevi Indians wintered in this area of San Diego County, but otherwise there was no civilization in these parts. It would be 1860 before Death Valley had visitors interested in something more than just passing through as quickly as possible. Mining and scientific expeditions in the early 1860s brought the first people to place any value on the area that today makes up Death Valley National Park.

Sites to Visit in Southeastern Inyo County

Death Valley National Park, Death Valley 760.786.2331

Death Valley Chamber of Commerce, P.O. Box 157, Shoshone, CA 92384-0157
760.852.4524

Notes ꙮ SAN DIEGO

1
The Old Point Loma Lighthouse, the first lighthouse to be built on the West Coast, would be built at the southern tip of Point Loma in 1854.

2
See Pico sidebar on page 59.

3
Miguel de Pedrorena was a delegate of the State Constitutional Convention.

4
See Forster sidebar on page 46.

5

Camp Pendleton was established by the U.S. Marine Corps in 1942.

6

See Stearns sidebar on page 52.

7

The San Pasqual Battlefield State Historic Park is well-worth a visit to gain an understanding of the bloodiest battle of the Mexican-American War fought in California.

8

Today, however, San Diego is the second most populated county in the state.

9

Oliver Meredith Wozencraft was a delegate of the State Constitutional Convention.

10

All of the area in present-day Riverside County is covered in this section.

11

The Cahuilla Indian Reservation located in the San Jacinto Mountains southeast of Hemet today is the area that would inspire Helen Hunt Jackson to write her best-selling novel, *Ramona*. The 1884 book did much to bring attention to the plight of the American Indian in southern California. The Ramona Pageant, based on Jackson's book, has been held in an outdoor amphitheater in Hemet every April and May since 1923.

12

In 1851 Los Angeles County absorbed much of San Diego and Mariposa counties.

13

See Wilson sidebar on page 53.

14

California horses and mules were especially valued for their size and stamina, and became an important trade item throughout the Southwest.

15

The rest of Inyo County is described in the 1850-Mariposa County chapter.

San Diego Mission

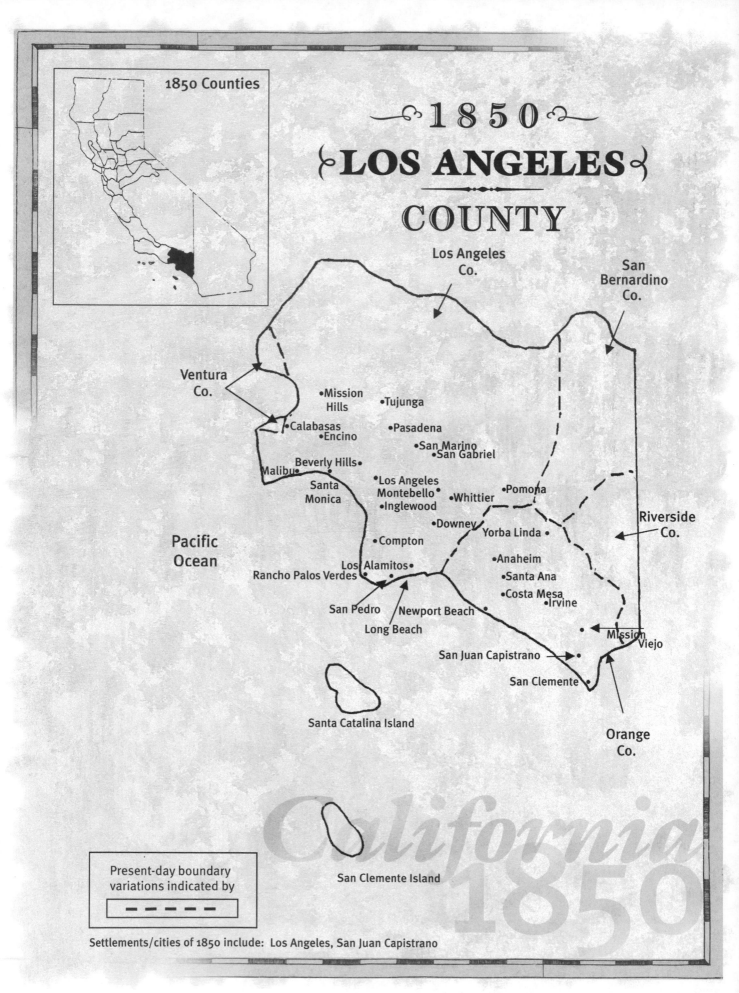

1850 Counties

1850
LOS ANGELES
COUNTY

Los Angeles
Co.

San
Bernardino
Co.

Ventura
Co.

•Mission
Hills

•Tujunga

•Calabasas
•Encino

•Pasadena

•San Marino
•San Gabriel

•Beverly Hills•
Malibu•

•Pomona

•Los Angeles
Montebello•
•Inglewood

•Whittier

Santa
Monica

•Downey

Yorba Linda

Pacific
Ocean

•Compton

•Anaheim

Los Alamitos•
Rancho Palos Verdes•

•Santa Ana

•Costa Mesa
•Irvine

Riverside
Co.

San Pedro

Newport Beach

Long Beach

Mission
Viejo

San Juan Capistrano

San Clemente

Santa Catalina Island

Orange
Co.

California
1850

Present-day boundary
variations indicated by

- - - - -

San Clemente Island

Settlements/cities of 1850 include: Los Angeles, San Juan Capistrano

LOS ANGELES COUNTY
1850

Small western portions of present-day Riverside and San Bernardino counties were located within the geographical area of 1850-Los Angeles County and are included in the chapter on 1850-San Diego County. Orange County would not be formed from the southern portion of Los Angeles County until 1889, and surprisingly, 1850-Mariposa County extended south through five present-day counties and encroached on the Antelope Valley area of present-day Los Angeles County.

Los Angeles County's 3,530 residents counted in the 1850 U.S. Census included Californios, Americans, and Europeans. Primarily the Gabrieliño Indians made up the uncounted Native American population. Spanish was still the area's common language.

AREA WITHIN PRESENT-DAY ORANGE COUNTY

In 1850 the area within present-day Orange County consisted of the former Mission San Juan Capistrano, the San Juan Capistrano community, the famous harbor now called Dana Point that Richard Henry Dana described in his book *Two Years Before the Mast*, three small communities called *Pueblo de Santa Ana, Santa Ana Arriba,* and *Santa Ana Abajo,* as well as 14 ranchos.

Mission San Juan Capistrano

Misión San Juan Capistrano, the seventh California mission, was established in 1776. The Great Stone Church[1] that had been one of the most elaborately adorned of the mission churches, lay in ruins in 1850—never having been repaired following the earthquake of 1812. The Serra Chapel that was built in 1777 was still standing, however, and the chapel remains the oldest standing church in California today. *Don* Juan (John) Forster had purchased the mission for $710 in 1845, and his family lived in part of the mission and stored trade goods in the Serra Chapel until 1865, when President Lincoln returned the mission to the Catholic church. The occupied portions that were protected would survive the elements, but the north and west wings eroded from exposure to the elements.

This mission is considered the "Jewel of the Missions," and is known especially for the annual migration of the cliff swallows from Goya, Argentina every March 19th. Their yearly return to build their nests under the eaves of the mission for lodging through October 23rd has been recorded every year since 1777.[2] The mission site brings the Spanish era to life through museum rooms depicting various periods of the mission's history, as well as outdoor displays.

Sites to Visit in Orange County

Ávila Adobe, 31831 Camino Capistrano, San Juan Capistrano (exterior only)

Blas Aguilar Adobe, 31806 El Camino Real, San Juan Capistrano

Domingo Yorba Adobe, 31871 Camino Capistrano, San Juan Capistrano (exterior only)

El Adobe de Capistrano, 31891 Camino Capistrano, San Juan Capistrano (restaurant)

Garcia Adobe, 31861 Camino Capistrano, San Juan Capistrano (exterior only)

Heritage Hill Historical Park, 25151 Serrano Rd., Lake Forest 949.855.2028

Los Ríos Historical District, Los Ríos St., San Juan Capistrano 949.489.0736

Mission San Juan Capistrano, 31882 Camino Capistrano, San Juan Capistrano 949.248.2048

Orange County Marine Institute—The Pilgrim, Dana Point Harbor, Dana Point 949.496.2274

Sepúlveda Adobe, Estancia Park, 1900 Adams Av., Costa Mesa

Costa Mesa Tourism & Promotion Council, P. O. Box 5071, Costa Mesa, CA 92628 800.399.5499

San Juan Capistrano

San Juan Capistrano had been a pueblo (*Pueblo San Juan de Argüello*) from 1841 to 1844; in 1850 it was a small community of Mexicans and American Indians. Squatters, drifters, and bandits constantly imposed themselves upon the quiet little settlement, because San Juan Capistrano was one of the few re-supply points between San Diego and Los Angeles. *Vaqueros* from the ranchos also frequented the town on Saturday nights, causing drunken brawls in the streets. Several stores and saloons were in operation in town and games of *monte* were always in progress. San Juan Capistrano's social scene closely rivaled that of Los Angeles to the north.

The Great Stone Church is the central focus of a preservation project currently under way at Mission San Juan Capistrano.

The Montanez Adobe, located in the Los Rios Historical District, is open to the public.

El Adobe de Capistrano was two separate structures in 1850. Today it is a restaurant in San Juan Capistrano.

The streets of the pueblo included present-day El Camino Real, San Juan's original main street; Spring Street, which was the route from the east mission gate to the San Juan Hot Springs; River Street, which was the path from the Los Ríos neighborhood to Trabuco Creek, a water source; and Los Ríos Street, the oldest continually occupied neighborhood street in California.

River Street today is the entrance lane to a commercial nursery. In 1850 it crossed Trabuco Creek and extended all the way to Dana Point, approximately four miles to the west. During the Spanish and Mexican times, cowhides were carted from the processing area at the mission down this road to the cliff tops above the harbor, where they were tossed down to the beach for loading on ships bound for the East Coast.

The present-day Los Ríos Historic District provides a glimpse of the San Juan Capistrano of 1850. The peaceful street housed about 40 adobe structures on six blocks. Three of the original adobe homes built in 1794 to house the employees of the mission still stand. The Silvas and Ríos adobes are private homes. The latter adobe was built for Feliciano Ríos, a Spanish soldier serving with the mission garrison, and is believed to be the oldest residence in California continuously occupied by the same family. The third remaining adobe, the Montanez Adobe, was named for a post-1850 resident, Polonia Montanez, who had charge of the religious instruction of the village children from 1886 to 1910. This adobe is open to the public. Board and batten homes were built on top of the old foundations of many of the other 30-plus adobes between 1887 and 1910 and remain standing today.

A block of pre-1850 adobes that remain today on Camino Capistrano may be viewed from the curb. *El Adobe de Capistrano* was two separate structures in 1850 owned by the Miguel Yorba family. The southern portion was the justice court and *juzgado* (jail), and would later serve as a store, stage depot, and overnight hotel. The northern portion was the Yorba family home. Today the single structure houses a restaurant of the same name.

The Domingo Yorba Adobe next door dates back to 1778. This adobe, with 12 to 20-inch thick walls and a wood shingle roof, is a private residence.

The García Adobe, a two-story adobe with exterior walls over three feet thick, was built in the 1840s by Manuel García, a Portuguese merchant. This private residence

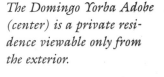
The Domingo Yorba Adobe (center) is a private residence viewable only from the exterior.

originally had a second story over only half of the ground floor area, but in 1880 a second floor was built over the rest of the ground floor and the Monterey-style balcony was added.

Finishing off the block, the Ávila Adobe, built in 1846, probably over older ruins, was the townhouse of *Don* Juan Ávila who was called *El Rico*, The Rich One. He owned the nearby *Rancho Niguel* and was well-known for his hospitality. A fire destroyed much of this adobe in 1879, and only a small part was rebuilt to serve as Ávila's home until his death in 1889. An extensive restoration to transform the former residence into a large commercial structure was completed in 1992.

The García Adobe is a private residence viewable only from the exterior. The Monterey-style balcony was added in 1880.

Three adobes once stood across the street on this block. They housed the José Aguilar, Demarco Forster, and James Durruel families.

The Blas Aguilar family owned two adjoining 1794 adobes on El Camino Real. The *Hacienda Aguilar* adobe is undergoing restoration to house a museum—the Blas Aguilar Adobe. The *Casa Tejada* adobe, which no longer stands, was located across a patio that served as the

The Blas Aguilar Adobe in San Juan Capistrano is undergoing restoration to house a museum.

working and entertainment area for the family.

A town plaza was located across the street where livestock grazed in neighboring public pastures, and crops were raised in fields on pueblo common land. The former mission's reservoir was located at El Camino Real and El Horno. *Zanjas* (aqueducts) ran from El Horno Creek to the mission.

Dana Point would not be named for Richard Henry Dana until 1884, two years following his death. Capistrano Bay was called San Juan Bay in 1850.

The Dana Point Headlands have always been a navigational landmark for ships; the sheltered cove was the anchorage for 19th century ships that brought supplies to exchange for hides and tallow.

The brig *Pilgrim* at the Orange County Marine Institute at Dana Point Harbor is a full-sized replica of the square-rigged vessel on which Dana sailed into this cove. A bronze statue of Dana is located on Dana Island. The development of Dana Point did not begin until the 1880s due to the lack of roads and water. (The government sold homesteads for $1.25 an acre in what today is a very upscale community.)

Orange County Ranchos

In 1850 eleven families controlled most of Orange County through land grants. More and more during the Gold Rush, the cattle raised on the ranchos were being driven north and sold at a great profit to feed the prospectors rather than being used for the hide and tallow trade. Horses were so abundant that they often were hunted down to save pasturage for the cattle. Several hundred horses were reportedly driven off the bluffs at Newport Beach at one time. Details about some of the more interesting ranchos follow.

In 1850 the land within the current city limits of Mission Viejo[3] belonged to two ranchos, *Rancho Mission Viejo* and *Rancho Trabuco*.[4] *Don* Juan (John) Forster owned both ranchos. These rancho lands had been used by the mission for cattle grazing and a number of structures built for the *vaqueros* stood here.

On the 10,000-acre *Rancho Cañada de Los Alisos*, *Don* José Serrano raised crops such as corn, beans, and watermelons, as well as cattle for hides and tallow. Serrano's adobe was built on El Camino Real and many other adobes were scattered along Aliso Creek for members of the Serrano family. In 1863 Serrano would build and move to the structure that has been restored and is now part of Heritage Hill Historical Park in Lake Forest. (No *circa* 1850 structures are part of this park, but displays contain factual information about early California.)

The Sepúlveda Adobe is a house museum located in Estancia Park in Costa Mesa.

Don Juan Ávila, the wealthy resident of San Juan Capistrano, and his sister, *Doña* Concepción, raised sheep on their *Rancho Niguel*. Ávila built his first home here before building his large residence in San Juan Capistrano.

Rancho San Joaquin lay in the present-day Costa Mesa area. The padres of San Juan Capistrano had constructed an adobe in the early 1800s as a shelter for the Native Americans who tended the mission's cattle in this region. *Don* José Andrés Sepúlveda used two walls of the original adobe in the 1820-23 construction of his house (the Sepúlveda Adobe) that he occupied after secularization and that still stands on the heights of Costa Mesa as a house museum in Estancia Park.

There was an intertwining ownership of *Rancho Santiago de Santa Ana* between the Yorba, Peralta, and Serrano families. Three distinct communities had developed on this rancho. The first adobe houses were built in *Pueblo de Santa Ana*, located where Olive lies today. All of the houses were simple structures with enclosed gardens. A stock ranch was in operation and a small store offered imported goods for sale. Hides and tallow were hauled from the rancho to San Pedro in Los Angeles where they were traded for goods from around the Horn and the Orient.

The Peralta settlement was located on the south side of the Santa Ana River and was called *Santa Ana Arriba* (Upper Santa Ana), or "Peralta." It consisted of approximately ten houses that also had gardens and corrals.

Another cluster of buildings was built on the riverbank just west of present-day Orange. This community was called *Santa Ana Abajo* (Lower Santa Ana) and was the agricultural center of the rancho. All of the residents of these three communities were related to the Yorba, Peralta, and Serrano families in some way.

Before his death in 1825, *Don* José Antonio Yorba, the original owner of the entire *Rancho Santiago de Santa Ana*, had diverted water from the Santa Ana River, beginning the transformation of this barren land into a prosperous agricultural region. Crops such as corn, beans, wheat, pumpkin, and even watermelons were grown. Grapes were planted for wine and many orchards produced fruits, walnuts, figs, and olives. In addition to cattle, other animals were raised, including sheep, mules, burros, oxen, and horses.

The 347-foot summit of Red Hill marked the intersecting boundaries of the *Santiago de Santa Ana*, *San Jouquin*, and *Lomas de Santiago* ranchos. It was an important landmark for early travelers and mapmakers. American settlers named it Red Hill because of the color of its soil that contained cinnabar (mercury).[5]

Rancho Cañon de Santa Ana—across the river from Peralta's portion of *Rancho Santiago de Santa Ana*—was located in Yorba Linda.[6] In 1834 *Don* Bernardo Yorba built his famous *Hacienda San Antonio*, a two-story, 50-plus-room adobe house on a bluff overlooking the Santa Ana River in Yorba Linda. Many people inhabited the rancho, including more than 20 family members and a number of servants, laborers, and craftsmen who performed a wide array of tasks that allowed the rancho to be almost entirely self-sufficient. The rancho even had its own chapel, store, and barroom. Yorba tapped the Santa Ana River for irrigation and built a water-powered gristmill. Orchards, vineyards, wheat fields, and gardens were planted along the river. Sheep and cattle grazed the nearby hills.

Rancho La Bolsa Chica was located on the Bolsa Chica Mesa north of present-day Huntington Beach on the Pacific Coast Highway. *Don* Joaquin Ruiz owned it. He grazed sheep on a low plateau between Huntington Beach and Sunset Beach. Swampland and the ocean surrounded the highland where he built a two-room adobe house. Mexican colonists had constructed ditches in 1838 to drain the water from the 8,000-acre swamp that extended inland several miles, but much of this rancho was still submerged by water in 1850 and remains so today as part of the Bolsa Chica Ecological Reserve.

Rancho Los Coyotes was owned by *Doña* Francesca Uribe de Leandry, the widow of the third owner of the property. An adobe house and corrals stood on the eastern part of the rancho; it was an important stopping place for travelers on a shortcut that led from El Camino Real, past the Coyote Hills, and eventually to Los Angeles. *Don* Andrés Pico acquired the deed to this rancho during 1850.

Ranching began to diminish in the late 1850s and 60s—a little earlier than San Diego County. The *rancheros* began to sell off their estates to the likes of Irvine,

Bernardo Yorba (1800-1858)

- Known throughout California for his wealth and hospitality; namesake for Yorba Linda
- Fathered 21 children by three wives, the first two having died
- Well-educated by Franciscan Fathers in San Diego, his birthplace

Stearns, Hansen, and Flint, Bixby and Company. Towns arose and the transcontinental railroad linked Anaheim with the rest of the country in 1875, leading to further growth. Vineyards, orange groves, and the discovery of silver in the Santa Ana Mountains in 1877, and coal in 1878, would bring further prosperity to the region. (Much later, of course, Orange County became the theme park capital of the world with the opening of Knott's Berry Farm in 1920 and Disneyland in 1955.)

Natural bodies of water are rare in Orange County. The Santa Ana River, the longest river lying wholly within southern California, empties into the Pacific Ocean between Newport and Huntington beaches. Its course changed constantly following major floods before it was channelized. The Prado Dam project would be completed in 1941; Orange County has a number of other man-made lakes and reservoirs.

ORANGE COUNTY RANCHOS

NAME OF RANCHO	GRANTEE AND/OR 1850 OWNER	1850 AND/OR CURRENT SITES
Rancho Boca de la Playa (Mouth of the Beach)	Emígdio Véjar	San Clemente
Rancho Mission Viejo	Juan (John) Forster	Mission Viejo
Rancho Trabuco (Musket)	Juan (John) Forster	Mission Viejo
Rancho Potreros (Pasture Land) de San Juan Capistrano	Juan (John) Forster	Santa Ana Mountains
Rancho Cañada de Los Alisos (Glen of Alder Trees and Wood)	José Serrano	Lake Forest
Rancho Niguel	Siblings Juan and Concepción Ávila	Leisure World, Aliso Viejo, Laguna Niguel, Laguna Hills, Laguna Beach
Rancho San Joaquin	José Andrés Sepúlveda	Newport Beach, Irvine, Corona del Mar
Rancho Lomas de Santiago (Hills of St. James)	Teodocio and Inocencia Reyes de Yorba	Orange, Tustin, Irvine, Santa Ana
Rancho Santiago de Santa Ana	Yorba, Peralta, and Serrano families	Orange, Santa Ana, Costa Mesa, Newport Beach
Rancho Cañon de Santa Ana	Bernardo Yorba	Yorba Linda, Chino Hills State Park in San Bernardino County
Rancho San Juan Cajon de Santa Ana	Juan Pacífico Ontiveros	Anaheim, Fullerton, La Habra, Brea, Placentia
Rancho Los Coyotes (Coyotes)	Francesca Uribe de Leandry and Andrés Pico	Stanton, Cypress, La Palma, Buena Park, La Mirada (L.A. Co.)
Rancho Las Bolsas [7] (Pockets)	Caterina Ruiz (widow of José Antonio Nieto)	Huntington Beach, Fountain Valley, Westminster, Garden Grove
Rancho La Bolsa Chica (Little Pocket)	Joaquin Ruiz	Bolsa Chica Mesa, Huntington Beach

AREA WITHIN PRESENT-DAY LOS ANGELES COUNTY

In 1850 the area within present-day Los Angeles County consisted of a prospering pueblo and a chaparral-covered countryside of ranchos. Included within the 1,610 population of this part of the county were three "American" families—families in which both spouses were American. Two Chinese, Ah Fou and Ah Luce, lived in Los Angeles in 1850; they were servants of a Robert Haley.

City of Los Angeles

The second pueblo to be established in Alta California, *El Pueblo de la Reina de Los Angeles* (The Town of the Queen of the Angels) was founded in 1781. Eleven families had been assigned land to farm in support of the Spanish soldiers stationed in southern California. The City of Los Angeles had its beginnings on the site of the pueblo and was incorporated on April 4, 1850. A. P. Hodges became the first mayor; *Don* Abel Stearns acted as the *alcalde* for the first six months of 1850. The community social life of all of southern California centered around the pueblo in Los Angeles (L.A.).

Lieutenant E. O. C. Ord,[8] with the assistance of William Rich Hutton, had surveyed the pueblo in 1849. Hutton sketched many scenes of the pueblo and drew the first map of L.A. from Ord's survey. Both the Spanish and English names for the streets were noted. Some residents found their homes standing halfway between two streets because adobes had been built in random locations with haphazard paths leading to them.[9]

A plaza was laid out in the early 1800s. It was the town's main meeting place and the center of its social activity. The streets near the plaza were *Calle Principal* (Main Street), which extended into the San Fernando Valley; *Calle Primavera* (Spring Street); *Calle Fortin* (Fort Street) (now Broadway); *Calle Loma* (Hill Street); *Calle Aceituna* (Olive Street); *Calle Caridad* (Street of Charity) (now Grand Avenue); *Calle de Las Esperanzas* (Hope Street); *Calle de las Flores* (Flower Street); and *Calle de los Chapules* (Street of Grasshoppers) (now Figueroa).

The Bella Union Hotel, owned by *Don* Benito (Benjamin Davis) Wilson, stood on *Calle Principal*. This one-story building also served as the courthouse; the first permanent court facility would not be built until 1861. The only other public buildings were a jail and the *Nuestra Señora la Reyna de los Angeles*—Our Lady Queen of Angels Catholic Church, which is still in use today.

El Campo Santo (The Sacred Ground), next door to the church, served as L.A.'s first cemetery. By 1836 it had become overcrowded, however, so burials began to occur on a small plot near the current site of Dodger Stadium. This plot was called the Old Calvary Cemetery; the remains of those buried there would be moved to other cemeteries in the 1920s.

The first Protestant sermon in L.A. was preached in June 1850 by a Methodist minister who had been part of the Death Valley party, but it would be 1853 before the first Protestant church was established. The first Jewish services were held in a home in 1854.

Although the children of the pueblo, the boys more than the girls, had been offered informal schooling in various venues since the 1820s, it would be 1855

Sites to Visit in Los Angeles County

Adobe de Palomares, 491 East Arrow Hwy, Pomona 909.620.2300

Arboretum of Los Angeles County (Hugo Reid Adobe), 301 North Baldwin Av., Arcadia 626.821.3222

Blanco Adobe, San Marino High School Athletic Field, 2701 Huntington Dr., San Marino

Campo de Cahuenga, 3919 Lankershim Bl., North Hollywood (Closed)

Casa de Adobe (c/o Southwest Museum), 4605 N. Figueroa St., Highland Park (Closed/Undergoing seismic retrofitting)

Centinela Adobe, 7634 Midfield Av., Inglewood 310.649.6272

Dominguez Adobe, 18127 S. Alameda St., Compton 310 631 5981

El Molino Viejo (California Historical Society), 1120 Old Mill Rd , San Marino 818.449.5450

El Pueblo de Los Angeles Historic Monument, Visitor's Center, Sepúlveda House, 622 N. Main St., Los Angeles 213.628.1274

La Casa de Lopez de Lowther, 330 North Santa Anita Av., San Gabriel

La Casa Primera, 1569 North Park Av., Pomona 909.620.2417

Leonis Adobe, 23537 Calabasas Rd., Calabasas 818.222-6511

Los Angeles Natural History Museum, 900 Exposition Bl., Los Angeles 213.763.3466

Los Encinos State Historic Park, 16756 Moorpark St., Encino 818.784.4849

Mission San Fernando Rey de Espana, 15151 San Fernando Mission Bl., Mission Hills 626.457.3048

Mission San Gabriel Arcangel, 537 West Mission Dr., San Gabriel 626.457.3048

Placerita Canyon State and County Park, 19152 West Placerita Canyon Rd., Newhall 805.259.7721

Pico Adobe, 10940 Sepulveda Bl., Mission Hills 818.365.7810

(continued next page)

Nuestra Señora la Reyna de los Angeles—Our Lady Queen of Angels Catholic Church—is an active parish located in El Pueblo de Los Angeles Historic Monument.

before the first public school was built. A proposal to establish L.A.'s first newspaper was presented to the city council in October 1850, but the first issue of *The Los Angeles Star* would not be published until May 1851.

A number of commercial establishments were in operation in the pueblo, established by recent arrivals to the growing city. John Goller, a member of the Manley party that survived the journey through Death Valley, was operating a profitable horseshoeing and wagon shop in town. Joseph Lancaster Brent, Jonathan R. Scott, and Benjamin Hayes were practicing law.[10] Arthur McKenzie Dodson manufactured soap and Edouard Naud baked pastries. Russell Sackett, a lawyer, established himself as a butcher, and Charles Ducommun, a watchmaker, operated a hardware business. Peter Biggs, an African American, opened the first barber shop in L.A. John Gately Downey ran a drugstore in partnership with Dr. James P. McFarland.

Don Juan (Jonathan) Temple and George Rice had opened the first general merchandise store in the pueblo, and in 1850 were in competition with *Don* Abel Stearns, Jonathan Trumbell Warner, John Schumacher, and Packard and Wilson.[11] Until a post office was established in April 1850, Packard and Wilson was the depository for all of the city's mail until it was claimed. People claimed their mail after sorting through a tub on the counter.

An auction of pueblo lands had been held in November 1849 in which almost all of the city's four square leagues were sold to bargain hunters in an effort to replenish the town's empty treasury. Only the park areas now called Pershing, Elysian, and the Plaza remained in the possession of the city. Even the site of the present city hall would have to be re-purchased in later years.

There was a large residential area in the pueblo. All of the houses were adobe, all but three were one-story, and all but a few had the typical mud and tar flat roofs.[12] In 1850 the pueblo was enjoying the prosperity brought about by the Gold Rush and the new demand for beef cattle in the north. Many of the homes around or near the plaza were "townhouses" of the wealthy *rancheros* profiting from this boom in

the economy. They would come into town to arrange cattle deals, visit the liquor shops, play a little *monte* in a gambling house, or perhaps see a horse race, bullfight, or bear and bullfight. The women of the ranchos came along to look for bargains in furniture and hardware from New England, shawls from China, or clothes from Mexico. Some of the *rancheros* were raising their families in town, leaving the management of their ranchos to their *mayordomos*.

There were too many residences to list, but some of the more outstanding ones are worth noting. *Don* Abel Stearns and his wife, Arcadia Bandini, the daughter of *Don* Juan Bandini,[13] lived in *El Palacio*, the large house located on *Calle Principal* near the plaza. Another social center of L.A., it included a 100-foot-long ballroom.

Captain Alexander Bell's two-story adobe, the largest house in the pueblo, stood at the southeast corner of Los Angeles and Aliso streets. Called "Bell's Row," it was another gathering place for public functions and grand balls.

Don Vicente Lugo and *Don* Vicente Sanchez lived in each of the other two-story houses on the plaza. *Don* Pío Pico's townhouse stood between Sanchez Street and the entrance to Ocampo's Plaza, and *Don* Andrés Pico's home stood just south of the burial ground of the church.

The townhouse of *Don* Ygnacio Del Valle was located where the Serra Statue stands today in the plaza.[14] Although he managed his *Rancho San Francisco* in the northwestern part of the county, he was spending most of his time in his plaza home in 1850 where he was raising his five children. Most of the political meetings of the early American period were held in his home.

The tile-roofed adobes belonged to: José Antonio Carrillo,[15] whose house stood on the plaza across from the church on *Calle Principal*, where the Pico House (1870) stands today; the heirs of José António Rocha, the Portuguese family living on *Calle Primavera*; and the widow of *Don* José María Ávila. The Ávila Adobe, the oldest existing residence in the city, stands today on Olvera Street within the El Pueblo de Los Angeles Historic Monument. A restored, seven-room wing remains of what was once 18 rooms.

The long adobe of L.A.'s pioneer lawyer and first judge, Agustín Olvera, spanned the north side of the plaza. Court proceedings were often held in Olvera's house. Across the street from his house was a large adobe gambling house where the visiting *rancheros* played *monte*.

The town's water was obtained from the *Zanja Madre* [16](Mother Ditch). It started at the *Toma* (Great Water Wheel) that lifted the water from the Los Angeles River to the pueblo, running along the slope between Los Angeles and Alameda streets. At various points, smaller *zanjas* branched off the main canal to water the fields and vineyards of the settlers. Stringent laws were enacted in 1850 prohibiting bathing or washing clothes in the *zanjas*. A triple row of bricks may still be seen today running diagonally across Olvera Street, which denotes the path of the original *Zanja Madre*.

A few cottonwood trees grew in the plaza area, but, with the exception of a large *aliso* (sycamore) on Aliso Road and a large pepper tree northwest of the plaza, there were few other trees. Shrubs and vines grew along the garden adobe walls. A thicket of willows filled the river bottom from the hills of present-day Elysian Park down through town.

In the winter, the streets of the pueblo were knee-deep in mud and nearly impassable; in the summer, clouds of dust filled the air from the countless horsemen and ox-drawn *carretas* making their way through town. Hundreds of mongrel dogs ran around the plaza, barking at the hooves of horses. Sanitation was poor; rubbish was tossed into the streets; cattle were slaughtered in the house yards; and the remains of

Agustín Olvera (1820-1876)

- Arrived in California in 1834 from Mexico
- Commissioner of secularized Mission San Juan Capistrano in 1841 and judge
- Moved to L.A. in 1845
- Judge, county supervisor, and assemblyman
- Namesake of L.A.'s Olvera Street

The Ávila Adobe, located in El Pueblo de Los Angeles Historic Monument, is the oldest existing residence in Los Angeles.

This is an interior view of the Ávila Adobe.

Jonathan Temple (1798-1866)

- Massachusetts trader; arrived in L.A. from Hawaii in 1827
- Opened first general store in the pueblo and encouraged use of hides as currency
- Owned two ranchos
- Built first office building in L.A.
- Married to Raphaela Cota
- Namesake for L.A.'s Temple Street

Abel Stearns (1798-1871)

- Native of Salem, Massachusetts; became sailor when orphaned at age of 12
- Arrived in L.A. in 1829 as merchant/astute businessman—wealthiest man in southern California in 1850s
- Married to Arcadia Bandini, daughter of *Don* Juan Bandini; no children (Arcadia Bandini Stearns Baker died in 1912 at the age of 85 and was worth $8,000,000)
- Owned ranchos in San Diego, Riverside, San Bernardino, Orange, and Los Angeles counties—acquired primarily by foreclosing on mortgages he held—totaling over 200,000 acres
- Sent first California gold from Placerita to U.S. Mint
- Delegate of State Constitutional Convention
- *Alcalde*, state assemblyman, county supervisor, justice of the peace, L.A. city councilman, L.A. Board of Education member
- Generous philanthropist
- Partner in Robinson Trust set up by friends in 1868 to save him from debt

carcasses were thrown about for scavenger dogs and crows. The streets were periodically cleaned, however, in preparation for a variety of annual festivals.

Buildings constructed primarily of adobe and tile were resistant to fire, but the storage of large quantities of hay created hazardous conditions that sometimes resulted in fires. In 1850 the City Council was authorized to create a fire department, but no formal action was taken until 1871 when the Volunteer Fire Department was organized. In the meantime, neighbors formed "volunteer bucket brigades," working feverishly until the fires were extinguished. Volunteers were called to a fire by repeated gunshots fired into the air by the person discovering the fire.

El Pueblo de Los Angeles Historic Monument would be the inspiration of Christine Sterling in the mid-1920s. She worked for nearly two years to convert the old plaza that had become a slum and crime center into the Mexican social and commercial center it is today. It covers 44 acres, bounded by Alameda, Arcadia, Spring, and Macy streets.

Fort Moore, named for Captain Benjamin D. Moore, who had lost his life in the Battle of San Pasqual, stood above the pueblo on Hill Street. It was an earthwork with six embrasures for cannon, completed during the Mexican-American War by the Mormon Battalion. Four men killed when a powder magazine exploded were buried within the fort and a cemetery was started in 1850 due to the crowding within the pueblo. The fort fell into ruin and the graves would be moved in later years; today the Fort Moore Memorial commemorates the site of the fort.

Many Mexican miners from Sonora, Mexico, originally on their way to the gold fields in northern California, instead settled in the northern section of the pueblo, which came to be known as Sonoratown. Similarly, some Americans taking the southern routes from the eastern states and passing through the pueblo chose to remain here.

Farming operations—cornfields, vineyards, and groves of apples, pears, peaches, plums, and figs—were carried on in the river-rich area southeast of Main Street. Community-owned fields lay northeast of Aliso Street. Privately assigned fields extended to the southwest as far as present-day East Fourth Street.

William Wolfskill, a former trapper from Kentucky, had planted the first table grape vineyard on pueblo lands in 1838. In 1850 he was shipping thousands of boxes of these eating grapes to San Francisco and other northern towns. Wolfskill also pioneered the commercial citrus industry in California; in 1841 he planted the first commercial orange orchard in California located outside of mission property. Wolfskill lived in an adobe nearby with his wife, Magdalena Lugo of the Lugo family that owned the nearby *Rancho San Antonio*.

Salomon Pico had been leading a life of crime in L.A. since 1847 that would continue until 1857. He ruthlessly murdered and robbed Americans and was the inspiration for the mythical "Zorro." Pico led a band of marauders similar to those that were formed in the 1850s by the likes of Joaquin Murieta and Tiburcio Vásquez.

Los Angeles County Ranchos

More than 50 ranchos were located in present-day Los Angeles County in 1850. Details about some of the more interesting ones follow.

Don Abel Stearns owned *Rancho Los Alamitos*, originally part of the large 1784 *Los Nietos* concession subdivided by Nieto's heirs. It was the summer home for Stearns' wife, Arcadia. Thousands of cattle grazed on the grass-covered plain that stretched to the bluffs overlooking the Pacific Ocean.[17]

Don Juan José Nieto built the original 1806 adobe on the mesa overlooking Long Beach. Through the years, additions were made to this adobe as ownership changed hands. Today the *Rancho Los Alamitos* adobe and its frame additions remain as they looked when Fred and Florence Bixby[18] added the last building in 1906. The restored home is furnished with pieces from the 1800s and 1900s.

Rancho Los Cerritos was another of the ranchos created from *Los Nietos*. *Don* Juan (Jonathan) Temple owned a 27,000-acre portion of the rancho in 1850 on which he had built a two-story adobe in 1844. Temple imported bricks from the East Coast, shipping them around the Horn for use in the foundation, two long verandas, marking off the garden beds, lining a 60-foot well, and building a large cistern. He obtained hand-hewn redwood from northern California forests for the beams, floors, and other interior woodwork, as well as for the 12-foot fence around the garden. He used the common slabs of sun-dried adobe for the walls of the house.

The Monterey-style adobe which stands today was restored in 1929 by Llewellyn Bixby, a later owner, and reflects the life-styles of his father and mother when they managed an extensive sheep ranching operation here from 1866-1886. Llewellyn's daughter, Sarah Bixby Smith, described the history of the family and early California in her 1925 book *Adobe Days*.

Temple's *Los Cerritos* house was seven miles from Stearns' house on the adjoining rancho, but there were very neighborly relations developed between the two. A friendly rivalry existed between them as to the speed of their horses. Horse races were held annually between the two ranchos; the racecourse ran from present Signal Hill to the beach, a total of four miles. *Los Cerritos* and *Los Alamitos* also held joint rodeos and barbecues.

In 1850 the land below Cerritos Hill was wooded and swampy. The Los Angeles and San Gabriel rivers united at this point and poured into the lowland on their journey to the sea. (The 1860 and other later floods would change all of this.)

Rancho Santa Gertrudes, also originally part of the *Los Nietos* concession, was owned by *Don* Lemuel Carpenter, from Kentucky, who founded a soap and broom factory in the vicinity of present-day Downey. He, his wife, *Doña* María de los Angeles Domínguez, and five children lived on the rancho that he purchased from his wife's aunt. He raced horses and was known for his card-playing abilities. A village carried his name, but it would be swept away by the great flood of 1867.

Doña Joaquina Sepúlveda, *Dons* Bernardino Guirado and Pío Pico, and heirs of *Don* Juan Crispín Pérez owned *Rancho Paso de Bartolo*, originally part of the Mission San Gabriel lands. Pico owned the largest, 9,000 acre portion on which he built an adobe in 1850. The floods of 1883-84 would destroy this original adobe, but his second adobe remains today in Pio Pico State Historic Park. This property was Pico's favorite home place and his last possession.[19]

Doña Casilda Soto de Lobo owned *Rancho La Merced*. She built an adobe in 1845 on a bluff above the Rio Honda River. An expanded and restored version of her home known as the Sanchez Adobe stands as a house museum in Montebello.

Misíon San Gabriel Arcángel stood on R*ancho Potrero de la Misíon de San Gabriel.* The mission's first site (in Montebello) proved to be unsatisfactory; in 1776 the mission was moved to a safer location where it stands today in San Gabriel. Mission San Gabriel has been in continuous use for over 225 years, when not undergoing restoration activities following damage from numerous earthquakes. (The

An expanded and restored version of the original Sanchez Adobe stands as a house museum in Montebello.

Mission San Gabriel has been in continuous use for over 225 years, except when undergoing restoration activities following damage from numerous earthquakes.

La Casa de Lopez de Lowther, adjacent to Mission San Gabriel, may be viewed through an iron fence.

most recent was the Northridge earthquake in 1994.) In 1850 William Workman, a neighboring *ranchero*, was administering the mission.

A number of adobe homes stood in the area surrounding the Mission San Gabriel in 1850. Three remain today; two of them are private residences. One of the private residences was built as a home for mission friars three years before the Mission San Gabriel church was erected. As cactus "fences" were planted to protect the mission's crops from wild horses, the adobe came to be known as *Las Tunas* (Cactus) Adobe. The other private residence, the Ortega-Vigare Adobe, is the second oldest adobe in the region. It is now only half its original size.

The Juan Lopez family lived in the 1806 *La Casa de Lopez de Lowther*, adjacent to the mission, and continued to occupy it until 1964. Today the exterior of the house may be viewed through an iron fence.

James S. Waite owned the property on which the first water-operated gristmill in California was located, two miles north of the mission. *El Molino Viejo* only operated as a gristmill for a couple of years after it was built in 1816; it subsequently was converted into a residence, later enjoying a very colorful history. The structure still stands in San Marino, appropriately housing the southern California headquarters of the California Historical Society. [20]

In 1850, the same *Don* Miguel (Michael White) Blanco who owned the *Rancho Muscupiabe* in San Bernardino County, lived on a 77-acre grant directly north of the mission. He was married to the daughter of the former housekeeper of *Misíon San Gabriel.* His 1845 Blanco Adobe stands today on the campus of San Marino High

School in a fenced area between the swimming pool and baseball field. (There is discussion about opening this adobe to the public in the future.)

The Englishman *Don* Julian (William) Workman and his partner, *Don* Juan Roldan (John Rowland), owned the large *Rancho La Puente*. The two men had left New Mexico to lead the first southern California-bound overland expedition—the Workman-Rowland party—that included 40 American emigrants and several European immigrants. They arrived with pack animals, herds of cattle, and covered wagons filled with rugs, blankets, and other goods from New Mexico.

Shortly after arriving in 1841, Workman and Rowland acquired the rancho from the Mexican government for a sum of gold and the promise to care for the Native Americans already living on the land. Both families established cattle ranchos on the 48,000 acres. William and Nicolasa Workman's home was a simple three-room adobe in 1850, but with the success of their cattle ranch, and the wealth derived from their vineyards and wheat farming, they continued to remodel the house and add rooms. An 1870s remodeled version of the residence still stands on a six-acre site in the City of Industry as part of the Workman and Temple Family Homestead Museum.

El Molino Viejo houses the southern California headquarters of the California Historical Society in San Marino.

In 1850 Rowland lived in an adobe near the south bank of San Jose Creek in the Hacienda Heights area of today. Rowland and Workman supplemented their income from cattle ranching by the operation of a pair of gristmills along San Jose Creek.

Don Ygnacio Palomares and *Don* Ricardo Véjar were the primary owners of *Rancho San José*, the most northeastern rancho in Los Angeles County. The two soldiers had long been close friends and their children would later intermarry. Palomares had built *La Casa Primera* in 1837, which stands today in Pomona. In 1850 the Palomares moved into the first phase of what became the 13-room *Adobe de Palomares* by 1854, the restored version of which also stands in Pomona. The Palomares occupied the upper portion of the rancho, or *San José de Arriba*.

The Blanco Adobe stands on the campus of San Marino High School in a fenced area between the swimming pool and baseball field.

La Casa Primera is located in Pomona.

Véjar owned the lower half of the rancho referred to as *San José de Abajo*. In 1850, however, he lived on his other rancho, *Rancho Los Nogales*. Today several other adobes of this rancho remain as private residences in Pomona and in the foothills to the west.

Don Enrique (Henry) Dalton owned the extreme northwesterly portion of *Rancho San José*, as well as the neighboring *San José Adición* and *Rancho Azusa de Dalton*. Dalton constructed a *zanja* (aqueduct) from the San Gabriel River to his adobe house.

Dalton also owned *Rancho Santa Anita* on which the Arboretum of Los Angeles County is located today. The three-room adobe that lies within the park was unoccupied and falling into disrepair in 1850. It is known as the Hugo Reid Adobe, because Hugo Reid built it and his son lived in it until Reid sold it in 1847. The adobe has been reconstructed on its original 1840 foundation. Vineyards, a variety of fruit trees, and wheat had thrived on the fertile lands of this large rancho, as did many herds of cattle, until it was neglected by Dalton.[21]

The Palomares family lived in the first phase of their 13-room Adobe de Palomares in 1850. The restored adobe is located in Pomona.

The Hugo Reid Adobe was reconstructed on its original 1840 foundation in the Arboretum of Los Angeles County.

A remodeled version of the Dominguez Adobe is a house museum on the grounds of the Dominguez Memorial Seminary.

One of the two *Rancho San Antonios* in Los Angeles County lay just southeast of L.A. *Don* Antonio María Lugo owned this almost 30,000-acre rancho. His father, *Don* Francisco, had started construction of the *Casa de Rancho San Antonio* in 1780; *Don* Antonio completed it in 1810. It stood in present-day Bell Gardens and was the second oldest structure in southern California until it was destroyed by fire. A replica of it has been incorporated into the overall design of the Lugo Plaza shopping center. Another Lugo adobe that was built in 1840 remains in Bell Gardens today as a private residence.[22]

Rancho San Pedro occupied a vast expanse of hills, sand dunes, swamps, and sloughs that stretched from the mud flats that became Wilmington to the hills rising back of San Pedro Bay. A road connected the present-day Redondo Beach area with L.A. because residents traveled to a salt lake here to obtain salt, a valuable commodity in 1850.

The original owner of *Rancho San Pedro* was the former soldier, *Don* Juan José Domínguez. His heirs—grandnephews and grandnieces, as he had no children of his own— owned the rancho as tenants-in-common in 1850. They had built a house in 1827, the Domínguez Adobe,[23] and several other adobes and huts for the rancho *vaqueros*. Cattle and horses ranged on the slope of a hill overlooking the San Gabriel River—before it traded channels with the Los Angeles River. The Domínguez hacienda was known for its hospitality; it was a popular stopping point halfway between the San Pedro Bay and L.A.

Only a small portion of the current city of San Pedro is located within the former boundaries of *Rancho San Pedro*. The rest of San Pedro lies on property that was part of the *Rancho Los Palos Verdes*. Two brothers, *Dons* Juan Diego and José Loreto Sepúlveda, owned the rancho. They raised several thousand head of cattle and lived in a hacienda on the property.

McCulloch, Hartnell and Company, a trading company which was defunct by 1850, had built the first commercial structure on San Pedro Bay in 1823—a warehouse for hide storage. The warehouse was called *Casa de San Pedro*. San Pedro Bay was the major southern California port, especially after *Don* Abel Stearns built a road down to sea level in the mid-1840s. Stearns had taken up a collection from his friends to fund the road construction shortly after Richard Henry Dana's book was published describing the desolateness of the San Pedro port. Actually, Dana called San Pedro the "hell of California" because it was one of the worst places in the world for mariners to approach due to the shifting shoals and sandbars.

The Centinela Adobe, more reflective of its 1870s period, is tucked away in the middle of a residential neighborhood in Inglewood.

An island was situated near the mouth of San Pedro Bay in 1850. It was called Deadman's Island because six Americans killed in a Mexican-American War skirmish were buried there. The island would disappear in 1921 during harbor construction work. Other landmarks in the bay disappeared with other harbor improvements, including Timms Landing or Point, the first deep water landing established in San Pedro Bay in the 1830s. Cowhides were loaded onto ships at this landing.

The route of the present-day Harbor Freeway runs north/south through the former *San Pedro* and *Los Palos Verdes* ranchos. This route was first a Native American trail leading inland. Later it became the main pathway between the harbor and the Los Angeles pueblo 20 miles away. As more and more ships began visiting the harbor, traffic on the road increased. The first shipping line using oxen and wagons began in 1848, and in 1850 *Don* Diego Sepúlveda started the first stagecoach line between the harbor and the pueblo.

Don Bruno Ávila owned *Rancho Aguaje de la Centinela*. *Don* Ygnacio Machado had built the 1830s Centinela Adobe that still stands today tucked away in the middle of a residential neighborhood in Inglewood. He had grown tired of the isolation on his rancho and traded Ávila the rancho for a townhouse and fenced-in vineyard in L.A. (Today the adobe is more reflective of the 1870s period, but contains several artifacts from the earlier period.)

Rancho La Brea had the distinction of having the *La Brea* (tar) pits located on it. Scouts for the Portola expedition had discovered the pits and the tar was regularly mined for use as a roofing material; it would be 1906 before the remarkable discoveries of prehistoric animal bones were made. The bones occasionally found in the tar were first thought to be those of unlucky cattle. The sound of the bubbles bursting could be heard distinctly in town four miles away. The road between the tar pits and the pueblo, known as the "old road," lay along Wilshire Boulevard. Today the pits are located within Hancock Park.

Hugo Reid 1810-1852

- Arrived in Los Angeles in 1832

- Scotch trader, merchant, Mexican citizen

- Highly educated, active in the community, and kept books for many neighboring ranchos

- Married a widowed Indian; adopted her 4 children

- Delegate of State Constitutional Convention

- Provided Abel Stearns with the idea of selling cattle in northern California that spurred the practice of driving cattle to the north

- Grew tired of *ranchero* life; purchased a town lot in San Francisco and moved there

- Worked to improve the plight of the American Indians

- Died of tuberculosis in Los Angeles

The heirs of *Don* Antonio José Rocha and *Don* Nemesio Domínguez owned the *Rancho La Brea*. They were required to allow anyone from L.A. to take from the pits as much tar as they needed for the roofs of their adobe houses. Their *mayordomo* lived in an adobe, which Rocha had built in 1830. Today the remodeled adobe serves as the corporate offices of a business, but is not open to the public.

Doña María Ygnacia Verdugo owned and raised cattle on *Rancho Los Feliz*. She was the remarried widow of one of the heirs of the original grantee, Corporal José Vicente Feliz. The rancho consisted of mountains, hills, canyons, valleys, and streams that today make up Griffith Park—the largest municipal park and urban wilderness area in the U.S.[24]

A replica of the Campo de Cahuenga adobe, where the Treaty of Cahuenga was signed, may be viewed through an iron fence. It is located in North Hollywood.

The Treaty of Cahuenga ending the fighting in California between Mexico and the U.S. was signed in the *Campo de Cahuenga* in 1847, which was located on *Rancho Cahuenga*. A replica of this adobe built by *Don* Tomás Feliz in 1845 stands on the original site today, but may only be viewed externally through an iron fence.[25]

"Eagle Rock," located at the end of Figueroa Street in the town of Eagle Rock, was an early well-known landmark, so-named in 1880 because of its resemblance to an eagle in flight.

Rancho San Rafael was a combination of fertile farming and grazing lands and mountainous terrain with canyons and streams. In 1850 this rancho was owned by Julio and Catalina Verdugo, the children of the late *Don* José María Verdugo. The Verdugos were well-known for their fiestas and rodeos. Three or four families lived on the rancho in several homes and huts. Barley, wheat, corn, beans, and hay were raised, as well as large herds of cattle and horses.[26]

The prominent 150-foot high "Eagle Rock" located at the end of Figueroa Street in the town of Eagle Rock was an important and well-known landmark used by the American Indians, Spanish, and Mexicans, but it would not be named such until 1880. Despite the erosion that has occurred over the years, it still resembles an eagle in flight. (The rock and the land on which the rock sits are owned by the City of Los Angeles and the rock has been given the protective status of a historic monument.)

Doña María Rita Valdez De Villa owned the other *Rancho San Antonio* in Los Angeles County. She referred to it as *Rancho Rodeo de las Aguas* (Ranch of the Gathering of the Waters), because of the confluence of waters that flowed down from the streambeds of *Cañada de las Aguas Frias* and *Cañada de los Encinos*, which today are known as Coldwater and Benedict canyons. During the rainy season, streams cascaded down the canyons and gathered near the southern boundary where clear springs bubbled and a *ciénega*, or swamp, formed.[27] The 1831 home of *Doña* María Rita stood where Coldwater Canyon Park is located today, with another home located next door which had been built by a feuding relative whom she had already successfully expelled from the property by 1850. *Doña* María Rita and her son,

Mario, raised cattle and horses on this rancho of fertile, grassy plains, sycamore trees, and gently rolling hills and canyons. This rancho property would not begin its transition into the exclusive Beverly Hills of today until 1906.

Rancho San Francisco encompassed most of the western Santa Clarita Valley and extended into eastern Ventura County. When he was not at home with his family in the pueblo, *Don* Ygnacio Del Valle stayed at the *Asistencia de San Francisco Javier*, a branch of *Misión San Fernando Rey de España*. Del Valle raised cattle, sheep, and horses. An earthquake would destroy most of the early buildings in this region in 1857. Today remnants of the *asistencia* lie in Castaic Junction in an area that a development company has deeded to a non-profit organization for preservation.[28]

Several historic events took place on *Rancho San Francisco*. In 1842 a relative of the Del Valle family—Francisco Lopez y Arballo—had discovered gold. Lopez was running his cattle in Placerita Canyon one day and accidentally discovered gold particles clinging to the roots of wild onion bulbs growing around an old oak tree. It is estimated that $80,000 in gold was recovered by prospectors from Los Angeles and Sonora, Mexico between 1842 and 1847. The discovery of gold in Coloma in 1848 drew the miners away from this area, and work would not be resumed until 1855. Today the famous "Oak of the Golden Dream" is identified by a plaque in the Placerita Canyon State and County Park in Newhall.

Second, in January 1850, *Rancho San Francisco* is where William Lewis Manly and John Rogers obtained supplies and animals for the rescue of their comrades of the gold-seeking emigrant party stranded and starving in Death Valley some 250 miles to the northeast. Finally, *Rancho San Francisco*, in the vicinity of Newhall, would be the site of California's first successful commercial oil well, which was drilled in 1876 by Charles Alexander Mentry.

Returning to the San Fernando Valley, the 1797 *Misión San Fernando Rey de España* stood in disrepair. After secularization, it was sold to *Don* Eulogio de Celís. Its roof tiles were stripped by settlers and the adobe walls ravaged by the weather. Restoration of the mission was completed in the 1930s, but the 1971 Sylmar earthquake damaged it and the 1994 Northridge earthquake subsequently destroyed it. A replica of the mission stands today in Mission Hills. De Celís also owned *Rancho Ex-Mission de San Fernando*—116,000 acres of the San Fernando Valley.

What is known as the Pico Adobe stands in Mission Hills near the mission. De Celís enlarged and renovated the mission outbuilding built in 1834 by American Indians, and was living there in 1850. *Don* Andrés Pico was leasing a portion of the rancho in 1850 and would buy an undivided half interest in the rancho in 1854. He never actually lived in the Pico Adobe; he preferred staying in the *convento* building of the old mission complex when he was at the rancho. However, Romulo Pico, his adopted son, would live in the home with his family in later years. The Pico Adobe is the oldest adobe in the San Fernando Valley. The adobe had many owners and has undergone many renovations, but in 1969 it was restored to the Victorian era of Romulo Pico.

Don Vicente de la Osa owned *Rancho El Encino*, which included the foothills of the Santa Monica Mountains. De la Osa was a successful cattle rancher who made a great deal of money driving his cattle to the gold fields and selling them at inflated

Pico Brothers—African, Native American, Hispanic, and European ancestry

Pío Pico (1801-1894)

- Civil revolutionary during duration of Mexican Republic

- Last governor of Alta California; moved capital from Monterey to L.A.

- Married to María Ignacia Alvarado, niece of Mexican Governor Juan Bautista Alvarado; couple had five adopted children

- Owned two ranchos in San Diego County, one in L.A. County, and a townhouse in L.A.

- Became American citizen, but spoke little English

- Self-made, successful businessman, until he failed in his struggle to compete with American business methods

- Los Angeles city councilman

- Namesake of Los Angeles' Pico Boulevard

- Died penniless at the home of one of his adopted daughters

Andrés Pico (1810-1876)

- Military revolutionary during duration of Mexican Republic

- Mexican General who led *Californios* against Americans at Battle of San Pasqual

- Signed Treaty of Cahuenga with Lt. Col. John C. Frémont

- Large landowner of six ranchos in four counties

- Gold miner in 1849 and 1850

- State assemblyman and senator

- Member of California Rangers

- Brigadier general in California Militia

- Offered commission as a major of a calvary company in California during the Civil War, but declined due to illness

- Lost much of his land due to foreclosures

- Never married, but adopted several sons

prices. The De la Osa family hosted many travelers passing through here on El Camino Real.

The Los Encinos Historic State Park has preserved the 1848 De la Osa adobe ranch house (as it looked in the 1870s and 80s) standing beside a small lake, as well as other buildings built by earlier and later owners. Unfortunately, all of the buildings in the park were damaged by the 1994 Northridge earthquake; the park is open for other uses, however, and the buildings may be viewed from a distance through cyclone fences. Reconstruction will begin as soon as funds are available.

Three Chumash Indian brothers—Odon, Urbano, and Manuel—and *Don* Joaquín Romero owned the small *Rancho El Escorpión*, which was nestled between

The De la Osa adobe ranch house stands in Los Encinos Historic State Park, awaiting reconstruction following earthquake damage.

The Leonis Adobe, restored to its 1870s era, is located in Old Town Calabasas.

The Reyes Adobe is located on the grounds of a small neighborhood park in the City of Agoura Hills, awaiting restoration.

the Santa Monica and Santa Susanna Mountains. Many Native Americans made their homes in the canyons of this rancho where streams and springs nourished the wildlife. Massive, 500-700 year-old oak trees cover the rolling hills of this former rancho today. Since the valley was particularly ideal for sheep raising, many Basque families came to live in the area.

An adobe built in 1844 by an early settler on public land adjacent to this rancho remains in Old Town Calabasas today and is known as the Leonis Adobe.[29] El Camino Real passed in front of the adobe, and the area had been known as *Las Calabazas* (The Pumpkins) since 1824 when hundreds of pumpkin plants sprouted where a Basque farmer spilled a load of pumpkins on his way to the pueblo.

Don Juan Domínguez[30] owned *Rancho Las Virgenes*. Entitlement to different parts of this rancho was in dispute for over 30 years and various claimants occupied the property. *Doña* María Antonia Machado de Reyes lived in the Reyes Adobe that still stands today. This home welcomed many visitors, including the *vaqueros* driving cattle north to feed the miners in the gold fields. The City of Agoura Hills has plans to restore the two structures located on the grounds of a small neighborhood park as soon as funds are made available. The buildings are currently viewable through an iron fence.

Finally, the Island of Santa Catalina lies between the San Pedro and Outer Santa Barbara channels in the Pacific Ocean—directly to the west of San Clemente in Orange County. It is part of Los Angeles County, however. In 1850 *Don* José María Covarrubias owned the island. During the period of time when title of most of

California's ranchos was in doubt, various squatters laid claim to different areas of the island and began running sheep and cattle. Several coves still bear the names of these early squatters. It would not be until the 1880s and 90s, however, that adventurous mainlanders sailed across the channel to picnic on the shore and escape the heat of California's inland valleys.[31]

UNGRANTED LAND IN PRESENT-DAY LOS ANGELES COUNTY (PART OF 1850-MARIPOSA COUNTY)

Several explorers and expeditions had made their way through the Antelope Valley prior to 1850, but the area would remain relatively undisturbed until the 1870s with the completion of the railroad in 1876. Early travelers through the valley, geographically a part of the Mojave Desert, wrote of the distinctive trees (named by early visitors for their resemblance to the praying prophet, Joshua) and the glorious poppy fields in the spring. General Edward F. Beale[32] led his famous camel caravan along the southern end of this valley in 1857. The area was used as hunting grounds for antelope, thus its name. The thousands of antelope were practically eliminated by hunters and the severe winters of the 1880s.

EPILOGUE: LOS ANGELES COUNTY

In contrast to today, Los Angeles was behind northern California in 1850 in many respects—especially in terms of population. Los Angeles would grow, but not spectacularly until after 1870. It took 52 days to receive mail from San Francisco. A stage line was established between the Port of San Pedro and Los Angeles in 1852, but the San Francisco and Los Angeles sections of the Southern Pacific Railroad were not united near Saugus until 1876. Although Los Angeles is the entertainment capital of the world today, the first play was not presented in Los Angeles until 1860—much later than in northern California.

Water, the state's most valuable natural resource, has played a significant role in California's history, especially as it relates to Los Angeles County. The Los Angeles, San Gabriel, Rio Honda, and Santa Clara rivers have complicated histories involving course changes due to floods and man-made irrigation ditches. The 233-mile long Los Angeles-Owens River aqueduct running from the Owens River Valley in the Sierra Nevada mountains was not built until 1913. In 1940, the aqueduct was extended 105 miles north to tap the waters of the Mono Basin; in 1970, the Second Los Angeles Aqueduct from the Mono Basin was completed. (Currently, environmental lawsuits are pending in the courts over the water from the Mono Basin.)

LOS ANGELES COUNTY RANCHOS

NAME OF RANCHO	GRANTEE AND/OR 1850 OWNER	1850 AND/OR CURRENT SITES
Rancho Los Alamitos (Little Cottonwoods)	Abel Stearns	Seal Beach and Los Alamitos in Orange County; Long Beach
Rancho Los Cerritos (Little Hills)	Juan (Jonathan) Temple	Long Beach, Signal Hill, Lakewood, Paramount
Rancho Santa Gertrudes	Lemuel Carpenter	Downey
Rancho La Habre (Depression in the Hills)	Andrés Pico	East Whittier, La Habra Heights; La Habra in Orange County
Rancho Paso de Bartolo	Joaquina Sepúlveda, Bernardino Guirado, Pío Pico, heirs of Juan Crispín Pérez	Whittier, Pico Rivera
Rancho La Merced	Casilda Soto de Lobo	Montebello
Rancho Potrero de Felipe Lugo (Pasture Land of Felipe Lugo)	Teodoro Romero	Monterey Park, South El Monte, El Monte, Rosemead
Rancho Potrero Grande (Large Pasture Land)	Manuel Antonio	Monterey Park, South El Monte, El Monte, Rosemead
Rancho Potrero Chico (Little Pasture Land)	Mission property	San Gabriel
Rancho San Francisquito	Enrique (Henry) Dalton	Temple City
Rancho La Puente (Bridge)	Julian (William) Workman, Juan Roldan (John Rowland)	La Puente, City of Industry, Rowland Heights, Walnut, Covina, West Covina
Rancho Rincón de La Brea (Crude Tar)	Gil Ybarra	Walnut
Rancho Los Nogales (Walnut Trees)	Widow of José de la Luz Linares, Ricardo Véjar	Diamond Bar
Rancho San José	Ygnacio Palomares, Ricardo Véjar, Enrique (Henry) Dalton	Pomona, Claremont, LaVerne, San Dimas
Rancho San José Adición	Enrique (Henry) Dalton	Glendora
Rancho Azusa de Dalton	Enrique (Henry) Dalton	Azusa
Rancho Azusa de Duarte	Andrés Duarte	Duarte, Bradbury, Monrovia
Rancho Santa Anita[33]	Enrique (Henry) Dalton	Arcadia, Sierra Madre, Pasadena[34]
Rancho San Pascual	Manuel Gárfías	South Pasadena, Pasadena
Rancho San Antonio	Antonio María Lugo	Vernon, Huntington Park, South Gate, Lynwood, Bell Gardens
Rancho Tajauta	Anastasio Ávila	Watts
Rancho San Pedro	Heirs of Juan José Domínguez	Gardena, Compton, Redondo Beach, Torrance, San Pedro
Rancho Los Palos Verdes (Range of Green Trees)	Juan Diego and José Loreto Sepúlveda	San Pedro, Rancho Palos Verdes, Rolling Hills Estates
Rancho Sausal Redondo (Round Clump of Willows)	Antonio Ygnacio Ávila	Redondo Beach, Hermosa Beach, Manhattan Beach, El Segundo, L.A. International
Rancho Aguaje de la Centinela (Gathering Waters of the Sentinel)	Bruno Ávila	Inglewood

LOS ANGELES COUNTY RANCHOS (CONTINUED)

NAME OF RANCHO	GRANTEE AND/OR 1850 OWNER	1850 AND/OR CURRENT SITES
Rancho La Ballona	Brothers Ygnacio and José Agustín Machado; father and son, Felipe and Tomas Talamantes	Culver City, Playa Del Rey, Marina Del Rey, Venice, Santa Monica
Rancho Rincón de los Bueyes (Bull's Corner)	Brothers Francisco and Secundino Higuera	Culver City
Rancho Ciénega o Paso de la Tijera (Marshlands/Pass of the Open Pair of Scissors)	Vicente Sánchez and his son, Tomás A. Sánchez, following his death in 1850	Culver City, City of Los Angeles
Rancho Las Ciénegas (Marshes)	Januario Ávila	City of Los Angeles
Rancho San Antonio	María Rita Valdez De Villa	Beverly Hills
Rancho San José de Buenos Aires (St. Joseph of the Good Air)	Máximo Alanis	Bel Air, Westwood, UCLA
Rancho La Brea (Tar)	Heirs of Antonio José Rocha and Nemesio Domínguez	Hollywood
Rancho Los Feliz (Happy Ones)	María Ygnacia Verdugo	Griffith Park
Rancho La Providencia (Divine Providence)	Vicente de la Osa, J. Castro, and Luis Arenas	Burbank
Rancho Cahuenga	Tomás Feliz	North Hollywood
Rancho San Rafael	Heirs of José María Verdugo	Burbank, Glendale, Eagle Rock
Rancho La Cañada (Mountain Valley)	Ygnacio Coronel	La Canada Flintridge, La Crescenta
Rancho Tujunga	Brothers Pedro and Francisco Lopez	Tujunga, Sunland
Rancho San Francisco	Ygnacio Del Valle	Santa Clarita, Newhall, Placerita Canyon State Park, extended into Ventura Co.
Rancho Ex-Mission de San Fernando	Eulogio de Celís	116,000 acres of San Fernando Valley from Sylmar to Chatsworth to Van Nuys to Pacoima
Rancho El Encino (The Oak)	Vicente de la Osa	Encino
Rancho El Escorpión (Scorpion)	Brothers Odon, Urbano and Manuel; Joaquín Romero	Calabasas
Rancho San Vicente y Santa Monica	Francisco Sepúlveda	Santa Monica
Rancho Boca (Mouth) de Santa Monica	Isidro Reyes, Francisco Marquez	Pacific Palisades, Will Rogers State Historic Park
Rancho Topanga Malibu (Surf Sounds Loud) Sequit	Victor Prudhomme	Malibu
Rancho Las Virgenes (Virgins)	Juan Domínguez	Agoura Hills, Westlake Village

Notes ⤙ LOS ANGELES COUNTY

1

The Great Stone Church is the major focus of a preservation project currently under way at Mission San Juan Capistrano.

2

Great flocks of swallows no longer descend on Mission San Juan Capistrano en masse, because the development in the area has caused the swallows to locate away from the center of town.

3

There are conflicting historical suppositions about whether Mission Viejo was the original site of Mission San Juan Capistrano.

4

Supposedly the Trabuco Mesa of this area was named by one of the soldiers traveling with the Gaspar de Portola expedition in 1769 who lost his "trabuco" or musket here. The name has been associated with the mesa, the canyon, and the entire area ever since.

5

Ranchos *Lomas de Santiago* and *San Joaquin*, along with a strip along the southeast border of *Rancho Santiago de Santa Ana*, would become part of the Irvine Ranch in 1876, one of the last great ranches in California.

6

Originally known as San Antonio, the name of the community was changed to Yorba in honor of *Don* Bernardo Yorba. Later the word "Linda" was added, meaning beautiful. Yorba Linda would become the birthplace of the first native Californian president, Richard M. Nixon.

7

Las Bolsas and *Los Coyotes* ranchos originally were part of the 1784 Los Nietos concession granted to *Don* José Manuel Nieto, a soldier of the San Diego Presidio; it was subdivided by Nieto's heirs following his death in 1804.

8

See Ord sidebar on page 92.

9

An ordinance would be passed in 1854 to allow certain homeowners to take possession of the land between their houses and the nearest street.

10

Jonathan R. Scott became the first Justice of the Peace and Benjamin Hayes became the first County Attorney; the two also owned a rancho in the San Fernando Valley.

11

The Wilson of Packard and Wilson was Benjamin D. Wilson.

12

The first wooden building would be built in L.A. in 1851—a saloon, later to be used as a Methodist church; the first brick building was built in 1853.

13

See Bandini sidebar on page 34.

14

The original plaza in the L.A. pueblo stood a short distance from the present one; it was moved due to flooding.

15

José Antonio Carrillo was a delegate of the State Constitutional Convention.

16

As late as 1863, the citizens of Los Angeles were still poorly supplied with water hauled in carts from the Los Angeles River. The Los Angeles River would serve as the only water supply for Los Angeles until 1913 when the Los Angeles Aqueduct was completed. Today the river takes a much different route than it did in 1850 and much of it is contained within a concrete channel that protects the city from flooding. Long Beach, 50 miles from the mountains above the San Fernando Valley where the river originates, is the permanent destination of the river.

17

Alamitos Bay that surrounds the Naples portion of Long Beach today is man-made and did not exist in 1850.

18

The Bixbys were part of the prominent southern California family that acquired extensive ranch lands in Monterey, L.A., San Luis Obispo, and Orange counties.

19

Damaged by the Whittier Narrows Earthquake of 1987, only exterior viewing of the Pico adobe is generally allowed. Reconstruction will begin as soon as funds are available.

20

The preservation of *El Molino Viejo* is an extraordinary example of the sacrifice of a prime piece of real estate in the interest of history. The property is located in an exclusive residential neighborhood.

21

The elaborate Queen Anne cottage and Coach Barn that stand across the marshy lagoon from the Hugo Adobe today were constructed on the grounds in the 1880s.

22

Henry Taft Gage, a Supreme Court Justice and Governor, would live in this home, so it is often referred to as the Henry Gage Mansion.

23

The Claretian Missionaries, a Catholic order, would be deeded the adobe in 1924. The Dominguez Memorial Seminary was established and still operates on the property today. A remodeled version of the original adobe is a house museum open to the public on specified days of the week.

24

The renovated Los Feliz Adobe, which today serves as the Park Ranger's Headquarters in Griffith Park, would not be built until 1853. A much later owner of the rancho—Colonel Jenkins Griffith—donated part of the rancho to the City of Los Angeles in 1896 to be used as a park, thus its name.

25

A reenactment of the signing of the Treaty of Cahuenga takes place at the *Campo de Cahuenga* every January.

26

Casa Adobe de San Rafael would not be built until the 1870s; it stands today in Glendale. The *Casa de Adobe*, a 1925 replica of an early 1800s residence with authentic furnishings, stands today below the Southwest Museum in Highland Park. The adobe was built by the Hispanic Society of California to depict an early California-style adobe home of a wealthy *ranchero*, but has no connection with the Verdugo family. It currently is closed for seismic retrofitting.

27

The former streams in the Coldwater and Benedict canyons have subsided and the swamp is gone.

28

In 1853 Del Valle would build the ranch house that Helen Hunt Jackson chose to represent a typical Spanish-California residence in her famous 1884 novel, *Ramona*. The historic adobe, winery, chapel, schoolhouse, garage, and gardens of this Camulos (Juniper) Ranch, which is situated on the western edge of the former *Rancho San Francisco* along the Santa Clara River in Ventura County, are scheduled for preservation and restoration as soon as sufficient funds can be raised. In the meantime, the "Rancho Camulos" and "The Home of Ramona" exhibits created by the curator of the Ventura County Museum of History and Art tell the fascinating story about this famous rancho.

29

Don Miguel Leonis, a Basque immigrant who was a sheepherder for the *Don* Joaquín Romero when he first arrived in the area in 1858, and his American Indian wife (the daughter of Odon) would renovate the adobe in the 1870s, converting it to a Monterey-style home. Today the Leonis Adobe is restored to its 1870s era. The Agoure family lived in this home in the 1920s; Agoura Hills just west of Calabasas is named for them.

30

This is not the Juan José Domínguez of San Pedro.

31

Today, Santa Catalina is a popular travel destination, originally developed by William Wrigley, Jr. in the 1930s.

32

See Beale sidebar on page 255.

33

Santa Anita, one of the most famous thoroughbred horseracing tracks in the country, lies on the former *Rancho Santa Anita*, thus its name.

34

Pasadena would become the home of the famous Tournament of Roses Parade in 1890; the first Rose Bowl football game would be held here in 1902.

This is another view of the El Molino Viejo that houses the southern California headquarters of the California Historical Society in San Marino.

The Ortega-Vigare Adobe, a private residence located in San Gabriel, is the second oldest adobe in the region.

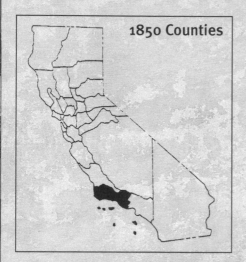

1850 Counties

ᏚᏃ 1 8 5 0 ᏓᏂ
SANTA BARBARA
COUNTY

San Luis
Obispo Co.

Los Angeles
Co.

Santa
Barbara Co.

• Santa Maria

• Guadalupe

• Los Alamos

Buellton • • Los Olivos

• Lompoc   Solvang

• Santa Inez

Ventura Co.

Gaviota

Carpenteria

Pacific
Ocean

Goleta   Santa
Barbara

• Ojai

• Simi Valley

• Ventura   Camarillo

Channel Islands

California
1850

Present-day boundary
variations indicated by

- - - - - -

Settlements/cities of 1850 include: Santa Barbara, San Buena Ventura (Ventura)

SANTA BARBARA COUNTY
1850

The geographical area of 1850-Santa Barbara County included present-day Ventura County. Its 1,185 residents counted in the 1850 U.S. Census included Californios, Americans, and Europeans. Chumash Indians made up the uncounted Native American population. Spanish was still the area's common language, although it alternated with English as the language of official records.

AREA WITHIN PRESENT-DAY VENTURA COUNTY

In 1850 the area that would later become Ventura County in 1873 consisted of the former mission community of San Buenaventura and 16 ranchos. The region's fertile valleys and beautiful coastline were not yet attracting settlers. As late as 1860, there were but nine American voters within the county.

The unique geological characteristics of the region contributed to the area's isolation. The Transverse Ranges stretch in a west/east direction from the Pacific Coast all the way to the Mojave Desert in San Bernardino County, and include Ventura County's Simi Hills, the Santa Susana Mountains, and the Santa Monica Mountains. The county also has the Santa Ynez and Topatopa mountains along its northern border. All of these mountains created a geographical barrier to travel.

Attempts had been made to establish a town on the lands of the Rancho Ex-Mission San Buenaventura in 1848, when *Don* José Arnaz made offers in East Coast journals of lots to those who would make improvements on them. However, the town of San Buenaventura (Ventura, today) would not be laid out until the 1860s. Some of the large ranchos were subdivided during this same period of time and a general influx of Americans finally began—many of whom were veterans of the Civil War taking advantage of the free land offered following passage of the Homestead Act of 1868. Agriculture on any large scale was not undertaken until this time. The Southern Pacific Railroad arrived in Ventura in 1887.

Mission San Buenaventura

Mission San Buenaventura was established in 1782. The first church was destroyed by fire; a second church was begun in 1792, but abandoned before completion because of faulty construction. The present mission church was completed in 1809.

Don José Arnaz owned the mission in 1850. Its deteriorating buildings, arranged in a quadrangle, still stood and were occupied by local merchants. President Lincoln

Sites to Visit in Ventura County

Albinger Archaeological Museum, 113 E. Main St., Ventura 805.648.5823

Mission San Buenaventura, 211 E. Main St., Ventura 805.648.4496

Olivas Adobe Historical Park, 4200 Olivas Park Dr., Ventura 805.644.4346

Ortega Adobe, 215 W. Main St., Ventura

Strathearn Historical Park and Museum, 137 Strathearn Pl., Simi Valley 805.526.6453

Ventura County Museum of History and Art, 100 E. Main St., Ventura 805.653.0323

Ventura Visitors and Convention Bureau, 89 S. California St., Ventura, CA 93001 805.648.2075

would return the mission holdings to the Catholic church in 1862. The church building was restored in 1957.

A seven-mile-long aqueduct was still bringing water from the Ventura River to the mission in 1850. Today, the 1780s brick water-filtration building located north of the Albinger Archaeological Museum[1] is the oldest standing structure in Ventura County. Water was distributed from here to the mission and neighboring homes. The remains of an adobe brick factory where bricks were made from 1845 to 1860 may also be seen on the museum grounds. Several adobe homes lined both sides of El Camino Real west of the mission.[2]

Ventura County Ranchos

Sixteen land grants had been made in present-day Ventura County. Details about the more interesting ones follow, beginning on the southeastern border. *Don* José de la Guerra of Santa Barbara owned *El Rancho Simi*, which he visited once a year in order to inspect his cattle and sheep. Today, a restored 1888 house that incorporates two rooms of the old Simi adobe that stood on the property in 1850 is located in the Strathearn Historical Park and Museum.

Three *Dons*—Ygnacio Rodríguez, José Polanco, and José de la Guerra—owned *Rancho El Conejo*. Thousands of rabbits roamed the land, thus its name. The valley

Mission San Buenaventura was restored in 1957.

The restored, two-story Olivas Adobe is located in Ventura.

of this rancho was remote and used primarily for pasturing livestock. There were only two or three small adobe buildings used by the *vaqueros* and occasional traveling *rancheros*. El Camino Real passed through *El Conejo*, but because of the rugged mountains, the majority of travelers between San Buenaventura and Los Angeles used the route through the neighboring *El Rancho Simi*. The road through *Simi* was less difficult and slightly shorter.

Dons Raymundo Olivas and Felipe Lorenzana, two retired soldiers, owned *Rancho San Miguel*. In 1847 Olivas built a hacienda on the banks of the Santa Clara River, which stands today as the restored, two-story Olivas Adobe in Ventura.[3] His family, with 21 children, was famous for its generous hospitality. Although this rancho was one of the smaller land grants in Ventura County, it offered enough good grazing land to make Olivas a very prosperous cattle rancher.

Don Fernando de Tico raised cattle and planted crops on *Rancho Ojai*, known as *Rancho Ojay* (Spanish spelling). Tico was active in the San Buenaventura community life as a merchant and government official.[4]

Don Carlos Carrillo owned *Rancho Sespe* where he raised cattle, horses, mules, and sheep, and planted vineyards. He and his family lived in Santa Barbara, but visited the rancho once a year—staying in the two-story house Carrillo built.[5]

Los Padres National Forest (Forest of the Fathers) and other protected wildlife areas occupy the rugged, northern portion of Ventura County. The Los Padres National Forest is also located in Santa Barbara, San Luis Obispo, and Monterey counties and is the largest national forest in California, with nearly two million acres.

The Channel Islands are located off the coasts of Ventura and Santa Barbara counties. The Chumash Indians had navigated around the Santa Barbara Channel for many years, Juan Rodríguez Cabrillo had explored the islands in 1542, and trappers had hunted seal and sea otters in the area in the early 1800s.[6] A U.S. Coast Survey party mapped the islands in 1850. Only the Anacapa[7] and Nicolas islands are part of Ventura County; the San Miguel, Santa Rosa, and Santa Cruz islands are part of Santa Barbara County.

VENTURA COUNTY RANCHOS

NAME OF RANCHO	GRANTEE AND/OR 1850 OWNER	1850 AND/OR CURRENT SITES
El Rancho Simi	José de la Guerra y Noriega	Santa Susana, Simi Valley,[8] Moorpark
Rancho El Conejo (Rabbit)	Ygnacio Rodríguez, José Polanco, José de la Guerra	Thousand Oaks, Newbury Park, Westlake Village
Rancho Gaudalasca	Ysabel Yorba	Point Mugu State Park, Santa Monica Mountains
Rancho Calleguas (Burial Ground)	José Gabriel Ruiz	Somis, Camarillo
Rancho Las Posas (Buttocks)	José Carrillo	Camarillo
Rancho Santa Clara del Norte	Juan Sanchez	Oxnard
Rancho Río de Santa Clara	Valentin Cota and eight fellow soldiers	Oxnard
Rancho San Miguel	Raymundo Olivas, Felipe Lorenzana	Ventura
Rancho Santa Paula y Saticoy	Manuel Jimeno Casarín	Santa Paula, Saticoy
Rancho Ex-Mission San Buenaventura (Good Fortune)	José Arnaz, M.A.R. Poli[9] during 1850	Area west of Santa Paula
Rancho Cañada Larga o Verde	Joaquina Alvarado	Foster Park area
Rancho Cañada de San Miguelito	Ramon Rodriguez	Foster Park area
Rancho Santa Ana	José Arnaz	Lake Casitas Recreation Area
Rancho Ojai	Fernando de Tico	Ojai
Rancho Sespe	Carlos Carrillo	Santa Paula, Fillmore
Rancho Temescal (Sweat Lodge)	Francisco Lopez	Lake Piru[10]

Area Within Present-Day Santa Barbara County

In 1850 the area within present-day Santa Barbara County consisted of a sleepy former mission/presidio town, two other former missions, and 38 ranchos. The Santa Barbara pueblo portion of the county would remain isolated from the north county and the rest of the state until the State Legislature appropriated money for construction of the first county road to be cut through the Gaviota Pass in 1860. In 1850 the Gaviota Pass was too narrow for wagons to be drawn through; a series of trails, a few of them wide enough only for horseback travel, served as the only roads through the area. A wagon road would not be built over San Marcos Pass until 1868-69. El Camino Real, a rough dirt road along the coastline, followed what is now the route of the Southern Pacific Railroad, but was not a very desirable alternative.

Santa Barbara Channel

Until 1872, when Stearns Wharf was built by John Stearns, cargo and passenger ships had to drop anchor out in the Santa Barbara Channel. Passengers were then rowed ashore or, if the sea was rough, carried the last several yards to the beach on the backs of strong sailors. Hides were carried atop sailors' heads and other types of freight had to be floated to the beach.

Whaling had begun in the Santa Barbara Channel in the 1820s. The whaling days would continue until the discovery of oil in Pennsylvania in 1859; at that time, kerosene began to replace whale oil for lamps. The last whaling station in the Santa Barbara region ended its operations in 1890.

City of Santa Barbara

The city of Santa Barbara is located on a narrow coastal plain between the Pacific Ocean and the Santa Ynez Mountains of the Los Padres National Forest. In 1850 the former presidio and pueblo lands of Santa Barbara consisted of the town proper and present-day Montecito, Summerland, and Carpinteria. Santa Barbara was incorporated in April 1850, with Lewis T. Burton serving as the first president of Santa Barbara's common council and *Don* Francisco de la Guerra serving as the first mayor. The new city government rented rooms in various adobe houses. The first Santa Barbara school under the American flag had been established in 1849, and the first post office was established in 1850.

There were more than 100 adobes in Santa Barbara. There were no streets or planned sites, so the adobes were located haphazardly. Captain Salisbury Haley would survey the city in 1851, at which time a committee composed of three city councilmen was appointed to name the streets. Some of Santa Barbara's streets are named in honor of men who held positions in state government and/or whose families were prominent in Santa Barbara's early history. Other names reflect the Spanish word for something common to the area of a particular street.

A number of historic adobe buildings still remain in the downtown Santa Barbara area. Most are now offices or private residences, but may be viewed from the exterior on the "Red Tile Tour."[11]

Sites to Visit in Santa Barbara County

Carpinteria Valley Museum of History, 956 Maple Av., Carpinteria 805.684.3112

El Presidio de Santa Barbara State Historic Park, 123 E. Canon Perdido St., Santa Barbara 805.965.0093

La Purisima Mission State Historic Park, Hwy 246 and Purisima Rd., Lompoc   805.733.3713

Mission Santa Barbara, 2201 Laguna St., Santa Barbara 805.682.4149

Mission Santa Inés, 1760 Mission Dr., Solvang   805.688.4815

Santa Barbara Botanic Garden, 1212 Mission Canyon Rd., Santa Barbara 805.682.4726

Santa Barbara County Courthouse 1100 Anacapa St., Santa Barbara 805.962.6464 (Red Tile Tour Map)

Santa Barbara Historical Museum, 136 E. de la Guerra, Santa Barbara 805.966.1601

Santa Ynez Historical Museum, 3596 Sagunto St., Santa Ynez 805.688.7889

Santa Barbara Conference & Visitors Bureau, 1 Santa Barbara St., Santa Barbara, CA 93103 800.676.1266

The Hill-Carrillo Adobe, on Carrillo Street, was built in 1825 by Daniel A. Hill for his bride, Rafaela Luisa Ortega y Olivera. She was the granddaughter of José Francisco Ortega, founder and first *commandante* of the Santa Barbara presidio. The adobe contained the city's first wooden floor and was the birthplace in 1833 of Isabella Larkin, the first child born in California of parents who were both Americans.[12] Captain John Wilson[13] and his wife, Ramona de Carrillo,[14] owned the home in 1850. When they were not staying at one of their properties in San Luis Obispo County, the Wilsons regularly welcomed traveling pioneers in this home.

The adobes on either side of the Wilson's house no longer remain. One of these adobes—*La Casa de Aguirre*—was built in 1841 by *Don* José Antonio de Aguirre, a wealthy Spanish-French merchant and ship-owner. It had a number of apartments arranged in a quadrangle around a paved patio and was one of the most famous of the Spanish-California homes of that day.

The Casa de la Guerra, located downtown, is one of Santa Barbara's oldest structures.

The *Casa de la Guerra* on East De la Guerra Street is one of the city's oldest structures.[15] It was completed in 1827 by *Don* José de la Guerra. The adobe was surrounded by buildings which included an oven larger than an ordinary room, a flour mill, a two-story building for storing supplies purchased from sailing ships, a carriage shed, and the *bodega* (wine cellar), in which not only wine, but potatoes and olives were stored. The *Casa* was the economic, political, and social center of the pueblo. The *Plaza de la Guerra* located across the street is where the first city council met in 1850.

The 1849 Oreña Adobe stood alone next door to the *Casa*, but today it is part of a three-building structure housing business offices and shops. *Don* Gaspar Oreña, a Spanish trader and wealthy resident, built the Oreña Adobe. (Oreña also owned the town's billiard parlor.)

Across Anacapa Street, still on East De la Guerra, *Don* Teodoro Arrellanes owned the first substantial home built outside of the presidio grounds in 1795. (The house was destroyed in the 1925 earthquake.) Today, the seven carved wooden porch pillars, brought around Cape Horn in 1800 and added to the house when the porch was built, are incorporated into the piazza of the community social service center located on Santa Barbara Street.

The 1812 Santiago de la Guerra Adobe, a remodeled office building today, also is located on East De la Guerra. The 1830 Lugo Adobe is nestled in a courtyard nearby.

Captain Alpheu B. Thompson, an early-American resident of Santa Barbara, lived on State Street in an 1834 two-story, pillared structure with a wooden-railed balcony extending around all four sides at the second-story level. It would later become the St. Charles Hotel. The Rodríguez family home was on the west side of State Street; next door was the San Carlos Hotel.

El Presidio Real de Santa Barbara lay astride Santa Barbara and Canon Perdido streets. (The streets were surveyed through the site of the original Presidio in 1851.) Founded in 1782, it was the last Spanish military outpost in California. The soldiers

José Antonio Julián de la Guerra y Noriego (1779-1858)

- Came to California in early 1800s from Spain
- Fifth *commandante* of the Spanish presidio in Santa Barbara, 1815-1842
- His home was the center of social life in Santa Barbara; host to Richard Henry Dana as noted in his book
- Married to María Antoniá Carrillo

Pablo de la Guerra (1819-1874)

- Most prominent of José's sons
- Administrator of Custom House in Monterey
- *Alcalde* in Santa Barbara
- Delegate of State Constitutional Convention
- State senator, acting Lieutenant Governor, U.S. Marshal and judge

and their families played an important role in the settlement of Santa Barbara County following the American occupation in 1846.

Most of the original presidio structures were lost in one of three earthquakes by the 1840s; others would be lost to the forces of progress, but El Presidio de Santa Barbara State Historic Park, in progress since the 1920s, has restored several of the buildings. Many of the Presidio's other foundations are now being uncovered and restored as part of an extensive excavation and reconstruction project.

The Presidio Gardens are located on the site of the former Presidio parade grounds on De La Guerra Street. The Presidio Chapel stood on Canon Perdido Street and has been reconstructed on its original foundations. The original chapel

El Presidio de Santa Barbara State Historic Park is located in downtown Santa Barbara. An extensive excavation and reconstruction project is ongoing.

was an active parish church until 1857 when it was destroyed by an earthquake. *El Cuartel*, the 1788 family residence of the Presidio guard, is the oldest building in Santa Barbara and the oldest building owned by the State of California. It houses exhibits, a small museum, and a gift shop. The adjacent Cañeda Adobe was also a part of the original Presidio quadrangle, housing Presidio soldiers and families. Today it contains museum exhibits. Portions of the Commandant's Quarters and Padre's Quarters have also been restored.

The Santa Barbara Historical Museum is part of an adobe complex where two 19th century adobes surround a courtyard. The *Casa Covarrubia* was constructed on this site by *Don* Domínguez Carrillo in 1817. His daughter married *Don* José María Covarrubias in 1838 and they owned the home in 1850. The other adobe, the Historic (or Malo) Adobe, was built on State and Carrillo streets in 1836 for Concepción Pico de Carrillo, sister of Pío Pico. It was moved to its current location in 1924 to make way for a commercial structure built on the adobe's original site.

Many other adobes stood within the pueblo area. Outside of the pueblo, along the Santa Barbara waterfront, a large 1840 adobe stood on the knoll known today as the Burton Mound. A mill was built next to the adobe and a sulfur spring was located nearby. The property had passed between a number of different American owners. Captain George C. Nidever, an American hunter and trapper, lived here in 1850.

There were many business establishments, including a very large number licensed to sell liquor.[16] There were few actual stores, however; most merchants simply had large rooms outside their homes where groceries, dry goods, tobacco, and liquor could be bought or exchanged for other commodities.

None of today's gorgeous trees graced the streets of Santa Barbara in 1850. It would be the late 1870s before any were planted. There were not even any large native trees in the surrounding area because a disastrous fire had swept through the hills in 1831.

Santa Barbara was barely affected by the gold-seekers following the coast route to the gold fields. It was still quite rural. The *Santa Barbara Gazette*, the city's first newspaper, would not be published until 1855 (and have a short life of less than two years). The Catholic religion of the Franciscan padres remained dominant until well into the 1860s. The first Protestant sermon was preached in Santa Barbara in 1854.

Sharing hospitality with visitors, horse racing, and gambling were commonplace. Santa Barbara also was among the haunts of the outlaws that began operating throughout the state in the late 1840s. Salomon Pico's gang was headquartered at the *Rancho Los Alamos* and the former *Misión la Purísima* in the north county.

Today Santa Barbara's heritage is evident in its many whitewashed, Mediterranean, tile-roofed buildings and Spanish street names. The 1925 earthquake was a blessing in disguise, providing the opportunity for Santa Barbara to start over and create the unified look that the city has today—a Spanish colonial revival style.

The church of Mission Santa Barbara has been used continuously for religious observances since its founding.

Prior to 1846, pueblo lands in the area of present-day Montecito, Summerland, and Carpinteria[17] had been given away in parcels of 50 acres each to soldiers of the Santa Barbara Presidio upon retirement as compensation for as many as 20 years of service without pay. Thus, this area never became a Mexican land grant. The soldiers used the area as garden plots where they planted summer crops of corn, beans, and pumpkins. Often whole families camped for the summer along the running streams. Quite a number of descendants of Presidio soldiers still reside on these parcels. Two remodeled original adobes stand as private residences in the area. One room of the 1829 *Casa San Ysidro* is incorporated into one of the buildings of the San Ysidro Guest Rancho.

Mission Santa Barbara

The original Mission Santa Barbara was built in 1786, but was replaced by two later adobe churches. The 1812 earthquake destroyed the third church; the church that stands today was finished and dedicated in 1820. After secularization, unlike most of California's other missions, the Mission Santa Barbara buildings were not completely abandoned, but used for a number of purposes. The church has been used continuously for religious observances since its founding.

Dr. Richard Somerset Den of Los Angeles, the brother of Nicholas A. H. Den, owned the mission in 1850, but it would be returned to the church by the federal government in the 1860s. The 1925 earthquake damaged the mission considerably, but in 1927 it was restored to its 1820 "Queen of the Missions" state.

Santa Barbara County Ranchos

Most of the land outside Santa Barbara's pueblo was rancho property, except for the mountain areas that were too steep for grazing cattle and the windswept desert area of the Santa Maria Valley. For the most part, Santa Barbara County's ranchos were undeveloped in 1850, except where the two other missions had been established. Some of the ranchos have since been transformed by development or exploited for their oil deposits, but a number of working ranches cover the inland valleys and coastal shelf today. In fact, ranching remains an important part of the county's economy. Details about some of the more interesting ranchos follow.

Nicolas A. H. Den (1812-1862)

- Irishman who dropped out of medical school in Dublin due to a family financial crisis
- Arrived in Santa Barbara in 1836
- Called "Doc" by townspeople and performed many phlebotomies
- Married to Rosa Hill, Daniel Hill's daughter; learned Spanish
- One of wealthiest and most influential men in California in 1850
- Chair of first grand jury in Santa Barbara and County Assessor
- Charter member, with his brother, Richard Somerset Den, of the Society of California Pioneers

Captain Thomas M. Robbins, who was married to the daughter of the prominent Carrillo family, owned *Rancho Las Positas y La Calera*. He also owned and operated a store in Santa Barbara that was a popular gathering place for traders and seafarers. Hope Ranch lies on this former rancho land today.[18]

The 28 swamp acres of *Rancho Las Cieneguitas* were located within *Las Positas y La Calera*, and were owned by *Don* Anastacio Carrillo. American Indians would worship in an *asistencia* (a branch of Mission Santa Barbara) located on an acre of this property until the late 1800s. Today the swamps are drained and two schools are located here.

Daniel A. Hill owned *Rancho La Goleta*. The remodeled version of the adobe he built in 1850 still stands today as a private residence in Goleta. Today this area is the most completely urbanized of Santa Barbara's former rancho lands.

Rancho Los Dos Pueblos has a rich history associated with its owner, Nicholas Den. He would not take up residence on his rancho until 1854 when he built an adobe on a bluff above the Dos Pueblos Creek, but he was raising livestock here in 1850. Dos Pueblos Creek was a favorite campsite for travelers at this time.

Don José Dolores Ortega and one of his brothers owned *Rancho Cañada del Corral* and built two primitive adobes in a grove of sycamores. The El Capitan State Beach Park located on this former rancho serves as a memorial to Santa Barbara's first rancher, *Don* José Francisco de Ortega, known as *El Capitan*.

Rancho Nuestra Señora del Refugio was owned by *Don* Antonio M. Ortega, another son of *Don* José Francisco. This was the original Ortega rancho and one of the few ranchos in Santa Barbara County that operated as an estate. The Ortegas employed *vaqueros*, farmers, and household workers. A number of adobes were built by the Ortega family over the years on various secluded parts of this rancho, several of which still stand today as remodeled private residences.[19]

The first site of *Misión la Purísima* was located in present-day Lompoc, but it was totally destroyed by the 1812 earthquake. A new church was built about four miles northeast of the first site where the restored mission stands today. After secularization and abandonment in 1834, the mission slowly fell into total ruin. The decay was the result of neglect and weathering, particularly rain damage to the adobe walls. *Don* Juan (Jonathan) Temple[20] of Los Angeles had purchased the mission in 1845 for $1,100, but he only used it as a stable. Traveling vagrants and outlaws inhabited its crumbling structures. The mission was transferred back to the Catholic church in 1874.

In 1934, through a combined effort of county, state, and federal agencies, the restoration of *La Purísima* began. La Purisima Mission State Historic Park was created to model the mission of 1820. It is considered one of the finest restorations in the United States.

Rancho Guadalupe, partially located in San Luis Obispo County, was the most northerly Santa Barbara County rancho on the coast. It was owned by *Dons* Diego Olivera and Teodoro Arellanes. The Arellanes' home was the first in the Santa Maria Valley. Guadalupe would become the first town of any importance in the northern part of the county in 1874, followed by Santa Maria the next year. Cattle were raised in the Santa Maria Valley as early as 1840, but there was little farming until the Americans began to arrive after the Civil War.

Today Gaviota State Park lies on the former lands of *Rancho Las Cruces*, which was owned by family members of Miguel Cordero, the former *majordomo* of *Misión La Purísima*. The hot sulfur springs to the south and the clear waters of Gaviota Creek made the area a natural stopover for travelers on the main road into the valley until the San Marcos Pass Turnpike was built in 1868-69.

Don Francisco Cota owned *Rancho Santa Rosa*. His father had built an adobe on a knoll overlooking the property in 1808. Chumash Indian laborers brought timbers down from the San Rafael Mountains. A greatly remodeled version of the original home still serves as a private residence today southwest of Buellton.

Misión Santa Inés (Saint Agnes)[21] was situated on seventeen acres of the former mission rancho. The chapel of *Misión Santa Inés* has been in continuous use since 1817. Although the 1812 earthquake destroyed much of the mission, eleven of the original 22 arches and over one-third of the original mission quad still stand. The ruins of a gristmill built in 1820 by Joseph Chapman[22] are a nearby historical landmark today.

In 1850 *Dons* José María Covarrubias and José Joaquín Carrillo owned the crumbling mission. Major repair and reconstruction of the mission was begun in 1947 and completed in the early 1970s.

The Franciscans left the mission grounds when it was sold to the *dons*, but continued to manage the first seminary in California, the College of Our Lady of Refuge, established in 1844. The college had been relocated to what was known as *Rancho Cañada de los Pinos* (College Ranch). The college was abandoned in 1881.

Rancho Tinaquaic, located at the eastern end of the Santa Maria Valley, was owned by the former English ship captain, *Don* Julián (William Benjamin) Foxen. He and his family were living with Daniel Hill on his rancho in 1850, however, because the Foxen adobe home had been burned in 1847 by *Californios* angry with Foxen. Grizzly bears, mountain lions, and wolves still roamed the rolling oak-covered hills.

Doña María Antonia Domínguez y Caballero, of the distinguished Domínguez family of Los Angeles, owned *Rancho Sisquoc*. The rancho was known for its annual barbecues and rodeos at cattle branding time. Today this rancho land is home to a 37,000-acre cattle ranch and vineyard that still is just as large as it was in 1850.

Don José Domínguez owned *Rancho Los Prietos y Najalayegua*. This land in the upper Santa Ynez River Valley was too rugged for cattle or sheep grazing. The property would be considered worthless until quicksilver (mercury) was discovered in the Santa Ynez Mountains in the early 1860s.

The Santa Cruz and Santa Rosa islands were land grants owned by *Dons* Andrés Castilleros and Antonio and Carlos Carrillo, respectively. The Mexican governor had wanted settlement there to protect the surrounding waters, but that never occurred. The Carrillo brothers raised sheep on their island. Castilleros deeded half of his island to James Alexander Forbes[23] and Isidoro de la Torre, both of whom were involved in Castilleros' Almaden quicksilver mine operations in Santa Clara County.

Samuel C. Bruce was grazing sheep on San Miguel Island in 1850; later in the year, George C. Nidever bought him out and began grazing sheep, cattle, hogs, and horses on the island. The isolation of the five islands has left them relatively undeveloped even to this day.

William Benjamin Foxen (1798-1877)

- Sailor and hide trader from Norwich, England
- Married to Eduarda Osuña, the stepdaughter of *Don* Tomás Olivera
- Built a schooner (goleta) for Capt. De la Guerra
- Aided Lt. Col. John C. Frémont and the California Battalion in 1846, bringing on the wrath of the *Californios*
- In 1847 his cattle were scattered and his house burned and ransacked
- After his return to his rancho seven years later, his adobe became a way-station for prominent travelers
- His family had the Sisquoc Chapel built in his memory
- Credited with bridging the gap between the Spanish and American cultures

SANTA BARBARA COUNTY RANCHOS

NAME OF RANCHO	GRANTEE AND/OR 1850 OWNER	1850 AND/OR CURRENT SITES
Rancho El Rincón (Corner)	Teodoro Arellanes	Ranchland on Santa Barbara/ Ventura County line
Rancho Las Positas y La Calera	Thomas M. Robbins	Hope Ranch
Rancho Las Cieneguitas (Little Marshes)	Anastacio Carrillo	Hope Ranch
Rancho La Goleta (Schooner)	Daniel A. Hill	Goleta,
Rancho Los Dos Pueblos (Two Towns)	Nicholas A. H. Den	Isla Vista, University of California, Santa Barbara, Ellwood
Rancho Cañada del Corral (Valley of)	José Dolores Ortega	El Capitain State Beach
Rancho Nuestra Señora del Refugio (Our Lady of Refuge)	Antonio M. Ortega	Gaviota, Refugio State Beach
Rancho Punta de la Concepción	Anastacio Carrillo	Point Concepcion
Rancho Lompoc (Little Lake or Laguna)	Joaquín and José Carrillo	Lompoc, Vandenberg Air Force Base
Rancho La Mission Vieja de la Purísima	Juan (Jonathan) Temple	La Purisima Mission SHP
Rancho Jesús María	Lucas and Antonio Olivera	Vandenberg Air Force Base
Rancho Casmalia	Lucas and Antonio Olivera	Vandenberg Air Force Base, Casmalia
Rancho Guadalupe	Diego Olivera and Teodoro Arellanes	Guadalupe, Point Sal State Beach, Guadalupe-Nipomo Dunes Preserve [24]
Rancho Punta de la Laguna	Luis Arellanes and Emígdio Ortega	Between Guadalupe and Santa Maria
Rancho Todos Santos (All Holy) y San Antonio	W. E. P. Hartnell [25]	Vandenberg Air Force Base
Rancho Los Alamos (Poplar Trees)	Gaspar Oreña, Cesario E. A. and María Antonia de la Guerra de Lataillade	Los Alamos
Rancho Santa Rita	José Ramon Malo	East of Lompoc
Rancho Cañada de Salsipuedes	Pedro Cordero	Southeast of Lompoc
Rancho San Julián	De la Guerra family	Southeast of Lompoc
Rancho Las Cruces (Crossroads)	Miguel Cordero family	Las Cruces, Gaviota State Park
Rancho Santa Rosa	Francisco Cota	Buellton
Rancho Nojoqui	Raimundo Carrillo	Santa Ynez Valley
Rancho Lomas de la Purificación (Hills of Purification)	Augustín Janssens	San Lucas Ranch
Misión Santa Inés and Rancho	José María Covarrubias and José Joaquín Carrillo	Santa Ynez
Rancho Cañada de los Pinos (College Ranch)	Franciscans	Santa Ynez
Rancho San Carlos de Jonata	José María Covarrubias and José Joaquín Carrillo	Buellton, Solvang
Rancho Corral de Quati	Gaspar Oreña, Cesario E. A. and María Antonia de la Guerra de Lataillade	Foxen Canyon
Rancho La Zaca	Gaspar Oreña, Cesario E. A. and María Antonia de la Guerra de Lataillade	Zaca Canyon
Rancho La Laguna [26]	Octaviano Gutierrez	Foxen and Zaca canyons
Rancho Tinaquaic	Julián (William Benjamin) Foxen	Los Olivos, Foxen Canyon

NAME OF RANCHO	GRANTEE AND/OR 1850 OWNER	1850 AND/OR CURRENT SITES
Rancho Sisquoc	María Antonia Domínguez y Caballero	East of Sisquoc
Rancho Tepusquet	Tomás Olivera	East of Garey
Rancho del Suey	Ramón Carrillo	North of Garey, extending into San Luis Obispo County
Two Cuyama ranchos	María Antonia de la Guerra y Lataillade	North of Los Padres National Forest, extending into San Luis Obispo and Kern counties
Rancho Tequepis	Antonio María Villa	Lake Cachuma
Rancho San Marcos	Nicolas A. H. Den and Dr. Richard Somerset Den	North of Lake Cachuma
Rancho Los Prietos y Najalayegua	José Domínguez	Upper Santa Ynez River Valley
Island of Santa Cruz	Andrés Castilleros	Island of Santa Cruz
Island of Santa Rosa	Antonio and Carlos Carrillo	Island of Santa Rosa
Island of San Miguel	Samuel C. Bruce; George C. Nidever	Island of San Miguel

Like its neighbors to the south, Santa Barbara County's history and traditions were shaped by its cattle industry. Cattle would continue to support the area until the floods of 1861-62 and the drought of 1863-64. Santa Barbara *rancheros* sustained major losses from these two natural disasters and were even forced to sacrifice the native coast live oak trees to provide a few more days of feed for the starving, dying herds of cattle.

The subsequent division of the vast ranchos into small farms and the influx of settlers would create the water supply problem in the county that persists to this day. Amazingly enough, the square stone reservoir, built in 1806 about 500 feet from the church of the Santa Barbara Mission to collect water for the mission orchards and gardens, was used as part of the city water system until as late as 1966. The 1807 Old Mission Dam (located in the Santa Barbara Botanic Garden near the redwood grove) and the stone aqueduct that carried water from behind the dam to the reservoir at the mission were still used until the early part of the 20th century.

Santa Barbara would not begin its initial expansion until the late 1860s when it became a winter travel destination. Further growth was spurred by the arrival of the Southern Pacific Railroad in 1887, linking the area with Los Angeles. In 1901 the railroad began travel through the Santa Maria Valley en route to San Francisco.

Notes ⌐ SANTA BARBARA COUNTY

1

The Albinger Archaeological Museum was opened in 1980, following archaeological investigations in the 1970s that uncovered more than 30,000 artifacts. The area was originally part of the Mission Plaza Urban Redevelopment Project, but when the cultural remains were discovered, the property was withdrawn from the project.

2

The Emigdio Ortega Adobe would not be built until 1857, but should be viewed in connection with the 1850 sites. It appears much as it did when first built, including its original dirt floors. (Many 1850 adobes are restored with the wooden floors of a later era.) The Ortega Chili Co. would begin operations here in the 1890s.

3

The Olivas Adobe would become the home of Major Max Fleischmann of the Fleischmann Yeast and Margarine Company in 1927. The dining room reflects this era, but the rest of the home reflects the earlier Olivas era.

4

The first, painstaking drilling for oil would begin in the early 1860s in the Ojai/Santa Paula area. Oil exploration in the Ojai Valley was never very successful, however.

5

Gold would be discovered in this area east of present-day Santa Paula in 1872.

6

The otter was almost extinct in the Santa Barbara Channel in 1850 due to the excessive hunting for their valuable furs.

7

Interesting note: James Whistler was a member of a U.S. Coast Geodetic team that surveyed Anacapa Island in 1854. He was fired for painting in a few sea gulls lurking over the island's picturesque arch rock. He would later become famous for painting Whistler's Mother.

8

The Ronald Reagan Presidential Library is located in Simi Valley on a 100-acre, hilltop site with panoramic views in all directions.

9

M.A.R. Poli would become Ventura's first land developer in the early 1850s. He also was the town's first practicing physician.

10

Lake Piru would not be created until a dam was constructed in 1955.

11

The "Red Tile Tour" map may be obtained at the Santa Barbara County Courthouse. Even though the courthouse was not built until 1929, it is included as a historical resource because murals depict early Santa Barbara history, the courthouse tour provides early history background information, and the views from the clock tower provide a useful (and beautiful) orientation to the city.

12

See sidebar about Thomas Larkin on page 128.

13

See Wilson sidebar on page 85.

14

Doña Ramona's son from a previous marriage, Romualdo Pacheco, would serve as acting Governor in 1875 when Governor Booth was elected to the U.S. Senate, thus becoming the only Hispanic Governor of California to date.

15

Since 1990 the *Casa de la Guerre* has been undergoing restoration to return it to its pre-1858 status.

16

Of the 50 business licenses issued from August of 1850 through February of the following year, 32 were for the sale of liquor.

17

The Carpinteria Valley received its name from the soldiers of the 1769 Portola expedition. They were impressed with the Chumash Indian's skill at boat building. *La Carpinteria* means the carpenter's shop. A former tar pit is located within the borders of Carpinteria Beach State Park and seepage can still be seen in the bluff where these natives lived. The Chumash used the tar to seal their boats.

18

The Hope Ranch of today was named for its third owner, Thomas W Hope, an Irishman who fell in love with the area when passing through Santa Barbara by wagon train on his way to San Francisco. He worked in San Francisco until he had enough money to buy 2000 sheep, which he brought, along with his new wife, to Santa Barbara in 1849.

19

One of the Ortega adobes would be rebuilt and remodeled several times, and was owned by actor John Travolta for a time. *Rancho del Cielo,* the "Western White House" of former President Ronald Reagan, is located in a secluded part of the Santa Ynez Mountains above the former Ortega rancho.

20

See Temple sidebar on page 52.

21

The Spanish word for Agnes is Inés; the Americans anglicized the spelling of the Spanish pronunciation and named the town Santa Ynez.

22

Joseph Chapman was a pirate who had been captured by the Spanish in Monterey in 1818. His skills as a millwright and boat builder soon made him welcome in California.

23

See Forbes sidebar on page 139.

24

The Guadalupe-Nipomo Dunes would be the movie set for six films, including Cecil B. DeMille's version of the Ten Commandments.

25

See Hartnell sidebar on page 101.

26

Rancho La Laguna would be divided up into large home sites in the 20th century for the likes of wealthy individuals such as singer Michael Jackson.

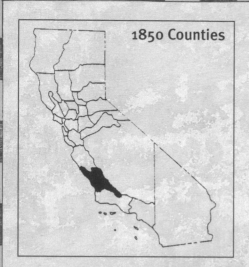

1850 Counties

∽ 1 8 5 0 ∾
⊱ SAN LUIS OBISPO ⊰
COUNTY

Monterey Co.

Kings Co.

• San Miguel

•San Simeon

• Paso Robles

•Cambria

•Atascadero

Kern Co.

•Cayucos

• Santa Margarita

•Morro Bay

Pacific Ocean

• San Luis Obispo

• Avila Beach

• Arroyo Grande

Nipomo•

Santa Barbara Co.

California
1850

Present-day boundary variations indicated by
— — — —

Settlements/cities of 1850 include: San Luis Obispo

SAN LUIS OBISPO COUNTY
1850

The 1850 boundary of San Luis Obispo County encroached ever so slightly into present-day Santa Barbara County on the south and present-day Monterey County on the north. In 1850 the county consisted of the small community of San Luis Obispo that had grown up around the former mission and 29 ranchos. Like its neighbor to the south, Santa Barbara County, its inaccessibility would delay its development for many years to come. Its mere 336 residents counted in the 1850 U.S. Census consisted of Californios and a few Americans and Europeans. The uncounted Native American inhabitants included members of the Chumash and Salinan tribes. Spanish still was the primary language spoken.

Morro Bay

The first known landing at Morro Bay by explorers from Europe was made by Pedro de Unamuno in 1587. Morro Rock (Crown-Shaped Hill) has served as an important mariner's navigational landmark in the bay for hundreds of years. Sometimes called the "Gibraltar of the Pacific," it is the last in the chain of nine volcanic plugs known as the "Nine Sisters" that start in the city of San Luis Obispo.[1]

Mission San Luis Obispo de Tolosa

Misíon San Luís Obispo de Tolosa, the fifth California mission, was founded in 1772 on a plain near San Luis Creek in the vicinity of present-day Nipomo and Dana streets. Flood, fire, and an earthquake required rebuilding it at its current site on Monterey Street. It was named for the French saint, Saint Louis (San Luis), the Bishop (Obispo) of Toulouse (Tolosa), France. John Wilson, James Scott, and James McKinley had purchased the mission and the one-acre ranch property for $510 in 1845. In 1850 Wilson was renting rooms in the mission to the county. The mission would become a parish church again later in the 1850s. It took on several different appearances over the years, but was fully restored to its early mission style in the 1930s. Today it is a working parish open to the public, set in the midst of the downtown business district.

Community of San Luis Obispo

San Luis Obispo had never achieved the status of a "pueblo," but it was made the county seat in 1850. The three mission rooms rented from Wilson by the county were used as offices, a courtroom, and a jail. The courtroom and offices would move to William Goodwin Dana's *Casa Grande*, built in 1851, but the jail facility remained in the mission until 1861.

Sites to Visit in San Luis Obispo County

Dana Adobe, 671 South Oak Glen Av., Nipomo 805.543.0638 or 805.929.2570

El Paso de Robles Area Pioneer Museum, 2010 Riverside Av., Paso Robles 805.239.4556

Mission San Luis Obispo de Tolosa, 782 Monterey St., San Luis Obispo 805.543.6850

Mission San Miguel Arcángel, 775 Mission St., San Miguel 805.467.3256

Murray Adobe, 747 Monterey St., San Luis Obispo

Rios-Caledonia Adobe, 700 Mission St., San Miguel 805.467.3357

San Luis Obispo County Historical Museum, 696 Monterey St., San Luis Obispo 805.543.0638

San Luis Obispo Chamber of Commerce, 1039 Chorro St., San Luis Obispo, CA 93401 805.781.2777 (Walking Tour Map)

Rancheros, especially those with ranchos in the isolated north coastal area, maintained homes in San Luis Obispo as headquarters for their necessary frequent business trips to town. Adobe and timber houses and some business buildings were built haphazardly around the immediate vicinity of the former mission, including two that may still be viewed today. A small portion of the large Murray Adobe built in 1850 lies adjacent to the mission. It belonged to Judge Walter Murray, an English jurist and journalist who came to California in 1846.[2]

The other remaining adobe downtown is one known today as the Butrón Adobe on Dana Street. A small portion of this adobe had been built in the 1840s.[3]

Numerous other structures once stood near the former mission, but have long

since disappeared. Among them were the Wilson's wooden two-story house on the corner of Monterey and Broad streets. The first frame building in San Luis Obispo, it was ready-cut and came from the East Coast around Cape Horn in 1850. The Garcia Adobe, which had been used as a mission outbuilding, was located at the corner of Osos and Higuera streets. A two-story adobe used as a Spanish restaurant and dance hall stood where Monterey and Chorro streets intersect today. A general store, Beebee & Pollard's, also was in operation.

One main road passed through the town from the southwest to the northeast, later becoming Monterey Street. William R. Hutton surveyed the town in August 1850, but the first map would not be produced until 1862.

San Luis Obispo County Ranchos

In 1850 San Luis Obispo County *rancheros* were just starting to occupy their ranchos in order to protect them from squatters, as well as to avoid the lawlessness which was becoming commonplace in town. However, previously relocated mission Indians and a few Mexican *vaqueros* were the only inhabitants of the remote northern coastal ranchos. Unsuccessful gold miners, some with families, were settled in the mountains east of the coastal ranchos. Details about some of the more interesting ranchos follow.

Between the Santa Maria and Nipomo valleys, *Don* Guillermo (William Goodwin) Dana and his family lived on *Rancho Nipomo*. Dana was the cousin of the author, Richard Henry Dana. William was known for his abilities in raising stock, farming, soap-making, furniture manufacture and trade, and also entertaining. His rancho was the center of trade for the region and the favorite stopover for those traveling between San Luis Obispo and Santa Barbara. His 1840, 13-room Dana Adobe remains standing in Nipomo today.[4]

Don Francisco Ziba Branch, a native of New York who came to California in 1831, owned *Rancho Santa Manuela* in the Arroyo Grande Valley. He was married to the daughter of his neighbor, Zefarino Carlón, having met the family when he was running a store and boardinghouse in Santa Barbara. Much of his property was an impenetrable swamp, but he built an adobe home for his family and raised livestock here.

Rancho Pismo had originally been granted to *Don* José Ortega, but in early 1850 Isaac J. Sparks acquired this rancho. Later in the year, Sparks gave half of it to John Price, an Englishman, instead of paying him wages in gold. Price would move horse and cattle herds onto the rancho and eventually build a home in which he and his wife, María Andrea Carlona, raised their 15 children.

One of the nine volcanic cones of the Nine Sisters chain was located on *Rancho Corral De Piedra*—the Islay Hill. *Don* José María Villavicencia owned this rancho that had previously been part of the grazing land used by the mission. Two adobes stood on this rancho, one of which sits vacant today awaiting restoration.[5]

Rancho San Miguelito was owned by *Don* Miguel Ávila. He was married to Pío Pico's[6] niece, María Inocenta. They lived with their children in the 1841 adobe Ávila built. He raised cattle, horses, and sheep, and grew corn, wheat, and vegetables. It is believed that he was operating a dairy as early as 1842.

A natural landing on the coastal bluffs of Ávila's property bordering the San Luis Obispo Bay served as a port for shipping and receiving supplies for the *rancheros* of the area. Cave Landing, a popular beach and hiking area on the bay today, functions as a natural pier that was used as early as mission times for shipping hides, tallow, and grain. In 1850 a number of former *asistencia* mission outbuildings were being used for private purposes in the area.

The large *Rancho Cañada de los Osos y Pecho y Islay* lay along the coastline and spread inland towards San Luis Obispo. John Wilson owned this rancho that contained *La Canada de Los Osos* (Valley of the Bears.)[7] Wilson built a large adobe ranch house in this valley, a portion of which remains in use as a barn on a private ranch today.

Wilson had purchased the tiny, 117-acre *Rancho Huerta de Romualdo* from a Chumash Indian named Romualdo[8] in 1846 to provide access between his *Chorro* and *Los Osos* ranchos. Another of the nine volcanic cones—Cerro Romualdo—lies on this former rancho.

Doña Concepción Boronda owned *Rancho Potrero*. A portion of the still standing La Loma Adobe may have been built prior to 1850. The adobe served as a respite to many dignitaries traveling through the county.[9]

Don Vicente Canet owned *Rancho San Bernardo*. The 1830 Canet Adobe was one of the largest in the county. About one-third of this adobe with wings added on in later years is now covered by clapboard to protect it and lies on private property alongside Highway 1.

Don Rafael Villavicencio owned *Rancho San Gerónimo*. He built several adobe structures, a gristmill, and looms on which the wives of his *vaqueros* wove blankets. The lands of this former rancho remain undeveloped, north of Cayucos and east of present-day Harmony.

Rancho Santa Rosa, one of the three ranchos that were formerly part of the coastal grazing lands of the Mission San Miguel Arcángel, was owned by *Don* Julian

William Goodwin Dana (1797-1858)

- Former Boston sea captain who traded with China, the Sandwich (Hawaiian) Islands, and Alta California

- Prominent businessman and public official in Santa Barbara before moving to San Luis Obispo

- Married María Josefa Carrillo of Santa Barbara, daughter of *Don* Carlos

- Fathered 21 children, leaving numerous descendants in the Santa Maria and San Luis Obispo areas

- Famous for taking in travelers who enjoyed the rancho so much, they never left

- Headed the San Luis Obispo vigilantes and was the first treasurer of San Luis Obispo County

John Wilson (18??-1860)

- Scotsman made famous by Dana's *Two Years Before the Mast*—he was the captain who saved *The Pilgrim* at San Diego in 1835

- Married widow, Ramona Carrillo Pacheco

- Stepfather to Romualdo Pacheco, Jr., 12th Governor of California and the only Hispanic Governor to date. (Pacheco advanced from lieutenant governor upon the election of Governor Newton Booth to the U.S. Senate.)

- Owned four land grants, including the largest in San Luis Obispo

- Wealthiest man in San Luis Obispo at one time (gauged by amount of taxes paid)

Estrada. Thousands of head of cattle grazed on this rancho of diverse terrain—cliffs and rocky coastal shorelines;[10] fertile, wooded valleys traversed by streams and creeks; marshland, and chaparral-covered dry hillsides.

Estrada's family had permanently moved to the rancho from San Luis Obispo in 1849. They had a large Native American workforce that lived on a neighboring *rancheria*. The natives maintained the garden, orchard, vineyard, and fields and performed domestic household tasks for the Estradas. The Estradas frequently entertained visitors and held fiestas with the usual bull and bear fights, dancing, and eating.

Today Highway 1 runs almost directly over the site of the Estrada adobe. Cattle still graze near the little town of Harmony, which stands on the southernmost portion of this former rancho. Copper, quicksilver, and lumber would draw settlers to this area in the 1860s and 70s.

Rancho San Simeon, also part of the former Mission San Miguel Arcángel grazing lands, was owned by Thomas A. Park, a sea captain, but neither he nor the original grantee, *Don* José Ramon Estrada, ever occupied it.[11] Even as early as the mission period, the sandy beaches of the San Simeon Bay had been used by the hide and tallow traders. John Wilson developed a landing here during that time. Regular and frequent runs to San Simeon Bay were established in 1850 following development of an ox cart road between the Bay, San Luis Obispo, and the neighboring ranchos.

Mission San Miguel is the only mission that has not undergone extensive renovations and restorations.

The 1846 Rios-Caledonia Adobe in San Miguel is a restored house museum.

Don Joaquín Estrada owned *Rancho Santa Margarita*. He lived on the rancho and raised cattle and horses. The former *Asistencia de Santa Margarita*, which had been an outpost of the Mission San Luis Obispo to serve the natives who lived north of the mission across Cuesta Pass, lay in ruins on the property in 1850. Today the ruins of the chapel and storehouse are covered by a barn, which stands on the private Santa Margarita Ranch.

Just ten miles south of the northern county line, *Misión San Miguel Arcángel* was located on the former mission rancho. Established in 1797, the mission was abandoned and plundered following secularization. It had been sold to William Reed,[12] Petronillo Rios, and Miguel Garcia in 1846. It would be returned to the church in 1859 and repaired in 1878 by secular clergy. It is the only California mission that has not undergone extensive renovations and restorations. Most of the mission, including the colorful interior murals, is original. Today the mission serves as a parish church.

Don Petronilo Rios lived in the 1846, two-story Rios-Caledonia Adobe that today is a restored house museum. It served as a home for his family and the headquarters for his sheep and cattle operations.

During the 1850s, San Luis Obispo County would produce much of the meat consumed by the miners in the Gold Country. The county's geographic isolation made getting that meat to market very difficult, however, and this same isolation continued to hinder the area's economy throughout the second half of the 19th century. The Southern Pacific Railroad finally arrived in 1894.

The majority of San Luis Obispo County's ranchos would suffer the same fate as their neighbors to the south following the severe drought of the mid-1860s that decimated the cattle population. Subsequently the large ranchos were subdivided and sold in smaller parcels to new settlers for agricultural uses.

SAN LUIS OBISPO COUNTY RANCHOS

NAME OF RANCHO	GRANTEE AND/OR 1850 OWNER	1850 AND/OR CURRENT SITES
Rancho Bolsa del Chamisal	Francisco Quijada	Oceano
Rancho Nipomo (Foot of the Hills)	Guillermo (William Goodwin) Dana	Nipomo
Rancho Huasna	Isaac J. Sparks	Arroyo Grande
Rancho Arroyo Grande (Wide Gulch)	Zefarino Carlón	Lopez Lake since 1969
Rancho Santa Manuela	Francisco Ziba Branch	Arroyo Grande Valley
Rancho Pismo (Tar)	Isaac J. Sparks, John Price	Pismo Beach, Grover Beach
Rancho Corral De Piedra (Stones)	José María Villavicencia	San Luis Obispo
Rancho San Miguelito	Miguel Ávila	Avila Beach
Rancho Cañada de los Osos (Valley of the Bears) y Pecho y Islay	John Wilson	Montaña de Oro State Park, Baywood Park, Los Osos
Rancho La Laguna (The Lake)	Miguel Ávila	Southwest of San Luis Obispo
Ranchito de Santa Fe	Victor Linares	Southwest of San Luis Obispo
Rancho Huerta (Orchard) de Romualdo	John Wilson	Northwest of San Luis Obispo
Rancho Potrero (Pasture) de San Luis Obispo	Concepción Boronda	Private ranchland
Rancho El Chorro (Stream)	James Scott and John Wilson	Private ranchland
Rancho San Luisito	José Guadalupe Cantua	Private ranchland, Cuesta College
Rancho San Bernardo	Vicente Canet	East of Morro Bay
Rancho Moro y Cayucos (Kayak or Canoe)	Martin Olivera and Vicente Feliz	Cayucos, Atascadero State Beach
Rancho San Gerónimo	Rafael Villavicencio	East of Harmony
Rancho Santa Rosa	Julian Estrada	Cambria, Harmony
Rancho San Simeon	Thomas A. Park	San Simeon, Hearst Memorial State Beach, Hearst Castle
Rancho Piedra Blanca (White Stone) [13]	José de Jesús Pico	Northern coastline
Rancho Santa Margarita	Joaquín Estrada	Santa Margarita
Rancho Atascadero (Muddy or Marshy Place)	Trifon García	Atascadero
Rancho Ascunción	Pedro Estrada	Atascadero
Rancho Huerohuero (Babbling Spring)	Mariano Bonilla	Creston
Rancho Santa Ysabel	Francisco Arce	East of Paso Robles
Rancho El Paso de Robles (White Oaks)	Pedro Narváez	Templeton, Paso Robles
Mission San Miguel Rancho	William Reed, Petronillo Rios, and Miguel Garcia	San Miguel
Rancho Cholame	Mauricio Gonzáles	Cholame, southern Monterey Co.

Notes ⟿ SAN LUIS OBISPO COUNTY

1

The other volcanic peaks are Black Hill, Cabrillo Peak, Hollister Peak, Cerro Romualdo, Chumash Peak, Bishop's Peak, San Luis Mountain, and Islay Hill. The dramatic shape of Morro Rock today is a result of the quarrying that was done in the 1930s when jetties and breakwaters were constructed. The rock is now a protected home for the Peregrine Falcon.

2

Walter Murray would co-found San Luis Obispo's first permanent newspaper, *The San Luis Obispo Tribune*, in 1869, and publish it from his home.

3

The Butrón Adobe is one of three local adobes that the volunteer community organization called the Friends of Las Casas de Adobe, in partnership with the City of San Luis Obispo, plan to preserve and rehabilitate.

4

The Dana Adobe Nipomo Amigos, a recently formed community organization, is working to restore the Dana Adobe and have it designated a State Historic Landmark. It may be toured by appointment.

5

The Rodriguez Adobe is one of the three local adobes of interest to the Friends of Las Casas de Adobe. It is slated to be developed as a city park and is the first priority at this time.

6

See Pico's sidebar on page 59.

7

Gaspar de Portola's 1769 expedition had named this valley because of the number of grizzly bears sighted. The grizzly population had been decimated in 1772, however, by another Spanish expedition that had come in search of meat to supply the starving missions to the north.

8

Romualdo was the only Native American to receive a land grant in San Luis Obispo County.

9

Today La Loma Adobe stands in very fragile condition and is one of the three adobes owned by the City of San Luis Obispo that local volunteers plan to rehabilitate.

10

Dried hides were dropped from the cliffs of *Rancho Santa Rosa* to the sandy beach 75 to 100 feet below and then loaded on waiting ships for transport to the East Coast.

11

Senator George Hearst would buy the *San Simeon* and *Piedra Blanca* ranchos in 1865. Hearst constructed the pier at San Simeon Point that same year. His son, the newspaper publisher William Randolph Hearst, would not begin building the Hearst Castle atop the 1600-foot mountain overlooking the Pacific Ocean until 1919.

12

The entire William Reed family was tragically murdered by gold prospectors returning from the Gold Country in 1849.

13

Several guano-covered rocks mark Piedras Blancas Point. The white rocks occupied by countless sea birds were so named by the explorer Juan Cabrillo in 1542. The rocks could be seen for many miles at sea and easily spotted from the high ridge of the coastal range.

Morro Rock has served as an important mariner's navigational landmark in Morro Bay for hundreds of years.

1850 Counties

·1850·
·MONTEREY·
COUNTY

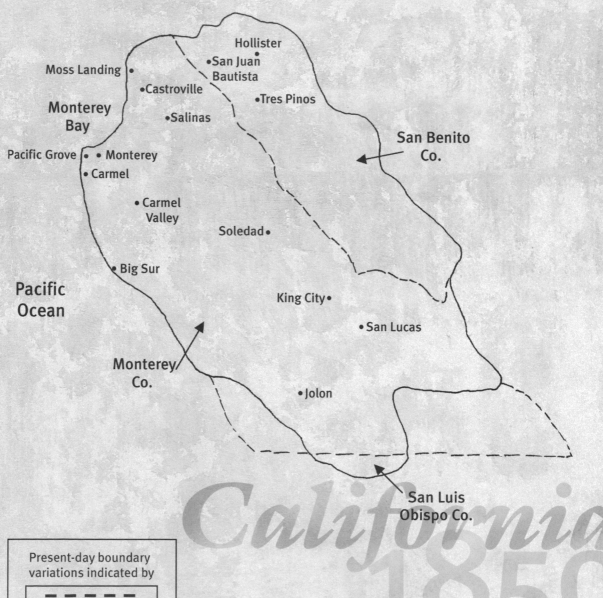

Hollister

San Juan
Bautista

Moss Landing

• Castroville

•Tres Pinos

Monterey
Bay

• Salinas

San Benito
Co.

Pacific Grove • • Monterey

• Carmel

• Carmel
Valley

Soledad •

Pacific
Ocean

• Big Sur

King City •

• San Lucas

Monterey
Co.

• Jolon

San Luis
Obispo Co.

California
1850

Present-day boundary
variations indicated by

- - - - - -

Settlements/cities of 1850 include: Monterey, San Juan Bautista

MONTEREY COUNTY
1850

The geographical area of 1850-Monterey County included most of present-day San Benito County and a sliver of present-day San Luis Obispo County. Between 1850 and 1873, the county's boundaries would change three times—two times gaining land from San Luis Obispo County and finally losing the area within San Benito County. Its 1,872 residents counted in the 1850 U.S. Census included Californios, Americans, and Europeans. The uncounted Native American inhabitants included members of the Salinan, Esselen, and Ohlone tribes. Spanish was still the area's common language.

AREA WITHIN PRESENT-DAY MONTEREY COUNTY

In 1850 the area within present-day Monterey County consisted of the city of Monterey, three other former mission communities, numerous ranchos, and several "county tracts." With a few brief interruptions, Monterey had served as the capital of Alta California for 75 years.

Monterey Bay

Point Piños had been sighted as early as 1542; Sebastián Vizcaíno was the first European to actually land at Monterey Bay and take possession of it for Spain in 1602. Monterey Bay's first pier, which connected to the Custom House, was built of stone by Thomas O. Larkin[1] in 1846. The Maritime Museum of Monterey provides a complete history of the seafaring heritage of the second largest bay in California.

City of Monterey

Monterey was founded in 1770 by Father Junipero Serra and Gaspar de Portolá with the establishment of the *Misíon San Carlos* and the *Royale Presidio de San Carlos de Monterey*. Spain established a formal pueblo government in 1791. When Richard Henry Dana visited Monterey in 1825, he described it as being "decidedly the pleasantest and most civilized-looking place in California."

The City of Monterey was incorporated by an act of the State Legislature on March 30, 1850.[2] It would serve as the county seat until 1872, when this honor was transferred to Salinas.

Previously, Monterey had been the cultural, religious, military, and social center of California, but in 1850 Monterey was still adjusting to its lessened stature. Since the discovery of gold in 1848 and the removal of the state capital to San Jose in

Sites to Visit in Monterey County

Boronda Adobe Casa, Boronda History Center, 333 Boronda Rd. at Calle del Adobe, Salinas 831.757.8085

Colton Hall Museum, civic center on Pacific St., Monterey 831.646.5640

Maritime Museum of Monterey, Stanton Center, 5 Custom House Plaza, Monterey   831.373.2469

Mission San Antonio de Padua, Mission Rd. off Jolon Rd., Jolon 831. 385.4478

Mission San Carlos Borromeo de Carmel, 3080 Rio Rd., Carmel 831.624.3600

Mission Nuestra Senora de la Soledad, 36641 Fort Romie Rd., Soledad   831.678.2586

Monterey State Historic Park: Stanton Center (see below); Pacific House (when it reopens in 2000), 20 Custom House Plaza; and Cooper-Molera Adobe, 525 Polk St., Monterey   831.649.7118

Presidio of Monterey Historic Park and Museum (when it reopens in late 2000), Pacific and Artillery streets, Monterey

Richardson Adobe (CLOSED), US 101 junction with Arroyo Seco Rd., Soledad

San Carlos Cathedral, 550 Church St., Monterey   831.373.2628

Stanton Center, 5 Custom House Plaza, Monterey   831.373.2469

Monterey Peninsula Visitors and Convention Bureau ("Monterey Path of History" map), 380 Alvarado St., Monterey, CA 93940 831.649.1770

1849, Monterey had been reduced to a non-productive adobe pueblo of mostly women, children, and men who stayed behind because they physically were unable to venture to the gold fields. The political prestige was gone, the economy had slowed, and only a few military officers remained to maintain the peace and security of the community.

The original presidio grounds consisted of a square of adobe buildings located in the vicinity of what is now downtown Monterey. The first mission building was built on the site where the restored 1794 San Carlos Cathedral now stands.[3] However, the proximity of the sometimes abusive soldiers and the lack of fertile land for growing crops led to the relocation of the mission in 1771, five miles away in Carmel. The original church then became the Royal Presidio Chapel where the king's representative worshipped, and after secularization, it served as the parish church of the mission in Carmel. The San Carlos Cathedral is the only surviving building of the original presidio complex, and is the oldest building on the Monterey Peninsula.

There were four cemeteries located near the Presidio. Two of these cemeteries are maintained today on the peninsula formed by the horseshoe-shaped El Estero (Salt Marsh)—a lake, which, in 1850, was an estuary that emptied into Monterey Bay.

What remained of the Presidio of Monterey in 1850 stood on Fort Hill—the present-day Presidio Hill at the southern end of Monterey Bay. The garrison had been moved to a newly constructed Mexican government building—*El Cuartel* (Barracks)—in 1840. After the American occupation in 1846, a blockhouse, called Fort Mervine, was built on the site of the original fort by Lieutenants Edward O. C. Ord and William Tecumseh Sherman. In subsequent years, the fort took on various other names, was abandoned during the Gold Rush, was only briefly occupied during the Civil War, and was abandoned again in 1866. Today, the Presidio of Monterey Historic Park contains several monuments to the area's early history.

The pine-covered hills of the city lands of Monterey were dotted haphazardly by several hundred white-washed adobe structures with tiled roofs. Many historic build-

The restored 1794 San Carlos Cathedral, which was the chapel of the original Mission San Carlos before the mission was relocated to Carmel.

The 1841 Custom House presided over Mexico's only port of entry on the Alta California coast during most of the Mexican era.

The 1847 Pacific House was a public tavern in 1850.

Edward O.C. (Otho Cresap) Ord (1818-1883)

- Arrived in Monterey in 1847 as a first lieutenant in the Mexican-American War
- Returned east in 1850 after surveying the pueblo in Los Angeles
- Returned to Monterey later in 1850 as a commander
- Distinguished Civil War general
- Commander of Dept. of the Pacific from 1868 to 1871
- Fort Ord was named for him in 1940

ings remain today that may be toured or viewed from the exterior within the Monterey State Historic Park and the rest of "Old Monterey." [4]

In 1841 the two-story stone and adobe Custom House[5] was built to replace the original deteriorated 1827 structure. The Custom House presided over Mexico's only port of entry on the Alta California coast during most of the Mexican era. Custom duties were paid here and goods from the U.S., England, and South America were traded for cowhides, tallow, and other locally produced items. However, in 1850 the Office of Customs was moved to San Francisco, and the Monterey office became unnecessary, eventually closing and becoming a residence. In 1850 the Custom House adjoined the pier built by Larkin, allowing ships to moor

The 1845 Casa Del Oro (House of Gold), where the first mercantile store in Monterey, the Boston Store, was operated.

alongside the building to make loading and unloading easier. The open space between the wharf and the Custom House was known as *Plaza del Muelle* (Pier or Wharf).[6]

Pacific House, a large two-story adobe located on the Custom House Plaza, was constructed by David Wight for Larkin in 1847. Originally it was used by the U.S. Quartermaster for offices, storing military supplies, and stabling army horses. By 1850 it had become a public tavern. It had a large horse corral that was used for Sunday afternoon bull and bear fights.

The 1847 First Brick House was the first structure built in California by the kiln-fired brick construction method.

Larkin built the *Casa Del Oro* (House of Gold) in 1845 for business purposes. He then sold it to José Abrego. Sometime between 1849 and 1850, Abrego leased it to Joseph Boston and Company to operate the first mercantile store in Monterey. Boston offered items ranging from kitchenware and food items to grinding stones. (David Jacks, who became a real estate tycoon in Monterey County, was a clerk here in 1850.) In later years, miners

The 1847 Old Whaling Station Adobe was serving as a rooming house in 1850.

would bring their gold dust to the store for safekeeping, thus its name. Today the Boston Store is operated by a historical organization.

The First Brick House was built as a modest home in 1847 by Gallant Duncan Dickenson. (He and his family were original members of the Donner party, but parted company before the tragic trek across the Sierras.) This home was the first structure built in California by the kiln-fired brick construction method. Dickenson had finished the portion of the building remaining today before leaving with his family for the gold fields in 1849. The Breens, another Donner party family, would buy the house in 1851.

The Old Whaling Station Adobe was built in 1847 by David Wight as a replica of his family's ancestral cottage in Scotland. He succumbed to gold fever and sold his home in 1849 to Alberto Trescony, who converted the home into a rooming house. In 1855 Trescony would lease the building to the Old Monterey Whaling Company, which used it as a headquarters and employee residence, thus its name. Today this structure is an official part of the State Historic Park, but it is leased to a non-profit organization for its headquarters and may only be viewed from the exterior.

The 1849 F. Doud House is an example of a local wooden house of the early American period in Monterey. Used as a headquarters by a local foundation today, it is not open to the public.

California's first theater was established in Jack Swan's 1846 saloon and boarding house for sailors. It was first used for amateur dramatics by four soldiers and a local group in 1847. In 1848 Stevenson's Regiment of New York Volunteers began performing live theater here as a moneymaking venture. Swan built a stage with benches and used whale-oil lamps and candles for footlights. The troupe had disbanded in 1849, however, to join the Gold Rush. Today "The Troupers of the Gold Coast" perform melodramas reminiscent of the days of '49 in The First Theatre.

The *Casa Soberanes* was built in 1842 by José Rafael Papías Estrada. His heirs lived here in 1850. This restored adobe is often called "the House with the Blue

Gate," because of its entrance gate.[7]

The two-story Merritt House Adobe was built in the 1830s; *Don* Juan Tierney owned it in 1850. The influential Merritt[8] family took ownership of the house in 1852. Today the house is significantly remodeled and is part of a hotel complex.

The Troupers of the Gold Coast still perform melodramas reminiscent of the days of 1849 in The First Theatre, which was built as a saloon and boarding house for sailors in 1846.

The 1842 Casa Soberanes Adobe is often called "the House with the Blue Gate." The Estrada family lived here in 1850.

Larkin began construction of the *Casa Serrano* in 1845. Later Florencio Serrano purchased and completed the house for his large family. Serrano succeeded Walter Colton as *alcalde* of Monterey. He also established a private school within his home and taught Spanish, even after losing his eyesight in later years. Today paintings and antique furniture may be viewed within this structure during specified times.

Doña Feliciana Lara owned the Lara-Soto Adobe built by Jésus Soto in the 1830s. *Doña* Feliciana was one of the few women to be granted a town lot. Many people, including John Steinbeck, would own this home through the years and today the greatly remodeled building houses a facility of the Monterey Institute of International Studies.

The adobe *Casa Alvarado*, now private property, was the residence of the first Monterey-born Governor of California under Mexican rule, *Don* Juan Bautista Alvarado. He lived here while he held office from 1836 to 1842. It was one of several homes he would occupy in the state. Manuel Dutra purchased the adobe in 1842 and it remained in his family until 1946.

Colton Hall was erected by Reverend Walter Colton in 1847-49 after he was appointed *alcalde* of Monterey by Commodore Robert Stockton. It was on the second floor of this town hall that the 48 delegates met in the fall of 1849 to draft the Constitution under which California was admitted to the Union. It also was here where one of the first public schools in California and the first in Monterey conducted classes on the first floor in 1849. Reverend Samuel Hopkins Willey, a pastor and educator from New England, was living and teaching in Colton Hall, until May of 1850 when he moved to San Francisco. (He also had served as chaplain to the Constitutional Convention.) While Monterey was the county seat, Colton Hall was the county courthouse, and a jail would be added on in 1854.

The State Constitution was drafted in Colton Hall in 1849 and the first Monterey County courthouse was housed here.

Don Joaquín Gutiérrez built the *Casa Gutiérrez* in 1846. It is one of the few remaining Monterey adobes built in the simpler Mexican style. The home originally had a wing to house his 15 children, but that portion has been torn down. (The adobe is currently vacant.)

One of the first houses built by Larkin in 1834 was the two-story adobe *La Casa de Los Cuatro Vientos* (House of Four Winds). Used as a residence and store, it would later become California's first Hall of Records. Jacob P. Leese[9] purchased this property sometime during 1850. The first weather vane in Monterey was installed on this house in the mid-1800s, thus the building's name. Today it serves as a meeting place for various organizations.

The 1834-37 Larkin House was the first two-story adobe built in California and the forerunner of the classic Monterey-style adobe that soon appeared all over California.

The two-story adobe Larkin House—the first two-story adobe built in California—was erected by Larkin in 1834-37. Its New England style of architecture with a wood-shingled hip roof, inside fireplaces, glass windows, and planked floors was a radical departure from the California Spanish-style homes and was the forerunner of the classic Monterey-style adobe—Monterey Colonial—that began appearing all over California.[10]

Larkin's home became the American Consulate and the center of social life in the capital after he was appointed U.S. Consul to Mexican California in 1844. Larkin had a beautiful garden—one of the few at the time. In January 1850, Larkin traded his house and some other Monterey properties for some of Jacob Leese's properties in San Francisco and moved his family there. Many original items from the Larkin family are among the furnishings and artifacts in this restored home that today is more a reflection of a granddaughter who owned the home in later years.

Don José Amesti built the *Casa Amesti* Adobe in 1834. Originally a single-story, two-room adobe, he would add to the building and construct a second story in 1853.

Reverend Walter Colton (1797-1851)

- Yale-educated, Congregationalist minister from Vermont

- Arrived in California in 1846 as a chaplain on the USS Congress

- Appointed as the first American *alcalde* of Monterey in 1846

- Impaneled the first jury in California

- With Robert Semple, in 1846 founded and edited *The Californian*, the first newspaper published in California (in English and Spanish). Publication moved to San Francisco in May 1847.

- Moved to Philadelphia; published his journal, *Three Years in California*, in 1850

- Died of tuberculosis

Amesti was a Spanish Basque married to Prudenciana Vallejo, a sister of *Don* Mariano Guadalupe Vallejo.[11] This restored house operates as a private men's club today.

The Gabriel de la Torre Adobe was built in 1836 for Gabriel de la Torre, a government official of both the Mexican and American periods. Today it is a private office building.

The Fremont Adobe is misnamed. One of the original adobes, it was long thought that John C. Frémont[12] had his headquarters here, but his memoirs have disputed that. Ownership of the adobe has been traced through several Monterey families. This adobe is a private law office today.

The original first floor portion of the Cooper-Molera Adobe was built in 1827.

The original portion of the Cooper-Molera Adobe was built in 1827 by *Don* Juan Bautista Rogerio (Captain John Rogers) Cooper as a gift for his bride. Over the years, he added a second floor and the many other structures that make up the three-acre complex today.[13]

The Robert Louis Stevenson House began as a two-story stone, wood, and adobe home built by *Don* José Rafael Gonzalez in 1841. He would sell it in 1856 and it had several new owners and uses in subsequent years. It acquired its fame and current name as a result of the famous Scottish writer's three-month stay here in 1879, when it was known as the "French Hotel." (Stevenson was only an infant in 1850.)

The Washington Hotel stood at the corner of present-day Pearl and Washington streets, but no longer exists. It had been converted from the 1832 home of the Eugenio Montenegro family to a hotel in the 1840s. It served as the headquarters for the delegates of the State Constitutional Convention in 1849.

The *Casa Abrego* Adobe was built of adobe bricks and wood by *Don* José Abrego in 1834. Abrego owned one of the three pianos brought from Baltimore in the first such shipment in California history. Today the adobe is a private women's club. Another private club is housed in the Francisco Pacheco House. This two-story adobe built by *Don* Francisco Pérez Pacheco[14] in 1840, once was used as a hospital.

Two adobe homes remain today on a hill southeast of downtown. A significantly remodeled version of one stands today as an art museum open to the public. La Mirada Adobe began as a four-room house in the early 1800s. General José Castro owned the adobe in 1850. Although he had returned to Mexico after the American occupation, his wife and daughter remained here. The adobe went through many owners and today bears no resemblance to its humble beginnings.

The *Casa Bonifacio* once stood on Alvarado Street at Bonifacio Place, but has been moved to Mesa Road. *Señorita* María Ygnacia Bonifacio lived here.[15] This is a private residence today.

The first post office west of the Rocky Mountains had been opened in Monterey in 1849[16] in *El Cuartel*. Captain William G. Marcy, a captain in Stevenson's Regiment of New York Volunteers, became the first postmaster in California. He would also serve as the secretary for the State Constitutional Convention.

John Rogers Cooper
(1792-1872)

- Native of the British Isles; grew up in Massachusetts
- Half-brother of Thomas O. Larkin
- Arrived in California in 1823 from New England as captain of a trading schooner
- Childhood injury left him with a withered left arm, earning him the name *Juan el Manco* (The Maimed)
- Married Encarnacion Vallejo, sister of General Mariano Vallejo
- Owned numerous businesses, including a mercantile store, hide and tallow trade operation, sawmill, grist mill, and small sailing fleet
- Owned three ranchos in Monterey County and other property in the Sacramento Valley and in Sonoma and Marin counties
- Moved to San Francisco in 1864, where he later died

California's first library also was opened in 1849 in *El Cuartel*. Reverend Willey, the New England pastor and educator teaching at Colton Hall, arranged for a collection of 900 books to be shipped around Cape Horn.

Another hotel, the St. Charles, had suddenly appeared when the State Constitutional Convention was in session, as well as several fully stocked saloons. The only restaurant in town was *La Fonda de la Union* (Union Inn). Several parlors where men could find casual female companionship stood on Alvarado Street.

Many other pre-1850 adobes, mostly private residences, are scattered throughout Monterey. Monterey heads the list of California cities that have vigorously preserved the tangible evidence of their past. The Monterey History and Art Association has marked nearly all of the city's historic buildings. Monterey and the Monterey Peninsula as a whole have been called the "Cradle of History" because of all of the "firsts" that occurred here and because of the many state historical landmarks.

Monterey County Ranchos

A rash of land grants, 28 in all,[17] had been bestowed on friends, family, and deserving supporters of the government by Governor Juan Bautista Alvarado between 1836 and 1842. For the most part, few families were living on their ranchos; they lived in Monterey instead. The ranchos were used primarily for grazing purposes and if there were any adobe structures, they were for the *vaqueros*, except during the annual rodeo times. Details about some of the more interesting ranchos follow.

Misión San Antonio de Padua—the third California mission—stood within *Rancho Milpitas*. The original church was built in 1771, but the church standing today was the third one that was completed in 1813 on a slightly different location closer to the San Antonio and San Miguel rivers. Dams, aqueducts, and reservoirs provided water for irrigation and for powering a gristmill. The mission had no resident priest in 1850, but would not fall into complete ruin until the 1880s. No one ever bid on Mission San Antonio when Governor Pío Pico declared all mission buildings in California for sale in 1845. The mission was returned to the church in 1863 by the U.S. government. The church was restored several different times, the final time in the 1950s, and today serves as an active Catholic parish open to the public, as well as a private retreat facility.

Ygnacio Pastor, a Native American from the mission, had been granted *Rancho Milpitas* in 1838. Juan M. Luco, a Chilean, was a claimant of a portion of the rancho. An adobe "inn" was built in the area by Antonio Ramirez in 1850 that later was enlarged and came to be known as the Dutton Hotel. An important stage stop at one time, today it is part of Fort Hunter Liggett.[18]

Don Mauricio Gonzáles lived with his family in an adobe of two apartments on *Rancho San Miguelito*, which was owned by his father, *Don* José Rafael Gonzáles of Monterey. Employing American Indians, the family raised sheep and cattle and manufactured scarves and shoes that they exported to Monterey.

Don Juan Bautista Rogerio (Captain John Rogers) Cooper owned *Rancho El Sur* and employed a Kentuckian, Francis Job Dye, to raise mules and cattle on the property. Cooper lived in Monterey and it is believed that the "pioneer cabin" still standing at Andrew Molera[19] State Park was not built until 1861.[20]

David Jacks (1823-1909)

- 1841 Scottish immigrant to New York
- Arrived in San Francisco in 1849 as customs inspector
- Moved to Monterey on New Year's Day 1850
- Worked and lived in The Boston Store until 1851, when he began his land acquisition through what some would term illegitimate means and for which he has been much maligned
- Acquired some of his 60,000 acres of property by lending money on the security of land and foreclosing
- Partner and treasurer of the Monterey and Salinas Valley Railroad—a narrow-gauge railway created to undercut the high shipping charges of Southern Pacific
- First to commercially market Monterey Jacks cheese in 1882, later shortened to Monterey Jack
- Benevolent contributor, benefactor, and Sunday school teacher—for 50 years
- Married to Maria Cristina Soledad Romie, daughter of German immigrants of Santa Barbara, and fathered seven children
- Having no grandchildren, much of his estate was dispersed to California colleges and universities and the City of Monterey upon the death of the last daughter in 1962

MONTEREY COUNTY RANCHOS

NAME OF RANCHO	GRANTEE AND/OR 1850 OWNER	1850 AND/OR CURRENT SITES
Rancho Pleyto (Lawsuit)	Mariano de Jesús Soberánes	Lake San Antonio since 1965
Rancho Los Ojitos (Little Springs)	Mariano de Jesús Soberánes	Fort Hunter Liggett
Rancho Milpitas (Several Little Gardens)	Ygnacio Pastor and Juan M. Luco	Jolon, Fort Hunter Liggett
Rancho San Miguelito (Little St. Michael)	José Rafael Gonzáles	Between Fort Hunter Liggett and Los Padres National Forest
Rancho El Piojo (The Louse)	José Joaquín Soto	Between Fort Hunter Liggett and Los Padres National Forest
Rancho El Sur (The South)	Juan Bautista Rogerio (John Rogers) Cooper	Big Sur, Andrew Molera State Park
Rancho San José y Sur Chiquito (St. Joseph and Little South)	José Castro	Point Lobos State Reserve[21], Carmel Highlands, Garrapata State Park,
Rancho Cañada de la Segunda (Second Canyon)	Lázaro Soto	Carmel, Carmel Valley, Fort Hunter Liggett
Rancho El Pescadero (Fishing Place)	Juan (John F.) Romie; Jacob P. Leese	Carmel, Pebble Beach
Rancho Punta de Pinos (Point of Pines)	José Abrego	Pacific Grove, Asilomar
Rancho Aguajito (Little Water Hole)	Gregorio Tapia	Adjacent to Monterey on east
Rancho Noche Buena (Christmas Eve)	Juan Antonio Muñoz	Monterey, Seaside, Sand City, Del Rey Oaks, Fort Ord
Rancho Saucito (Little Willow)	Graciano Manjares	Monterey Airport
Rancho Laguna Seca (Dry Lake)	Catalina Manzaneli de Munrás	Laguna Seca Recreation Area
Rancho El Potrero de San Carlos (Pasture of St. Charles)	Fructuoso del Real	Carmel Valley
Rancho San Francisquito (Little St. Francis)	Heirs of William R. Garner	Carmel Valley
Rancho Los Tularcitos (Little Tules)	Josefa Antónia Gómez de Wolter	Carmel Valley
Rancho Los Laureles (The Laurels)	José Manuel Boronda and Vicente Blas Martinez	Carmel Valley
Rancho Los Laurelitos	Thomas O. Larkin; Jacob P. Leese	Carmel Valley
Rancho Corral de Tierra (Earth Corral)	Daughter of Francisco Figueroa Guadalupe	Northeast of Carmel Valley
Rancho El Toro (The Bull)	Charles Luis Wolter	Southwest of Salinas
Rancho El Chamisal (Chamise Brush)	Felipe Vásquez	Southwest of Salinas
Rancho Nacional	Vicente Cantúa	Salinas
Rancho Las Salinas (Salt Marsh)	Gabriel Espinosa	East of Salinas
Monterey County "tract"	Simeón Castro	Castroville
Rancho El Tucho	Joaquín Arroyo and Tomás Blanco (Tom White)	East of Castroville
Rancho Rincón de las Salinas (Corner of the Salt Marshes)	Christine Delgado	West of Prunedale
Rancho Bolsa del Potrero y Moro Cojo (Pocket of the Pasture and Lame Moor)	Juan Bautista Rogerio (John Rogers) Cooper	Prunedale
Rancho Bolsa Nueva y Moro Cojo (New Pocket and Lame Moor)	José Simeón Juan Nepomucena Castro and María Antonia Pico de Castro	Castroville, Prunedale, Elkhorn Slough[22]

NAME OF RANCHO	GRANTEE AND/OR 1850 OWNER	1850 AND/OR CURRENT SITES
Rancho Bolsa de San Cayetano	José de Jesús Vallejo	Pajaro, Las Lomas, Moss Landing, and Zmudowski beaches
Rancho Vega del Río de Pajáro (Meadow Along the Pajaro River)	Antonio Miguel Castro family	Aromas
Rancho Los Carneros (Mutton Sheep) (1 of 2)	Heirs of Francisco Javier (David) Littlejohn	East of Las Lomas
Rancho Cañada de la Carpenteria (Valley of the Carpenter Shop)	Joaquín Soto	South of Aromas
Rancho Los Carneros (Mutton Sheep) (2 of 2)	María Antonio Linares	West of San Juan Bautista (San Benito County), across county line
Rancho Los Vergeles (The Flower Gardens)	José Joaquín Gomez	Foot of Sugarloaf Peak
Rancho La Natividad (The Nativity)	Manuel Josef Butrón and Nicolás Alviso	West of Fremont Peak
Rancho Bolsa de las Escarpines (Pocket of the Sock or Perch)	Salvador Espinosa	North of Salinas
Rancho Rincón del Zanjón (Deep Ditch)	José Eusebio Boronda	Salinas
Rancho Sausal (Willow Grove)	José Tiburcio Castro	Salinas
Rancho El Alisal (Alder Grove) (1 of 2)	Juan Bautista Alvarado	Salinas
Rancho El Alisal (Alder Grove) (2 of 2)	Guillermo (W.E.P.) Hartnell	Salinas
Rancho Encinal y Buena Esperanza (Live Oak Grove and Good Hope)	David Esteban Spence[23]	East of Spreckles
Rancho Llano de Buena Vista (Plain of Good View)	José Mariano Estrada and José Santiago Estrada, his son	Spreckles
Rancho Buena Vista (Good View)	José Mariano Estrada and José Santiago Estrada, his son	Chualar
Rancho Guadalupe y Llanitos de los Correos (Guadalupe and Little Plain of the Messengers)	Juan Malarín; his heirs following his death in 1850	West of Gonzales
Rancho Chualar (Patch of Pigweed)	Juan Malarín; his heirs following his death in 1850	Chualar
Rancho Zanjones (Ditches)	Juan Malarín; his heirs following his death	Northwest of Gonzales
Rancho Rincón de la Punta del Monte (Corner of Mountain Point)	Teodoro Gonzáles	Gonzales
Rancho Paraje de Sanchez (Sanchez Place)	Francisco Lugo	South of Gonzales
Rancho San Vicente	Feliciano Soberánes	Soledad, Camphora
Rancho Los Coches (Pigs)	María Josefa Soberánes	Soledad
Rancho Arroyo Seco (Dry Creek)	Joaquín de la Torre	Greenfield
Rancho Posa de los Ositos (Pool of the Little Bears)	Carlos Cayetano Espinosa	West of King City
San Lorenzo (1 of 3)	Feliciano Soberánes	King City
San Lorenzo (2 of 3)	Rafael Sanchez	East of Greenfield
Rancho San Lorenzo (3 of 3)	Francisco Rico	East of San Ardo
Rancho San Bernabé (St. Barnabas)	Petronillo Ríos	King City
Rancho San Benito (St. Benedict)	Francisco García; James Watson	San Lucas
Rancho San Lucas (St. Luke)	José Rafael Papías Estrada	San Lucas
Rancho San Bernardino (St. Bernard)	José Mariano	San Ardo

- Married to María Juana Cota de Boronda

- Parents and 15 children were all industrious and hard-working

- *Doña* Juana was the first in the Monterey area to make the popular round yellow cheese in mounds that missionaries brought from Spain to California in the 1700s. She made it to support her family after José Manuel suffered an injury. One version of history states that Monterey Jack cheese acquired its name when David Jacks began producing the cheese for American buyers.

Don Lázaro Soto owned *Rancho Cañada de la Segunda*. The *Misión San Carlos Borroméo del Rio Carmelo* had been relocated here in 1771. The building still standing in Carmel today was begun in 1793 and dedicated in 1797.

The Carmel Mission, as it is known today, was Father Serra's favorite and he is buried within the sanctuary. The mission stood in neglected ruins in 1850, but would be restored and rededicated in 1884. Further restoration took place in the 1920s and 30s.

The western borders of two ranchos, *Rancho El Pescadero* and *Rancho Punta de Pinos* fell within the 8400-acre forested area known today as the Del Monte Forest through which the famous Seventeen Mile Drive winds. *Don* Juan (John F.) Romie owned *El Pescadero* and *Don* José Abrego owned *Punta de Pinos* until he sold it to Jacob P. Leese and others in April 1850.

Rancho Aguajito[24] was owned by *Don* Gregorio Tapia. The Americans called a portion of this rancho opposite the Catholic cemetery "Washerwoman's Canyon" because the women washed their clothes in the springs located here.

Of the 32 ranchos in the Salinas Valley, 26 lay adjacent to the Salinas River in southern Monterey County. None of these ranchos were particularly noteworthy.

Rancho Bolsa de San Cayetano was located in the lower Pajaro River Valley bordering Santa Cruz County. *Don* José de Jesús Vallejo had inherited the rancho from his father, *Don* Ignacio Vicente Ferrer Vallejo, but a brother, Juan Antonio, was living here in 1850. All of the Vallejo children, including the influential *Don* Mariano Guadalupe Vallejo, had grown up here in what has been called the *Casa Materna* (Mother House) of the Vallejos because this home was the first of many parcels of property owned by the Vallejo family. The family's 1824 adobe would later be known as the "Glass House" because of the many glass windows added to enclose the upper porch. (Attempts to save this historic structure were unsuccessful.)

Rancho Los Vergeles was owned by *Don* José Joaquín Gomez. His two-story adobe stood near Lagunita Lake at the foot of Sugar Loaf Peak and was a favorite

The 1844-48 Boronda Adobe Casa is the oldest structure in Salinas and is part of the Boronda History Center.

stop for travelers on their way to San Juan Bautista.

Don José Eusebio Boronda owned *Rancho Rincón del Zanjón*. He and his family originally lived on a hill in an adobe with a red-tiled roof that could be seen for miles by travelers crossing the Salinas plain. That house no longer stands, but the Boronda Adobe Casa built between 1844 and 1848—the oldest structure in Salinas—remains and is part of the Boronda History Center[25]

Don Juan Bautista Alvarado, the former Governor, owned *Rancho El Alisal* that he had purchased from *Dons* Feliciano and Mariano Soberánes (brothers) in 1841. He and his wife, María Martina Castro de Alvarado, had retired here in 1842, but in 1850 they were living in Contra Costa County.

Don Guillermo (William Edward Petty (W.E.P.)) Hartnell, who was married to a De la Guerra daughter from Santa Barbara, had obtained a grant of land on the bank of Alisal Creek in 1833 for the purpose of building a summer home. Realizing the need for education for the youth of the Salinas-Monterey area, he established a school in a portion of his home—*El Colegio de San José* (College of St. Joseph). One of the school's first 15 pupils was Pablo de la Guerra, who was a delegate of the State Constitutional Convention and later a state senator. The school only remained in operation until 1836, however.[27]

Don Feliciano Soberánes owned *Rancho San Vicente* and resided here with his family until he sold it to *Don* Estéban Munrás in September 1850. Mission Soledad, which was founded in 1791, lay in complete ruins on this rancho in 1850 and would remain that way for another century. Restoration, still in progress today, did not begin until 1954.

Rancho Los Coches was owned by *Doña* María Josefa Soberánes, eldest daughter of Feliciano Soberánes. She was married to William Brenner Richardson, formerly from Maryland, who built the now state-owned 1843 Richardson Adobe.[28] In 1846 Richardson planted the locust trees that surround the adobe.

The same drought and flood cycles that ruined the ranchos in the counties to the south affected the *rancheros* of Monterey County. Squatters added to the problems of these *rancheros* by costing them huge attorney's fees in attempting to void the squatters' claims.

Shore whaling would help to keep Monterey afloat economically during the 1850s and '60s. The entry of the Southern Pacific Railroad into the Salinas Valley in 1872 spurred the growth of the agricultural and tourism industries and had a significant effect on the development of the county. In the 1920s, sardine harvesting led to the establishment of Monterey's famous Cannery Row, a major tourist attraction today—especially since the opening of the Monterey Bay Aquarium in 1985.

AREA WITHIN PRESENT-DAY SAN BENITO COUNTY

Most of present-day San Benito County would be part of Monterey County until 1874. In 1887 San Benito's boundaries were expanded on the east to include portions of Fresno and Merced counties.

The Diablo and Gabilan mountain ranges cover much of the county. The Pajaro River originates here on its way to the Pacific, forming the boundary between present-day San Benito and Santa Clara counties. After passing the junction of Pescadero Creek, the river forms the boundary between Monterey and Santa Cruz counties on its way to the ocean.

In 1850 the San Joaquin and Panoche valleys contained an estimated 25,000 wild horses that ran in herds. The notorious Joaquin Murieta and his gang also drove stolen horses through this area.

San Benito County has one particularly remarkable natural site located west of the town of San Benito. The Pinnacles National Monument is an unusual mountain range of yellow Miocene sandstone set aside by President Theodore Roosevelt in 1908. It is believed that it was sighted as early as 1794 by the English navigator George Vancouver.

A former mission and pueblo were located within the current boundaries of San Benito County, as well as a small number of ranchos. It would be 1860 before many English-speaking people settled in the area.

W.E.P. Hartnell (1798-1854)

- Englishman who arrived in California in 1822 as a hide trader
- Resident manager in Monterey for McCullough, Hartnell and Company, agents for a British trading firm
- Married to María Teresa, daughter of José de la Guerra y Noriega of Santa Barbara; they had 25 children
- Tried to improve California culture by offering educational opportunities for sons of merchant class *Californios*
- Appointed inspector of missions during secularization and held various other government positions
- Official Interpreter of State Constitutional Convention; translated deliberations for Spanish-speaking members

Sites to Visit in San Benito County

Mission San Juan Bautista, Hwy 156, San Juan Bautista 831.623.4528

San Juan Bautista State Historic Park, Hwy 156, San Juan Bautista 831.623.4881

San Juan Bautista Chamber of Commerce, 402-A Third St., San Juan Bautista 831.623.2454 (Walking Tour Map)

Mission San Juan Bautista

Misión San Juan Bautista, the fifteenth California mission, was established in 1797. The San Andreas earthquake fault runs along the base of the hill lying below the mission cemetery; an earthquake in 1803 destroyed the original church. The new mission church built afterwards, the largest of its kind in California (with three aisles), has been in continuous use since 1812 as a parish church. The buildings suffered further damage during the 1906 earthquake, but were later restored.

Following secularization, San Juan Bautista[29] became a pueblo, known temporarily as San Juan de Castro because José Tiburcio Castro became the civil administrator of the mission. Acting in accordance with the mission secularization decree issued

Mission San Juan Bautista is located in the San Juan Bautista State Historic Park.

that year, he divided up the mission property and auctioned it off to friends, neighbors, and relatives. The mission buildings and 55 acres would be returned to the Church by federal decree in 1859.

Today the San Juan Bautista State Historic Park contains the only original Spanish plaza remaining in California, as well as one of the state's few preserved stretches of El Camino Real. The section of road lies on the edge of the plaza, right along the rift zone of the San Andreas fault.[30]

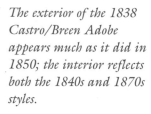

The first story of the Plaza Hotel was built in 1813 to serve as a barracks for the mission's Spanish guard.

The Historic Park also contains two buildings remaining from the pre-1850 era, and several later buildings. The adobe Plaza Hotel stands kitty-corner from the mission. The second story of the hotel was built in 1858 atop the solid walls of a one-story barracks that was built in 1813 for the mission's Spanish guard. The building has been restored to look as it did in the 1860's. Next door, Patrick and Margaret Breen and their seven children lived in the two-story Castro/Breen Adobe, which was

The exterior of the 1838 Castro/Breen Adobe appears much as it did in 1850; the interior reflects both the 1840s and 1870s styles.

built by Castro around 1838. The exterior appears much as it did in 1850; the interior reflects both the 1840s and 1870s styles.[31] The Breens established an inn that was a favorite stopping place for travelers between Monterey and the mines in 1849-50. They also owned 400 acres of prime agricultural land in the San Juan Valley.

The Breens were the first English-speaking settlers in San Juan. They had been among the members of the Donner Party who survived the tragic winter of 1846-47 in the Sierras. Their very first home in California actually was a room in the Mission San Juan Bautista that today is used as a gift shop.

Across the plaza from the mission, the Plaza Hall is believed to have first housed unmarried mission Indian women and later cavalrymen. It is restored today as it looked in 1868 when the first floor served as Angelo Zanetta's family home and the second floor served as a public meeting place.

San Juan Bautista was a trade and supply center for cattle and sheep ranchos. It also would become a stop on the way to the San Benito Mountain quicksilver mines following the establishment of such mercury mines as the New Idria Mine in the early 1850s. San Juan also was a major stop for the stage and wagon traffic between San Francisco and Los Angeles, until the railroad, which bypassed it, was built in 1876.[32]

San Benito County Ranchos

Fifteen ranchos were located within the current boundaries of San Benito County. Several ranchos crossed county lines into Monterey, Santa Cruz, and Santa Clara counties. The ranchos lying exclusively in San Benito County were concentrated in the north. A number of San Benito County's ranchos had been mission ranchos. Irrigation systems were never established because springs running from the elevation of Gavilan Peak, known today as Fremont Peak[33], irrigated the mission gardens, vineyards, and cornfields. Details about the more interesting ranchos follow.

Dons Juan M. Anzar and Manuel Larios owned *Rancho Santa Ana y Quién Sabé*. Anzar was an absentee landowner; he paid Larios to oversee his portion of the rancho. Larios owned and lived on the lower part of the rancho in the Santa Ana Valley, where he built a large adobe house with a chapel and fortress along the Santa Ana River. One of the original purposes of the grant was to prevent the American Indians from attacking San Juan Bautista. Larios became quite the Indian fighter and bear hunter. Bears inhabited the nearby Quien Sabe Hills and often were caught for bull and bear fights.

The Pinnacles National Monument is an unusual mountain range of yellow Miocene sandstone located west of the town of San Benito.

Dons Angel Castro and his son-in-law, José Antonio Rodríguez, owned *Rancho Ciénega de los Paicines*. The family lived in a two-story adobe built by Castro. The San Benito River and its tributary, Pescadero Creek, ran through this rancho.

Don Francisco Peréz Pacheco owned *Rancho Ausaymas y San Felipe*, which extended into Santa Clara County. He lived in a two-story adobe and employed laborers to raise his thousands of horses, cattle, and hogs, as well as various crops. The rancho was fairly self-sufficient. Pacheco Pass, which links the Santa Clara and San Joaquin valleys, runs through this former rancho.

SAN BENITO COUNTY RANCHOS

NAME OF RANCHO	GRANTEE AND/OR 1850 OWNER	1850 AND/OR CURRENT SITES
Rancho Real de las Aguilas (Royal Ranch of the Eagles)	Francisco Arias and Saturnino Carriaga	East of Paicines near county border
Rancho Santa Ana y Quién Sabé (Who Knows!)	Manuel Larios and Juan M. Anzar	Northeast of Tres Pinos
Rancho Ciénega de los Paicines	Angel Castro and José Antonio Rodríguez	Tres Pinos, Paicines
Rancho Ciénega del Gabilán (Marsh of the Hawk)[34]	Antonio Chavez; Joseph Limantour	Fremont Peak State Park
Rancho San Justo[35]	Francisco Pérez Pacheco	Hollister
Rancho Las Aromitas y Agua Caliente (Little Odors and Warm Water)	Juan M. Anzar	Northwest of San Juan Bautista, Aromas (Santa Cruz County)
Rancho Lomerias Muertas	José María Sanchez	North of San Juan Bautista
Rancho Llano del Tequesquita (Alkali Plain)	José María Sanchez	San Felipe Lake, Santa Clara County
Rancho Bolsa de San Felipe	Francisco Pérez Pacheco	Hollister
Rancho San Joaquin	Cruz Cervantes	East of Dunneville
Rancho Ausaymas y San Felipe	Francisco Peréz Pacheco	North of Dunneville, Bell Station in Santa Clara County

Notes —∽ MONTEREY COUNTY

1

See Larkin sidebar on page 128.

2

Due to several repeals of the law in subsequent years, Monterey's official year of incorporation is 1889.

3

San Carlos Cathedral is the fourth version of the first church. The first two were pole and brush and the third was adobe with a stone foundation that was destroyed by fire.

4

Arrangements for several different guided tours may be made at the Stanton Center Visitor Center, the Cooper-Molera Adobe, or the Pacific House when it reopens in 2000.

5

The following discussion of the Monterey adobes is organized geographically. When visiting Monterey, refer to the "Monterey Path of History" map which may be obtained from the Visitors and Convention Bureau, and follow the Path of History markers embedded in the sidewalks.

6

Plaza del Muelle was where Commodore John Drake Sloat raised the American flag on July 7, 1846, officially making California part of the U.S.

7

The prominent Feliciano Soberánes family would live here from 1860 to 1922, thus its name. Many of their additions and improvements to the property may be seen on the tour of the interior.

8

Josiah Merritt was a New York lawyer, and later a judge in Monterey, who arrived in Monterey in 1850 and played a significant role in organizing the county.

9

See Leese sidebar on page 173.

10

In the late 1930s and post-World War II-1940s, many of the features of Larkin's house would become part of a new style for mass housing called "the ranch house style."

11

See Vallejo sidebar on page 170.

12

See Frémont sidebar on page 253.

13

Cooper's married daughter, Amelia Molera, and her family lived here briefly at various times, thus the hyphenated name. His granddaughter willed the property to the National Trust for Historic Preservation.

14

Francisco Pérez Pacheco was one of the largest landowners in California at one time, owning property in Monterey, San Benito, Merced, and Santa Clara counties.

15

Robert Louis Stevenson's fiancée, Fanny Osbourne, would live here with *Señorita* María in later years, so he was a visitor to this home and did some writing here.

16

California's second post office was opened in San Francisco less than a week later.

17

Approximately 40 other land grants were made before or after Governor Alvarado's.

18

Fort Hunter Liggett was established as a troop-training site on lands acquired from William Randolph Hearst during World War II.

19

Andrew M. Molera was the grandson of John Rogers Cooper.

20

In 1850, under ideal conditions, it took 11 to 14 hours to reach *Rancho El Sur* from the site of present-day Carmel. The Coast Highway (Highway 1) passing through Big Sur today, including the famous Bixby Creek Bridge, would not be completed until 1937.

21

Point Lobos derives its name from the offshore rocks at Punta de los Lobos Marinos (Point of the Sea Wolves) where the barking sea lions may be heard.

22

The Elkhorn Slough emptied into the Salinas River in 1850 and the river then emptied into the ocean north of Moss Landing. In 1909, the river changed its course. It now empties into the ocean south of Moss Landing. Elkhorn Slough is one of California's largest wetlands and part of the National Estuarine Reserve.

23

David Esteban Spence devised a way of salting and packing beef for shipment to the gold fields.

24

The *El Pescadero, Cañada de la Segunda,* and *Aguajito* ranchos were located where some of the most valuable pieces of property in Monterey County lie today, and which the illustrious David Jacks began acquiring after his arrival in Monterey in 1850.

25

The Salinas River originates in San Luis Obispo County, bisecting Monterey County as it runs in a northwesterly direction to the Monterey Bay. The Salinas Valley is an elongated area approximately ten miles wide, lying between Sierra de Salinas and the Santa Lucia Range on the west and southwest, and the Gabilan and Diablo ranges and Cholame Hills on the east and northeast. The valley extends for 120 miles from just south of Moss Landing to Santa Margarita in San Luis Obispo County.

26

The Boronda Adobe was damaged in the 1989 Loma Prieta Earthquake, but has been repaired and is undergoing renovation. It should reopen for visitors shortly.

27

Today, Hartnell College in Salinas commemorates the pioneer educator of *El Alisal,* W. E. P. Hartnell.

28

The Richardson Adobe currently is boarded up and closed to the public.

29

Helen Hunt Jackson began writing her best-selling novel, *Ramona,* during her stay in San Juan Bautista in 1883. Also, the final scenes of Alfred Hitchcock's movie, *Vertigo,* were filmed here.

30

A small seismograph which registers the tectonic activity of the San Andreas fault is located on this preserved section of El Camino Real.

31

Succeeding generations of the Breen family would live in the Castro/Breen Adobe until 1933 when the adobe became part of the State Historic Park.

32

One of California's most famous outlaws would be associated with San Juan Bautista during the 1860's and '70's. Tiburcio Vasquez lived in San Juan for a time and had many friends in the San Benito and Gavilan Mountains around present-day Hollister and San Juan Bautista.

33

John Frémont raised the American flag on Fremont Peak in 1846 during the Mexican-American War.

34

The ranch still in operation today on a portion of the former *Rancho Ciénega de los Paicines* is hidden away in the Gabilan Mountains, but when a certain cigarette company sighted the beautiful valley from an airplane, it asked permission to film its famous Marlboro advertisements here.

35

This *Rancho San Justo* would become the famous sheep ranch of W. W. Hollister and Flint, Bixby, and Company (later of Los Angeles/Orange counties) in 1855.

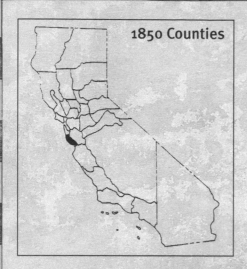

1850 Counties

❧ 1 8 5 0 ❧
❧ SANTA CRUZ ❧
COUNTY

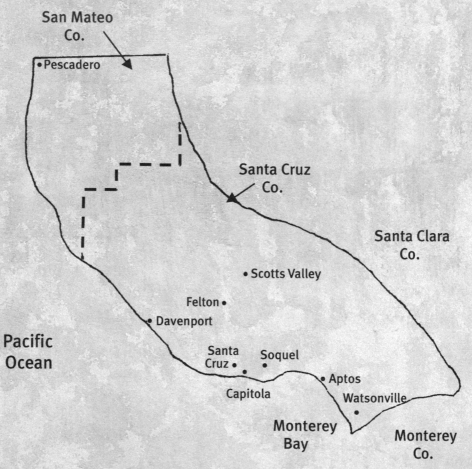

San Mateo Co.

• Pescadero

Santa Cruz Co.

Santa Clara Co.

• Scotts Valley

Felton •

• Davenport

Pacific Ocean

Santa Cruz •

Soquel •

Capitola

• Aptos

Watsonville

Monterey Bay

Monterey Co.

California
1850

Present-day boundary variations indicated by

– – – – –

Settlements/cities of 1850 include: Santa Cruz

SANTA CRUZ COUNTY
1850

The geographical area of 1850-Santa Cruz County included the southwestern portion of present-day San Mateo County until San Mateo County annexed that area in 1868.[1] Branciforte County was created on February 18, 1850, but the name was changed to Santa Cruz (Holy Cross) County in April.

Santa Cruz County's 643 residents counted in the 1850 U.S. Census included Californios, Americans, and Europeans who lived primarily around the former mission. The uncounted Native American inhabitants included members of the Salinan, Esselen, and Ohlone tribes, which as a group were called the Costanoans. (Very few American Indians remained in this area, however.) Spanish still was the dominant language, but a little less so than the other counties to the south.

Santa Cruz County consisted of the former mission and pueblo, the county seat of the county at the time—Santa Cruz, and 20 ranchos. Physical evidence of Santa Cruz' heritage is scant due to a number of natural disasters, including a disastrous fire in 1894 and the earthquakes of 1857, 1906, and 1989. Also, later settlers, unappreciative of the Spanish adobe architecture, attempted to transform Santa Cruz into a New England town.

Santa Cruz Mission

Misión la Exaltación de la Santa Cruz, the 12th California mission, was founded in 1791. Discovering that the original site was too close to the flood prone San Lorenzo River, the mission was constructed on a bluff above the river and completed in 1794. The mission and its several out buildings still stood in 1850 on the mission lands of *Rancho Misión Santa Cruz*, but were in great disrepair due to neglect and the heavy rains of 1840. The final destruction would occur in the 1857 earthquake. Today a 1932 concrete replica of the original mission stands just off of Mission Square, identical in proportions to the first structure, but about half its size. The brick Holy Cross Catholic Church that today stands on the site of the original chapel was built in 1889.

With secularization, the administration of the mission had been given to the authorities of *Villa de Branciforte*—the former pueblo that had been established across the San Lorenzo River to help fortify the coast. The last Franciscan priest left the mission in 1849. One adobe building constructed in 1824 as a row house for the mission Indians was divided into two residences and was occupied in 1850 by the Roman Rodríguez and Félipe Armas families. Today known as the Neary-Rodriguez Adobe, it is part of the Santa Cruz Mission State Historic Park.

Sites to Visit in Santa Cruz County

Museum of Art & History, The McPherson Center, 705 Front St., Santa Cruz 831.429.1964

Santa Cruz Mission State Historic Park, 144 School St., Santa Cruz 831.425.5849

Mission Santa Cruz, 126 High St., Santa Cruz 408.426.5686

Wilder Ranch State Park, 1401 Old Coast Rd., off Hwy 1, Santa Cruz 831.426.0505

Santa Cruz County Conference and Visitors Council, 701 Front St., Santa Cruz 95060 800.833.3494

Town of Santa Cruz

The town of Santa Cruz had grown up around the plaza of the mission on Mission Hill—first near the Upper Plaza, then later on "the flats" near the Lower Plaza. The town of 600 included the *Villa de Branciforte*. The third Spanish secular town established in Alta California in 1797, *Villa de Branciforte* was intended to be a retirement community for Spanish soldiers. Young soldiers finishing their ten-year enlistments were also encouraged to settle at the new pueblo. Many Brancifortans acquired ranchos after secularization, as well. The two communities of Branciforte and Santa Cruz merged into one after secularization; they would split off when Santa Cruz incorporated in 1876, and then rejoin as one city in 1907.

Two prominent California families made their start in Branciforte—the José Antonio Rodríguez and Joaquin Castro families. Rodríguez and Castro had come to Branciforte in 1798 as veterans of the Spanish Army. Their children became the "aristocrats" of the villa. By 1846, more than 60 Americans also lived in Branciforte or its vicinity, more than 20 of whom established families and stayed until their deaths.

Adobe houses lined a mile-long horse racetrack, which today is North Branciforte Avenue. A bull and bear fight arena was located on the flats near the present-day Soquel Avenue Bridge, between the San Lorenzo River and Branciforte Creek. Fights would continue here until as late as 1867. (Grizzly bears for the fights were captured in the valley located on the north coast of the county.)

The 1932 concrete replica of the original Mission Santa Cruz stands just off of Mission Square, identical in proportions to the first structure, but about half its size.

This 1824 mission row house was occupied in 1850 by the Roman Rodríguez and Félipe Armas families. Known as the Neary-Rodríguez Adobe today, it is part of the Santa Cruz Mission State Historic Park.

A subdivision map of the Town of Santa Cruz had been prepared by surveyor Jacob Rink Snyder[2] in 1847 at the request of the Town Council in order to establish the town and gain revenue from land sales. None of the streets that connect the flats with the hill today existed in 1850, however. Green and Mission streets were mere foot paths or wagon tracks that were dusty in the summer and deep in mud in the wet winter months. Elihu Anthony laid out Water Street in 1848; the street led to a ford across the San Lorenzo River and was known as the San Jose Road.

Anthony and a partner, Adna Hecox, ran a store in the foundry Anthony built in 1849 between Mission Hill and the San Lorenzo River. This was the first commercial building erected in Santa Cruz. The town's other 30-plus adobe structures were gradually converted to commercial uses. A structure built on the Upper Plaza by Thomas Fallon in the 1840s as a residence and saddlery shop was serving as a hotel. The Eagle Hotel, owned by Joseph L. Majors, was operating across the street. It served as the county's first courthouse, as well. The Santa Cruz Post Office was established on April 9, 1850.

The Frenchman John Baptise Arcan was operating a shop in his residence on the corner of present-day Pacific and Soquel avenues. (He and his wife were two of the survivors of the Death Valley party.) The Cooper brothers, from Pennsylvania, were operating a mercantile store that stood on Main Street (now Front Street). Francisco Alzina, from Menorca, one of the Spanish Balearic Islands, and his wife, María Gonzales, built a home in 1850-52 that still stands on Holy Cross Plaza today as a private residence. Lumber for the house was brought down the coast from *Rancho Pescadero*, which was owned by María's father. Alzina was the county's first sheriff in 1850, a job he performed well since he was fluent in both English and Spanish.

The Case family lived on what is known today as Neary's Lagoon, which in 1850 was a fairly large body of open water. The lagoon was subject to the ocean tides that backed up the river and swelled the lagoon. Benjamin A. Case was from Connecticut and his wife, Mary Amney Case, was from Vermont. They built a home on Neary Lagoon in 1848 in which Mrs. Case established the first American school in Santa Cruz. She had taught a dozen children during the summers of 1848 and 1849.

During the period between when Mrs. Case finished teaching and the establishment of the first public school, the Methodists maintained an academy in a little building on the bluff overlooking the river on School Street. The academy moved to the new First Methodist Church on Green Street in December 1850. The Methodist church was the first Protestant church in Santa Cruz. The church had its beginnings in a private residence in 1848, and its first full-time minister was Reverend James W. Brier, another Death Valley survivor.

Water for drinking, laundering, and irrigating vegetable gardens was obtained from Santa Cruz Creek, which originated on upper High Street as three springs called *Tres Ojos de Agua* (Three Eyes of Water). The creek crossed the plaza in front of the church. Santa Cruz' first municipal water system would draw on the same stream to fill up the reservoir installed in 1859 at the end of School Street.

Sandstone hills surround the city of Santa Cruz and were commonly called "chalk-rock." These hills gave the area one of its earliest and most important industries—limestone. Lime was to become an essential element in construction in the new state. It was the principal ingredient in mortar, plaster, and stucco. The redwoods and a wealth of other types of virgin timber located throughout the county would form the basis of another lucrative industry—lumber. The enormous demand for lumber in nearby San Francisco and the mining districts of the Gold Country kept timber prices high during most of the 1850s and early 1860s. *Don* Rafael Castro had been producing lumber since the 1830s, but in general, the Spanish made little use of the timber before the Americans started arriving in the 1820s.[3] They were accustomed to using adobe and tile as building materials.

Santa Cruz County Ranchos

In Santa Cruz County there were no Spanish land grants; all grants had been made under Mexican rule from 1822 to 1848. The 20 land grants had gone to Branciforte residents, with half of them going to the Castro and Rodríguez families. Details about the more interesting ranchos follow.

Along the Monterey/Santa Cruz border, *Don* Manuel Jimeno Casarín, a former secretary of state and former acting governor of Alta California, owned *Rancho*

Elihu Anthony (1818 –18??)

- Methodist minister and hardware merchant from Indiana
- He and his family arrived in Santa Cruz in 1847 by wagon train
- Served as the first Methodist minister in Santa Cruz and helped found the first Protestant church in Santa Cruz
- First postmaster; county treasurer, a member of the Board of Supervisors and the State Assembly
- Built the third foundry on the Pacific Coast in 1848 and made the first cast iron plow and first miners' picks in California
- Builder of first wharf (a plank chute on which goods slid into waiting rowboats) in Santa Cruz in 1849
- With F.A. Hihn, had reservoirs dug on Mission Hill bluff in 1856; redwood logs served as pipes to transport water from the storage tanks to the town of Santa Cruz
- Laid out Santa Cruz' first two real estate subdivisions

Adna Andress Hecox (1806-1883)

- Methodist Episcopal lay minister and carpenter from Michigan/Illinois
- Arrived in Santa Cruz in 1847
- Preached the first Protestant sermon in California at Mission Santa Clara in 1846 and the first Protestant sermon in Santa Cruz County at Soquel in 1847; instrumental in founding Protestant worship in Santa Cruz County; organized the first Temperance Society in California in Santa Cruz in 1848
- Repaired and operated the Lodge family's sawmill
- Tried his hand in the gold fields in 1849
- Operated a store with Elihu Anthony
- Served as justice of the peace, county treasurer, and lighthouse keeper (His daughter took over the post after his death.)

Salsipuedes. This rancho extended to the south from the Pajaro River and north to the mountains, and on into a small portion of Santa Clara County. Casarín was married to one of the daughters of the Santa Barbara De la Guerra y Noriega family, Agustías. The Casaríns raised their family here, sending two of their sons to the East Coast for their education.

Don José Amesti owned *Rancho Los Corralitos.* He was living in Monterey in 1850, but in later years after his death, his heirs would build an adobe on this rancho. Amesti manufactured shingles and timbers in the area as early as 1832, and a profitable sawmill industry would arise here in the 1860s.

Along the shores of Monterey Bay, *Don* José Joaquín Castro owned *Rancho San Andrés,* which was the most southerly of the ranchos owned by the Castro family. This rancho's beach had served as a Mexican-era embarcadero for shipping lumber. Castro's first house was located not far from the beach, but in 1833 he built a large, two-story adobe house on a hill above Larkin Valley. This adobe, which stood on the present-day Old Adobe Road in Watsonville, was the region's center for business, political, and social activities.

Don Rafael de Jesús Castro, son of *Don* José Joaquín, owned *Rancho Aptos,* which adjoined his father's rancho and extended north along the bay to Borregas Creek. *Doña* Martina Castro Lodge, the sister of *Don* Rafael, owned *Rancho Soquel* and *Rancho Soquel Augmentación,* which extended northeast into Santa Clara County. Her rancho was the largest single land grant in the county and contained vast forests of redwood, live oak, and madrone that today are located within The Forest of Nisene Marks State Park.[4] A sawmill was operating on the Soquel Creek.

Doña Martina had been widowed in 1849 when her husband was murdered on the way home from the gold fields. She remarried in 1850 to Louis Depeaux. She divided her property evenly between herself and her eight children, retaining her three-room adobe and its garden on the bank of the stream in Capitola.

John Daubenbiss, a Bavarian, and John Hames, a New Yorker, had acquired title to *Rancho Arroyo del Rodeo* in 1847, just prior to the death of the original grantee, *Don* Francisco Rodríguez. The Rodríguez and Castro families had conducted roundups of their herds in a natural amphitheater on this rancho, thus its name.

Don Juan José Crisóstomo (Joseph L.) Majors owned *Rancho San Agustín.* Majors built a large home for his wife, Maria de los Angeles Castro, and a gristmill on this rancho. Burros and mules loaded with grain would come over the mountains from Santa Clara County to the mill. Scotts Valley is located here today, named for a later owner, Hiram Scott.

Isaac Graham owned *Rancho Zayante.* A colony had developed within this rancho due to the inattention of the original 1834 grantee, *Don* Joaquin Buelna. Buelna let his claim lapse after conferring timber rights on Ambrose Tomlinson and Job Francis Dye in 1835. The colony rapidly grew, attracting many of the pioneers who came over the Santa Fe Trail in the 1830s and across the plains in the early 1840s. Joseph L. Majors had become a Mexican citizen, requested and received the grant for the rancho, and subsequently signed an agreement with Graham, Frederick Hoeger, and Peter Lassen[5] to build a mill. A gristmill, a small whiskey still, and an 1841 sawmill were in the center of a group of cabins. In 1843 Graham and Henry Neale built a slightly larger mill a mile north of present-day Felton.

Graham also built a steep road for hauling his lumber from the rancho to the beach at Santa Cruz for shipment, which has been in continuous use ever since. Today, improved and slightly realigned, it is known as Graham Hill Road.

Graham had given his small *Rancho Potrero y Rincón de San Pedro de Regalado* to Thomas J. Farnham in 1846 in appreciation for some assistance that Farnham had provided him. Farnham's widow, Eliza, came to Santa Cruz from New York in 1850 to settle his affairs following his recent death. She and a friend, Georgiana Bruce, would build an unusual cottage on the property in 1851 and shock their neighbors by wearing bloomers while working on their property—a practice that has earned them the label of 1850-style feminists.

Don José Antonio Bolcoff, one of the earliest foreign settlers in Spanish California, owned *Rancho Refugio*. A deserter from a Russian sailing vessel when it visited Monterey Bay in 1815, he settled in *Villa de Branciforte* and married one of the daughters of *Don* José Joaquín Castro in 1822, thus his fortuitous ownership of the rancho. Part of his adobe, roofed with tiles taken from the Santa Cruz Mission, still stands on Meder Creek at the Wilder Ranch State Park.

Finally, *Dons* Ramón Rodríguez and Francisco Alviso owned *Rancho Agua Puerca y las Trancas* that was the northern-most coastal rancho located in current Santa Cruz County.[6] The valley north of *Agua Puerca y las Trancas* had been named *Cañada de la Salud* (Hollow of Health) by Portola's expedition in 1769. This land was never included in any Spanish or Mexican grants. It was renamed Waddell Creek Valley after William W. Waddell, who established a sawmill here in 1862. This would become a very active lumbering area between 1850 and 1880 and today is part of Big Basin Redwoods State Park.[7]

Squatters and settlers (many who were discouraged 49ers) would descend on Santa Cruz County in the early 1850s and begin extensive farming of wheat and potatoes, and later fruit. Elihu Anthony was shipping potatoes to the mines in 1850 for a lucrative price. Other industries sprang up such as dairy farming and tanning.[8]

An Irish quartermaster of the British army, Charles Henry McKiernan, arrived in the present-day Summit Road area of the Santa Cruz Mountains in 1850. The only resident in this area for two years, he was known as "Mountain Charley." He became a sheep and cattle rancher, orchardist, hunter, woodsman, lumber mill operator, road builder, and stagecoach owner/operator. Today the Mountain Charley Road runs along the old Native American trail on which McKiernan established a toll road.

El Camino Real ran approximately where the highway connecting Watsonville and Santa Cruz and running up the coast to Ano Nuevo Point is located today. A former Native American trail or two traversed the rugged mountains covered by virgin timber, but it would be the late 1850s before the first stage roads were built allowing travel between Santa Cruz and the Santa Clara Valley. In fact, the only way to export the goods that were being produced in excess of the area's needs was by sea. Elihu Anthony had built a wharf in 1849 near the mouth of the San Lorenzo River in Santa

José Antonio Bolcoff (1790-1866)

- Only Russian to settle permanently in Alta California and the only Russian to receive a Mexican land grant
- Mission administrator in 1839
- Married to Candido Castro, one of the prominent Castro sisters
- Alcalde and justice of the peace in Santa Cruz

Part of José Antonio Bolcoff's adobe, roofed with tiles taken from the Santa Cruz Mission, still stands on Meder Creek at the Wilder Ranch State Park.

Cruz.[9] The wharf was used extensively by schooners transporting the many products produced during the early pioneer days to San Francisco.

Santa Cruz was considered a main shipping point. The Pacific U.S. Mail Steamship Company, which was subsidized by the federal government to carry U.S. mail to and from California, regularly visited Santa Cruz. Soquel Landing, a forerunner of Capitola Wharf, was built in 1849 at the mouth of the Soquel River. Several other landings would be established in later years for the same purpose.

Ship construction had begun in Santa Cruz as early as 1846. Spikes, bolts, blocks, sails, and rigging were manufactured on the spot. Other components were obtained from the Sandwich (Hawaiian) Islands.

The Southern Pacific Railroad arrived in the county in the 1880s, linking Santa Cruz with the Santa Clara Valley. Santa Cruz became home to the famous Santa Cruz Boardwalk in 1904, the first amusement park built west of the Mississippi River.

SANTA CRUZ COUNTY RANCHOS

NAME OF RANCHO	GRANTEE AND/OR 1850 OWNER	1850 AND/OR CURRENT SITES
Rancho Bolsa del Pájaro (Pocket of the Pajaro)	Sargento Sebastián Rodríguez	Watsonville [10]
Rancho Salsipuedes (Get Out If You Can)	Manuel Jimeno Casarín	East of Watsonville, extending into Santa Clara County
Rancho Los Corralitos (Little Corrals)	José Amesti	Freedom, Watsonville Airport
Rancho Laguna de las Calabazas (Pumpkin Lake)	Félipe Hernandez	West of Freedom
Rancho San Andrés	José Joaquín Castro	Watsonville
Rancho Aptos	Rafael de Jesús Castro	Seacliff State Beach, Aptos
Rancho Soquel and Rancho Soquel Augmentación	Martina Castro Lodge	Capitola, Aptos, The Forest of Nisene Marks
Rancho Arroyo del Rodeo (Stream of the Rodeo)	John Daubenbiss and John Hames	Capitola, Soquel
Rancho Tres Ojos de Agua (Three Springs) and Rancho Mesa de Ojos de Agua	Nicholás Dodero and Thomas W. Russell, respectively	Santa Cruz, University of California, Santa Cruz
Rancho La Carbonera (Place Where Charcoal is Made)	William Buckle (aka "Guillermo Bocle" or "Thompson")	Pasatiempo
Rancho San Agustín	Juan José Crisóstomo (Joseph L.) Majors	Scotts Valley
Rancho Zayante	Isaac Graham	Felton, Big Trees Park, Mount Hermon
Rancho Potrero y Rincón (Corner Pasture) de San Pedro de Regalado (Delicate)	Eliza Farnham	South of Zayante
Rancho Cañada del Rincón en el Río de San Lorenzo de Santa Cruz	Pierre Sainsevain	Henry Cowell Redwoods State Park, Gold Gulch,[11] University of California, Santa Cruz
Rancho Refugio (Refuge)	José Antonio Bolcoff	Wilder Ranch State Park
Rancho Arroyo de la Laguna (Stream of the Lake)	Gil Sánchez	South of Davenport
Rancho San Vicente	Blas A. Escamilla	Ben Lomond Mountain
Rancho Agua Puerca y las Trancas (Muddy Water and the Bars or Barriers)	Ramón Rodríguez and Francisco Alviso	Davenport, Swanton

1

See San Mateo County for a description of this area.

2

Jacob Rink Snyder was a delegate of the State Constitutional Convention.

3

The Mexicans even had the same concern for preserving the redwoods that the Americans would develop in later years. In fact, in 1830 a government *reglamento* was issued restricting the cutting of timber and imposing a duty of ten percent on its export.

4

The parkland of The Forest of Nisene Marks State Park would be clear-cut of redwoods between 1893 and 1925 by the Loma Prieta Lumber Company, but second-growth forests replaced them. The epicenter of the Loma Prieta Earthquake of 1989 is located in this park.

5

See Lassen sidebar on page 192.

6

Two more ranchos, *Punta del Año Nuevo* and *Butano* were located in 1850-Santa Cruz County, but that area would become part of San Mateo County in 1868 and is described in the next chapter.

7

Big Basin Redwoods State Park, originally called the California State Redwood Park, was the second California state park, established in 1902 at the behest of early California environmentalists. Today it is the oldest state park, because the first, Yosemite State Park, is now a national park. Big Basin and the Henry Cowell State Park contain most of the remaining old growth forest in the county. Loggers stripped 18 million board feet of lumber from the Santa Cruz Mountains between 1850 and 1880.

8

Tan oaks grew in Santa Cruz County, which accommodated the tannery industry. Pulverized, cooked bark from these trees made a chemical bath used for processing hides.

9

Elihu Anthony also built the county's first wagon bridge in 1849 to enable loaded wagons to climb the bluff to use his wharf.

10

On October 18, 1850, cannon shots announcing that California had been admitted to the Union as the 31st state were fired on the site that would become the city plaza in Watsonville.

11

Gold would be discovered in a small creek in this area in 1855. No fortunes were made here, however.

1850 Counties

❧ 1 8 5 0 ❧
❧ SAN FRANCISCO ❧
COUNTY

City and
County of
San Francisco

Pacific
Ocean

•San
Francisco

San
Francisco
Bay

•Colma

Pacifica •

San Bruno •

Millbrae •
San Mateo

• Burlingame

San Mateo
Co.

• Montara

• Princeton

• Half Moon Bay   Redwood City •

Menlo Park •

Woodside •

Portola Valley •

Santa Clara
Co.

• San Gregorio

• La Honda

Santa Cruz
Co.

California
1850

Present-day boundary
variations indicated by

━ ━ ━ ━ ━

Settlements/cities of 1850 include: San Francisco, Woodside, San Benito (Half Moon Bay)

SAN FRANCISCO COUNTY
1850

The geographical area of 1850-San Francisco County included the area of present-day San Mateo County. The 1850 U.S. Census was destroyed by fire; the 1849 census had counted 5,000 and the 1852 census counted 34,766, which provides a perspective on the population growth for that three-year period. The uncounted Native American population consisted of the Ohlone Indians. English had replaced Spanish as the dominant language.

AREA WITHIN PRESENT-DAY SAN MATEO COUNTY

San Mateo County would be formed in 1856 from the southern portion of San Francisco County. Part of northern Santa Cruz County was transferred to San Mateo County in 1868, because the Pescadero residents disliked the long trek over narrow, mountain roads required to reach the county seat of Santa Cruz County.

San Mateo County occupies most of the peninsula south of the present-day San Francisco/San Mateo County line. The county is bordered by the San Francisco Bay on the east and the Pacific Ocean on the west. Its rugged, forested mountains and a rocky shoreline with only occasional stretches of beach made access to the western San Mateo coast by both land and sea difficult in 1850. This same terrain has preserved the rural nature of this part of the county to this day.

The economy of the area located in present-day San Mateo County had been interdependent with San Francisco's since mission times. San Mateo County needed the mercantile goods that were only available from San Francisco, and San Francisco relied on San Mateo County for its water supply and lumber. In fact, the building boom caused by the influx of new settlers and commerce to San Francisco during the Gold Rush, as well as the frequent destructive fires in San Francisco, spurred the development of San Mateo County's first industry, lumber milling.[1]

Before the Gold Rush, the Spanish had done little or no logging, but even as early as 1850 there were about a dozen sawmills operating in San Mateo County. During the 1860s and 1870s there would be 30 sawmills in the county. Most of the trees that were accessible and usable were logged by the early 1900s.

There had been an *asistencia* (a branch of Mission Dolores) on one rancho, but a mission was never located in San Mateo County. One settlement of sawyers was located in Woodside and the "Spanishtown" of San Benito was situated where the city of Half Moon Bay lies today. Most of San Mateo County's buildings of this era

Sites to Visit in San Mateo County

San Mateo County Historical Museum, 777 Hamilton St., Redwood City 650.299.0104

Sanchez Adobe Historic Site, 1000 Linda Mar Blvd., Pacifica 650.359.1462

Woodside Store Historic Site Museum (Dr. Tripp's 1854 Store), Kings Mountain and Tripp roads, Woodside 650.851.7615

San Mateo County Convention and Visitors Bureau, 888 Airport Blvd., Burlingame, CA 94010 650.347.7004

would be lost in the 1868 and 1906 earthquakes, and others were destroyed before California began valuing its historical landmarks.

San Mateo County Ranchos

Sixteen ranchos had been granted in the area that makes up San Mateo County today. Details about the more interesting ones follow.

Don José Simeon de Nepomuceno Castro, a prominent resident of Monterey, owned *Rancho Punta de Año Nuevo*, the southernmost rancho. This rancho had been a Mission Santa Cruz outpost used as pastureland. Grizzly bears were once common at *Año Nuevo* and were a substantial danger for Spanish, Mexican, and early Euro-American settlers. Today the point and beach are part of Ano Nuevo State Reserve, a protected breeding ground for northern elephant seals.[2]

Don Antonio Buelna's widow and her new husband, Francisco Rodríguez, owned *Rancho San Gregorio*. Buelna's widow also owned a rancho in Santa Clara County. Her late husband had built a road over the hills connecting his two ranchos. Known today as La Honda Road and Old La Honda Road, it was the first connecting route across the mountains. During 1850 *Don* Salvadore Castro acquired an eastern portion of *Rancho San Gregorio* from *Doña* Rodríguez to settle some debts.

The Candelario Miramontes family owned *Rancho Miramontes*. Ten houses would eventually be built along Pilarcitos Creek in the present-day city of Half Moon Bay for the large extended Miramontes family.

Bordering the shores of Half Moon Bay,[3] *Rancho El Corral de Tierra*, which had been a horse and oxen ranch of Mission Dolores, was granted in two parts. *Don* Tiburcio Vásquez owned the southern portion of the rancho; he built an adobe home on the north bank of Pilarcitos Creek across from the Miramontes' adobe. The cattle ranching Vásquez and Miramontes families lived in harmony in this area and provided the basis of the settlement that began to take shape in the 1840s called San Benito. The original Mexican settlers came here to escape harassment from Euro-

The Sanchez Adobe Historic Site, located in Pacifica, is the only pre-1850 building open to the public in San Mateo County.

American settlers on the San Francisco Bay side of the mountains. They lived in relative isolation because of the lack of decent roads over the mountains. The Americans would start calling the settlement "Spanishtown" in the early 1850s when the first squatters tried to move in; they were subsequently forced to settle in Purisima instead. The post office designation was changed to Half Moon Bay in 1872.

Don Francisco Guerrero Palomares owned the northern and larger part of *Rancho El Corral de Tierra*. He built a four-room adobe ranch house on a hillside northeast of present-day Princeton.

Don Francisco Sánchez, a native of San Francisco, owned *Rancho San Pedro*. The large, restored, two-story 1846 adobe—the Sanchez Adobe Historic Site—in Pedro Valley in present-day Pacifica, is the only pre-1850 building open to the public in San Mateo County today.

Rancho Buri Buri was owned by the heirs of *Don* José Antonio Sánchez, the father of Francisco. The Sanchez family built two identical adobe houses where Millbrae lies today. This rancho originally was a Mexican government cattle ranch to supply meat to the Presidio of San Francisco. José Antonio had been one of the most prosperous and influential *rancheros* on the peninsula, even constructing an embarcadero on a nearby slough for his shipments of hides and tallow.

The first of many roadhouses was built on El Camino Real in present-day San Bruno. John Thorpe's 14-Mile House was reported to have been a primitive, flea-infested place, but a place to rest for the night, nonetheless. It would become one of the Peninsula's landmark inns and restaurants in later years. Many other country inns sprang up along the old mission trail, most named according to their distance from San Francisco. They furnished food, drink, lodging, and livery stables.

Robert T. Ridley owned *Rancho Cañada de Guadalupe, la Visitación y Rodeo Viejo*. Several adobe structures stood on the property that the previous owner, Jacob P. Leese,[4] had built for his foreman and Native American herdsmen. Leese and Ridley had swapped ranchos in 1843—Ridley's being located in Sonoma County. However, Ridley never lived on the Bay property or developed it in any way. In 1850 Henry Schwerin was in the process of establishing a dairy ranch in Visitation Valley in present-day Bayshore where the Cow Palace exhibition hall is located.

William Davis Merry Howard, a San Francisco merchant from Boston, owned *Rancho San Mateo*. He would build a small villa in the hills near San Mateo Creek and El Camino Real in the early 1850s with materials shipped around the Cape from Boston. It was the first of many mansions to be built in San Mateo County.

Rancho San Mateo had been part of the rancho of Mission Dolores on which the ruined San Mateo outpost of *Misión San Francisco de Asis* called "The Hospice" still stood in 1850. The large building housed a small chapel. The 1868 earthquake would destroy it.

In 1849 Nicholas DePeyster, from New York, operated a store and public house called the San Mateo House in the old mission outpost, but in 1850, W. D. M. Howard forced him out. DePeyster moved across San Mateo Creek onto the Argüello's *Pulgas* rancho. A tall wooden structure served as a stopping place for travelers along El Camino Real, midway between San Francisco and Santa Clara.

The prominent Argüello family owned the vast *Rancho de las Pulgas*. El Camino Real traversed this rancho into Santa Clara County. Several of the heirs of *Don* Luis Argüello had recently moved from San Francisco to live in a small adobe house located on the site of present-day San Carlos in order to protect their rights of ownership.

A number of squatters were already established in the Pulgas Redwoods in 1850 and would be forced to compensate the Argüello family when the court later found the original grantees to be the legal owners. Other squatters settled in the vicinity of present-day Menlo Park. Isaiah C. Woods, a San Francisco speculator and banker, established docking facilities at Ravenswood on the Bay in present-day East Palo Alto. Most of the other squatters were sawyers working in the nearby redwoods.

A little creek that ran through *Rancho de las Pulgas* within present-day Redwood City[5] emptied into a slough of the San Francisco Bay, forming a natural embarcadero. Mathias Parkhurst and his partner in the shingle business, Dr. Robert Orville Tripp, developed the Redwood Creek inlet as the port—the "Red Woods[6] Embarcadero" or Redwood Landing—from which lumber from the Woodside mills was transported up the Bay. Oxen dragged the logs down to the slough; the logs were then tied together and floated out as far as the tide would carry them. Sailboats then pulled the logs the rest of the way to San Francisco.

Irishman John Coppinger had been granted *Rancho Cañada de Raymundo*, which extended to the summit of the Santa Cruz Range. Coppinger was the first English-speaking person to settle in the area, arriving in 1836 after jumping ship in San Francisco. He built a millpond and dam in 1840 and was one of the first to use waterpower to run a sawmill. His 1841 adobe ranch house stood at the intersection of present-day Woodside and Kings Mountain roads in Woodside. Shortly before his death in 1847, Coppinger began selling off his heavily timbered land in small parcels. His widow, María Luisa Soto Coppinger, and children remained in the area and María married the Irish Presbyterian sea captain, John Greer, in August 1850.

The Irish Catholic Dennis Martin had purchased a thousand acres from Coppinger in 1846 and built a gristmill on the San Francisquito Creek in 1850. Unfortunately, floodwaters carried it away, forcing him to build another one. He also would build a lumber mill in 1852-53 and a small church in 1856—St. Denis Chapel, which was the only place of worship between San Francisco and Santa Clara for almost 20 years. Martin, his father, and brother had been members of the Stephens-Townsend-Murphy party, the first group to arrive in California by wagon train across the Sierras in 1844.

Charles Brown, from Baltimore, had built a sawmill in 1849 near Woodside on the banks of Alambique Creek. Brown and his wife lived in an 1838 adobe house located where the Mountain Home Ranch lies today. Upon the death of his wife in 1850, Brown moved to San Francisco. His property soon was purchased at a sheriff's sale by John Coffee Hays and two partners, James Galbraith and Major John C. Caperton. Isaac Branham assumed Brown's interest in the sawmill and soon replaced the water wheel with a 40-horsepower steam engine.

The 1854 Woodside Store in Woodside houses a museum.

South of the Coppinger-Greer property, Edward A. T. Gallagher was operating two lumber camps that employed 115 men. North of the Coppinger-Greer property, Mathias Parkhurst had purchased 127 acres from Coppinger where he and his partner, Dr. Tripp, were operating their shingle and lumbering operation. There was a settlement in the Woodside area as early as 1836 and the residents of a lumber camp began calling it Woodside in 1849.

Tripp was a dentist from Massachusetts who had planned to establish a dental practice in Sacramento. However, a mishap on the Sacramento River left him ill with pneumonia, so he returned to San Francisco. While still quite ill, he met Parkhurst, who convinced him to move to the warmer climate of Woodside. Tripp recovered, joined Parkhurst in his business, and built a house on the corner of Kings Mountain and Tripp roads. He became a member of the Court of Session of San Francisco, County, riding his horse to the meeting each Monday and returning home the following day. It occurred to him that on his trips to San Francisco he could be purchasing items for resale in Woodside and thus began the Woodside Store. Tripp first sold items to the growing community from the shed he and Parkhurst shared. In 1851 a store was built where the Tripp home would later be built, and in 1854, the Woodside Store, which today houses a museum, was built across the street.

During 1850, the Hungarian Agoston Haraszthy, one of the later founders of the commercial wine industry in California, planted his first California vineyard in the now-flooded Crystal Springs Valley. The climate proved to be too damp for wine grapes, however, and he would move to Sonoma in 1860.

When the San Francisco-San Jose Railroad was built down the Peninsula in 1863, many wealthy San Francisco businessmen would begin to build their luxurious country homes here. The growth of bay fisheries and commerce coincided with the completion of the transcontinental railroad in 1869. The 1906 earthquake prompted a further population migration down the Peninsula.

SAN MATEO COUNTY RANCHOS

NAME OF RANCHO	GRANTEE AND/OR 1850 OWNER	1850 AND/OR CURRENT SITES
Rancho Punta de Año Nuevo (New Year's Point)	José Simeon de Nepomuceno Castro	Ano Nuevo State Reserve
Rancho Bútano (Cow's Horn Drinking Cup)	Ramona Sánchez	Bean Hollow State Beach
Rancho El Pescadero (The Fishing Place)	Juan José Gonzales	Pescadero, Pescadero State Beach
Rancho San Gregorio	Antonio Buelna's widow, Francisco Rodríguez; Salvadore Castro	Pomponio and San Gregorio state beaches, San Gregorio, La Honda
Rancho Cañada Verde y Arroyo de la Purísima (Green Wood and the Creek of Purisima)	José Antonio Alviso	Lobitos and Martins Beach
Rancho Miramontes	Candelario Miramontes family	Half Moon Bay
Rancho El Corral de Tierra (Earth Corral)	Tiburcio Vásquez, Francisco Guerrero Palomares	Miramar, El Granada, Princeton, Moss Beach, Montara, two state beaches
Rancho San Pedro	Francisco Sánchez	Pacifica, Pacifica State Beach
Rancho Buri Buri	Heirs of José Antonio Sánchez	Colma, South San Francisco, San Bruno, Millbrae, Burlingame
Rancho Cañada de Guadalupe, la Visitación y Rodeo Viejo (Hollow Where Rodeos Were Held Long Ago)	Robert T. Ridley	Daly City, San Francisco
Rancho San Mateo	William Davis Merry Howard	San Mateo, Burlingame, Hillsborough
Rancho Feliz	Domingo Feliz	San Andreas Valley
Rancho de las Pulgas (Fleas)	Luis Argüello family	San Mateo, Belmont, San Carlos, Redwood City, Atherton, Menlo Park, East Palo Alto
Rancho Cañada de Raymundo	María Luisa Soto Coppinger, John Greer, Dennis Martin	Woodside
Rancho El Corte de Madera (Place Where Lumber is Cut)	Maximo Martínez	Portola Valley,[7] extended into Santa Clara County
Rancho Cañada del Corte de Madera (Glen Where Wood is Cut)	Maximo Martínez, Cipriano Thurn	Portola Valley, extended into Santa Clara County

Sites to Visit in San Francisco

California Historical Society, 678 Mission St., San Francisco 415.357.1848

Chinese Historical Society, 644 Broadway, Ste. 402, San Francisco 415.391.1188

The Museum of the City of San Francisco, 2801 Leavenworth St., San Francisco   415.928.0289

Presidio of San Francisco Museum, Main Post, Lincoln Blvd. and Funston Av., San Francisco 415.561.4323

San Francisco Maritime Museum, Beach & Polk streets, San Francisco   415.556.3002

Society of California Pioneers Museum, 300 Fourth St., San Francisco   415.957.1849

Wells Fargo History Museum, 420 Montgomery Street, San Francisco 415.396.2619

San Francisco Convention & Visitors Bureau, 201 Third St., Ste. 900, San Francisco, CA 94103 415.974.6900

AREA WITHIN PRESENT-DAY CITY AND COUNTY OF SAN FRANCISCO

In 1850 the area within the present-day City and County of San Francisco[8] was in the midst of a population explosion. In its earliest days, San Francisco had consisted of three settlements separated from one another by the city's more than 40 hills, many of which were quite steep–some even much steeper than they are today.[9] The three original settlements were the Presidio of San Francisco, *Misión San Francisco de Asís*, and the small coastal village called *El Parage de Yerba Buena* (The Place of the Good Grass).[10] Yerba Buena had been renamed San Francisco in 1847, echoing the name of its bay, presidio, and mission.

San Francisco Bay

Sergeant José de Ortega was the first non-Native American to view San Francisco Bay in 1769, while on a land expedition in search of the "lost" bay of Monterey. But neither he nor his leader, Gaspar de Portolá, appreciated the value of the discovery because they were focused on locating the Monterey Bay. In 1775 Juan Manuel de Ayala and José Cañizares were the first to enter San Francisco Bay by ship. Ayala's exploration of the bay led to the siting of the presidio and mission here in 1776. The Spaniards had called the entrance to the bay *La Boca del Puerto de San Francisco* (The Mouth of the Port of St. Francis), but General John C. Frémont[11] named it *Chrysopylae* (Golden Gate) in 1846.[12]

A number of islands are located in San Francisco Bay, three of which lie within the boundaries of the City and County of San Francisco.[13] Yerba Buena Island has had many names, including Sea Bird Island, Goat Island, and Wood Island. When the State Legislature established the boundaries of San Francisco County in 1850, the island was named Yerba Buena. After 1895 it would again be known as Goat Island, until the U.S. Geographic Board renamed it Yerba Buena in 1931. The island has a convoluted history of claimants seeking ownership rights; Thomas J. Dowling and John C. Jennings are believed to have been living here in 1850. U.S. troops would take possession of Yerba Buena Island in 1867. (Today the tunnel connecting the two spans of the San Francisco-Oakland Bay Bridge that was built in 1936 passes through a hill of this island.)

Adjoining Yerba Buena Island is 400-acre Treasure Island that would not be constructed by the Army Corps of Engineers from mud dredged off the bottom of San Francisco Bay until 1936-37 in preparation for hosting the 1939-40 Golden Gate International Exposition here. It is one of the world's largest artificial islands.

Finally, Alcatraz Island had been named *La Isla de los Alcatraces* in 1775 by Ayala for its original inhabitants, pelicans.[14] The island originally had no soil, vegetation, or water. A few grasses were introduced from the mainland by birds, and in 1848, when the American military began setting up fortified buildings to defend San Francisco Bay, dirt from nearby Angel Island was brought over to form gun battery emplacements. With this dirt, many native grasses and annuals were coincidentally introduced and later, military personnel and inmates of a military prison would bring many other new types of vegetation to the island. (The famous federal Alcatraz Prison was located here from 1934 to 1963.)

Far west of the mouth of San Francisco Bay, the Farallon Islands were discovered by Spanish ships more than two centuries before the bay itself was discovered. They were known by several different names before taking on the name the Farallones (Rocky Islets) in 1774.

The Farallones have always been a breeding ground for birds. During the Gold Rush when eggs were a scarce commodity desired by the miners, the islands became a profitable source of supply for egg hunters. A pharmacist from Maine known as "Doc" Robinson had opened a drug store in San Francisco in 1849 with money he earned selling "murre" eggs collected from the Farallones. Rival egg companies would be established on the islands in 1851, which prospered until all were ousted in 1881 by the federal government.[15]

One adobe wall of the original San Francisco Presidio is encased in the former Officers' Club.

San Francisco was the main port of entrance for the prospectors and mining supplies arriving by sea, as well as being the main port of departure when the miners were ready to return home. In 1850 San Francisco Bay was full of several hundred ships that had been abandoned by their crews who fled to join the rush to the mines. A few of the smaller ships were subsequently used for bay and river traffic or in coastal shipping. Charles Minturn, for example, was operating his side-wheeler *The Senator* and other steamers as a shuttle service between San Francisco and Sacramento. Some of the larger ships served as hotels, stores,[16] offices, or warehouses, and even as jails in San Francisco and Sacramento. Still other ships were dismantled for their canvas and cordage, or used as foundations for new construction. However, most of the ships rotted, sank, or later were used as landfill in order to expand the city into the shallow bay.[17]

The waterfront land and wharves situated on San Francisco Bay were prime pieces of real estate in 1850. Owners built piers lined with shanties and charged exorbitant tolls and taxes on anything that passed over their property—people, animals, vehicles, and cargo. The Central Wharf (also called Long Wharf) had been built in 1848 where present-day Leidesdorff Street, between Clay and Sacramento streets, is located. In 1850 the wharf extended 2,000 feet into the Bay, and Pacific Mail steamers and other large ships anchored here. Other wharves were located on all of the other streets that today are located east of Montgomery between Broadway and California.[18]

In 1844 *Alcalde* William Sturgis Hinckley had built San Francisco's first bay bridge to permit Yerba Buenans, at all stages of the tide, to walk to the embarcadero at Clark's Point at Broadway and Battery streets. Transbay ferry service on the *Kangaroo* began in 1850, with the establishment of a route between San Francisco and the Oakland Estuary.

Presidio of San Francisco

Juan Bautista de Anza had done the original surveying and chose the sites for the Presidio of San Francisco and *Misíon San Francisco de Asís* in early 1776, but it was his lieutenant, José Joaquín Moraga and Father Francisco Palou who actually established the two institutions during the summer of that year. The presidio was never adequately maintained, and its adobe buildings and fortifications had stood in ruins since 1840. When the Mexican-American War broke out in 1846, U.S. military forces occupied Yerba Buena and the Presidio, and in 1850 the U.S. government formally established a military reservation here.[19] All that remains of the original Presidio today are a few durable cannon barrels and one adobe wall encased in the former Officers' Club. In 1850, unlike today, the hills on the Presidio land were barren sand dunes; the eucalyptus, acacia, pine, cypress, and bamboo trees would not be planted until the 1880s. Today many post-1850 historical structures remain that may be viewed on the Main Post Walk, including one that houses the Presidio Museum.

Mission Dolores

Misíon San Francisco de Asís, also known as *Misíon de los Dolores*, was established in 1776. The mission, located five miles from the city center, had been linked to the village by a road approximating today's Grant Avenue–the city's oldest street. The mission was sited at the edge of a lake, now filled in, and close to a fresh-water stream, but it lacked many of the other amenities essential for maintaining a mission–wood, grazing land, good soil, and an adequate climate for growing crops. For this reason a southern outpost was established in the southern portion of the county in present-day San Mateo County.

In 1850 the mission consisted of a few deteriorating buildings, including the former convent in which a tavern was operating. The Mission Dolores structure standing today was constructed between 1788 and 1791.

Fort Mason and Fort Point

Fort Mason was established as a military reservation in 1850 on the site of a 1797 Spanish fortification. It would become a major shipping point for American soldiers during the Civil War. Several homes built in the 1850s remain today in the Fort Mason Historic District.

Fort Point was built between 1853 and 1861 where the Spanish had built their adobe fort known as *El Castillo de San Joaquin* in 1793-94, but which the Mexican Army abandoned in 1835. The Spanish built their fort atop a high white cliff, but the Americans leveled off the cliff and constructred Fort Point at sea level.[20]

City of San Francisco

The English Captain William A. Richardson[21] had settled Yerba Buena Cove under an agreement with the Mexican government to teach the young Spaniards the skills of navigation and carpentry. After marrying the daughter of *Don* Ignacio Martínez, *commandante* of the San Francisco Presidio, and starting his family, Richardson settled his family in a tent on a site along present-day Grant Avenue–the first structure of any kind beyond the presidio and mission. Three months later he built a board house, and in 1836 he built the adobe *Casa Grande* of Yerba Buena, which would remain the largest building in the town until 1848. His home survived several fires, but not the 1906 earthquake and fire. By 1850 Richardson and his family had moved to Marin County.

Jacob Primer Leese, San Francisco's second settler, built a redwood house in 1836 where Grant Avenue and Clay Street intersect today—next to the tent occupied by Richardson. It was the center for a large trading business that he and his partners, Spear and Hinckley, operated with the nearby ranchos.

The first *alcalde* of San Francisco, *Don* Francisco de Haro, commissioned the Swiss artist Jean-Jacques Vioget to map out streets for the growing town in 1839. Vioget created the grid pattern north of Market by mapping out the eight-block area between Montgomery, Sacramento, Grant, and Pacific streets. In 1847 Jasper O'Farrell surveyed lots for the city so that they could be sold to raise revenues. By 1849 most of the lots were sold.

Mission Dolores is one of the oldest buildings in San Francisco.

O'Farrell deviated from Vioget's grid pattern in order to include the trail to the mission, which was at a diagonal to the grid. The confusing result was that San Francisco's Market Street runs at acute angles to all streets to the north, but at right angles to all streets to the south. O'Farrell also mapped the beach and "water" lots located in Yerba Buena Cove. The original line of Yerba Buena Cove's beach is marked by Montgomery Street; O'Farrell's map showed several hundred lots that were actually submerged at high tide. The city auctioned off subdivided mudflats in the cove's shallows, thus encouraging the new owners to fill the "water lots" with refuse and sand from leveled sand hills.[22] These lots would eventually become valuable pieces of property. By 1854 the shoreline moved six blocks to the east and was finally fixed by a seawall construction project that continued from 1877 to 1914.

O'Farrell was the first to name any streets. He chose the names of prominent townspeople like Brannan, Bryant, Howard, Harrison, Leavenworth, and Hyde; prominent Californians like Vallejo, Larkin, and Sutter; or men prominent in the American conquest of California like Kearny, Stockton, Fremont, Jones, Montgomery, Dupont, and Taylor.

In 1850 San Francisco's roads were unpaved and thus, muddy in the winter and dusty in the summer, and always cluttered with litter as well as cargo due to the shortage of warehouses. Enacting ordinances for street improvements was one of the first orders of business undertaken by the governmental bodies created in April 1850. (San Francisco county government was established on April 1, 1850, and the city was incorporated on April 15th.) By the end of the year, many of the streets in the business district were graded and planked.

In 1850 few of the buildings were personal residences, although more and more prefabricated houses were being imported to fill the void left when carpenters departed for the Gold Country. The owners of these houses rented them out for profit.

Hotels, restaurants, and other business establishments abounded. The hotels were expensive, but not because they were luxurious. The hotels and makeshift lodging houses were mere plank and canvas structures with narrow bunks for the guests to sleep on in their own bedding. The St. Francis Hotel was the only hotel providing sheets on its beds.

Jasper O'Farrell (1817-1875)

• Civil engineer from Ireland

• Arrived in San Francisco in 1843

• Appointed Surveyor-General of Alta California

• Laid out several Mexican ranchos; surveyed Benicia and San Francisco

• Street in his gridiron plan was later named for him

The spacious adobe Custom House with a red tile roof[23] was located on Portsmouth Square, San Francisco's oldest public plaza, named in honor of the USS Portsmouth, the ship from which Captain John B. Montgomery and his men disembarked to occupy the town in 1846.[24] The treeless plaza located between Kearny, Washington, Grant, and Clay streets was the social center of the city, sporting a flagstaff and a platform for public speaking; it usually was cluttered with provision booths, piles of building materials, and roving animals. (A slaughterhouse and corral were built about a half mile from Portsmouth Square where cattle and sheep were butchered daily.)

A number of two-story wood and adobe buildings, primarily gambling houses, but secondarily hotels, surrounded the plaza, including the Portsmouth House, the City Hotel, the American Hotel, the Parker House, and the El Dorado. The latter two were among the most famous saloons and gambling establishments in the city. The Jenny Lind Theater replaced the Parker House during 1850. Most of these buildings were destroyed by fire several times, but invariably rose again out of the ashes.

Also sited on the plaza were a store that sold stationery, newspapers, and books (8,000 volumes) and the post office. Long queues of people seeking word from home formed several lines at the post office once every two weeks. "Steamer Day," an institution peculiar to San Francisco in the 1850s, took place on the first and the sixteenth of each month. The week before these two days, mail and millions of dollars-worth of gold dust were prepared for loading on the outgoing steamer, and the homesick residents anxiously awaited the arrival of letters, newspapers, and business communications on the steamer inbound from the East Coast.

Union Square, the heart of San Francisco's downtown area today, was set aside for public use in January 1850 by the city's first mayor, John White Geary. (It did not take on its name until 1860 when pro-Union meetings were held here.) Nearby, on Maiden Lane, Mygatt, Bryant & Co. opened the first bathhouse. Those who lived in bathless hotels and homes could bathe here, indulging in a once a week cleansing, usually on Saturday or Sunday night.

Many of the hills in San Francisco, especially Pacific Heights and Russian, Rincon, and Nob hills, have colorful, interesting histories–but not until after 1850. However, the history of Telegraph Hill, originally known as *Loma Alta* (High Hill), began as early as 1846. In that year, Captain Montgomery had a battery–a fortification equipped with heavy guns–built on the east side of the hill. This battery is the derivation of the name for Battery Street.

Since 1849 *Loma Alta* had been used as a point from which to observe incoming vessels; it sometimes was called "Signal Hill." In September 1849, a two-story house was built on the top from which the resident observers could report about the incoming ships; a semaphore–a mechanical apparatus for giving signals–sat on top of the house. It was from Signal Hill that, on October 29, 1850, the signal to announce the news that California had been admitted to the Union was given.[25]

Finally, *Loma Alta* was quarried for ship ballast, which would be used to build streets in ports throughout the world upon the ship's return to its homeland.[26] Houses were beginning to be built near the base of the hill in 1850, first by Chileans and Mexicans, and later by Italian families.

At the outskirts of the city, encampments of canvas shanties and tents housing men on their way to the mines were sheltered from the winds by the sand hills surrounding three little hollows, named "Happy," "Pleasant," and "Contented" valleys. Happy Valley, for example, was located between First, Second, Market, and Mission streets; and Pleasant Valley lay between Mission and Howard streets. In the winter of 1849-50 close to a thousand tents populated each valley. Unfortunately, the overcrowding and unsanitary conditions resulted in a high incidence of dysentery and cholera, often fatal. Dr. Peter Smith owned the private City Hospital, where many of the sick were treated. He contracted with the city to care for the destitute for $4 per person, per day. The hospital was destroyed by fire in October 1850.

The Mission Bay district of today was a marshland in 1850. Marshes, with intersecting sloughs, penetrated as far north as present-day Mission Street between Seventh and Eighth streets, and Folsom Street between Fourth and Eighth streets. The marshland extended to the foot of the Potrero Hills, as well. Mission Creek, which was a navigable stream between 1854 and 1874 but exists no longer, was the cause for the eastward curve of the numbered streets south of Eleventh Street.

Several cemeteries had been laid out in San Francisco before 1850, but with the Gold Rush and the swelling population, land became such a precious commodity that in order to create more space, cemeteries were first moved farther to the west and finally south to San Mateo County. San Francisco would ban cemeteries in the city in 1900.

Between December 1849 and June 1851, six major fires destroyed various parts of San Francisco—at a cost exceeding $9.5 million. Sadly, many of the city's fires were intentionally set, either to destroy a competitor's merchandise or as a means for water purveyors to earn enormous sums by inflating the price of water sold in cartloads to extinguish the fires.

By mid-1850, seven volunteer fire companies were organized, alarm boxes were installed throughout the city, and a number of city ordinances were passed to organize a fire department, establish fines for refusing to assist in extinguishing flames, and to require every household to keep six water buckets in readiness for future fires. Following the fires of the early 1850s, wood construction would be banned from the central district and brick buildings were fitted with iron shutters. Cisterns for collecting and storing rainwater also were built at strategic locations.

Nonetheless, most of San Francisco's Gold Rush era housing was destroyed in subsequent fires, or later in the great earthquake and fire of 1906. The Jackson Square Historic District, located between Sansome, Washington, Kearny, Columbus, and Broadway streets, was the only exception. Having escaped the disastrous fire of 1906, today it is home to a neighborhood of surviving 1850s and 60s Gold Rush-era buildings. Some of these buildings were brick warehouses that wholesale interior decorating firms have renovated; others were hotels or other types of establishments, including the French consulate, that today serve as offices for law firms, advertising agencies, and antique dealers.[27]

In January 1847, Sam Brannan had published the first issue of *The California Star,* San Francisco's first newspaper. In 1849 it joined with *The Californian*[28] and was called the *Alta California.* Both newspapers had temporarily suspended publication during the early days of the Gold Rush because their staff, subscribers, and

Sam Brannan (1819-1889)

- Arrived in San Francisco in 1846 as the leader of a contingent of 238 Mormons, including 100 children, to found a colony outside the U.S. to escape persecution—only to discover that California had been taken over by the U.S.

- Established California's first flour mill and San Francisco's first newspaper, *The California Star*

- Embezzled church money and was tried by California's first jury (a dead locked jury resulted)

- After noticing people paying with gold for purchases in his Sutter's Fort store, he bought up all of the tools needed to mine for gold and then passed through the streets of San Francisco announcing the discovery of gold on the American River

- Invested heavily in carpet tacks, which turned out to be much in demand in the era of canvas and muslin housing

- Organized the Society of California Pioneers; president of the 1851 Vigilance Committee

- Owned and built most of the first buildings in Sacramento along Front Street

- Became the state's first millionaire through real estate and other investments, but heavy drinking led to his demise

- Died in poverty in San Diego County

**Thomas Oliver Larkin
(1802-1858)**

• Born in Massachusetts; orphaned at 15; became store-keeper and office holder by age of 20

• Arrived in California in 1832 as a merchant at the prodding of his half-brother, John Rogers Cooper

• Quickly became a successful merchant and clearing house for notes and drafts of other traders in the area

• One of few foreign residents to become wealthy and powerful without becoming a Catholic and Mexican citizen and without marrying a Mexican woman

• First U.S. Consul to Mexican Province of California, 1844-48; hoped to bring California peaceably into the Union

• Delegate of State Constitutional Convention

• Married to widowed Rachel Holmes, the first American woman to live in California

• Fathered first child of American parents to be born in California and eight more. (First child died in infancy, one month following her parents' marriage.)

• Operated a wheat mill, involved in lumbering and ranching, extensive landowner throughout northern California, bought and sold building lots, chief founder and promoter (with Semple) of the town of Benicia, invested in railroads and a quicksilver mine; international trader—one of the first millionaires in California

• Moved to San Francisco in January 1850, moved to New York in April 1850, returned to San Francisco in 1853 and died there as one of the richest and one of the most highly respected men in California

advertisers left for the gold fields; the *Alta California* would continue publication until 1891. During 1850 a number of smaller newspapers began publication, including the French *Le Californien*, *The Journal of Commerce*, the *San Francisco Daily Herald*, the *California Courier*, *La Gazette Republicaine*, and the *Public Balance*.

A private school for children had been established in San Francisco in 1846 and a semi-public school—one that charged some tuition and was not under complete government control—was opened in 1847. In October 1849, John C. Pelton, a young Massachusetts schoolteacher and Baptist church layman, opened California's first free "common school" that depended entirely on voluntary subscriptions and donations for its support and was free to poor children. In the spring of 1850 the city council adopted an ordinance making his school a free public school, the first in California, and providing a salary of $500 a month, payable in city scrip, which had a cash value of about 30 cents on the dollar. Another school opened in 1850 in Happy Valley and would become the first school operated under the city public school system in November 1851. The founders of this school were W. D. M. Howard, a prominent merchant; Thomas J. Nevins, a lawyer from New Hampshire and later the first superintendent of schools in San Francisco; and Reverend Samuel Hopkins Willey. (Reverend Willey was the pastor and educator from New England who, until moving to San Francisco in the spring of 1850, taught in Monterey's first public school and established the state's first public library there.)

A number of churches had been established in San Francisco by 1850. St. Francis Church was established in 1849 and today is the second oldest Roman Catholic parish in San Francisco. (The present building was erected in 1859.) The First Presbyterian Church was established in 1849 and in the fall of 1850 a church building was brought around the Horn from New York. The freight, building, and lot cost an estimated $16,000. Other churches established in 1849 included the First Baptist Church, the First Congregational Church, the Episcopalian Trinity Church, and Grace Chapel, a Protestant Episcopal church. Upon his arrival from Monterey in the spring of 1850, Reverend Willey established the Howard Street Presbyterian Church in a carpenter's shop in Happy Valley. The Congregation Emanu–El was founded in July. The first Jewish religious services were held in 1849 when 40 pioneers celebrated Yom Kippur.

The churches' primary goal during 1850 was to abolish Sunday gambling. Gambling had become a profession for some with stakes sometimes rising as high as $16,000 in gold dust. However, the ordinary stakes of from 50 cents to five dollars allowed even the common man to play. In September 1850, the Town Council prohibited gambling on Sunday and, in November, the Grand Jury condemned all gambling and urged, as well, that something be done about the numerous houses of prostitution. One Methodist street preacher, the Reverend William Taylor, was a particularly effective reformer. He would set up a box in front of a gambling house and sing Methodist hymns or deliver a sermon.

The Englishman, Stephen C. Massett, had been the first professional entertainer in San Francisco, running a one-man show in 1849. A minstrel company and Joseph Rowe's Olympic Circus followed him. The circus opened in October 1849, performing in a crude amphitheater on Kearny Street that seated up to 1500 patrons.

San Franciscans sampled the first legitimate theater in January 1850 when the Eagle Theater Company, flooded out of business in Sacramento, performed *The Wife and Charles II* at Washington Hall. The positive response to this type of entertainment prompted the opening of additional venues throughout 1850, including the National, Phoenix, and Jenny Lind theaters. Rowe placed a platform across one end of his circus tent and substituted actors for gymnasts and animal acts in a new and improved Olympic Circus, and Dr. D. G. Robinson started a "dramatic museum" in partnership with James Evrard, performing satires.

The existence of numerous gambling houses, saloons, wholesale liquor establishments, houses of prostitution, rival ethnic gangs, as well as the occurrence of suspicious fires and bribery schemes meant that crime was rampant in San Francisco, thus providing ample work for the numerous attorneys in town. A host of other entrepreneurs were profiting from the Gold Rush and the burgeoning population in San Francisco in 1850. Manufacturing industries such as Levi Strauss & Co. were operating, meeting the needs of the gold seekers by making "Levi" blue jeans–canvas pants made from sail canvas–and supplying tent material. The Selby Smelter–with its blast furnaces that separated metals from their ores–was established by Thomas Selby during 1850, and an iron foundry company, Pacific Iron Works, conducted an iron molding trade.

Isodore Boudin had been creating the "Original San Francisco Sourdough French Bread" since 1849. His original French recipe is still used today by the Boudin Bakery. Domenico "Domingo" Ghirardelli, an experienced Italian confectioner and chocolate trader, had established a base supply store on Battery Street in 1849 to complement the two chocolate stores he was operating elsewhere, one in Hornitos in Mariposa County and one in Stockton in San Joaquin County. He would permanently settle in San Francisco late in 1850 and later became the world famous chocolate maker and builder of the landmark Ghirardelli Square.

Grocers, butchers such as Charles H. Rice and George W. Scribner, and other enterprising merchants like the New York jeweler, Immanuel Charles Christian Russ, were operating out of tents. Russ and his family would build a hotel near the site of the Russ Building located on Bush Street today.

Henry M. Naglee had opened the first bank in the city on Portsmouth Square in 1849 and was followed by the banking house of Palmer, Cook & Co. in 1850. Adams & Co. Express, an established East Coast company, provided banking and mail services to the mines. (Tycoons Henry Wells and William Fargo would open their first Wells, Fargo & Co. bank in 1852.)

Finally, other early entrepreneurs included land agents such as Glayson & Co. and Stevenson & Parker; merchants like Mellus and Howard (W. D. M. Howard); W. H. Davis; Ward & Smith; Roland, Gelston & Co.; and Sherman & Ruckel; and ship chandlers Webster, De Graaf & Owens.

Chinese immigrants had been arriving in San Francisco since 1848, but slowly at first. They were seeking their fortunes in California, which was referred to as *Gum San* (Land of the Golden Mountain). Most soon left the city for the gold fields, however, and it would be 1851 before many returned to San Francisco to take advantage of the enterprise opportunities available in the booming city. Chinese restaurants such as Celestial Jon-Ling on Jackson Street had opened in the area of present-day

Jean-Jacques Vioget (1799-1855)

- Swiss-born soldier, sailor, surveyor, and artist
- Arrived in San Francisco in 1837 as master of his own ship to trade with *Californios*
- Made first official survey of Yerba Buena in 1839, with the streets not at right angles by 2-1/2 degrees
- His survey was later incorporated into the survey made by Jasper O'Farrell
- Mapped *Nueva Helvetia* for John A. Sutter
- Spent his last years in San Jose

William Davis Merry Howard (1819-1856)

- Boston-born merchant who arrived in San Francisco in 1839
- Owned a rancho in present-day San Mateo County and dealt in the hide trade
- Formed a general merchandise trading company partnership with Henry Mellus that became one of the most active and successful businesses in San Francisco
- Organized the first fire company
- Active in creating schools
- First president of the Society of California Pioneers; one of organizers of the first Vigilante Committee
- Served on Board of Supervisors

Chinatown as early as 1849 and Chinese laundries soon began operations. Although most Chinese never intended to settle in California permanently, many eventually did and Chinatown would become the rich cultural center that it remains today. The museum of the Chinese Historical Society of America provides evidence of the important role of the Chinese in the settlement of the city and other parts of the West.

Laundry services in San Francisco were very expensive in 1850. The average price was $8 for each dozen items, regardless of whether the article was a handkerchief or a shirt. It was not uncommon for linen to be sent by ship to Honolulu or Canton to be washed and ironed, a process that took several months. The first washerwomen in San Francisco had been Mexicans and Native Americans. They worked at a pond located at the foot of Russian Hill that came to be known as Washerwomen's Bay. Because the pay was good, a number of men began setting up a large-scale industry, using large kettles for boiling the clothes and doing the ironing in tents.

Several celebrations were held in San Francisco in 1850. A grand Fourth of July celebration was held on the Portsmouth Square. Reverend Taylor delivered the oration and the firemen wore their new uniforms for the first time. On this day, the original Mexican flagstaff was replaced by a gift from the citizens of Portland, Oregon, an 111-foot high flagpole. (The Mexican flagstaff was relocated to the new Custom House at the corner of California and Montgomery streets.)

October 29th was a full-day admission-to-the-Union celebration that began with a sunrise 13-gun salute, a parade, which included a group of Chinese dressed in their colorful clothing and carrying gaily painted paper umbrellas; a sunset 31-gun salute, and finally, an evening grand ball sponsored by the citizens of San Francisco. (Unfortunately, the happy occasion was marred by the explosion of the steamer *Sagamore*, on which 40 people lost their lives as it cast off from the Central Wharf on its way to Stockton.)

San Francisco County Ranchos

Little land within the current boundaries of the City and County of San Francisco had been granted to individuals during the Spanish-Mexican rancho days. Most of it either was reserved for mission and presidio use or it was covered with sand dunes that were unfit for grazing or any type of agriculture. Of the three ranchos granted, *Rancho Rincon de las Salinas y Potrero Viejo* was the most interesting. A great portion of it was marshland penetrated by an estuary of San Francisco Bay known as Islais Creek. A portion of it may even have been a peninsula in 1850. The 938-foot Mount Davidson, the highest peak in San Francisco, was situated on *Rancho San Miguel.*

San Francisco would continue its development as an important industrial, travel, and financial center after 1850. Its colorful history requires entire books, but some of the more significant events not mentioned elsewhere in this chapter include the invention by the Scottish wire cable manufacturer Andrew Hallidie in 1873 of the world's first cable car; the creation of Golden Gate Park on the 1,017 acres of sand dunes by John McLaren in the 1890s; and the birth of the United Nations in the War Memorial Opera House in 1945.

SAN FRANCISCO COUNTY RANCHOS

NAME OF RANCHO	GRANTEE AND/OR 1850 OWNER	1850 AND/OR CURRENT SITES
Rancho Rincon de las Salinas y Potrero Viejo (Corner of the Salt Marshes and Old Pasture)	Carmen Cibrian de Bernal and her son, José Jesús Bernal	Potrero district
Rancho San Miguel	José de Jesus Noé	Noe Valley, Twin Peaks
Rancho Laguna de la Merced (Lake of Mercy)	Heirs of Francisco de Haro	Lake Merced, extending into San Mateo County

Notes ❧ SAN FRANCISCO COUNTY

1

In later years, San Francisco would also need San Mateo County as a place to bury its dead. Land became such a precious commodity during the Gold Rush that in order to create more space, cemeteries were first moved farther to the west and finally south to San Mateo County. Colma became the central burial ground for the area when the first cemetery opened in 1887.

2

The seals were almost extinct by 1869 due to wholesale slaughtering. After the State of California purchased the property in 1971, the seals began coming ashore once again.

3

Half Moon Bay officially lies between Pillar Point and Miramontes Point. The man-made rock breakwater would not be built in Princeton's Pillar Point Harbor until 1962.

4

See Leese sidebar on page 173.

5

Today Redwood City is quite different than it was in 1850. Redwood Creek flows under the city, and Redwood Slough is filled in. City Hall stands on what used to be called "The Island" because the area was an acre of firm land located between two branches of the slough. The neighboring Redwood Shores and Foster City, to the north and adjacent to San Mateo, would be created from extensive landfill dredged from the bottom of the Bay within the last 35 years. Levees were built in the mud flats adjacent to San Mateo and the enclosed area was permitted to dry. Farmers subsequently grew hay here and in 1964, Foster City was built. Redwood Shores adjacent to and part of Redwood City took a similar course and had its first structures by 1968.

6

The lumbering area called "the Red Woods" lay between the foothills and the top of the mountains. By 1855, there were close to a dozen sawmills and shingle mills in the area. As the timber was removed from the lower levels, the mills were moved up the canyons and over the mountain. The timber industry, which supplied the settlers of Santa Clara Valley and San Francisco with building materials for houses, commercial buildings, and wharves, would flourish into the late 1860s and early 1870s, when the best redwood timber was depleted. The trees located in these lumbering areas today include second-growth redwoods.

7

The Alpine Beer Garden that operates today on Alpine Road would be built in 1852 by Félix Buelna, the son of Antonio, and serve as the gathering place for local Mexicans. It was conveniently situated at Alpine Road's intersection with Arrastradero Road, which had been a short cut to Santa Clara and San Jose since the 1830s. The tavern has been known by many different names and owned by various owners throughout its long history.

8

When San Mateo County was created from the southern portion of San Francisco County in 1856, the government began operating as the consolidated City and County of San Francisco.

9

Quarrying and grading in the 1860s and 70s would reduce the size of many of San Francisco's hills.

10

The minty *yerba buena* was among the few plants that grew on the sand dunes. The name Yerba Buena had been given to a cove in 1792 by Captain George Vancouver, the first Englishman to sail into San Francisco Bay.

11

See Frémont sidebar on page 253.

12

John C. Frémont was comparing San Francisco Bay to the harbor of Byzantium (later Constantinople) known as *Chrysoceras* (Golden Horn).

13

Two tiny points of Angel Island lie within the northwestern boundary of the City and County of San Francisco, but the rest of the island is located in Marin County; Angel Island is described in that chapter.

14

Actually, a Spanish mapmaker's error may have confused Alcatraz with Yerba Buena Island.

15

Biologists today estimate that 500,000 adult murres raised chicks on the island before the Gold Rush. Today only about 80,000 adults remain where a wildlife refuge has been created for the protection of seabirds, elephant seals, and sea lions.

9

In 1850 the French Verdier brothers opened a store aboard the ship *Ville de Paris*. This store became the famous City of Paris dry goods store that later operated in the 1896 landmark building on Union Square until 1962. (Neiman Marcus is located here today.)

17

Historians have pinpointed the location of buried ships, and occasionally, as new construction replaces older buildings, remnants of these ships are uncovered.

18

This whole area along the Bay would later be filled in, mostly with sand from the nearby dunes. Meiggs Wharf would be built in 1853 in the area between Mason and Powell streets. This wharf was enclosed by a seawall in 1881 and today the famous Fisherman's Wharf is located just to the east.

19

The U.S. Army would remain in control of the Presidio until 1994 when, as a result of the Base Closure and Realignment Act, the Presidio was transferred to the National Park Service. Parts of the Presidio had earlier become part of the Golden Gate National Recreation Area, the largest park in the world, which was established in 1972 by an act of Congress.

20

Today Fort Point National Historic Site stands beneath the 1937 Golden Gate Bridge and is part of the Golden Gate National Recreation Area.

21

See Richardson sidebar on page 163.

22

Sand fill provided a questionable base; in the winter of 1852, parts of Jackson Street would sink four to five feet. After the 1906 earthquake and fire, rubble from the downtown area–brick, rock, and mortar–was used to fill in the Marina District on the northern edge of the Bay. There were few legal restraints on filling until the Bay Conservation and Development Commission, a state-mandated agency that tightly regulates filling and promotes the recreational use of the Bay, was formed in 1965.

23

A new Custom House was opened during 1850 on the corner of California and Montgomery streets; the old Custom House was then rented out for offices.

24

The American flag was raised in Portsmouth Square in July of 1846 to establish possession of Yerba Buena, and it was through this plaza that Sam Brannan paraded holding a bottle of gold dust above his head shouting, "Gold! Gold! Gold from the American River!"

25

Eight year-old Lillie Hitchcock, the future wealthy eccentric Mrs. Coit, would arrive in San Francisco in 1851. The famous 210-foot Coit Tower, which was built through a $125,000 bequest left to the city by Mrs. Coit upon her death in 1929, has stood atop Telegraph Hill since 1933. Coit Tower commemorates the Gold Rush era semaphore, originally also called a telegraph, not Samuel F. B. Morse's electronic telegraph that later linked the two coasts of the U.S. in 1861.

26

Sansome Street would be cut through Telegraph Hill in 1853. Quarrying and street grading to accommodate San Francisco's grid pattern of streets scarred many of the city's hills. Rincon Hill, in the area between Spear, Second, Folsom, and Brannan streets, was nearly leveled, much of it going into Mission Bay as fill in the 1870s. The "Steam Paddy," a steam-powered shovel attached to a railroad car, was typically employed to grade the sand hills.

27

The district on the perimeter of Jackson Square would become known as the Barbary Coast in the 1860s when its wickedness was compared to the treacherous, pirate-infested waters of the Mediterranean Barbary Coast off Africa. An 1851 building on Montgomery Street, known today as the Belli Building, was originally a tobacco warehouse and later a Barbary Coast melodeon where Lotta Crabtree sang. She was a gold miner's daughter who went on to become one of the wealthiest performers in America. Today, as a result of a California Historical Society-sponsored project spear-headed by local San Franciscan Daniel Bacon, a series of bronze plaques and painted emblems mark a historical 3.8 mile walk called the "Barbary Coast Trail" that connects 20 historic sites. Two printed trail guides are available for purchase at most San Francisco bookstores. (The California Historical Society has a museum and offers programs devoted to various aspects of California history–all open to the public.)

28

The Californian was the first newspaper published in California on August 15, 1846 in Monterey. It had moved to San Francisco in May 1847.

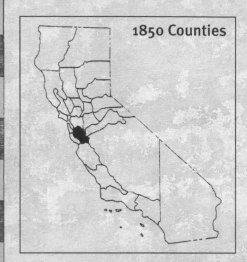

1850 Counties

∝ 1850 ∝
⟨ SANTA CLARA ⟩
COUNTY

Alameda Co.

• Fremont
• Newark

• Palo Alto Alviso •   • Milpitas

Santa Clara Co.

San Mateo Co.

Sunnyvale •

• Santa Clara

• Cupertino   • San Jose
Campbell •

Stanislaus Co.

• Saratoga
• Los Gatos
• New Almaden

Morgan Hill •

• San Martin

Santa Cruz Co.

• Gilroy

San Benito Co.

California
1850

Present-day boundary
variations indicated by

‒ ‒ ‒ ‒ ‒

Settlements/cities of 1850 include: Santa Clara, San José, New Almaden, Gilroy, Alviso, Redwoods
(Saratoga/Campbell area)

SANTA CLARA COUNTY
1850

The geographical area of 1850-Santa Clara County included a portion of present-day Alameda County, namely Rancho Agua Caliente, portions of ranchos Potrero de los Cerritos, Arroyo de la Alameda, and Valle de San Jose, as well as Misión San José. (The ranchos and the mission are included in the Alameda County section of the chapter on Contra Costa County.)

The official U.S. Census of 1850 for the City of San José and Santa Clara County was lost en route to the Census Office; the 1849 county population of nearly 4,000 and the 6,764 counted in 1852 provides a basis for estimating the 1850 population. Californios, Americans, and Europeans were living here, and the uncounted Native American population included the Ohlone and Northern Valley Yokuts. English had recently become the primary language spoken in Santa Clara County.

In 1850 within the current boundaries of Santa Clara County, the former Misión Santa Clara de Asís was located in the township of Santa Clara and the city of San José was serving as the state capital. There were three other townships—Washington, Redwoods, and Gilroy, as well as a port at Alviso, the quicksilver mining settlement of New Almaden, and over 40 ranchos.

Mission Santa Clara

Misión Santa Clara de Asís, founded in 1777, was relocated four times, variously to avoid flooding from the Guadalupe River and then to rebuild after the earthquakes of 1812 and 1818. The fifth church was completed in 1825. After secularization, the buildings fell into disrepair and squatters began occupying most of the land. In 1850 the American government returned the mission to the Catholic church and the Jesuit order of priests took it over.

What may be seen today of the mission is a 1929 concrete replica of the 1825 church that was destroyed by fire in 1926. Part of the altar of the adobe church was saved from the fire and incorporated into the replica, which serves as a church for the community and Santa Clara University. Located in the garden behind the church are an adobe wall from the original cloisters of 1822 and one reconstructed adobe building—the Adobe Lodge—that now serves as the faculty club for the university.

The only original mission building remaining today is the 1800 adobe dwelling that was part of the third mission compound—a continuous row of 30 homes built for Native American families of the Mission Santa Clara. Today the adobe is called the Santa Clara Women's Club Adobe, having served as their clubhouse since 1907.

Sites to Visit in Santa Clara County

Gilroy Historical Museum, 195 Fifth St., Gilroy 408.848.0470

Higuera Adobe, Rancho Higuera Park, Wessex Pl., Milpitas (exterior only)

Mission Santa Clara, Santa Clara University, 500 El Camino Real, Santa Clara 408.554.4023

New Almaden Quicksilver Mining Museum (Casa Grande), 12350 Almaden Rd., New Almaden 408.268.1729

Peralta Adobe, 175 West St. John St., San Jose 408.993.8182

Roberto-Sunol Adobe, 770 Lincoln Av., San Jose (exterior only)

San Jose Historical Museum, Pacific Hotel, 1650 Senter Rd., San Jose 408.287.2290

Santa Clara Women's Club Adobe, 3260 The Alameda, Santa Clara

San Jose Convention and Visitors Bureau, 333 W. San Carlos St., San Jose 95110 408.295.9600

Santa Clara Convention and Visitors Bureau, 1850 Warburton Av., Santa Clara 95050 408.244.9660

Don José Peña owned the adobe in 1850 and his widow would live here until her death in 1883.

Township of Santa Clara

In 1850, American settlers, including previous residents who had ventured to the gold fields, were arriving in large numbers in the township of Santa Clara. No town government was established until 1852, but William Campbell surveyed the town into equal size lots in 1850. Citizens were given one lot on which they were required to build a house within three months. Peleg Rush set up 23 houses, which he imported from Boston.

This is the 1929 replica of the 1825 Mission Santa Clara de Asis that was destroyed by fire in 1926.

This adobe wall is the only remaining portion of the original 1822 cloisters of the Mission Santa Clara. It is located in the garden behind the church.

The Santa Clara Women's Club, the 1800 adobe dwelling that was part of the mission compound, is the only original mission building remaining today.

The Union Hotel was built in 1850, and a tannery was in operation on El Camino Real across from the mission. Dr. H. H. Warburton was Santa Clara's first physician, having established his practice in 1848.

During the winter of 1846, Mrs. Olive Mann Isbell, niece of Horace Mann, the pioneer American educator, had opened the first English language school in California. It was located on the Mission Santa Clara grounds in a former adobe stable, but it was no longer in operation in 1850. A schoolhouse was built during 1850 on Liberty Street and was known as the "little brick schoolhouse." It also was used as a place of worship by all denominations. The first Protestant church would be organized in 1851—the Christian Church, and the first Protestant church building was built in 1853 by the Methodists.

Another educational first would occur in Santa Clara in 1851—establishment of the first college in California—Santa Clara College (Santa Clara University, today). It was founded on the grounds of the decaying mission by the Jesuits. The mission buildings were adapted for use by the school, but were later modified or replaced.

City of San José

In November 1777, Lieutenant José Joaquin Moraga, with 14 settlers and their families, arrived in the Santa Clara Valley to found *El Pueblo de San José de Guadalupe* (Town of San Jose on the Wolf River),[1] the first purely civil community in California. Originally established on a different site closer to the river and the mission, *El Pueblo* became the City of San José by an act of the State Legislature on March 27, 1850, and was serving as the first state capital.

In 1847 two brothers, William and Thomas Campbell, had surveyed the former mission lands. A town plat of equal size lots was drawn up and the parcels sold.

San José had a population of approximately 1,000 in 1850. A few wooden houses were built just outside town; the old adobes in the center of town were partially hidden by the many wooden shacks and tents that had sprung up with the arrival of the State Legislature on December 15, 1849. The first state capitol—the State House—was located in an 1849 adobe located across from the town plaza on Market and San Antonio streets. The two-story building, built as a hotel by Pierre Sainsevain[2] of Santa Cruz County and Zepheryn Rochon, a fellow Frenchman, was the only building in San José large enough to serve as the State House.

In 1850 the cost of living in San José was higher than normal due to supply and demand. Not only was there a sudden increase in population due to the Legislature being in session here, but also many fields had gone untended when the local men fled to the gold fields in 1848 and 1849. Consequently, staples had to be shipped in from San Francisco. The legislators were paid $16 per day in state scrip, which only San José merchants redeemed at face value. In other cities, such scrip was only worth 40 cents on the dollar.

Heavy rains between December 1849 and March 1850 kept the legislators captive in San José, as impassable roads prevented them from returning home, even for the three-day Christmas recess. A few social events took place during the members' time in San José, including the first state ball (which few women were able to attend due to the inclement weather), a bull and bear fight in the old pueblo ring, a short-lived "gold rush" on Coyote Creek, and a $10,000 horse race. On October 19, 1850, Governor Peter Burnett personally delivered the news to the Legislature that California had been admitted to the Union on September 9th.

The legislators were generally under-whelmed by the offerings in San José. After some debate, both houses voted to move the capital to General Manuel Vallejo's donated property in Vallejo in Solano County. Thus, San José was the seat of state government only from late 1849 to mid-1851. The third Legislature would convene at Vallejo on January 5, 1852.

A town hall stood in the intersection of present-day Market and Post streets. It served as the first courthouse until the city council declared it a public nuisance in 1850 and had it razed. The courthouse was then moved to the 1849 adobe jail on Market Street next to the State House. Dr. Joshua Winn Redman was the first county judge. A considerable number of attorneys from all parts of the world were practicing here. Austrian John W. Kottinger was acting as an interpreter for the court. The jail was owned by the City of San José and also housed the county administration office until late in 1850 when both the court and the administration offices were moved to a building on First Street opposite Fountain Alley. Josiah Belden, a mercantile businessman from St. Louis, was serving as San José's first mayor. He had arrived in California in 1841 with the Bidwell-Bartleson party and established a successful mercantile store here in 1848.

The town plaza was located where Plaza Park is enclosed by South Market Street today. Bull and bear fights were held on Sundays either in this town plaza or in St. James Park.

Peter Hardeman Burnett (1807-1895)

- Native of Tennessee; lawyer in Missouri before leaving for Oregon in 1843
- Arrived in California from Oregon in 1848, mining in Butte County for awhile
- Established a successful law practice in San José and speculated in the development of Alviso
- First Governor of the American State of California
- Resigned in late 1850 as a result of certain personal prejudices
- Justice of the State Supreme Court
- President of the Pacific Bank in San Francisco

Zachariah Jones was operating a hotel in an adobe just east of the plaza called Half Moon; the City Hotel was located on First Street and the Bella Union Saloon stood on Santa Clara Street. Several stores were conducting business, including Lightson & Weber on Santa Clara and Lightson streets; a Chilean firm on San Pedro Street; Hoppe, Hawkins & Company, a two-story general merchandise store on Market Street; and Antonio Suñol's general merchandise store that he operated out of his residence on Market Street.

San José would have some educational firsts like Santa Clara, its neighbor to the west. In 1851 the first chartered institution of higher learning in California—the California Wesleyan College—was established at the corner of San Fernando and Second streets. After several name changes and moves, it operates today as the University of the Pacific in Stockton. The College of Notre Dame, a Catholic college for young women, was organized in the same year. It was relocated in 1923 from San José to Belmont in San Mateo County.[3]

There were no public elementary schools in San José in 1850, but the Moreland School, the oldest known rural school district in California, would be established in 1851 as a subscription school, meeting in private homes in San José. The first public schools of the county were organized in San José in 1853.

A small adobe Catholic church had been established by the Franciscan Fathers in 1803; it existed where the 1877 St. Joseph's Catholic Church stands today at Market and San Fernando streets. The First Presbyterian Church and the Methodist Episcopal Church were organized in 1849, and the Baptist Church was formed in 1850. The Presbyterian services were held in the town hall until it was torn down; the Baptists met in the State House, and the Methodists constructed a building during 1850 on Third Street.

The California State Library was created on January 24, 1850 by the State Legislature. By July, 135 volumes were acquired through donations made by Colonel Jonathan Drake Stevenson, Senator Thomas Jefferson Green, and General John C. Frémont.

The *State Journal* was the first newspaper published in Santa Clara County—the first issue rolled off the press on December 19, 1850. Published by James B. Devoe, it was discontinued when the Legislature adjourned in 1851. The first theater would not be established in San José until 1859.

Since 1847, a fire regulation had been in effect prohibiting the use of straw, grass, tules, mustard, reeds, willows, canvas, or cotton cloth in new construction within the downtown area. Haystacks were also prohibited. The tradition of bucket brigades and fire wardens began during 1850 and a volunteer fire company called Fire Engine No. 1 was formed. It would be 1854 before an engine actually was purchased. Harry Bee performed the duties of marshal, constable, and sheriff.

Since mission times, an *acequia* (irrigation ditch) about four feet wide had run in a zigzag course from the Guadalupe River between present-day San Pedro and Santa Clara streets. A city officer supervised this stream so that everyone who was entitled to water was provided a fair share. Building sites were chosen along the course of the *acequia*, which supplied water for the houses and garden plots. An 1850 town ordinance provided for a bridge across the *acequia* at Santa Clara Street. The *acequia* would serve San José's needs until it was replaced by the successful boring of artesian wells in the early 1850s.

A marshy frog-pond was located near the corner of present-day First and Santa Clara streets. Hundreds of squirrels lived in the pueblo and fleas were common. Cattle and horses wandered about the streets that were muddy in the winter and dusty in the spring and summer. Mustard grew everywhere—the stalks as high as young trees.

A number of Europeans had settled in and around San José in the 1830s and many overland pioneer families arrived in the early 1840s. Like many other towns in California, San José lost much of its male population with the discovery of gold, but by 1850 many had returned and many newcomers arrived to take advantage of the commercial opportunities available in the area. John W. Whisman, for example, had established California's first stage service in the fall of 1849—a nine-hour run between San José and San Francisco. The winter rains forced him to modify his route; he transported his passengers to Alviso where they boarded steamers bound for San Francisco, Oakland, and Sacramento. Whisman reestablished his stage route up the peninsula in the spring of 1850, and the firm of Ackley & Maurison established a similar service three times a week. That summer, Whisman sold his business to Warren F. Hall and Jared B. Crandell, two stage operators from Mexico.

Peter Quivey had brought his family to San José from New York in 1847. He built the first frame house in San José from redwood timber he cut in the Santa Cruz Mountains. His family had originally been part of the Donner party, but by traveling Sundays and late at night, they arrived at Sutter's Fort much before tragedy struck the rest of the party. Quivey became a prosperous and influential citizen, owning the first hotel in San José. With a partner, William Wilson, he owned thousands of acres of cattle land on the slopes of the Mount Hamilton range.

James F. Reed and his family completed the journey with the ill-fated Donner party, arriving in San José in 1846. After a successful visit to the gold fields in 1848, Reed returned to San José and invested heavily in real estate. A large portion of downtown San José, south of San Jose State University, was originally land subdivided by Reed, who named the streets for family members.

Adolf Pfister was a prominent merchant who had arrived in 1847. Pioneer nurseryman and silk culturist Louis Prevost had arrived from France in 1849, as had pioneer gunsmith Felix Sourisseau. The Frenchman Louis Pellier also arrived in 1849. After trying his luck at mining, he established a nursery in the fall of 1850 called "City Gardens." In 1856, he and his brothers would introduce the French prune and become the founders of California's prune industry.

Judge Henry Skinner arrived in 1850, bringing the Skinner seedling for the cultivation of apples. Dr. Benjamin Cory, San José's first physician, had arrived in 1847 from Ohio. He combined a career of medicine, public service (including state legislator), and mining.

Another doctor, Dr. Bascom, from Kentucky, and his wife and children had arrived in San José in 1849. Dr. Bascom had difficulty competing with Dr. Cory, but Mrs. Bascom supplemented their income by running a high-class boarding house out of their home, which came to be known as "Slapjack Hall." They had an African American cook whom Dr. Bascom had purchased for $800 even though he was legal-

James Alexander Forbes (1804-1881)

- Scottish; arrived in California in 1831 after living in Chile for awhile; fluent in Spanish
- Served as manager and attorney for Mission Santa Clara
- Served as Hudson Bay Company's agent
- British Vice-Consul in Monterey
- Sometimes acted as intermediary between fighting *Californios* and Americans
- Married into prominent Galindo family; 12 children
- Investor in his uncle's New Almaden Quicksilver Mine and real estate in Santa Clara Valley
- Builder and operator of Santa Rosa Flour Mill in Forbestown—present-day Los Gatos
- Declared bankruptcy, losing the mill and a large fortune
- Developed fruit orchards in the valley

ly free in California. He would stay with the family for four years. While the Legislature was in session, legislators, ministers, and teachers were among Mrs. Bascom's many guests. Many other homes served as "inns" during the first session of the Legislature, as well. There usually was a party at some home every evening of the week during this time.

More than 100 adobes were built in the area of the Market Plaza, but today little remains of San José's earliest days. All but one of the early buildings were either lost in the 1906 earthquake or razed before Californians began regarding such structures as historical landmarks worth saving.

Only two of the original rooms of the Peralta Adobe, the one surviving building,

The Peralta Adobe is San Jose's earliest building, but only two of its original rooms remain.

remain. The earliest known occupant, and likely the builder in the late 1790s, was Manuel González, an Apache Indian. The second owner of the adobe, *Don* Luis María Peralta, raised his large family here. On the lot that ran back to the *acequia* and beyond its bank to the Guadalupe River, Peralta planted orchards of pear, peach, apple, and apricot trees, which would become the forerunners to the later orchards that made the valley famous. Peralta preferred to live here rather than on his *Rancho San Antonio* in present-day Alameda County.

Brooks, marshes, small lakes, and especially roaming wild cattle had made travel difficult between Mission Santa Clara and the pueblo of San José. To help alleviate this problem, in 1799 Father Magin de Catala of the Mission Santa Clara had planted the entire three miles of what came to be called *La Alameda* (Grove of Shade Trees) with black willows on both sides to protect pedestrians from the wild cattle. Irrigated by a ditch dug from the Guadalupe River and Mission Creek, the trees flourished, their top boughs eventually meeting to form a natural canopy. They were undisturbed for 75 years, but during the 1870s, in order to make way for houses and cross streets, the trees were removed. The present-day street, The Alameda, runs along the same route.

Lumbering was one of the most important businesses in Santa Clara County in 1850. The forested areas above the valley floor supplied lumber for the growing valley population. In 1848, Isaac Branham and Julian Hanks[4] had built the first operating sawmill and lumber camp in Santa Clara County in the vicinity of the present-day Lexington Dam and Reservoir.

Vineyards planted by using mission grape cuttings from the old Mission Santa Clara vineyard were under cultivation in Santa Clara County in 1850. Using European wine grape cuttings, Charles LeFranc would establish the first winery in the county—the Almaden Vineyards—in 1852.

Santa Clara County Ranchos

Between 40 and 50 land grants were made in Santa Clara County. Several of the ranchos extended across county lines into Santa Cruz and present-day Alameda, San Mateo, San Benito, and Merced counties. Other land grants were pueblo tracts.

Luis María Peralta (1759-1851)

- Retired military sergeant; held various government positions

- Married to María Loreto Alviso

- Fathered 17 children, but only nine attained adulthood

- Four sons were heirs of *Rancho San Antonio*—Hermenegildo Ignacio, José Domingo, Antonio María, and José Vicente—in Alameda County

Most of the ranchos had been devoted to cattle raising until the foreigners started arriving and began taking advantage of some of the most fertile land in California—the Santa Clara Valley. Details about the more interesting ranchos follow.

Don Mariano Castro's widow, Josefa Romero, owned *Rancho Las Animas*. During 1850, James Houck of Ohio established a small inn and livery stable along a wagon trail between San José and Monterey on the eastern edge of this rancho. A trading post and saddler's shop would follow and Gilroy became a town in 1851, with Houck serving as the first postmaster. *Don* José María Sanchez also owned a portion of *Las Animas* and operated a thriving soap business from here. Part of Gilroy is located on the former *Rancho San Ysidro*. *Don* Quentin Ortega, son of the late *Don* Ignacio, owned the southern portion of this rancho and his sister, María Clara, and brother-in-law, John (Cameron) Gilroy[5] owned the northern portion.

A small settlement of adobes called San Ysidro—now known as "Old Gilroy"—stood along the dividing line between the two portions of the rancho roughly following the Pacheco Pass Road of today. Julius Martin purchased a portion of this rancho in 1850. He built three houses in San Ysidro and operated a small flourmill.

Bernard Murphy, of the pioneer Martin Murphy, Sr. family,[6] owned *Rancho La Polka* located in the hills northeast of Gilroy. He had acquired it from *Doña* Ysabel Ortega, the sister of Quentin and María Clara. It was her one-third of their father's *Rancho San Ysidro* that he had split for his three children.

The Murphy family also owned *Rancho Ojo de Agua de la Coche*, located where the town of Morgan Hill lies today.[7] The family adobe accommodated travelers along the former mission road that ran through it. The Murphy family, known for its generosity, would eventually control six of Santa Clara County's largest ranchos.

The heirs of *Don* José de los Reyes Berreyesa[8] owned *Rancho San Vicente*. Two of the sons lived with their families in separate homes on the rancho. Part of an extremely valuable quicksilver mine—*Nuevo Almaden* owned by the Barron, Forbes Company—was located on this rancho. This actually was the first mine of any kind in California and, in the end, the richest of all. Quicksilver, or mercury, which is condensed from crushed and roasted cinnabar, was used to extract gold and silver from impure ores. As the first such mine to be worked on the North American continent, it was extremely profitable and could not have been discovered at a more opportune time. It was named after a rich quicksilver mine in Almaden, Spain and broke an international monopoly held by the English banking house of Rothschild that operated the mine in Spain. Its discovery saved every gold and silver mine in the West from probable domination by foreign capital.

Nuevo Almaden was a primitive Mexican-style mining camp until West Point graduate and San Francisco lawyer, Henry Wager Halleck,[9] was hired as general manager in 1850. During the year, furnaces were constructed that were able to reduce large quantities of ore into quicksilver. The town of *Hacienda de Beneficio*, today known as New Almaden, would emerge and flourish off and on during many closures and reopenings of the mine between 1912 and 1975. Several adobes had been built by Mexican workers brought to the mine in 1847. The *Casa Grande*, still standing in New Almaden today, was built in 1854. The New Almaden Quicksilver Mining Museum is housed in this building.

Antonio María Sunol (1797-1865)

- French-speaking Spaniard; cadet in French navy; came to San José in 1818
- *Alcalde* of Pueblo San José
- Successful businessman and gold miner
- Owned rancho in Alameda County
- First postmaster in San José from 1826 to 1829
- His son-in-law, Pedro Sainsevain, planted some of the earliest grapevines in the Santa Clara Valley on Sunol's rancho
- One of few Spanish-California *Dons* not to be bankrupted by Americans—died a very wealthy man

The Roberto-Sunol Adobe houses a private law practice in San Jose today.

An 1863 U.S. Supreme Court decision actually placed the quicksilver mine on the neighboring *Rancho Los Capitancillos*. *Don* Justo Larios owned this rancho in 1850.

Dons José María Hernández and Sebastián Peralta, his brother-in-law, owned *Rancho Rinconada de Los Gatos*. Many mountain lions and wildcats inhabited the nearby hills, thus its name. Three adobe houses were built along Los Gatos Creek and sawmills were operating in the canyons above this rancho.

Don José Zenon Fernandez and his son-in-law, *Don* José Noriega, owned *Rancho Quito*. The little settlement of Toll Gate, later known as McCartysville, was developed in this area by Martin McCarty, a former U.S. Army wagon master, who had gleaned $20,000 in the gold fields in 1849. Anticipating the need for a settlement in the vicinity of William Campbell's[10] Redwoods and sawmill, McCarty acquired 230 acres here. Along Saratoga Creek, he built a road to the mill, put up a tollgate, and laid out his town.[11]

Don Joaquín Bernal owned *Rancho de Santa Teresa*. His 1840s house was built of hand-hewn timbers. Several adobes stood on the property as well, and there was also an arena for bull and bear fights. Bernal would live to be 97 and his wife, 110, leaving behind a total of 78 children and grandchildren.

Don Antonio Suñol had acquired *Rancho de Los Coches* in 1847 in payment of a debt owed him by a Christianized Indian, Roberto Balermino. Suñol divided the

rancho into thirds, keeping a third for himself, giving a third to his daughter and her husband, Pierre Sainsevain, and selling a third to Henry Morris Naglee. Suñol entertained lavishly on his rancho, especially during California's first legislative session. The Roberto-Sunol Adobe, which houses a private law practice in San Jose today, is a combination of the small one-room adobe built by Balermino, the adjoining kiln-fired adobe brick, three-room house built by Suñol in 1847, and the full second story frame addition and balcony added in 1853 by Captain Stefano Splivalo.

Don Juan Prado Mesa owned *Rancho San Antonio* in the foothills between Stevens and San Antonio Creeks. He built a fort-like adobe house and corral on a hill located in present-day Los Altos. In 1848 Captain Elisha Stephens,[12] co-leader of the 1844 Stephens-Townsend-Murphy party had settled on Cupertino Creek,[13] just east of *Rancho San Antonio*. He built a split shake house and planted fruit trees, mission grapes, and blackberries. He would leave his Blackberry Farm in 1864 to escape the "crowds."

Doña Juana Briones de Miranda owned *Rancho La Purísima Concepción*. She built a large adobe dwelling and several out buildings and lived here with her seven children. She grazed cattle, sold and leased land, and sheltered the needy.

Dons Teodoro and Secundino Robles owned *Rancho Rincón de San Francisquito*. The brothers had traded their one-eighth interest in the New Almaden Mine for this rancho with *Don* José Peña, the original grantee. In order to accommodate his wife and 29 children, Secundino enlarged the former Peña adobe built in the 1840s. The hacienda was always open to travelers passing through the Santa Clara Valley.

Doña María Antonio Mesa, the re-married widow of *Don* Rafael Soto, owned *Rancho Rinconada del Arroyo de San Francisquito*. *Don* Rafael, the original grantee, had built a landing on the San Francisquito Creek in the 1830s for the loading and unloading of boats that navigated the creek. Palo Alto's[14] town site was laid out here in 1891 for the benefit of the newly founded Stanford University.

Old Chief Yñigo was living on *Rancho Posolmi*. He was granted title to the rancho in 1844, one of the few natives to be so fortunate. Although Robert Walkinshaw had purchased the rancho in the late 1840s, Ynigo lived here until he died in 1864 at the age of 104.

The Mariano Castro family owned *Rancho Pastoría de las Borregas*. The southeastern half of the ranch had been purchased in 1849 by Martin Murphy, Jr., eldest son of the large Murphy clan. Murphy lived in a home located in present-day Sunnyvale that was cut and framed in Boston and brought around the Horn in 1849. The Murphys were famous for entertaining prominent public figures.

The Fremont House, the first of California's country inns, stood on *Rancho Pastoría de las Borregas*. It was originally established by George Harlan, but in 1850 Washington Moody and his father-in-law, James Lynn, both from Missouri, were operating it.

Rancho Rincón de los Esteros was owned by the *Don* Ignacio Alviso family. In 1849, four enterprising Americans who dreamed of a city at the southern tip of the San Francisco Bay had purchased parcels of this property. Jacob D. Hoppe, Charles H. Marvin, Kimball H. Dimmick,[15] and Robert B. Neligh called the place Alviso and had Chester S. Lymon lay out the town site. Several docks and warehouses were built along the Guadalupe River for the schooner trade and a toll road was built between the port and San José for transporting produce and passengers. Alviso was the busiest port on the south end of the Bay and served as the main link between northern and southern California in 1850, but the construction of the railroad in 1865, which bypassed Alviso, changed the path of travel and freight. Today the Guadalupe Slough in the area of Alviso is landfill, the marina is full of silt, reeds, and grass, and Alviso resembles a ghost town.

Finally, the heirs of *Don* José Loreto Higuera owned *Rancho Los Tularcitos*. Seven adobe houses surrounded by orchards, a vineyard, and vast grain fields stood near the banks of Calero Creek north of present-day Milpitas. They raised cattle, as well. Valentin, the second oldest son, lived in the 1828 family adobe that was a popular stopping spot on the Emigrant Trail between Sutter's Fort and San José, via the Livermore Pass. The completely reconstructed Higuera Adobe stands in a Milpitas city park today at the edge of a residential neighborhood adjacent to a field of grazing cattle.

The Higuera Adobe stands in a Milpitas city park at the edge of a residential neighborhood.

SANTA CLARA COUNTY RANCHOS

NAME OF RANCHO	GRANTEE AND/OR 1850 OWNER	1850 AND/OR CURRENT SITES
Rancho Juristac (At Juris)	Antonio and Faustino German	South of Gilroy
Rancho San Ysidro (St. Isidore)	Quentin Ortega, John and María Clara Ortega Gilroy, and Julius Martin	Gilroy
Rancho La Polka	Bernard Murphy	Gilroy
Rancho San Francisco de las Llagas (St. Francis of the Wounds)	Martin Murphy, Sr. family	San Martin
Rancho Solis	Mariano Castro family	West of Gilroy
Rancho Las Uvas (Grapes)	Lorenzo Pineda	West of Morgan Hill, Uvas Reservoir
Rancho Ojo de Agua de la Coche (Pig's Spring)	Martin Murphy, Sr. family	Morgan Hill
Rancho Cañada de San Felipe y Las Animas (Glen of St. Philip and the Souls)	Charles M. Weber[16]	North of Morgan Hill
Rancho La Laguna Seca (Dry Lake)	William Fisher	Northwest of Morgan Hill
Rancho San Vicente	Heirs of José de los Reyes Berreyesa	New Almaden, New Almaden Quicksilver County Park
Rancho Los Capitancillos (Little Captains)	Justo Larios	New Almaden
Rancho Rinconada de Los Gatos (Corner of the Cats)	José María Hernández and Sebastián Peralta	Los Gatos, Monte Sereno, Campbell
Rancho Quito	José Zenon Fernandez and José Noriega	Saratoga, Campbell, Cupertino
Rancho San Juan Bautista	José Agustín Narváez	San Jose
Rancho de Santa Teresa	Joaquín Bernal	San Jose, Santa Teresa County Park
Rancho Yerba Buena (Good Herb)	Antonio Chaboya	San Jose, Evergreen Valley College
Rancho Los Huecos (Hollows)	Luis Arenas and John Roland	Isabel Valley south of Mt. Hamilton
Rancho Cañada de Pala (Shovel Glen)	José de Jesús Bernal	West of Mt. Hamilton
Rancho Pala (Shovel)	Charles White	East of San Jose
Rancho El Potrero de Santa Clara (St. Clare's Colt Pasture)	James Alexander Forbes	San Jose
Rancho de Los Coches (Pigs)	Antonio Suñol	San Jose
Rancho San Antonio	Juan Prado Mesa	Los Altos, Los Altos Hills
Rancho La Purísima Concepción (The Holy Virgin)	Juana Briones de Miranda	Los Altos Hills
Rancho Rincón de San Francisquito (Corner of the Little St. Francis)	Teodoro and Secundino Robles	Palo Alto, Stanford University
Rancho San Francisquito (Little St. Francis)	Antonio Buelna's widow	Stanford University, extended into San Mateo County
Rancho Rinconada del Arroyo de San Francisquito (Corner of the Stream of the Little St. Francis)	María Antonio Mesa	Palo Alto
Rancho Posolmi	Robert Walkinshaw	Mountain View, Moffett Field

SANTA CLARA COUNTY RANCHOS (CONTINUED)

NAME OF RANCHO	GRANTEE AND/OR 1850 OWNER	1850 AND/OR CURRENT SITES
Rancho Pastoría de las Borregas (Sheep Pasture)	Mariano Castro family, Martin Murphy, Jr.	Sunnyvale
Rancho Ulistác	Jacob D. Hoppe	Sunnyvale
Rancho Embarcadero de Santa Clara (St. Clare's Port)	Barcilia Bernal	Alviso
Rancho Rincón de los Esteros (Estuaries Corner)	Ignacio Alviso family, Jacob D. Hoppe, Charles H. Marvin, Kimball H. Dimmick, Robert B. Neligh, and Nicolás Antonio Berryessa	Alviso
Rancho Los Tularcitos (Little Tule Thickets)	Heirs of Don José Loreto Higuera	Milpitas
Rancho Milpitas (Little Corn Fields)	Nicolás Antonio Berryessa and José María de Jésus Alviso	Milpitas

Notes ⁊· SANTA CLARA COUNTY

1

The Guadalupe River originates in the Santa Cruz Mountains and flows northwest into San Francisco Bay. Seven tributary streams feed the river.

2

Pierre Sainsevain was a delegate of the State Constitutional Convention.

3

Of additional significance, in 1871 San José would become the new home of the first normal school (teachers' college) established in California. Minns' Evening Normal School had its beginnings as a private school in San Francisco in 1857, moved to San Jose, and changed its name to San Jose State College in 1935. Since 1972 it has been known as San Jose State University.

4

Julian Hanks was a delegate of the State Constitutional Convention.

5

John Gilroy, a Scotsman, and his shipmate, "Deaf Jimmy," were the first English-speaking settlers in Alta California—having arrived in 1813 at Monterey. Gilroy was baptized Juan Bautista María Gilroy at Mission San Carlos.

6

Martin Murphy, Sr. was one of the co-leaders of the Stephens-Townsend-Murphy party from Missouri that brought the first wagon train across the Sierra in 1844. Two years later, the ill-fated Donner party used cabins built by the Murphys in the Sierras.

7

Morgan Hill was named after Hiram Morgan Hill (who married a Murphy granddaughter) not after the cone-shaped peak which is located here called El Toro.

8

José de los Reyes Berryessa had been killed by Kit Carson and several other men under Captain Frémont's command following the Bear Flag uprising.

9

Henry Wager Halleck was a delegate of the State Constitutional Convention.

10

The City of Campbell would be named for Benjamin Campbell, the son of William Campbell, the surveyor of Santa Clara and San José. Benjamin was only 19 in 1850, but he purchased land northeast of the mill his father built in 1847 and later subdivided the tract and sold lots for the town of Campbell.

11

Pacific Congress Springs, a mineral springs resort modeled after the famous Congress Springs of Saratoga, N.Y., would open here in 1866 and the area would become known as Saratoga.

12

Elisha Stephens was the first man to guide a wagon train across the Sierras and the first to blaze a trail up the Truckee River route—the central immigration road to California. Many have argued that Donner Pass should be called Stephens Pass.

13

This creek was later renamed for Elisha Stephens, misspelled "Stevens." Many other county place names are named for him with his name misspelled, as well.

14

Palo Alto means "tall tree;" the lone, very tall redwood still standing alongside San Francisquito Creek today was a landmark from earliest times for travelers between San Francisco and the missions of Santa Clara and San José. Its height was calculated at about 140 feet. The tree originally had two trunks, but one of the trunks has since fallen and lightning has lopped off the top of the other.

15

Kimball H. Dimmick was a delegate of the Constitutional Convention.

16

See Weber sidebar on page 262.

Peter Hardeman Burnett—First Governor of the American State of California

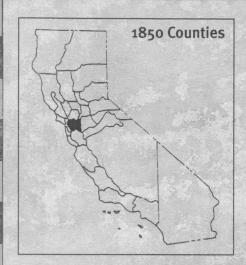

1850 Counties

❧ 1 8 5 0 ❧
❧ CONTRA COSTA ❧
COUNTY

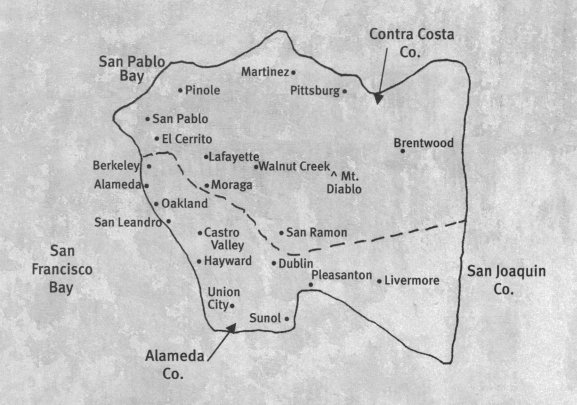

Contra Costa
Co.

San Pablo
Bay

• Martinez

• Pittsburg

• Pinole

• San Pablo

• El Cerrito

• Brentwood

• Lafayette

Berkeley •

• Walnut Creek

^ Mt.
Diablo

Alameda •

• Moraga

• Oakland

San Leandro •

• San Ramon

San
Francisco
Bay

• Castro
Valley

• Hayward

• Dublin

San Joaquin
Co.

• Pleasanton

• Livermore

Union
City •

Sunol •

Alameda
Co.

California
1850

Present-day boundary
variations indicated by

– – – – – –

Settlements/cities of 1850 include: San Antonio (Oakland), Mission San José (Fremont), New Haven/Mt. Eden
(Union City), Squattersville (Hayward)

CONTRA COSTA COUNTY
1850

The geographical area of 1850-Contra Costa County included the northern portion of present-day Alameda County, which included all of the large Rancho San Antonio and the entirety or portions of eight other ranchos. The 1850 U.S. Census for Contra Costa County was lost en route to the Census Office. The number of Contra Costa County residents counted in 1852 was 2,786 and included Californios as well as Americans and Europeans who had been attracted to the area by the lumber industry booming in the nearby redwood groves. Other settlers were unsuccessful miners who came to the area to take up farming, especially grain cultivation. The uncounted Native American population inhabiting the county included the Ohlone and Miwok tribes.

AREA WITHIN PRESENT-DAY ALAMEDA COUNTY

Alameda County would be created in 1853 from portions of Santa Clara and Contra Costa counties. In 1850 the area contained within its current boundaries included *Misión San José*, several settlements—San Antonio, Mission San José, Squattersville, Union City, New Haven, and Mt. Eden; and a dozen ranchos. Little remains to be seen of this era due primarily to the devastation of the 1868 earthquake.

The shores and sloughs of San Francisco Bay border the western edge of present-day Alameda County; in 1850 at least 20 shell mounds were scattered along these shores. Shell mounds were piles of shell-fish shells thrown aside by the early inhabitants of the area—the Ohlone Indians. Only one mound can still be seen today—in Coyote Hills Regional Park in Fremont.[1]

There still were many marshes and tidelands, but the shoreline had been undergoing change in recent years due to the filling by American settlers to create deep-water harbors for ships transporting and supplying miners. Lake Merritt, a salt-water lake covering 155 acres today, was a tidal marshland and arm of the Oakland estuary in 1850 where San Antonio Creek flowed into the bay. The marshland was dammed by Dr. Samuel Merritt in 1869. In 1850 The Embarcadero—a walkway and landing place for hide and tallow merchants in their flat-bottomed barges—was located on the northeast end of present-day Lake Merritt.

Americans and Europeans had begun settling in the East Bay Area in the 1840s. Although they had no right to any of the land or the trees, by 1842 these newcomers had established full-scale logging operations in what is known today as the

Sites to Visit in Alameda County

Hayward Area Historical Society Museum, 22701 Main St., Hayward 510.581.0223

Mission San Jose Chapel and Museum, 43300 Mission Bl., Fremont 510.657.1797

Oakland Museum, 1000 Oak St., Oakland 510.238.2200

The Bancroft Library, University of California, Berkeley, Berkeley 510.642.6481

Oakland Metropolitan Chamber of Commerce, 475 – 14th St., Oakland, CA 94612 510.874.4800

Oakland-Berkeley Hills. The first steam-powered sawmill was constructed on Palo Seco Creek. Approximately 200 acres of the redwood forest, known then as the San Antonio Redwoods, were lumbered to supply San Francisco with its wood needs—until the last tree was cut in 1854. Captain Thomas Gray established a two-trips-a-week ferry service late in 1850 to transport lumber from San Antonio (present-day Oakland) to San Francisco on his propeller steamer *Kangaroo*.

During the Gold Rush, Oakland would become the main staging area for passengers and cargo traveling between the Bay and the Sierra foothills. Ferry service between Oakland and San Francisco began operation in 1852; the first train arrived in Oakland in 1869.[2]

Mission San José

The 1797 *La Misión del Gloriosisimo Patriarcha Señor San José* (the Mission of the Most Glorious Patriarch St. Joseph) was the 14th mission to be built in California. Over the years, a number of earthquakes caused major damage to the mission, resulting in the erection of three different structures on the site in present-day Fremont. Only a portion of the padres' living quarters of the original mission remains today; it has been incorporated into the Mission San Jose Museum. The reconstructed replica of the 1809 adobe chapel was completed in the early 1980s.

The reconstructed replica of the 1809 Mission San Jose is located on Mission Boulevard in Fremont.

Dons Andrés Pico[3] and former Governor Juan Bautista Alvarado had purchased the mission in 1846 for $12,000, but by 1850 most of the mission lands had been sold to newcomers. The greater part of Mission San José was acquired by Elias Lyman Beard, who established a homestead behind the mission.

In 1850 the mission was a wayside station for the gold seekers using the land route from San Francisco to the mines by way of the Mission and Livermore passes. Henry C. Smith[4] was operating a trading post in the old adobe mission building, and others soon opened stores, lodging quarters, restaurants, and saloons in other adobe buildings. A post office was established during 1850 and a settlement called Mission San José or "Mission St. Joe" would be built around the mission in 1851 on the former mission rancho. The mission orchards were still well-tended and the old Mission Garden became the source for many seeds, cuttings, and grafts for starting orchards and vineyards elsewhere in northern California.

Alameda County Ranchos

Besides the mission rancho, there were eleven other ranchos in present-day Alameda County. Details about the more interesting ones follow.

Don Fulgencio Higuera owned *Rancho Agua Caliente*, which extended over the present-day Alameda/Santa Clara County line. Hot springs were located in the foothills of this rancho, thus its name. The Higuera family homes were located a short distance south of Mission San José. The Higueras sold various portions of their rancho in 1850. Clemente Columbet purchased the part of the rancho containing the springs—present-day Warm Springs—and built a resort there. Simeon Stivers, from New Jersey, settled near Lake Elizabeth, which was a swampy lagoon overgrown with tule until it was made into a lake in 1968. Perry and William Morrison, from Indiana, had settled in Morrison Canyon in the hills east of the mission in 1849.

Origin Mowry, a Mormon farmer and mason from Rhode Island, settled on Mowry Slough on the public lands bordering the southwestern portion of *Rancho Agua Caliente*. He built a warehouse and landing at the foot of present-day Mowry Avenue in Fremont.

Dons Agustín Alviso and Tomás Pacheco owned *Rancho Potrero de los Cerritos*, which was located on the current sites of Fremont, a portion of Newark, and the Alvarado and Decoto districts of Union City. The prime location of this rancho on the San Francisco Bay made it very appealing to squatters in 1850.

The Spaniards of the Mission San José and the Russians of Fort Ross in Sonoma County had built the first embarcadero on this side of the Bay—on present-day Newark Slough—in the 1820s. In 1850, Elias Lyman Beard built a wharf on the slough (then known as Beard Slough).

John M. Horner purchased 110 acres of previous mission grazing lands located on *Rancho Potrero de los Cerritos* during 1850 and laid out a town site on the south side of Alameda Creek. He named the town Union City after a river steamer that he purchased. *The Union* was used to carry agricultural products from Union City to San Francisco. The first lots of the new town were sold in September and the first building was a small warehouse that Horner built in 1850-51. Horner farmed thousands of acres of land and was recognized as "the great California farmer."

Henry D. Smith purchased 465 acres of *Rancho Potrero de los Cerritos* late in 1850 and laid out the town of New Haven in the present-day Alvarado district of Union City. New Haven would change its name to Alvarado in 1853 and today Union City is composed of the former cities of Alvarado, Union City, and Decoto, which were incorporated into one city in 1959.

Don José de Jesús Vallejo, Mariano Vallejo's[5] older brother, owned *Rancho Arroyo de la Alameda*. It was located on fertile valley land situated in the Niles district of Fremont. Vallejo lived in the settlement of Mission San José where he served as the postmaster, rather than on his rancho. Overseers ran the rancho for him, including the operation of a flourmill built in 1850.

Rancho San Lorenzo was divided between two owners. *Don* Francisco Soto owned the portion that today includes San Lorenzo and part of Hayward. His rancho was referred to as *Rancho San Lorenzito*. Squatters were so prevalent on this rancho along the San Lorenzo Creek that by 1850 the community was called Squattersville. Most people innocently believed the rancho lands to be government land, but some willfully encroached.

Mt. Eden, a town located southwest of present-day Hayward, was founded in 1850 on another portion of *Rancho San Lorenzo* by an association of farmers called the Mount Eden Company. Roberts Landing also was established early in the year on the San Lorenzo Creek of this rancho. Known at first as Thompson's, it soon became Roberts. Captains William Roberts, Robert Thompson, and Peter Anderson were the three founders of this embarcadero. Roberts, from Liverpool, England, would operate the landing for 30 years.

Don Guillermo Castro owned the other half of *Rancho San Lorenzo*. He built an adobe where Hayward[6] lies today, and raised cattle on the slopes and hillsides of present-day Castro Valley. Roads through this rancho led east to the valley and south to Mission San José.

Don Luis María Peralta[7] had divided his *Rancho San Antonio* among his four sons in 1842. One of the most valuable and largest land grants made in Alta California, it extended along the eastern shore of San Francisco Bay from San Leandro Creek on the south to El Cerrito Creek on the north. *Don* Luis had always preferred living in the pueblo in San José, but his sons lived on his land in an adobe in present-day Oakland. After the rancho was divided, the sons and their families gradually began occupying their own portions. Each son had his own embarcadero.

In 1830, Antonio María Peralta was the first son to permanently move onto his property, having built a small adobe in 1821 facing Peralta Creek in present-day East Oakland. In 1840 he built a second adobe and two other structures, one of which was a guesthouse. His portion of the rancho also included the oak-studded peninsula of the present-day island city of Alameda; the peninsula was called *Encinal* (Live Oaks) *de San Antonio*.[8]

During 1850, two Frenchmen, Le Maitre and Depachier, were leasing a tract of this land to cut firewood for the San Francisco market. Their enterprise failed and they subleased 160 acres on the eastern end of the *Encinal* fronting San Leandro Bay to W. W. Chipman, an Ohio lawyer and schoolteacher, and Gideon Aughinbaugh, a Pennsylvania carpenter. The two gentlemen pitched their tent here and would purchase the entire peninsula from Peralta in 1851 for $14,000.

José Vicente Peralta and his wife, Encarnacíon Galindo, built their large *casa* in the late 1830s on the *Encinal de Temescal* (Live Oaks of the Sweat House). The three wings of their adobe formed a patio so large that a carriage could turn around within it. A chapel was added to the adobe in which church services, baptisms, and funerals were held for friends and relatives. Vicente's share of the rancho comprised the north and central portions of Oakland, as well as Piedmont and Emeryville.

Vicente had his own embarcadero, but another one–*Embarcadero de San Antonio*, had been built in 1849 by lumbermen who shipped redwood from the hills behind San Antonio to San Francisco. It was located at the foot of present-day 13th Avenue on the Oakland Inner Harbor[9] known today as the Oakland Marina.

Temescal Creek, located on this rancho, supplied fresh water and food for the Peraltas. Until the 1880s, Temescal Creek even had salmon runs. Lake Temescal would not become a reservoir until the late 1860s when Anthony Chabot and William F. Boardman built a dam on Temescal Creek for a new water supply. The site of this manmade lake once was the center of logging activities in the East Bay. The Spaniards, who began this logging, gave the area its Aztec name—the words for sweat house—because they saw American Indian sweat houses nearby. They sent trees downstream to the Bay, as did the Mexicans and Americans who followed them.

Hermenegildo Ignacio Peralta lived along the north bank of San Leandro Creek on the southern portion of *Rancho San Antonio*. He built his first house in 1835 and a second adobe in 1842. Today his residence is a private clubhouse in San Leandro.

Finally, José Domingo Peralta was given the northern section of *Rancho San Antonio* where Berkeley and Albany now stand. He built an adobe in 1841 on Codornices Creek.

As early as 1847, strangers had started killing the Peralta's cattle for food and chasing other cattle away. At least 20,000 gold miners viewed the Peralta's prime piece of property on the way to the gold fields; after 1849, unsuccessful gold miners began squatting on the property, including Horace W. Carpentier,[10] Edson Adams, and Alexander Moon. The presence of squatters clouded the title of the property and eventually led to the subdivision of the rancho. In 1851, Carpentier, Adams, and Moon would lay out a town called Contra Costa—meaning opposite coast, relative to San Francisco. Their town took on the name of Oakland when it was incorporated in 1852. The Broadway Wharf located at the foot of Broadway on the Oakland Inner Harbor today was called Moon and Adams Landing because the two built a cabin and settled there in 1850.

Four relatives owned *Rancho Valle de San José*, which was located on the west side of the Livermore Valley. *Dons* Antonio María Suñol and Antonio Pico[11] were both married to sisters of Agustín and Juan Pablo Bernal, and the four *rancheros* shared ownership of this rancho. Suñol never lived on the rancho, living instead in San José; his son of the same name and Agustín Bernal did live on the rancho in their own adobes. A portion of Bernal's 1850 adobe remains today, incorporated into a private residence. Pico sold his portion to Suñol who later transferred it to Juan Pablo, but Juan would not settle on the rancho until 1852.

ALAMEDA COUNTY RANCHOS

NAME OF RANCHO	GRANTEE AND/OR 1850 OWNER	1850 AND/OR CURRENT SITES
Rancho Agua Caliente (Hot Water)	Fulgencio Higuera	Fremont, Warm Springs, Milpitas in Santa Clara County
Rancho Potrero de los Cerritos (Pasture of the Little Hills)	Agustín Alviso, Tomás Pacheco, John M. Horner, Henry D. Smith	Fremont, Newark, Union City
Rancho Arroyo de la Alameda (Tree-lined Stream)	José de Jesús Vallejo	Fremont
Rancho San Lorenzito	Francisco Soto	San Lorenzo, Hayward
Rancho San Lorenzo	Guillermo Castro	Hayward, Castro Valley
Rancho San Leandro	José Joaquín Estudillo	San Leandro, Lake Chabot
Rancho San Antonio	Luis María Peralta family	San Leandro, East Oakland, Alameda, Oakland, Piedmont, Emeryville, Berkeley, Albany
Rancho Valle de San José	Antonio María Suñol, Bernal Antonio Pico, Agustín and Juan Pablo	Pleasanton, Sunol
Rancho Santa Rita [12]	José Dolores Pacheco	Dublin
Rancho San Ramon	José María Amador	Dublin, San Ramon in Contra Costa County
Rancho Las Positas (Little Wells)	Robert Livermore	Livermore

Don José María Amador owned the southern portion of *Rancho San Ramon*, the majority of which lay within present-day Contra Costa County. He built his 1826 two-story adobe where Dublin is located today. Besides being engaged in cattle raising, Amador was one of the first manufacturers in Alameda County—employing Mexicans to make leather, soap, saddles, harnesses, blankets, shoes, and wagons in adobe workshops situated on his rancho. His house would become an inn on the road from the Mother Lode. Amador was drawn to the gold fields himself for a while and the area where he mined, with a company of mission Indians he organized, took on his name when it became a county in 1854.

Finally, Robert Livermore owned *Rancho Las Positas* on which he raised cattle and grew grapes, fruit, and grain. The eastern-most rancho in the valley, it often was in danger from American Indian raids. The Livermores often had to take refuge at their neighbor's to the west, José María Amador. The two gentlemen had traded favors and helped one another build their adobe homes. Livermore's home became a popular stopping place between San Francisco and the Mother Lode for travelers on the Stockton Road through the Altamont Hills and the area became known as Livermore or Livermore's. Livermore would build the first frame building in the area in 1851 from wood shipped around the Horn.

The brothers Jacob and Nathaniel Greene Patterson, from Tennessee, settled in the Patterson Pass east of Livermore. Nathaniel was renting Livermore's adobe for a hotel in 1850. The Pattersons later built a house known as "Negley's Place." Not far from here, Thomas Goodale was operating a "house of entertainment" in a "Blue Tent" near the point where the present-day Contra Costa, San Joaquin, and Alameda counties meet.

AREA WITHIN PRESENT-DAY CONTRA COSTA COUNTY

In 1850 the area within present-day Contra Costa County consisted of its county seat, Martinez, which straddled two ranchos, and 13 other ranchos. Details about the more interesting ones follow.

Don José María Amador's portion of *Rancho San Ramon* straddled the present-day Alameda/Contra Costa County line. Leo Norris, from Kentucky, purchased a small portion of Amador's rancho and, in the fall of 1850, settled in the canyon named for him—Norris Canyon, with his son William, and another relative, William Lynch, a journeyman carpenter from New York. There was an adobe located on the property, but Lynch would help Norris build the first frame dwelling in the San Ramon Valley from lumber hauled from the nearby redwoods. Heavy logging operations were underway in this redwood forest area between 1849 and 1851.

A third, long and narrow portion of *Rancho San Ramon* was owned by *Don* Mariano Castro and the widowed Rafaela Soto de Pacheco. Castro actually lived on his Santa Clara County rancho, but the Pacheco family lived on their portion of *San Ramon*. Several settlers—farmers seeking fields for grazing stock and sowing grain—settled in the Green, Sycamore, and Tassajara valleys located on this portion of *Rancho San Ramon*.

Don José Joaquín de la Santisima Trinidad Moraga[13] and the heirs of his cousin, Juan Bernal, owned *Rancho Laguna de los Palos Colorados*. The 1841 Moraga adobe home stood on a hill overlooking the Moraga Valley. One unique feature of this adobe was a salon with a redwood floor where all-night dancing frequently took place. The restored adobe is a private residence in Orinda today. A shallow tule lake created by the run-off from the surrounding hills was located on the present site of the high school located in Rheem Valley, thus the rancho's name.

Several lumber mills were operating in the redwood groves located on and adjacent to this rancho. William H. Taylor and James Owen were two mill operators who respected the property rights of Moraga and the Bernals, locating their mill instead on public land. Others were not so considerate and squatters were prevalent. So many men were working in all three of the redwood groves—the Moraga, San Antonio, and Middle redwoods—that a Contra Costa County voting precinct was established at the site of present-day Canyon for the first state election in 1850. The settlement was called Sequoia until 1927. All three of the redwood groves would be almost totally clear-cut by 1856.

Elam Brown owned the small *Rancho Acalanes*. He left New York as a widow with four children; along the way he married Margaret Allen, whose husband had died on the trip west. She had 11 children of her own. The lack of adequate water required the Browns to move three times. They finally built their redwood house along Lafayette Creek where downtown Lafayette is located today. The site of the Plaza at the corner of Mount Diablo Boulevard and Moraga Road was Brown's gift to the village.

Brown sold a small part of his rancho to his son-in-law, Nathaniel Jones of Tennessee, for $100. Jones built his home in Happy Valley and introduced the black locust tree to California, a few of which may still be seen on Lower Happy Valley Road, north of Lafayette. Jones and Brown grew wheat, which they transported by oxen-pulled wagons to a flourmill in San José. Jones would become sheriff, public administrator, and a supervisor of Contra Costa County.

Rancho San Pablo was bordered on the west and north by the San Francisco and San Pablo bays.[14] Dotted with groves of huge oak trees, it had been home to the *Don* Francisco María Castro family since the early 1820s. Francisco died in 1831, but his wife and 11 children continued to live in the little Mexican village established here. They raised cattle and planted the first fruit trees and grape vineyards in the county from mission cuttings. One of the sons, Victor Ramon, built a two-story adobe in 1839 on the north bank of El Cerrito Creek in present-day El Cerrito, and another son, Jesús María, built an adobe in 1842 for his mother. It stood in present-day San Pablo and came to be known as the Alvarado Adobe because one of the Castro daughters, Martina, moved into it in 1848 with her husband, the former Governor Juan Bautista Alvarado. In the 1970s a replica of the Alvarado Adobe was built and today it serves as a museum of the San Pablo Museum and Historical Society.

Another Castro daughter, Jovita, and her husband, Candido Gutiérrez, lived on the south bank of San Pablo Creek within the city limits of present-day Richmond. They built their adobe in 1850 and it was considered one of the finest mansions of its day. Schooners came up the creek right to their back door, bringing supplies and taking on products from the rancho.[15]

Rancho El Pinole was owned by the heirs of *Don* Ignacio Martínez, who had died in 1848. The modernized 1849 Vicente Martínez Adobe stands today at the John

Elam Brown (18??-1889)

- Arrived in California in 1846 as captain of a 16-wagon emigrant company

- Worked his first summer whip-sawing lumber in the San Antonio redwoods

- Moved his family to his rancho in 1848—the second American family to settle in the county

- Journeyed to San José to mill his wheat and barley into flour until he set up a horse-powered mill near his house in 1853

- Member of the State Constitutional Convention and the first two legislative sessions (Assemblyman)

Muir[16] National Historic Site in Martinez. Samuel J. Tennant, an English doctor, married Martinez' daughter in 1849, inherited a vast part of the rancho, raised ten children, and rode horses around his own racetrack.

Settlers had begun to arrive to the area in 1849 and Vicente Martinez had asked his brother-in-law, Colonel William M. Smith, to make some of his property into a town. That year, the town took the Martinez family name and was surveyed and laid out by Thomas A. Brown, one of Elam Brown's sons. He plotted 120 acres into streets and building sites that San Franciscans and others were anxious to buy. In 1850-51 he laid out 500 acres more for Martinez' neighbor, Maria Galindo Welch. Her *Rancho Las Juntas* had been granted to her late husband, the Irishman William

The modernized 1849 Vicente Martinez Adobe stands on the John Muir National Historic Site in Martinez.

Welch, in 1844. Her lots were located in the center of present-day Martinez.

Martinez was named the county seat on April 25, 1850. The town consisted of three stores, a blacksmith shop, a hotel, and various other buildings. One building served as a combination school, church, courthouse, and hotel. Oliver C. Coffin was the first postmaster and F. M. Warmcastle was the first judge. Sometimes court trials were held in private homes. The town's first newspaper, the *Contra Costa Gazette*, would not be published until 1858.

The remodeled 1844 Salvio Pacheco Adobe serves as an office building for a credit union in Concord.

Various types of primitive ferries had been operating to transport passengers across the Carquinez Strait to Benicia since 1846. Dr. Robert Semple [17] had started a ferry service in 1847. The ferries transported livestock to pastures in the north, as well as miners headed for the Mother Lode. In August 1850, Oliver Coffin began operating a steamboat he brought out from the East, and Charles Minturn of San Francisco organized the Contra Costa Ferry Company. Sloops, schooners, and steam vessels

The 1848 Fernando Pacheco Adobe serves as the headquarters for a horsemen's association in Concord.

were carrying shipments of produce, grain, and hay up the Sacramento River.[18]

Don Salvio Pacheco owned *Rancho Monte del Diablo*. His 1844 adobe house (Salvio Pacheco Adobe) has been modernized and serves as an office building for a credit union in Concord today. The adobe his son Fernando built in 1843—the Fernando Pacheco Adobe—has also survived and serves today as the headquarters for a horsemen's association. A number of outbuildings, a bull ring, and a dance pavilion were also located on the rancho. Francisco Galindo came to live on the rancho in 1850 and married Salvio's daughter, Manuela.

Mount Diablo is located on this former rancho. The volcanic cone of this mountain served as a landmark for explorers and pioneers from the earliest days. A government cabin and telescope would be placed on the 3,849-foot summit of Mount Diablo in 1851, when it was chosen as the base point for U.S. surveys in California.[19]

Doña Juana Sánchez de Pacheco owned *Rancho Arroyo de las Nueces y Bolbones* on the western side of Mount Diablo. One squatter had already settled in this area. William Slusher built a house on the bank of what was known as "Nuts Creek" in 1849. The creek would be renamed Walnut Creek in 1862. The Corners—so-named because four ranchos came together at this spot and because it was the main crossroads of Contra Costa County—was established here. Today it is known as the city of Walnut Creek.

Rancho Los Medanos, which bordered the Carquinez Strait, was owned by Colonel Jonathan Drake Stevenson, the leader of the regiment of volunteers from New York. Lieutenant William Tecumseh Sherman surveyed and laid out a town site named "New York of the Pacific." Stevenson had great hopes that his town site would become a large and prosperous seaport and even made an attempt to locate the state capital here, to no avail. New York Landing[20] was little more than an overnight stopping place for miners on their way to the foothills.

Twin brothers from New Hampshire, William Wiggins Smith and Joseph Horton Smith—both carpenters and ordained ministers in the Christian Church—had been doing carpentry work in New York of the Pacific since their arrival in 1849. They founded the New York House—a hotel and restaurant located at Smith's Landing. They also acquired property where Antioch[21] is located today, broke ground for a settlement, and set up tents. Unfortunately, Joseph died of malaria in February 1850, but William proceeded with their plan, inviting a group of New England frontier families to come to Smith's Landing. A street plan was laid out and Smith offered a lot to each family desirous of building a home here. George W. Kimball, the captain of the ship that brought the families to California, built the first house. In 1850 John Nicholls was operating a boarding house in an old converted ship in Smith's Landing.

Rancho Los Meganos had been the home of Dr. John Marsh since 1837. He was living in the four-room adobe built for him by the neighboring Native Americans. A few Mexican helpers assisted him with his orchard of grapes, figs, pears, and olives. His successful medical practice earned him fees paid in cattle, creating one of the largest herds in early California. Marsh had established a landing on the San Joaquin River called Marsh's Landing; it was a busy stop on the river for gold miners. He also built a smokehouse and slaughterhouse nearby and profited greatly from his beef and produce sales to miners as well as shipments to San Francisco.

Several public roads were designated in Contra Costa County during 1850, linking *Rancho El Sobrante* with *Rancho Acalanes*, the Canyon area with Oakland through the redwoods, and the redwoods with Martinez by way of Lafayette. Lumber was hauled from the redwoods to the port at Martinez. A narrow and dark tunnel would be built through the Oakland Hills between Alameda and Contra Costa counties in 1903, which improved Contra Costa County's access to San Francisco. The Caldecott Tunnel was built in 1937. The railroad reached Martinez from Oakland and the San Joaquin Valley in 1869.

John Marsh (1799-1856)

- Harvard graduate, studied medicine under a doctor in Minnesota for two years, but the doctor died before a certificate was issued

- Taught school and worked with Sioux Indians in Wisconsin

- Common-law marriage produced a son, whom he lost track of following the death of his wife

- Arrived in Los Angeles in 1836 with a small medical and agriculture library and his medicine bag

- First physician in California, due to his luck in passing off his Harvard B.A. degree as a doctorate in medicine

- Housed the first hospital in the San Joaquin Valley in his primitive home, and doctored patients on the ranchos in the valley, traveling as far as Monterey and Merced

- Previous experience with Native Americans allowed him to befriend the hostile tribe adjacent to his rancho and enlist their assistance in house-building and farming

- Influential in persuading President Polk to go to war with Mexico to acquire California; lured Americans to California with his published letters in Missouri newspapers, but offered little hospitality when they arrived

- Drove a hard bargain for medical fees and accommodating travelers (demanded high prices for supplies); impatient with *Californios*

- Married Abbie Tuck, a New England school teacher, in 1851

- Murdered near Martinez in 1856 by some *vaqueros* over a payment dispute for cattle branding charges; Abbie had died earlier, so a very young orphaned daughter remained, but she was united with her adult half-brother

- The Stone House that Marsh and Abbie began constructing in 1852 remains today awaiting restoration

CONTRA COSTA COUNTY RANCHOS

NAME OF RANCHO	GRANTEE AND/OR 1850 OWNER	1850 AND/OR CURRENT SITES
Rancho San Ramon	José María Amador, Leo Norris, Mariano Castro, Rafaela Soto de Pacheco	Alamo, Danville, San Ramon, Dublin in Alameda County
Rancho El Sobrante de la San Ramon (Surplus Ranch of San Ramon)	Inocencio and José Romero	Walnut Creek, Rossmoor Leisure World, Alamo, Danville
Rancho Laguna de los Palos Colorados (Lake of the Redwoods)	José Joaquín de la Santisima Trinidad Moraga, heirs of Juan Bernal	Orinda, Moraga, Canyon, Rheem, Lafayette
Rancho Acalanes	Elam Brown, Nathaniel Jones	Lafayette
Rancho San Pablo	Francisco María Castro family	San Pablo
Rancho La Boca de la Cañada de Pinole (Mouth of the Valley of Pinole)	Widow of Felipe Briones	Briones Regional Park, Briones and San Pablo reservoirs
Rancho El Sobrante (Surplus)	Juan José and Victor Castro, Colonel William M. Smith	Orinda, El Cerrito, El Sobrante
Rancho El Pinole	Heirs of Ignacio Martínez, Samuel J. Tennant	Pinole, Martinez
Rancho Las Juntas	Maria Galindo Welch	Martinez, Pleasant Hill
Rancho Cañada del Hambre Las Bolsas (Valley of the Hungry Purse)	Teodora Soto	Crockett
Rancho Monte del Diablo (Devils' Willow Thicket)	Salvio Pacheco	Concord, Clayton, Mt. Diablo
Rancho Arroyo de las Nueces y Bolbones (Creek of the Nuts)	Juana Sánchez de Pacheco	Walnut Creek
Rancho Los Medanos (Sand Banks)	Colonel Jonathan Drake Stevenson	Pittsburg
Rancho Los Meganos	Dr. John Marsh	Brentwood
Rancho Cañada de los Vaqueros (Canyon of the Cowboys)	Robert Livermore and José Noriega	West of Byron; north of Altamont in Alameda County

Notes ⟿ CONTRA COSTA COUNTY

1

Dredged shells from the shell mounds were utilized by the cement industry and chicken feed manufacturers for many years.

2

It would be 1936 before the San Francisco-Oakland Bay Bridge would open.

3

See Pico sidebar on page 59.

4

Henry C. Smith became a legislator in 1852 and aided in the organization of Alameda County.

5

See Vallejo sidebar on page 170.

6

Hayward's namesake, William Hayward, arrived from Massachusetts late in 1850.

7

See Peralta sidebar on page 140.

Notes ⁊ CONTRA COSTA COUNTY

8

In 1902 the Alameda peninsula became an island when the tidal canal was cut through joining the harbor of Oakland and the San Leandro Bay. Bay Farm Island was originally an island on the tidal flats, located south of Alameda, but today it is a peninsula and the Oakland International Airport is located on the southern portion of it.

9

The Oakland Inner Harbor is the water channel between Oakland and Alameda. In 1850 it was called San Antonio Creek or San Antonio Slough.

10

Horace W. Carpentier would earn the reputation of "land-grabber."

11

Antonio Pico was a delegate of the State Constitutional Convention.

12

The 1844-45 Francisco Solano Alviso Adobe located on the former *Rancho Santa Rita* was the first adobe to be built in the Pleasanton Valley. It recently was acquired by the City of Dublin and plans are underway to renovate it.

13

Joaquín was the grandson of José Joaquín Moraga, founder and first *commandante* of the Presidio of San Francisco.

14

Today San Pablo Bay is considerably smaller and shallower, owing to extensive diking, filling, and siltation over the past 150 years.

15

Nicholl Knob in Point Richmond was originally an island, separated from the mainland by sloughs and marshland, which allowed boats to navigate the channel during high tide.

16

John Muir, one of the earliest champions of the American wilderness and founder of the Sierra Club, would not arrive in California until 1868.

17

See Semple sidebar on page 181.

18

The first span of the Carquinez Bridge would be completed in 1927; the Benicia-Martinez vehicular bridge would not be built until 1962.

19

With the exception of southern California and the Humboldt County district, the locations of all lands in California are determined by their situation with reference to the Mount Diablo "base and meridian" lines. From its summit, more square miles of the earth's surface are potentially visible than from any other place except Mount Kilimanjaro in Africa.

20

New York of the Pacific became known simply as New York Landing and Black Diamond during the early coal-mining period of the late 1850s. After the Pittsburg Coal Company was established in the early 1860s, the name was changed to Pittsburg Landing and later, Pittsburg.

21

William Smith named the new community Antioch in 1851. He chose the Biblical name in memoriam to his brother. Antioch was the Syrian town where the followers of Jesus Christ were first called Christians.

1850 Counties

∼ 1 8 5 0 ∼
⊱ MARIN ⊰
—————
COUNTY

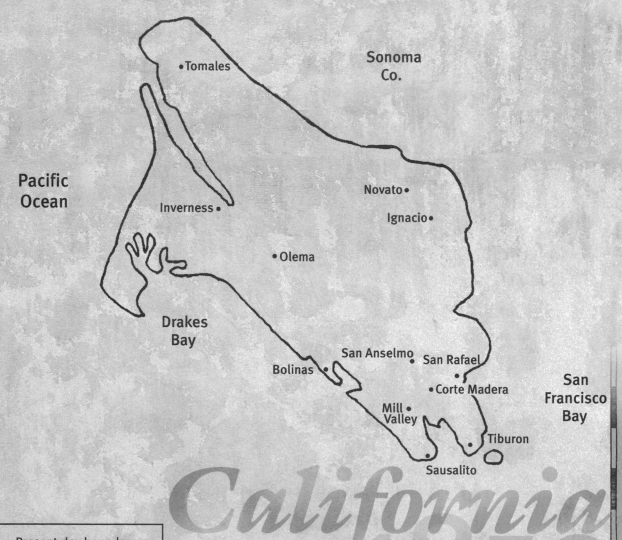

Sonoma Co.

•Tomales

Pacific Ocean

Inverness •

Novato •

Ignacio •

•Olema

Drakes Bay

San Anselmo •   San Rafael •

Bolinas •

• Corte Madera

Mill Valley •

San Francisco Bay

Tiburon •

Sausalito •

California
1850

Present-day boundary variations indicated by

— — — —

Settlements/cities of 1850 include: Tomales, Novato, Bolinas, San Rafael, Sausalito

MARIN COUNTY
1850

Marin County's boundaries have not changed since 1850. Its 323 residents counted in the 1850 U. S. Census included Californios, Americans, and Europeans. The uncounted Native American population was entirely from the Coast Miwok tribe.

The Pacific Ocean forms the western border of Marin County and the San Francisco Bay forms the county's eastern boundary. Sonoma County to the north is the only neighbor of this triangular peninsula. The Sisters and Marin islands, as well as San Rafael Rock, Red Rock, and almost all of Angel Island lie within the boundary lines of Marin County. In 1850 *Don* Antonio Maria Osio owned Angel Island, on which he grazed his cattle and horses and cut timber to sell in San Francisco. He never lived on the island, but he did build four houses and a dam, and raised some crops on the island.[1] Today, Angel Island is a state park.

The early settlement of Marin County by the Spanish was a defensive response to the presence of the Russians who had established Fort Ross in present-day Sonoma County in 1812. In 1850 Marin County consisted of a former mission and five townships located on ranchos. The townships of San Rafael, South Salieto, Boulinas, Navat, and Tomales would later become the present-day cities of San Rafael, Sausalito, Bolinas, Novato, and Tomales, respectively.

Mission San Rafael

Misión San Rafael Arcángel was founded in 1817 in an effort to provide a healthier place for the Mission Dolores Indians of Yerba Buena (San Francisco) to live. Originally only an *asistencia* to Mission Dolores and known initially as the "hospital mission," it became self-supporting by 1823. After secularization in 1834, the neglected mission deteriorated until nothing of the original buildings remained. *Dons* Antonio María Pico and Antonio Suñol[2] had purchased the mission property in 1846 for $8,000, but this purchase would not survive the U.S. Land Commission's ruling in later years and the Catholic church obtained a land patent for some of the land in 1859. A replica of the mission was built near the former site in San Rafael in 1949 and includes three of the original bells.

City of San Rafael

In 1850 Myers & McCullough surveyed San Rafael, the county seat, and laid out the town. The county was using part of the dismantled mission as the courthouse, the town meeting hall, and the jail. Other buildings included the San Rafael Hotel, several residences, stables, barns, and other agricultural structures built by the

Sites to Visit in Marin County

Mission San Rafael Arcangel, 1104 Fifth Av., San Rafael 415.454.8141

Old Mill Park, Throckmorton and Cascade Drive, Mill Valley

Olompali State Historic Park, 8901 Redwood Hwy, north of Novato 415.892.3383

Marin County Convention & Visitors Bureau, 1013 Larkspur Landing Cir., Larkspur, CA 94939 415.499.5000

Virginia and Baltimore companies. Late in 1850, the Davis & Taylor store began operations, stocking supplies that were transported in small sloops from San Francisco. The principal trade of San Rafael was shipping cattle. A slaughterhouse was operating on the San Rafael Creek; carcasses were shipped from here to San Francisco on the sloop *Boston* for further butchering.

Marin County Ranchos

Seventeen ranchos had been granted in Marin County. Details about the more interesting ones follow.

Captain Guillermo (William) Antonio Richardson owned *Rancho Saucelito*. He built Marin County's first house on a site in present-day Sausalito. His wharf at Shelter Cove was the maritime center of early Marin and his adobe home was the social center. He established the Saucelito Water Works during 1850, which piped water from springs located on his rancho to a boat on the waterfront that transported the water to San Francisco. From here, the spring water was distributed to San Francisco residents on mule and horse-drawn carts.

Several other structures stood in the township of Sausalito, including a hotel called the Fountain House, a government store, Captain Leonard Story's frame house brought around the Cape, and Robert Parker's home and adjacent building housing

This is a replica of the original Mission San Rafael Arcangel located in downtown San Rafael.

John Thomas Reed's mill was reconstructed in Old Mill Park in Mill Valley in 1990.

a bowling alley. Parker also owned a steam sawmill that had been milling timber for shipment by raft across the bay to San Francisco since 1849.

In 1850 the U.S. Army was in negotiations with Richardson to buy most of the peninsula portion of his *Rancho Saucelito* to create a military presence in the area, but it would be 1866 before a deal was struck with the then owner, Samuel Throckmorton. Today this area of coastal hills, valleys, steep cliffs, and uninhabited shoreline is known as the Marin Headlands and is part of the Golden Gate National Recreation Area. Fort Baker would be established as a harbor defense in 1897.

The heirs of Irishman John Thomas Reed owned *Rancho Corte de Madera del Presidio*.[3] Before his untimely death in 1843 at the age of 38, Reed had operated the first passenger ferry across the bay and built the first sawmill in Marin County in the mid-1830s to supply the Presidio of San Francisco. Some of the old timbers still stand in Old Mill Park in Mill Valley where Reed's mill was reconstructed in 1990. Reed's widow was Hilaria Sanchez, the daughter of the Sanchez family of San Mateo County. One of Reed's daughters inherited the larger house he had begun to construct that stood in Mill Valley until 1916.

Other sawmills were in operation in the area, including a government sawmill located on the wharf on Corte Madera Creek. One sawmill had been shipped around the Cape in 1849 by the Baltimore and Frederick Mining and Trading Company, originally formed by 30 Maryland businessmen who had since left for the gold mines.

A steamboat was operating on Corte Madera Creek between present-day Larkspur and San Francisco several times a week. It carried lumber, hides, beef, and produce from Marin County and returned with merchandise purchased in San Francisco.

Don Juan Bautista Rogerio (John Rogers) Cooper[4] of Monterey County owned *Rancho Punta de Quintin*, but spent little time here. The Irishman James Miller was lumbering the redwood forests located on the rancho and tending to Cooper's cattle. The U.S. government leased a section of the point for a sawmill. Benjamin Rush Buckelew purchased the rancho in late 1850.[5]

Don Timoteo (Timothy) Murphy owned *Rancho San Pedro, Santa Margarita y las Gallinas.* He had built a two-story adobe in 1839 in San Rafael, but he was living in the mission buildings and renting his home to *Don* Antonio María Osio. The first settler in the county, James Miller, owned 680 acres of the *Las Gallinas* portion of Murphy's rancho and built several small houses on it.

Don Domingo Sais owned *Rancho Cañada de Herrera.* Dr. Alfred W. Taliaferro was developing an estate on 40 acres of this rancho on the bank of Corte Madera Creek that Sais had given him in 1849.

Captain Stephen Smith, a native of Maryland, owned *Rancho Punta de los Reyes,* which consisted of two parts separated by *Rancho Tomales y Baulenes* and *Rancho Punta de los Reyes Sobrante. Don* Antonio María Osio owned the latter rancho, which was largely surrounded by water—Drakes Bay,[6] the Pacific Ocean, and Tomales Bay. Osio and his family did not live on the rancho, as they were renting Timothy Murphy's house in San Rafael. Squatters were invading these rancho lands that later became valuable dairying country, as well as a significant source of limestone.[7]

Don Gregorio Briones owned *Rancho Baulenes.* He grazed longhorn cattle on the rolling hills and the valley. Briones also leased logging rights on Bolinas Ridge to Euro-American lumbermen. Nearly 200 of Marin County's mere 323 residents in 1850 were located in the vicinity cutting timber. Lumber was shipped from Bolinas and Stinson Beach to San Francisco for the construction of wharves and warehouses. The first sawmill would be built in the area in 1851. Within ten years all of the redwoods were stripped from Bolinas Ridge.

Don Rafael Garcia owned *Rancho Tomales y Baulenes.* He and his family lived in a large adobe he built in 1837. Several other adobes and frame buildings stood on the property for his employees. Garcia owned over 400 horses and raised cattle, sheep and swine. His employees wove cloth from the wool sheared from the sheep and made boots and shoes from the leather tanned from the hides of the cattle. The Irishman John Keys was one of the many squatters that swarmed into the area to establish farms, graze cattle, and build fences, wharves, and roads. He and Alexander Noble established the town of Tomales in 1850. Keys owned and operated the schooner *Spray* that transported passengers and produce to San Francisco.

The Miwok leader José Camilo Ynitia owned *Rancho Olompali,*[8] which bordered Sonoma County. He raised cattle, grew grain, and had a small vineyard. The ruins of his 1837 adobe (Camilo Ynitia Adobe) stand next to the burned ruins of a later mansion in the Olompali State Historic Park. A shed was built over the ruins to protect them from further damage, but the ruins may be viewed through glass windows.

William Antonio Richardson (1795-1858)

- Arrived in Yerba Buena (San Francisco) in 1822 from London

- Built the first house at Yerba Buena and served as *commandante* of San Francisco Presidio

- Married daughter of Ignacio Martinez—María Antonia

- Operated cattle, produce, and wood trading business centered on Richardson's Bay

- First port captain of San Francisco—guided ships through bay; took first boat up Sacramento River

- Vast landholder in Marin, Mendocino, and San Diego counties

- Died penniless and in debt due to unwise investments

Alfred W. Taliaferro (1827-1885)

- Surgeon who arrived in San Francisco with Virginia Company in 1849

- Rented mission lands from Timothy Murphy where he farmed and doctored on the side, usually free of charge

- Established a medical office and drugstore in San Rafael

- Served as prison doctor at San Quentin and as Marin's first county physician

- State assemblyman and senator

- Largely responsible for establishment of Mount Tamalpais Cemetery where he is buried

Marin County would remain somewhat isolated until trains and ferries began operations in the 1880s and 90s. The Golden Gate Bridge was not built until 1937 and the Richmond-San Rafael Bridge not until 1956.

MARIN COUNTY RANCHOS

NAME OF RANCHO	GRANTEE AND/OR 1850 OWNER	1850 AND/OR CURRENT SITES
Rancho Saucelito (Little Willow)	William Antonio Richardson	Sausalito, Marin Headlands, Mill Valley, Muir Woods, Mt. Tamalpais [9]
Rancho Corte de Madera del Presidio (Where Wood is Cut for the Presidio)	Heirs of John Thomas Reed	Greenbrae, Larkspur, Belvedere, Tiburon, Mill Valley, Corte Madera
Rancho Punta de Quintin	John Rogers Cooper, Benjamin Buckelew	San Anselmo, Ross, Kentfield, Larkspur
Rancho San Pedro, Santa Margarita y las Gallinas (Saints Peter and Margaret and the Hens)	Timothy Murphy	San Rafael, Terra Linda, Marinwood, Lucas Valley, Gallinas
Rancho Cañada de Herrera (Vale of the Blacksmiths)	Domingo Sais, Alfred W. Taliaferro	Fairfax, San Anselmo
Rancho Punta de los Reyes (Point of the Kings)	Stephen Smith	Inverness
Rancho Tomales y Baulenes	Rafael Garcia	Olema, Golden Gate National Recreation Area
Rancho Punta de los Reyes Sobrante (Leftover Land)	Antonio María Osio	Drakes Beach, Tomales Bay State Park, Point Reyes National Seashore
Rancho Las Baulenes	Gregorio Briones	Bolinas
Rancho Cañada de San Gerónimo (Valley of Saint Jerome)	Joseph Warren Revere; late 1850-Rodman Price	San Geronimo, Lagunitas, Forest Knolls, Woodacre
Rancho Nicasio	Pablo de la Guerra, John Rogers Cooper, Jasper O'Farrell; late 1850-Benjamin Buckelew, Henry W. Halleck, Jasper O'Farrell	Marshall
Rancho Soulajule	José Ramon Mesa; late 1850-George Cornwell and Lewis D. Watkins	South of Tomales
Rancho Corte Madera de Novato (New Place Where Wood is Cut)	John Martin	San Marin, Novato
Rancho Olompali	José Camilo Ynitia	Olompali State Historic Park north of Novato
Rancho Novato (New)	Bezer and Benjamin Franklin Simmons	Novato
Rancho San José	Ignacio Pacheco	Ignacio; Hamilton Air Force Base (closed)
Rancho Buacocha	Teodora Peralta Duarte	Between Point Reyes Station and Petaluma in Sonoma County

1

Angel Island would become part of the public domain in 1856 through court proceedings and have a varied history—serving as a Civil War fortress, an immigration station, a quarantine station, a prisoner of war detention camp, an embarkation point for World War II troops, and a Nike missile site.

2

See Suñol sidebar on page 142.

3

Actually, Benjamin R. Buckelew took possession of *Rancho Corte de Madera del Presidio* in the fall of 1850, but the court found him in violation of probate court orders in 1851, so the Reed family regained ownership. In the brief time Buckelew thought he owned the rancho, he purchased the Baltimore and Frederick Trading and Mining Company in Baltimore Canyon, built a mile of fence, and laid out "California City" on 320 acres bordering the present-day Corte Madera shoreline. He moved a prefabricated hotel and several houses on the site of his city.

4

See Cooper sidebar on page 96.

5

Subsequently, Buckelew would sell 20 acres on the eastern part of *Rancho Punta de Quintin* to the State of California and San Quentin (Americans changed the spelling) Prison was established here in 1853. Previously, California's convicts had been housed on hulks of ships anchored off Angel Island.

6

Historians cannot agree on where Francis Drake landed when he arrived in Marin County in 1579 and claimed the land he called Nova Albion (New England) for the British crown. He is generally considered to have landed at what is known today as Drakes Beach.

7

The Russians had built kilns near present-day Olema to make whitewash, bricks, and tiles during their residence in Sonoma County. In 1850 lime was in demand for the construction of fireproof brick buildings in San Francisco.

8

Oak and laurel grew on *Rancho Olompali* and two neighboring ranchos, but the timber industry would ultimately denude the areas in order to serve both the local population and San Francisco.

9

The redwood forests of Muir Woods, located in a remote ravine, escaped logging during the building spree in San Francisco and today contain some trees estimated to be over 1,700 years old. A team of U.S. geological surveyors would make the first recorded climb of Mt. Tamalpais in 1862. Some of the existing hiking trails were originally made by Native Americans and early pioneers.

1850 Counties

⚬ 1850 ⚬
⚬ SONOMA ⚬
COUNTY

Lake
Co.

Mendocino
Co.

Cloverdale •

Geyserville •

Healdsburg •

Sonoma
Co.

Pacific
Ocean

Mark West •

Napa
Co.

Occidental •   • Sebastopol

Bodega •

Glen
• Ellen

Sonoma •

• Petaluma

Marin
Co.

California
1850

Present-day boundary
variations indicated by

— — — —

Settlements/cities of 1850 include: Sonoma

SONOMA COUNTY
1850

In 1850 Sonoma County included a small southern portion of present-day Mendocino County, and Mendocino County included the northwestern portion of present-day Sonoma County—part of a rancho and public lands to the east.[1] Its 560 residents counted in the 1850 U.S. Census included some Californios, but a larger number of Americans and Europeans. The uncounted Native American inhabitants included members of the Pomo and Coast Miwok tribes.

Sonoma County is comprised of coastal plains and three valleys divided by hills and mountains. The Pacific Ocean borders it on the west and a portion of San Pablo Bay lies on its southern border. In 1850 the county consisted of its county seat in Sonoma,[2] the former Mission San Francisco Solano, Fort Ross, and 25 ranchos.

Mission San Francisco Solano and Town of Sonoma

Like Marin County, the early settlement of Sonoma County by the Spanish occurred as a result of their fear of the Russian settlement at Fort Ross. (See below.) In an effort to deter the Russians from moving into the interior north of San Francisco, the last and northernmost of the 21 California missions—*Misión San Francisco Solano de Sonoma*—was established in 1823. After secularization in 1834, the mission suffered from neglect and looting. In 1838, while its roof was under repair, an unexpected rainstorm completely destroyed the mission. General Mariano G. Vallejo had built a smaller adobe church in 1840, which in 1850 was serving as the parish church of Sonoma. The church would be sold to a private citizen in 1881 and used for secular purposes until 1903, when a public fund was raised and the old mission deeded to the State of California for restoration. Sonoma's oldest structure, the 1825 padres' quarters, as well as the 1840 adobe church next door, are today part of the Sonoma State Historic Park.

In a further effort to discourage the Russians from venturing inland, General Vallejo was directed to establish the *Pueblo de Sonoma* in 1835. Vallejo laid out the new pueblo around a plaza.[3] The two-story Sonoma Barracks was built for Vallejo's soldiers in 1840-41. In 1850 the barracks was an important U.S. military post known as Camp Sonoma—the U.S. military headquarters for the entire Pacific Coast.[4] It was serving as a supply depot for military units heading north into Native American country, and also as a hospital. Today the barracks has been restored to its original form and houses a museum in the Sonoma State Historic Park.

The Mexican painter, Augustin Davils, had drawn the first map of the plaza and adjoining blocks of Sonoma in 1840. In 1847, at the direction of *Alcalde* Lilburn

Sites to Visit in Sonoma County

Petaluma Adobe State Historic Park, 3325 Adobe Rd. at Casa Grande, Petaluma 707.762.4871

Petaluma Historical Library/Museum, 20 Fourth St., Petaluma 707.778.4398

Sonoma County Museum, 425 Seventh St., Santa Rosa 707.579.1500

Sonoma State Historic Park, 20 East Spain St., Sonoma 707.938.1519

- Blue Wing Inn, 133 East Spain St. (Private Residence)
- Padres' House and Mission San Francisco Solano
- Sonoma Barracks/Museum
- Servants' Quarters
- Swiss Hotel, 18 West Spain St.
- Salvador Vallejo Adobe, 417 First St. West (Hotel & other businesses)
- Leese-Fitch Adobe, 487 First St. West, Sonoma (Private Residence)
- John G. Ray House, 205 East Spain St., Sonoma (Private Residence)
- Nash-Patton Adobe, 579 First St. East, Sonoma (Private Residence)
- La Casita, 143 West Spain St., Sonoma (Private Residence)

Sonoma Valley Historical Society Depot Park Museum, 270 First St. West, Sonoma 707.938.1762

Vallejo Home State Historical Monument (1851-52), Spain at Third St. West, Sonoma 707.938.1519

Sonoma Valley Visitors Bureau, 453 First St. East, Sonoma, CA 95476 707.996.1090

W. Boggs, Jasper O'Farrell[5] and J. M. Hudspeth had surveyed the pueblo into town lots that were then sold to those who had already built on them for $5 per acre. The remaining vacant lots were sold to the highest bidder.

Sonoma was incorporated on April 4, 1850. Male settlers and deserting soldiers had left Sonoma for the gold fields in 1848, but by 1850, many had returned disappointed, broke, and tired.

John Cameron, a former member of Stevenson's Regiment, was the first American mayor of Sonoma. Captain John E. Brackett was practicing law and representing Sonoma in the first State Legislature. The former state governor of Missouri, Lilburn W. Boggs, and William Scott were operating a general merchandise store in town, as was Captain John Frisbie, the husband of one of Vallejo's daughters.

In 1850 the Sonoma Barracks was an important U.S. military post known as Camp Sonoma—the U.S. military headquarters for the entire Pacific Coast.

The two-story adobe used as a kitchen and servants' quarters is all that remains of Vallejo's Casa Grande Adobe. It is located in the Sonoma State Historic Park.

The Salvador Vallejo adobe is located across from the plaza in downtown Sonoma.

Several private schools were operating in the Sonoma area in 1850, but it would be 1857 before a public school system was established.

General Mariano Vallejo's large two-story *La Casa Grande*, where he and his family lived until he built his famous *Lachryma Montis* (Tears of the Mountain) at the edge of town in 1851, stood next door to the barracks. The complex was the center of social and political life north of the San Francisco Bay. Vallejo owned one of the first three pianos brought to California from Baltimore. He produced prize-winning wines from the original mission vineyard located behind his adobe.[6] Only the two-story adobe used as a kitchen and servants' quarters remains today, as a fire would destroy the main wing in 1867.

Other adobes stood around the open plaza and a few remain today, some protected by wood siding, including the Swiss Hotel[7] that was a newly constructed wing of Captain Salvador Vallejo's original 1840 adobe; another Salvador Vallejo adobe, which he had built in the early 1840s; and the 1841 Leese-Fitch adobe, which was serving as the headquarters for the U. S. Army in 1850 and is a private residence today. The second story on the Leese-Fitch adobe would not be added until 1851 when it was serving as a hotel.

Several other adobes remain today in Sonoma, although not on the plaza, including Captain Juan Castenada's 1846 *La Casita*, the 1840 Blue Wing Inn–a combination hotel, restaurant, and casino;[8] the 1847 John G. Ray House, and the 1847 Nash-Patton Adobe, where Nancy Bones Patton Adler, a survivor of the Donner party, lived. All of these buildings are private residences today.

Many other one and two-story adobes were once located on the plaza and around the town, including the 1849 H. A. Green Courthouse, the 1847 Union Hotel operated by three former members of Stevenson's Regiment, *La Casa Del Billiar*—a recreation hall, an adobe jail, and Nicholas Carriger's house on First Street East, which was Sonoma's first redwood frame house.

Christian and Marie Brunner, a Swiss-German couple who had moved to Sonoma in the late 1840s, were operating a dairy. They were also caring for their two adopted daughters, orphans of the Donner family, who survived the tragic trip across the Sierras. "Grandma" Brunner also had been operating Sonoma's first hospital in her home since 1848—treating ailing miners returning from the gold fields. In 1850 she was supplementing the health care provided at the barracks.

In 1850 the Blue Wing Inn was a combination hotel, restaurant and casino. Today it is a private apartment building located across from the mission.

Since 1847, various sloops had been making the voyage between San Francisco and Sonoma, landing at the Port of Sonoma among the swampy bull rushes of a slough of the Napa River located two miles south of town. But in 1849 much of the traffic was diverted to the Sacramento River when boat operators that could navigate that river found it to be the quickest route to the gold fields.

The John G. Ray House is a private residence viewable from the exterior only.

Although Sonoma had only limited industry or commerce in 1850, settlers were attracted to the area because there was an abundance of food and water, as well as redwood and oak for firewood and building materials. Many settlers earned spending money by making shingles, fence posts, barrels, and wheels.

The Nash-Patton Adobe is a private residence viewable from the exterior only.

Fort Ross

Fort Ross had been founded in 1812 by Alaska-based Russians to serve as a southern post to hunt otter and seal and to grow food for the Russian colonies in Alaska. Constructed of redwood, the fort consisted of 60 to 70 buildings around a central structure. Russia had withdrawn its colonists from California in 1839 because the sea otters were decimated and because the colonists were unsuccessful in their agricultural pursuits never being able to produce enough for substantial exports.

All of Fort Ross, including the improvements and supplies, was sold to Captain John A. Sutter[9] of New Helvetia in 1841. Sutter dismantled many of the buildings and transported his purchases to his fort in the Sacramento Valley. In 1850, Native Americans were living in the buildings that were not razed—the Russian chapel, the commandant's house, and a few other buildings. The State of California acquired the

- Member of the Ignacio Vallejo and María Antonia Lugo family of Monterey County

- Married Francisca Benicia Carrillo

- Commander of northern Mexican frontier

- Secularized Mission San Francisco Solano and founded Pueblo of Sonoma

- Offered American soldiers and settlers advice on how to handle Native Americans and get along with Mexican officials

- Imprisoned at Sutter's Fort after Bear Flag Revolt

- Delegate of State Constitutional Convention, state senator, two-term mayor of Sonoma, head of State Lands Committee

- Owned ranchos in Sonoma and Solano counties where he raised cattle and sheep and various crops

- Partner with his son-in-law, Captain John B. Frisbie, in merchandising goods for miners and developing towns of Benicia (named for his wife) and Vallejo

- Offered lands and money to establish the state capital at Vallejo

- Avid reader and collector of official Mexican government papers in his later years

- Wrote a five-volume history of California, which he donated to Hubert Howe Bancroft for his research library

- Supporter of California Horticultural Society

- One of wealthiest and most influential men in California; one of few literate *Californios*; unfailingly generous and gracious even when taken advantage of

- Went broke after backing the financial failures of his son-in-law, John B. Frisbie, to whom he mistakenly gave full power of attorney; at his death, his adobe *Lachryma Montis* was his only holding

fort in 1906, but less than a month later, the 1906 earthquake would severely damage the buildings. Today, the reconstructed stockade, blockhouses, a Russian chapel, officers' barracks, a Russian well, and a storehouse make up Fort Ross State Historic Park.

Sonoma County Ranchos

Sonoma County's 25 Mexican land grants had been awarded primarily to General Vallejo's relatives or friends; a few were granted to retired soldiers. Details about the more interesting ones follow.

General Mariano Vallejo and the German musician, Andreas Hoeppner, owned *Rancho Agua Caliente* along Sonoma Creek adjacent to the town of Sonoma. Vallejo transplanted his grapevines from his town lot and planted an assortment of fruit and shade trees. In 1851-52 he would build his *Lachryma Montis* (Tears of the Mountain) frame/adobe house and the special warehouse for storing wine, fruit, and other produce, known today as the Swiss Chalet. The house was prefabricated on the East Coast and shipped around the Horn. The exterior of the Swiss chalet was built of brick and specially prefabricated timbers imported from Europe in 1849-50. Both buildings are preserved today in the Vallejo Home State Historical Monument. These post-1850 structures are included as sites to visit because so much can be learned about Vallejo—a significant figure in California's pre- and post-1850 history.

Hoeppner gained his portion of the rancho in payment for providing piano lessons to the Vallejo children over a five-year period. He had built a small bathhouse in 1847 and tried to attract San Franciscans to visit for curative miracles, but the business floundered. Thaddeus N. Leavenworth, a chaplain for Stevenson's Regiment of New York Volunteers, owned another portion of the rancho.

Vallejo also owned the large *Rancho Petaluma*. Between 1834 and 1840, he built the grandest adobe in northern California in the foothills of the Sonoma Mountains above Petaluma Valley. Although never completed, the adobe was then nearly twice as large as it is today. The original thatched roof was replaced in the early 1840s when George Yount[10] was commissioned to provide hand-split shingles for an all-wood roof on the adobe building. In September of 1850, Vallejo leased the rancho to a group of French colonists. The restored adobe is located today in the Petaluma Adobe State Historic Park.

Don Juan Miranda owned *Rancho Roblar de la Miseria*, which was located on the current site of the city of Petaluma. Beef from Miranda's and Vallejo's neighboring ranchos was in great demand in the gold mining camps.

In 1847 the German doctor Johann F. A. Heyermann had been the first to bring a sloop up Petaluma Creek, a slough called Petaluma River today, which runs northward from San Pablo Bay to Petaluma. He built a log cabin at the present location of McNear Park, practiced some medicine, and speculated on small parcels of land in the area.

A settlement of hunters' camps and trading posts was set up on the banks of the Petaluma Creek. Hunters and trappers, including Tom Lockwood, who would later help establish Petaluma, worked the nearby hills to obtain fresh meat—geese, ducks, quail, elk, deer, antelope, rabbits, grizzly bears, and mountain lions—to supply the hoards of people passing through San Francisco. A hunter with meat for sale could usually make more money than the average miner. The site of present-day Petaluma was a major point of commerce between San Francisco and the gold fields. A warehouse to store produce, chiefly potatoes, for shipment to San Francisco was built during 1850 and a few other buildings would be built in 1851. Many disappointed gold miners returned to Petaluma—having gazed upon the beautiful valleys surrounding it on their way to the mines.

Stephen Smith, of Maryland, owned *Rancho Bodega*, located on the coast. He built a sawmill in the redwood region east of Bodega Head and a house near Salmon Creek. Smith was in control of Bodega Bay in 1850.[11]

Don Juan German Peña owned *Rancho Tzabaco*, where Geyserville is located today. The geysers and hot springs in the hills outside Geyserville had been discovered in 1847 by former North Carolinians William Bell Elliott and his son while on a bear hunt. The medicinal value of the springs was advertised in San Francisco newspapers and they would become the second most popular natural attraction in California—behind Yosemi-te—in the 1850s. Today a major utility company uses the geyser steam as a source of thermal power.

In 1850 Native Americans were living in the few buildings remaining at Fort Ross. Alaska-based Russians had founded the fort in 1812, but sold it to John A. Sutter in 1841.

Before his death in 1849, Captain Henry Delano Fitch, a San Diego businessman and brother-in-law of General Vallejo, owned *Rancho Sotoyome*. He had hired Cyrus Alexander, a trapper and trader, to live on the rancho. Alexander raised horses, cattle, orchards, and wheat. His restored adobe now stands as a private residence in Alexander Valley.

The Vallejo Home State Historical Monument, Vallejo's Lachryma Montis (Tears of the Mountain) frame/adobe house, was erected in 1851.

Don Juan Bautista Rogerio (John Rogers) Cooper owned *Rancho Molinos*. In 1834 he had built the first waterpower-operated commercial sawmill in California along Mark West Creek north of present-day Forestville. The sawmill had been destroyed by a flood in 1840.

In 1850 a group of French colonists was leasing Vallejo's adobe that remains in the Petaluma Adobe State Historic Park today.

The heirs of *Señora* María Ignacia López de Carrillo owned *Rancho Cabeza de Santa Rosa*. The *Señora* and her eight unmarried children had moved here from San Diego following her husband's death in 1836. She had passed away in 1849. One of her married daughters was Francisca Benicia Carrillo Vallejo. Another daughter, Juana de Jesús Carrillo Mallagh and her husband, David, lived in the 1838-39 adobe ranch house along the Santa Rosa Creek. A portion of the house ruins remains today and efforts are being made to restore it.

Don José de los Santos Berryessa, General Vallejo's former sergeant, owned *Rancho Mallacomes*, which extended across the Sonoma/Napa County line. He built an adobe "hunting lodge" in Knight's Valley. Thomas Knight, from Arkansas, purchased a large portion of the rancho from Berryessa and added a second story to the adobe. He grew fruit and wheat and raised sheep.

Today Sonoma County is famed for the Sonoma Valley, a federally-designated wine appellation region ranked as one of the top wine producing regions in the world. Wine grapes from Europe were first grown successfully in Sonoma County, bringing the area recognition as the birthplace of the California wine industry. Colonel Agoston Haraszthy, the Hungarian nobleman who lived in San Mateo County in 1850, would plant European grape varieties and discover that vines in the coastal regions of California do not require irrigation to flourish. He established the Buena Vista Vineyard east of the town of Sonoma in 1856.

SONOMA COUNTY RANCHOS

NAME OF RANCHO	GRANTEE AND/OR 1850 OWNER	1850 AND/OR CURRENT SITE
Rancho Huichica	Jacob P. Leese	Southeastern Sonoma County and southwestern Napa County
Rancho Agua Caliente (Hot Water)	Mariano Vallejo, Andreas Hoeppner, Thaddeus N. Leavenworth	Sonoma
Rancho Petaluma	Mariano Vallejo	Petaluma
Rancho Roblar de la Miseria	Juan Miranda	Petaluma
Rancho Laguna de San Antonio	Bartolome Bojourques	Two Rock; extended into Marin County
Rancho Blucher	Stephen Smith	Bloomfield; extended into Marin County
Rancho Cañada de Pogolimi	Various Americans recommended by John Rogers Cooper[12]	Valley Ford, Freestone
Rancho Estero Americano (American Salt Marsh)	Various Americans recommended by John Rogers Cooper	Bodega
Rancho Bodega (Wine Cellar or Storeroom)	Stephen Smith	Bodega Bay, Salmon Creek, Carmet, Sereno Del Mar, Ocean View, Bridge Haven
Rancho Muñiz	Manuel Torres	Sea Ranch
Rancho Rincón de Musalacon	Francisco Berryessa	Cloverdale
Rancho Caslamayomi	Eng Montenegro	East of Cloverdale
Rancho Tzabaco	Juan German Peña	Geyserville
Rancho Sotoyome	Francisca Benicia Carrillo Fitch	Alexander and Russian River valleys, Healdsburg
Rancho Molinos (Mills)	John Rogers Cooper	Summer Home Park, Forestville
Rancho Cañada de Jonive	Jasper O'Farrell	East of Occidental
Rancho Llano de Santa Rosa	Joaquín Carrillo	Sebastopol
Rancho Cotati	Juan Castañada	Cotati
Rancho Los Guilicos	John Wilson[13]	Kenwood, Glen Ellen[14]
Rancho Cabeza de Santa Rosa (Head of Saint Rose)	Heirs of María Ignacia López de Carrillo	Santa Rosa
Rancho San Miguel	William Mark West	Mark West, Fulton
Rancho Mallacomes	José de los Santos Berryessa, Thomas Knight	Knight's Valley; extended into Napa County

1

All of the area in present-day Sonoma County is covered in this chapter.

2

The Sonoma County seat would be moved to Santa Rosa in 1854.

3

Sonoma is where the Bear Flag Revolt of 1846 took place. A monument in the old Sonoma Plaza memorializes the site where the flag was first raised.

4

One of the officers stationed at Camp Sonoma—Colonel Joe Hooker—remained in Sonoma after the post closed in 1851. His legendary behavior is said to have added the word "hooker" to our language. When two recruits asked about "loose" women, they were told there were none. Inquiring about two women suggestively attired standing nearby, the recruits were informed that they "were Hooker's."

5

See O'Farrell sidebar on page 126.

6

Today Vallejo's vineyard is part of the Samuel Sebastiani Vineyard and Winery.

7

The Reegers were living here at the time; it would not become the Swiss Hotel until the 1880s.

8

In 1850, the Blue Wing Inn was known as The Sonoma House.

9

See Sutter sidebar on page 226.

10

See Yount sidebar on page 177.

11

Bodega Bay was discovered in 1603 by the Sebastian Vizcaíno expedition searching for harbors, but not named until 1775 when the Spanish explorer Juan Francisco de la Bodega y Cuadra entered the bay. It was established as a port by the Russian settlers who settled at Fort Ross and also at a settlement called Kuskov in Salmon Creek Valley.

12

See Cooper sidebar on page 96.

13

See Wilson sidebar on page 85.

14

In 1905, author Jack London would establish his ranch on the former *Rancho Los Guilicos* in the *Valle de la Luna* (Valley of the Moon), so named as early as 1841, and he would entitle a romance novel *Valley of the Moon*.

Jacob Primer Leese (1809–1892)

- Santa Fe trader from Ohio who arrived in Yerba Buena (San Francisco) in 1836
- Built the first frame building in San Francisco in 1836
- Opened a mercantile business on the corner of present-day Clay Street and Grant Avenue in San Francisco
- Married a sister of General Vallejo; their daughter was first Anglo child born in Yerba Buena
- Moved to Sonoma in 1841; served as *alcalde*

Lilburn W. Boggs (1798 -1861)

- Wealthy Missouri landholder, pro-slavery politician, former Missouri state governor
- Came to California in 1846 with his wife, son, and daughter-in-law in hopes of being appointed governor of the territory
- Stayed at Vallejo's home in Petaluma for a time, developing a close, mutually beneficial relationship
- *Alcalde*, postmaster, state assemblyman, general store owner
- Purchased a ranch in Napa Valley in 1854 and lived there until his death

1850 Counties

❧ 1 8 5 0 ❧
❧ NAPA ❧
COUNTY

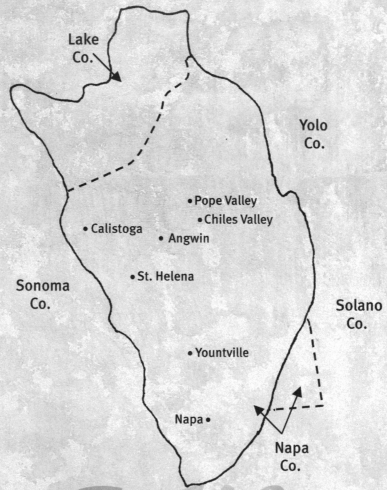

Lake Co.

Yolo Co.

• Pope Valley

• Chiles Valley

• Calistoga   • Angwin

• St. Helena

Sonoma Co.

Solano Co.

• Yountville

Napa •

Napa Co.

California
1850

Present-day boundary
variations indicated by

— — — — —

Settlements/cities of 1850 include: Napa

NAPA COUNTY 1850

The geographical area of 1850-Napa County included a small southern portion of present-day Lake County until 1861 when the latter county was established. Napa County's 405 residents counted in the 1850 U.S. Census included Californios and a large number, proportionately, of Americans and Europeans. Many of the pioneers and adventurers who were unsuccessful in their search for gold had drifted into Napa County. The uncounted Native American population included members of the Pomo, Lake Miwok, Wappo, and Patwin tribes.

In 1850 Napa County consisted of its county seat, Napa, and a dozen ranchos. Quite a number of American farmers had settled on the property of one of the ranchos—*Rancho Carne Humana*—during the mid-1840s. (See below.) Wild oats covered the areas where vineyards grow today in the Napa Valley; the hills and mountain areas were heavily forested with redwoods, pines, and firs and densely populated with deer and bear.

City of Napa

The city of Napa was laid out in 1847 by Nathan Coombs, from Massachusetts, on property he had purchased from *Don* Nicolás Higuerra. The city consisted of two blocks with five cross streets—First through Fifth. Harrison Pierce had built the first frame building—a saloon—in 1848 on the south side of Third Street near the Napa River. J. P. Thompson was operating Napa's first store at the foot of Main Street. William Russell had been operating a ferry across the river since 1848 and Turner G. Baxter began operating a steamship between Napa and San Francisco in 1850. A tent city sprang up along Main Street in late 1850 when disappointed miners arrived seeking refuge from severe winters in the gold fields. They found plenty of work in the valley on cattle ranches and in sawmills.

Napa County's first courthouse was built in 1849 on the corner of Coombs and Second Streets. It would be 1855 before a public primary school opened in Napa and 1856 before a newspaper began publication—*The Napa Reporter*.

Napa County Ranchos

A dozen ranchos had been granted in Napa County. *Rancho Tulocay* was among the more noteworthy. *Don* Cayetano Juárez, a native Californian, high-ranking Mexican military officer, and former *alcalde* of Sonoma, owned this rancho. He and his family had moved here from Sonoma in the early 1840s. The second adobe home he built in 1847 houses a tavern today in Napa—the Old Adobe Bar and Grill.

Sites to Visit in Napa County

Bale Grist Mill State Historic Park, 3801 St. Helena Highway (SR 29), Calistoga 707.942.4575

Old Adobe Bar and Grill, (Juarez Adobe), 376 Soscol Av., Napa

Napa Historical Society Museum and Library, 1219 First St., Napa 707.224.1739

Napa Valley Museum, Veterans Home, 55 Presidents Cir., Yountville 707.944-0500

Napa Valley Conference and Visitors Bureau, 1310 Napa Town Center, Napa, CA 94559 707.226.7459

Don Jorge Concepción (George Calvert) Yount owned *Rancho Caymus*, which was heavily populated with Native Americans and grizzly bears. He lived alone on his property in the heart of the Napa Valley. Neighboring American Indians helped him build his Kentucky log blockhouse and later additions along the Napa River in 1836. His two-story adobe was often called the "fort" because the thick walls contained portholes along their 100-foot lengths. Yount planted a variety of fruit trees, vineyards, oats, barley, and wheat, and he raised cattle, sheep, and horses. He also built a sawmill and flourmill on his rancho.

The widow and six children of Dr. Edward Turner Bale owned *Rancho Carne Humana.* The English doctor had practiced medicine in Monterey during the

Today the Old Adobe Bar and Grill is housed in this 1847 adobe in Napa.

The reconstructed gristmill, built by Dr. Edward Turner Bale in 1846, stands today in Bale Grist Mill State Historic Park in Calistoga.

1830s, married Carolina Soberanes, a niece of General Vallejo; and acquired this rancho in 1843. In the short time until his untimely death in 1849, he built an adobe along a small stream known today as Bale Creek and had Ralph L. Kilburn build a sawmill and F. E. Kellogg build a gristmill along the banks of the Napa River. The gristmill would operate for 25 years—supplying flour for the settlers—and still stands today in Bale Grist Mill State Historic Park.

American settlers—Wells and Ralph Kilburn, Peter Storm, John T. York, Enoch Cyrus, William and David Hudson, William Fowler and sons, Frank Bidwell, William Hargrave, John Grigsby, Benjamin Dewell, Bartlett Vines, and Elias Barnett; and Benjamin and Nancy Kelsey—had purchased portions of Bale's rancho in the mid-1840s. Most lived in log cabins where St. Helena and Calistoga are located today. (Nancy Kelsey was the first Anglo woman to cross the plains in 1841 with the Bidwell-Bartleson party.)

Two other families had originally been members of the ill-fated Donner party, but separated before tragedy befell the party and arrived safely before the early snows in 1846. One of those families—William H. Nash, his wife, and 14 children—lived on their ranch called Walnut Grove south of present-day Calistoga. Nash built a board house with lumber cut at Bale's mill, and planted an orchard from seedlings brought by Elias Barnett from Kentucky. The other family—the surviving Reason P. Tucker family—lived further south, as did F. E. Kellogg, who had built Dr. Bale's gristmill. The Kellogg's 1849 house, built of lumber cut at Bale's sawmill, still stands as a private residence today. It is the oldest house in the Upper Napa Valley.

With the considerable population of Americans, *Rancho Carne Humana* became the site of a few of Napa County's first public buildings. An 1849 building built by William H. Nash across from the gristmill was serving as a private school until the first public school opened in 1854. Sarah Graves Fosdick, another survivor of the Donner party, had been teaching the children of the area since 1847. The first church in the valley, the White Church, a Methodist Episcopal church named after its pastor, would be built in 1853 on the site of Bothe-Napa Valley State Park.

The remarried widow of Julian Pope, Maria Juliana Barnett, owned *Rancho Locoallomi*. She and her new husband, Elias J. Barnett, and her five children lived on the rancho. Cinnabar would be discovered on this rancho in the 1860s and a large Chinese community arose in the area. The well-made stone fences that line many of Napa County's roads date from the period following the closure of the Aetna cinnabar mine when the skillful Chinese stonemasons sought other work.

Joseph Ballinger Chiles owned *Rancho Catacula*. Chiles' 1846 adobe still stands on a private ranch today, but the gristmill he built collapsed into the Chiles Creek.

Today the Napa Valley is one of California's most famous wine-producing regions. Early Spanish and American settlers, including George Yount, had made wine from small vineyards, but it would be 1858 before Charles Krug made the first commercial wine in the county at Napa. In addition to the cinnabar found in 1860 that influenced the development of Napa County, two silver discoveries occurred in 1858 and 1874-75. The railroad arrived in 1865.

Mineral springs were discovered on public lands in the foothills west of present-day St. Helena in 1848. The first mineral springs resort in California—White Sulphur Springs—would open in 1852. Sam Brannan opened his Calistoga Hot Springs in 1868. Calistoga is still famous today for its mineral waters and health resorts.

George Calvert Yount (1794-1865)

- Native North Carolinian who came to California from New Mexico in 1831
- Left his wife behind who was seeking a divorce when she died in 1850
- Hunted sea otter on Santa Barbara Channel Islands
- First to make shingles in California in 1833 in Santa Barbara
- Trapped beaver in San Francisco Bay area and along San Joaquin River
- Employed by missions in San Rafael and Sonoma to make repairs
- First American settler in the Napa Valley
- Commissioned a surveyor to lay out a city in 1855—Sebastopol, even though one already existed in Sonoma County; town was renamed Yountville in 1867
- Gracious host and encourager to other American pioneers in the area

NAPA COUNTY RANCHOS

NAME OF RANCHO	GRANTEE AND/OR 1850 OWNER	1850 AND/OR CURRENT SITES
Rancho Rincon de Los Carneros (Sheep)	Nicolás Higuera	South of Napa
Rancho Entre Napa	Nicolás Higuera and Nathan Coombs	Napa
Rancho Napa	Salvador Vallejo	Napa, Yountville
Rancho Tulocay	Cayetano Juárez	Napa
Rancho Yajome	Damaso Antonio Rodríguez	Napa Valley
Rancho Caymus	George Calvert Yount	Yountville, Oakville
Rancho Carne Humana (Human Flesh)	Widow of Dr. Edward Turner Bale	Calistoga, St. Helena
Rancho de la Jota	George Calvert Yount	Howell Mountain, St. Helena, Deer Park, Angwin
Rancho Locoallomi	Maria Juliana Barnett	Pope Valley
Rancho Catacula	Joseph Ballinger Chiles	Chiles Valley
Rancho Las Putas	José de Jesús and Sisto Berryessa	Berryessa Valley, Lake Berryessa (1954)
Rancho Chimiles	Ignacio Berryessa	Gordon and Wooden valleys

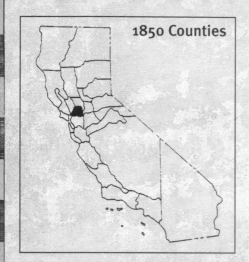

1850 Counties

1850
❦ SOLANO ❧
COUNTY

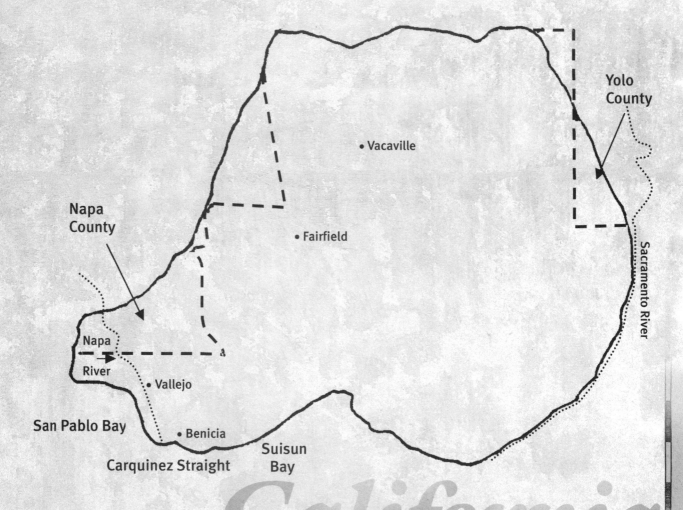

Yolo
County

• Vacaville

Napa
County

• Fairfield

Napa
River

• Vallejo

San Pablo Bay

• Benicia

Carquinez Straight

Suisun
Bay

Sacramento River

California
1850

Present-day boundary
variations indicated by

— — — — —

Settlements/cities of 1850 include: Benicia, Vallejo

SOLANO COUNTY 1850

The geographical area of 1850-Solano County was fairly close to what it is today. Only a few minor changes were subsequently made to its boundary lines. Its 580 residents counted in the 1850 U.S. Census included Californios, Americans, and Europeans. The uncounted Native American population inhabiting the county included the Patwin and Wappo tribes.

Solano County consisted of Benicia, its first county seat, and Vallejo. It only had five ranchos, one of which extended over the Solano-Yolo County line.

Benicia

Incorporated on March 27, 1850, Benicia would serve as the county seat until 1858 when the honor was transferred to Fairfield. Benicia was the brainchild of Dr. Robert Baylor Semple and Thomas Oliver Larkin.[1] Hoping to establish an inland competitor for San Francisco, they had obtained the deed to part of *Rancho Suscol*[2] in 1847, which was owned by General Mariano Vallejo.[3] They hired surveyors to lay out lots and streets, and named their city in honor of Benicia, the General's wife.

The U.S. Army had established the Benicia Barracks in 1849; also known as the "Post near Benicia," it would remain a garrison installation until 1898. The barracks also provided protection for miners and settlers. The Benicia Arsenal would be established as an ordnance depot in 1851. The latter played a major role in U.S. military history from the Civil War to the Korean War and remained in operation until 1964.

In an adobe building on the west side of First Street, Captain Edward H. Von Pfister was operating a general store by day and a bar/hotel at night, with sleeping arrangements on the store's floor. This 1846-47 adobe was the site where the first word of the discovery of gold was leaked by Captain John A. Sutter's courier on his way to Monterey to have the gold samples tested.

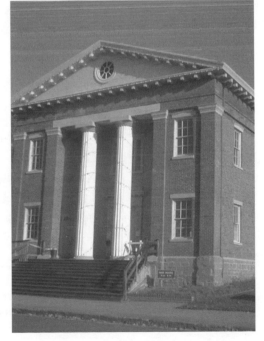

Benicia's 1852 City Hall served as California's third State Capitol from 1853 to 1854.

Sites to Visit in Solano County

Benicia Camel Barn Museum, 2024 Camel Barn Rd., Benicia 707.745.5435

Benicia Capitol State Historic Park, 115 West G St., Benicia 707.745.3385

The Brewery, 120 West H St., Benicia

Captain Walsh Home, 235 East L St., Benicia 707.747.5653 (Bed & Breakfast)

Masonic Lodge Hall, 110 West J St., Benicia

Peña Adobe, Peña Adobe Rd. and I-80, Vacaville

Vallejo Naval and Historical Museum, 734 Marin St., Vallejo 707.643.0077

Washington House, 333 First St., Benicia (private businesses)

Fairfield Suisun Chamber, 1111 Webster St., Fairfield, CA 94533 707.425.4625

Two "formal" hotels were also in operation, as Benicia was a way-station to and from the mines. The 1847 adobe California House, located on West H Street, was built for Major Stephen Cooper, the first mayor of Benicia. His daughter married Dr. Semple in this building—the first recorded marriage in Benicia's history. The rebuilt structure standing today (The Brewery) contains murals depicting Benicia's history; it is believed that the west wall of the current building was part of the original adobe before fire destroyed it.

The 1850 Washington House on First Street would have a colorful history involving state legislators, Chinese gamblers, violators of Prohibition, and prostitutes. Today the remodeled building houses a restaurant and several shops.

A restaurant and several shops are located in the remodeled 1850 Washington House.

Benicia's 1852 City Hall served as California's third State Capitol from 1853 to 1854. This vintage public building is part of the Benicia Capitol State Historic Park, and features a display about the history of California's state houses.

The first Protestant church to have an ordained resident pastor in all of California was built in 1849 where Benicia City Park is located today. Reverend Sylvester Woodbridge, Jr., a Presbyterian missionary from New York, held services on Sunday in a Gothic revival-style church and conducted Benicia's first public day school on weekdays. The first Catholic church would not be built in Benicia until 1852. In 1850, Catholic families were still driving by *carreta* to the Sonoma Mission 40 miles away to attend Mass.

California's first Masonic Lodge Hall stands in Benicia where it was constructed in 1850 of lumber and hardware shipped around the Horn.

California's first Masonic Lodge Hall stands today where it was constructed in 1850 of lumber and hardware shipped around the Horn. The lower floor was used as the county courthouse until 1852. The Peabody Hospital stood on West H Street; Dr. W. F. Peabody had been treating returning miners since 1849. The hospital was rebuilt and serves as a private residence today.

The Captain Walsh Home was one of three identical houses shipped around the Horn from Boston in 1850. Today it is a bed and breakfast in Benicia.

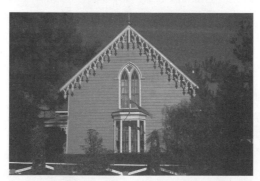

The Captain Walsh Home, today operating as a bed and breakfast, was a prefabricated house erected in 1850 by Captain John Walsh, a retired sea captain.[4] Walsh's wife, Eleanor, was the first woman in Solano County to be registered as a "married woman doing business in her own name." She managed her husband's shipping interests in Chile.

Two other prefabricated residences brought around the Horn from New England and reassembled in 1848 remain in Benicia today. Both are private residences.

Dr. Semple had established ferry service across the Carquinez Straits to Contra Costa County in 1847. Horses frequently accompanied their owners on the small, flat-bottomed boat. In 1850 the Pacific Mail and Steamship Company began operating a fleet of six side-wheelers from the Benicia docks. Regular trips were made from Benicia to the Isthmus of Panama carrying mail and supplies. Benicia also temporarily became an important distribution center for mail and supplies going to the mines. The transcontinental railroad would cause the demise of these operations in 1869, however. Steamboats were able to transport rail cars and a locomotive in one trip across the Suisun Bay to Contra Costa County. (The Southern Pacific Railroad bridge was not completed until 1929.)

City of Vallejo

General Mariano Vallejo founded Eureka (later Vallejo) in 1844. He saw promise in the area due to its central location. Originally part of his *Rancho Suscol*, which was never confirmed, Vallejo had the site of the city surveyed in 1850. Subsequently, corrugated iron homes were imported from Liverpool, England, and the settlement began to expand. One building with an iron roof was serving as a small general store and primitive lodging accommodations.[5]

Mare Island[6] is located across the Napa River from Vallejo. It was granted to Victor Castro in 1850, but he sold it during the year to Vallejo's son-in-law, Captain John B. Frisbee, and his partner, Captain Bezer Simmons. Later in the year, the U.S. Navy commissioner recommended Mare Island as the best location for an arsenal and in 1853-54 the Navy would take over the island and establish the West Coast's first shipyard. (The U.S. Naval Shipyard was closed in 1996 under provisions of the Base Reuse And Closure Act.)

Solano County Ranchos

Seven land grants were made in Solano County, but only five were confirmed. Vallejo's *Rancho Suscol* has already been noted. Another grant—the *Sobrante* grant—was never patented to brothers José and Juan Luco. The property they thought they owned in 1850 is the site of present-day Birds Landing, Collinsville, Denverton, and Montezuma. In 1846, Lansford W. Hastings, a lawyer from Ohio and agent for the Mormons, had selected a site for a colony and built an adobe for himself east of present-day Collinsville. But when the U.S. obtained possession of California in 1846, the Mormons lost interest in the site and Hastings went on to other endeavors. Hastings' one-room house was called "Montezuma House" and stands today, sheathed in redwood, on private property.

The 1843 Vaca-Peña Adobe stands southwest of Vacaville.

Don José Francisco Armijo, and his son Antonio upon José's death in 1850, owned *Rancho Tolenas*. A very small portion of this rancho crossed over the county line into Napa County. The Armijo family lived in an adobe home built northwest

Dr. Robert Semple
(1806-1854)

- Native Kentuckian; arrived in California in 1845 with Lansford Hastings party
- Took part in Bear Flag Revolt
- Co-published the first newspaper in California, *The Californian*
- President of the State Constitutional Convention at Monterey
- Co-founder of Benicia
- Died from injuries sustained in a fall from a horse

of present-day Fairfield and, per the specific requirement of the grant, allowed the American Indians already located on the rancho to remain.

Dons Juan Manuel Vaca and Juan Felipe Peña owned *Rancho Los Putos*, the largest of the county's grants. They built adobe homes southwest of present-day Vacaville. The 1843 Vaca-Peña Adobe stands today along I-80 and is the site where family members, most of whom live in Davis in neighboring Yolo County, continue to gather for family reunions. In 1850 Vaca deeded a portion of *Los Putos* to William McDaniel, who paid $3,000 and agreed to lay out a town site on one square mile of it, name it Vacaville, and give Vaca certain town lots.

William Wolfskill, of Los Angeles, owned *Rancho Río de los Putos*, which was partially located in Yolo County. In 1842, his brother, John Reed Wolfskill, had driven 96 head of cattle from Los Angeles to the banks of Putah Creek and built a wattle hut— a hut made of poles intertwined with twigs, reeds, and branches. John and three other brothers would eventually take ownership of the rancho and plant a variety of orchards from fruit seeds and cuttings they brought from Los Angeles. An avenue of gnarled olive trees remains today on property John's grandchildren willed to the University of California, Davis, for an agricultural experimental station in Yolo County.

SOLANO COUNTY RANCHOS

NAME OF RANCHO	GRANTEE AND/OR 1850 OWNER	1850 AND/OR CURRENT SITES
Rancho Los Ulpinos	Robert Semple	Rio Vista
Rancho Suisun	Chief Francisco Solano[7]	Suisun Valley, Fairfield
Rancho Tolenas	José Francisco and Antonio Armijo	Fairfield
Rancho Los Putos	Juan Manuel Vaca, Juan Felipe Peña, William McDaniel	Vacaville, Vaca Valley, Lagoon Valley
Rancho Río de los Putos	William Wolfskill	North of Allendale, Winters in Yolo County

1

See Larkin sidebar on page 128.

2

Rancho Suscol is not described in the rancho section of Solano County because it never was patented to Vallejo or anyone else. This rancho not only included the site of Benicia, but the site of Vallejo and present-day Cordelia.

3

See Vallejo sidebar on page 170.

4

The Captain Walsh Home was one of three identical houses shipped around the Horn from Boston. One of the houses was erected in San Francisco and the third would become the residence of General Vallejo in Sonoma in 1851.

5

At the close of the first legislative session in San Jose in 1851, Vallejo would offer $570,000 and 156 acres to the State of California for the relocation of the state capital to his city. In gratitude for his donation, his fellow representatives chose to call the state capital Vallejo. A new frame building was built and the Legislature met for the first time on January 5, 1852. Vallejo was unable to obtain financing to fulfill his agreement with the State for additional buildings, however, so the state capital was moved to Sacramento on January 12th. The Legislature would meet in Vallejo one more time, in 1853, due to a flood in Sacramento, and then move to Benicia until Sacramento claimed the final right in 1854.

6

Although originally named *Isla de la Plana* in 1775, General Vallejo named the island *La Isla de la Yegua* (Mare Island) in 1835 following a mishap with his wife's prized white mare on a barge transporting men and stock between land on either side of the Carquinez Straits.

7

Solano County was named after Chief Solano at the suggestion of General Vallejo, a close friend.

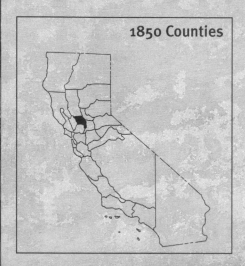

1850 Counties

❧ 1850 ❧
❧ YOLO ❧
COUNTY

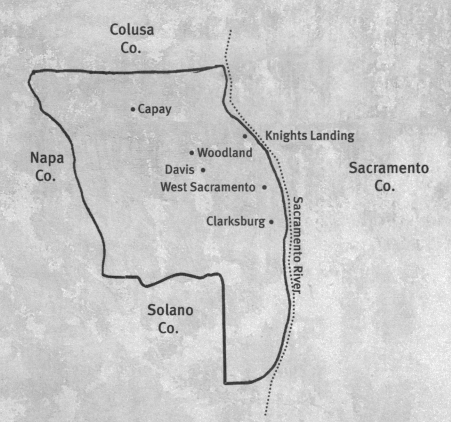

Colusa
Co.

• Capay

Knights Landing

Woodland

Napa
Co.

Davis •

West Sacramento

Sacramento
Co.

Clarksburg •

Sacramento River

Solano
Co.

California
1850

Present-day boundary
variations indicated by

— — — —

Settlements/cities of 1850 include: Knights Landing

YOLO COUNTY
1850

The geographical area of 1850-Yolo County was roughly the same as its current area, with only minor boundary line changes. Its 1,086 residents counted in the 1850 U.S. Census included Californios, Americans, and Europeans. The uncounted Native American inhabitants were primarily from the Patwin tribe.

In 1850 Yolo County consisted of its first county seat located in Fremont, a number of small communities along the Sacramento River, all of which exist today, and several ranchos. The county abounded with swamplands, marshes, and sloughs.

Jonas Spect had established the town of Fremont in 1849. He operated a ferry across the Sacramento River and a sand bar allowed fording across the Feather River. Fremont grew rapidly with miners passing through on their way to the gold fields. When popular vote transferred the seat of government to Washington[1] in 1851, however, its demise was imminent. Some of Fremont's buildings were moved to Knights Landing, Marysville, or to new ranches in the area. (Today the area of former Fremont is privately owned farmland.)

In 1843 William Knight, from Maryland, had built a primitive tules and willow pole house atop an ancient American Indian shell mound at a natural landing place on the Sacramento River. He attempted to start the town of Baltimore in 1849, but disagreements over the sale of lots prevented success. Knight moved to Stanislaus County later that year and founded Knight's Ferry. (Knights Landing would be laid out in Yolo County in 1853.)

Thomas Cochran operated a hotel for travelers along the Sacramento River. The place grew and would later become known as Cochran's Crossing, then Cacheville, and today, Yolo.

In late 1849, "Uncle Johnny" Morris and his family, from Kentucky, settled in what would become Woodland in 1857. They lived in a log cabin on the south side of Cache Creek. Morris planted the first mission variety of grapes in the county. Henry Wycoff was another early settler, who opened a trading post here.

In 1849 Frederick Babel, from Germany, and a Judge Clark settled on the Sacramento River where Clarksburg lies today. Other farmers who discovered that the fertile soil produced rich crops would soon join them. Annual flooding was a constant problem until high levees and canals were built in the 1920s.

Jerome C. Davis, from Ohio, had been a part of John C. Frémont's topographical survey expedition of 1845. After briefly trying his hand at mining, he settled in Yolo County and developed a profitable rope ferry across the Sacramento River in partnership with his father-in-law, Colonel Joseph B. Chiles of Napa County. He also

There are no 1850 Sites to Visit in Yolo County

Woodland Chamber of Commerce, 307 First St., Woodland, CA 95695
530.662.7327

Jonas Spect (1817-1883)

- Arrived in San Francisco from Ohio via Missouri and Oregon in 1848
- Discovered gold on the Yuba River in June 1848
- Established a trading post on the Yuba, trading primarily with American Indians
- Opened a store in Sacramento City in late 1848
- Settled Fremont on the Feather River, a general-store business, and the first public ferry in California in 1849
- Member of the committee that drafted the first mining laws that would subsequently be legalized by statute
- Settled in Colusa in 1868 where he invested in real estate that embroiled him in lawsuits

established Yolo County's first dairy north of Putah Creek, on property where the Dairy Industry Building of the University of California, Davis, is located today. Even though Davis had given up farming and moved to Sacramento in 1866, when the town of Davisville, later Davis, was established in 1868, it was named for him.

Yolo County Ranchos

Five land grants were made in Yolo County. Two of them crossed county lines— *Rancho Río de los Putos*, which is covered in the Solano County chapter, and *Rancho Jimeno*, which is included in the list of Colusa County ranchos. William Gordon's *Rancho Quesesosi* was the only marginally interesting rancho in Yolo County. Gordon had come to California from Ohio with the Workman-Rowland party in 1841 and settled here the following year. His home was a popular rendezvous point for settlers and hunters and everyone knew him as "Uncle Billy Gordon." Yolo County's first school had been started in a rustic building near Gordon's home in 1847.

The railroad would come to Yolo County in the 1860s and 1870s. The University Farm that later became the University of California, Davis, was not established by an act of the State Legislature until 1905. The popular recreational Lake Berryessa was created in 1957 when the Monticello Dam was completed. The Port of Sacramento for deep-sea traffic was constructed between West Sacramento and Collinsville in Solano County in 1963.

YOLO COUNTY RANCHOS

NAME OF RANCHO	GRANTEE AND/OR 1850 OWNER	1850 AND/OR CURRENT SITES
Rancho Cañada de Capay	George Dickson Stephens	Madison, Esparto
Rancho Quesesosi	William Gordon	Woodland
Rancho Río de Jesús María	James H. Harbin and others	Former Fremont, north of Woodland

1

Washington, later called Broderick and now part of West Sacramento, became the county seat in 1851. Cacheville, now called Yolo, became the county seat in 1857. In 1861, Washington regained the honor. Finally, in 1862, Woodland was chosen as the permanent county seat.

1850s Letter Sheet–"Bar Room in the Mines"

COURTESY OF THE SACRAMENTO ARCHIVES AND MUSEUM COLLECTION CENTER; THE ELEANOR MCCLATCHY COLLECTION

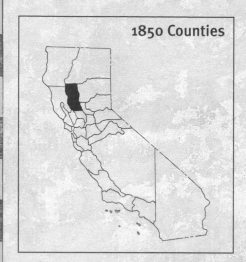

1850 Counties

Shasta
Co.

Tehama
Co.

Trinity
Co.

Red Bluff •

Tehama • • Los Molinos

Corning • • Vina

Orland • • Hamilton City

Glenn
Co.

Mendocino
Co.

Stony Creek

Willows •

Sacramento River

Princeton •

Colusa •

Colusa
Co.

Lake
Co.

Grimes •

California
1850

Yolo
Co.

Present-day boundary
variations indicated by

‒ ‒ ‒ ‒

Settlements/cities of 1850 include: Colusa

COLUSA COUNTY
1850

The geographical area of 1850-Colusa County included the areas that today make up both Colusa and Glenn counties, as well as the western half of Tehama County. It actually was called Colusi County until 1854. Its 115 residents counted in the 1850 U.S. Census were Americans, Europeans, and a few Californios. The uncounted Native American inhabitants included members of the Konkow, Nomlaki, and Yana tribes. In contrast to most other counties, there still was quite a large number of Native Americans—most living along the Sacramento River.

AREA WITHIN PRESENT-DAY COLUSA COUNTY

In 1850 the area within present-day Colusa County consisted of the town of Colusa[1] and three ranchos. Few settlers had been drawn to this area by this time.

Colusa County Ranchos

Colonel Charles D. Semple, a brother of Dr. Semple[2] of Benicia, owned *Rancho Colus*. He founded the city of Colusa along the Sacramento River in 1850. A few streets were laid out and a house built on one of the lots. Semple, his wife, and Will Semple Green, an 18-year old, lived here and operated a small store to supply the basic needs of travelers passing through. They raised vegetables to sell to the miners, and grew grain, which they shipped to San Francisco. Barges and steamboats such as the *Colusa*, owned by Semple's brother, had just started coming up the river from Sacramento, and in later years the Northern Mines would create a flourishing trade economy in Colusa.

The first land grant made in Colusa County was one that John Bidwell[3] mapped out in 1844 that came to be known as the Larkin Children's Rancho because it was secured for the Thomas O. Larkin[4] children. The grant extended along the west bank of the Sacramento River north of Colusa and into present-day Glenn County. In 1850 Charles B. Sterling assumed the job that John S. Williams had held since 1847 of attending to the grant and raising cattle and grain. Sterling had been Larkin's secretary while he was the U.S. Consul at Monterey. Williams built the first house in Colusa County located just below present-day Princeton. In 1850 he was living along Butte Creek.

There are no 1850 Sites to visit in Colusa County

Colusa Area Chamber of Commerce, 258 Main St., Colusa, CA 95932 530.458.5525

Will Semple Green (1832-1905)

- Arrived in San Francisco in 1849 from Kentucky

- Worked in Benicia briefly and delivered mail from Benicia to Sonoma

- Moved to Colusa in 1850 where he performed a variety of odd jobs and did some farming

- Self-taught to become qualified to serve as county surveyor, which he did for ten years

- Free-lance writer for several publications; purchased the *Colusa Sun* in 1863, with John C. Addington

- Moved to San Francisco in early 1870s to dabble in real estate and journalism

- Returned to Colusa in 1873 to devote his energies to the *Colusa Sun*

- State assemblyman, U.S. surveyor general, state treasurer

- Posted first water notice for diversion of miners' water for irrigation of lands on west side of Sacramento Valley

COLUSA COUNTY RANCHOS

NAME OF RANCHO	GRANTEE AND/OR 1850 OWNER	1850 AND/OR CURRENT SITES
Rancho Jimeno	Manuel Jimeno Casarín	Sycamore, Grimes, Tyndall Landing in Yolo County
Rancho Colus	Charles D. Semple	Colusa
Larkin Children's Rancho	Thomas O. Larkin	Princeton, Butte City in Glenn County

There are no 1850 Sites to Visit in Glenn County

Willows Area Chamber of Commerce, 123 S. Tehama St., Willows, CA 95988 530.934.8150

Granville Perry Swift (1821-1875)

- Arrived in Glenn County from Kentucky in 1842

- Trapper whose grandmother Swift was a sister of Daniel Boone

- Took part in Bear Flag Revolt and served as a captain in Frémont's army

- Oversaw a successful mining operation by working "his docile" American Indians on Bidwell Bar on the Feather River in Butte County

- Returned to Kentucky in 1849 to bring some of his family back to California

- Married in 1858; built an elaborate stone house in Sonoma County, which became an entertainment spot for high society San Franciscans

- Suffered through financial difficulties and divorce proceedings, but was on his way to making a second fortune when he met an accidental death on a mule

AREA WITHIN PRESENT-DAY GLENN COUNTY

Glenn County would not be separated from Colusa County until 1891.[5] In 1850 the area within its borders consisted of Monroeville, two complete ranchos, and a portion of a third. The trail that connected Sacramento with Shasta in Shasta County crossed through present-day Glenn County along the Sacramento River.

Granville Perry Swift was living in Stony Creek Valley, which remained in the public domain because it had been considered worthless except for grazing. He built an adobe home in the mid-1850s north of present-day Orland. This was the first structure to be built in Glenn County and he subsequently built another adobe west of present-day Willows and a stone corral, the ruins of which still stand near present-day Maxwell. In 1849, Swift and his cousin/brother-in-law, Franklin Sears, had purchased the cattle and brand from the Larkin Children's Grant. Mexican and American Indian *vaqueros* herded their cattle and rodeos were held. Swift and Sears also planted barley, the first in the northern Sacramento Valley.

Glenn County Ranchos

Glenn County's ranchos ran along the eastern edge of the county in an orderly line bordering Butte County. Today these areas are primarily farmland.

W. H. McKee owned *Rancho Jacinto*.[6] He hired William B. Ide to survey the tract in 1850 and intended to subdivide it, but difficulties establishing ownership arose when the U. S. Land Commission was created, so this never was completed.

Doña María Josefa Soto owned *Rancho Capay*. She did not reside on the rancho, but several settlers were living there. Uriah P. Monroe laid out the town of Monroeville in 1850. Monroe would be the instigator behind siting the Colusi County seat in his town in 1851. It became a popular stopping place on the road from Colusa to Shasta, but when the county seat was removed to Colusa, the town went into decline and today it no longer exists.

In 1845, W. C. Moon, Ezekiel Merritt, and Peter Lassen had quarried and manufactured many grindstones on Grindstone Creek several miles north of the present-day town of Elk Creek at the edge of Mendocino National Forest. They packed the grindstones on mules to the Sacramento River and from there transported them to Sutter's Fort and San Francisco.

Glenn County would become the producer of some of the most sought after wheat in the world. So fine in color and texture, it became known as "California White Velvet."

GLENN COUNTY RANCHOS

NAME OF RANCHO	GRANTEE AND/OR 1850 OWNER	1850 AND/OR CURRENT SITES
Rancho Jacinto	W. H. McKee	Glenn
Rancho Capay	María Josefa Soto	Hamilton City, former Monroeville, Kirkwood in Tehama County

AREA WITHIN PRESENT-DAY TEHAMA COUNTY

Tehama County would be organized in 1856 from parts of Colusa, Butte, and Shasta counties. Many explorers, hunters, traders, and trappers had passed through the present-day county from the 1820s through the 1840s. The gold miners used the same trails in the 1850s that connected Sacramento with Shasta, a distance of 180 miles. Many of the settlers in the county in 1850 had come across the plains with either the Bidwell-Bartleson or the Workman-Rowland parties of 1841

Tehama County Ranchos

In 1850 Tehama County consisted of Benton City and six ranchos. Peter Lassen owned the entire *Rancho Bosquejo* until sometime in 1850 when he sold half of it to a Mr. Palmer; he later sold the other half to Henry Gerke of San Francisco. Lassen's rancho was at the end of the Lassen Trail across the Sierra Nevada, the first northern emigrant route into California from the East.[7] Lassen had a vineyard and grew cotton and wheat on his rancho. In 1847 he had laid out Benton City on his rancho, named after Senator Thomas H. Benton of Missouri, who was John C. Frémont's[8] father-in-law. The population dwindled after the 1848 discovery of gold in Coloma and today Benton City no longer exists.

William C. Moon and Ezekiel Merritt, former "Bear Flaggers," as well as Henry L. Ford were "squatting" on lands west of *Rancho Bosquejo*. Moon, a famous hunter from Tennessee, was operating a ferry across the Sacramento River where Squaw Hill Bridge is located today on the road from Vina to Corning.

Robert Hasty Thomes, from Maine, owned *Rancho Saúcos*. He had built an adobe on his property in 1846 or 1847 on the site of the present-day town of Tehama. Known as Hall's Ranch, it was an important center of trade for miners headed for the northern gold fields. The principal ferry crossing between Marysville and Shasta was also located here. But Red Bluff[9] would become the head of navigation on the Sacramento River soon thereafter when the steamer *Orient* landed there in late 1850. Stage lines started operating in the area in 1851.

Sites to Visit in Tehama County

Tehama County Museum, C & 3rd Streets, Tehama   530.384.2595

William B. Ide Adobe State Historic Park, 21659 Adobe Rd., Red Bluff   530.529.8599

Red Bluff-Tehama County Chamber of Commerce, 100 Main St., P. O. Box 850, Red Bluff, CA 96080   530.527.6220

The 1846 (or perhaps 1852) pioneer adobe that still stands along the Sacramento River in Red Bluff is known as the William B. Ide Adobe.

Peter Lassen (1800-1859)

- Blacksmith from Denmark

- Arrived in California in 1839, becoming one of northern California's first Anglo settlers

- Lived for a time in Bodega Bay, Fort Ross, San José, Santa Cruz, and Sutter's Fort

- Obtained a charter for the first Masonic lodge in California and brought it across the plains in 1848

- Established a trading post (Benton City) near the mouth of Deer Creek on the east side of the Sacramento River near present-day Vina

- Blazed the Lassen Trail, but it was used very little

- First to bring a sternwheeler into Tehama County in 1849

- Lost his rancho in Tehama County and moved to the part of Plumas County that is now Lassen County

- May have climbed the peak that now bears his name

- Discovered gold in Honey Lake Valley in Lassen County in 1855

- Shot and killed by Native Americans while prospecting in Honey Lake region

William B. Ide (1796-1852)

- Originally from Massachusetts, the Ide family migrated to California via Kentucky, Ohio, and Illinois with a party led by the mountaineer Meek in 1845

- Settled his family in present-day Tehama County

- Helped organize the Bear Flag Revolt in 1846

- First and only President of the California Republic under the Bear Flag Party

- Primarily lived in Monroeville after 1850 and held all the Colusa County offices available at the time

- Died of smallpox at Monroeville

General William B. Ide owned *Rancho La Barranca Colorado*. He and his family had lived on other people's ranchos in several different log cabins he built with the circular saw and other tools he brought from Missouri, until he purchased this rancho from Josiah Belden in 1847. The 1846 (or perhaps 1852) pioneer adobe that still stands along the Sacramento River in Red Bluff today is known as the William B. Ide Adobe, but he probably did not build it and may not even have owned the property on which it stands. Someone established the Adobe Ferry that crossed the river at this point. It operated until 1876 when the Centennial Bridge across the Sacramento River at Red Bluff was built.

Job Francis Dye, a Kentucky trapper, owned *Rancho Primer Cañon o Río de los Berrendos*, the largest grant located in Tehama County. He lived in an adobe along Antelope Creek. He was quite the host, in the "Southern manner" of his native state.

Another view of the adobe locatd in the William B. Ide Adobe State Historic Park in Red Bluff.

TEHAMA COUNTY RANCHOS

NAME OF RANCHO	GRANTEE AND/OR 1850 OWNER	1850 AND/OR CURRENT SITES
Rancho Bosquejo (Wooded Place)	Peter Lassen	Vina, former Benton City, northwestern corner of Butte County
Rancho Saúcos (Elder Trees)	Robert Hasty Thomes	Tehama
Rancho Río de los Molinos (River of the Mills)	Albert G. Toomes	Los Molinos
Rancho Las Flores (The Flowers)	William George Chard	South of Red Bluff
Rancho La Barranca Colorado (Red Bluff)	William B. Ide	Red Bluff
Rancho Primer Cañon o Río de los Berrendos (The Antelopes)	Job Francis Dye	East of Red Bluff

Notes ～ COLUSA COUNTY

1

When Colusa County was created in 1850, it was attached to Butte County for judicial purposes. In 1851 the residents petitioned to establish their own county seat. After much political maneuvering, the county seat would be established in Monroeville in 1851, the former site of which is now located in Glenn County. The city of Colusa would not become the county seat until 1854.

2

See Semple sidebar on page 181.

3

See Bidwell sidebar on page 211.

4

See Larkin sidebar on page 128.

5

Glenn County was named for Dr. Hugh James Glenn, a Missouri physician, who became a prominent landowner and wheat farmer in the area in 1867.

6

Rancho Jacinto is the property that Dr. Hugh James Glenn would purchase in 1867.

7

Few people were emigrating over the Lassen Trail in 1850 because there were too many hardships in store for travelers on this route, and it took more than a month longer than other emigrant routes to reach the Sacramento Valley. As a result, little settlement was taking place in northern California.

8

See Frémont sidebar on page 253.

9

Red Bluff would be mapped in 1851 as a settlement in what was southern Shasta County at the time.

1850 Counties

~1850~
} MENDOCINO {
COUNTY

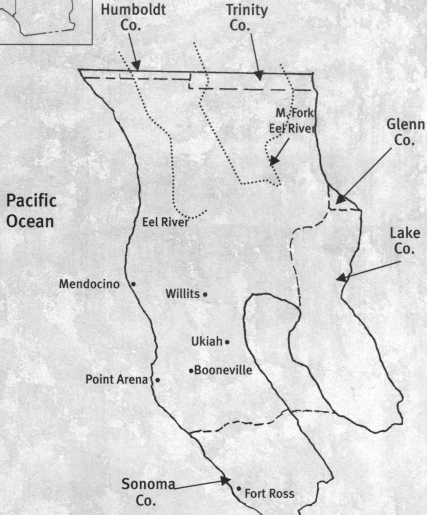

Humboldt Co.

Trinity Co.

M. Fork Eel River

Glenn Co.

Lake Co.

Pacific Ocean

Eel River

Mendocino •

Willits •

Ukiah •

• Booneville

Point Arena •

Sonoma Co.

• Fort Ross

California
1850

Present-day boundary variations indicated by
- - - - -

Settlements/cities of 1850 include: Fort Ross

MENDOCINO COUNTY
1850

The geographical area of 1850-Mendocino County included public lands and a portion of a rancho located within the current boundaries of Sonoma County; these areas are covered in the Sonoma County chapter. Mendocino County also included all but the most southern and most eastern portion of present-day Lake County. Its 55 residents counted in the 1850 U.S. Census included a few Californios, a few Americans, and a few Europeans. The uncounted Native American inhabitants included members of the Pomo and Patwin tribes.

AREA WITHIN PRESENT-DAY LAKE COUNTY

In 1850 present-day Lake County lay within a small northern portion of Napa County and the southeastern portion of Mendocino County. Its current eastern boundary also extended into a small portion of western Colusa County. For ten years, Napa County would gradually absorb more and more of present-day Lake County lands, but in 1861, Lake County separated from Napa County and named Lakeport as its county seat.

Lake County Ranchos

Three ranchos were granted within the boundaries of present-day Lake County. *Dons* Salvador and Juan Antonio Vallejo owned the most significant one, *Rancho Lupyomi.* They had been herding cattle in the Big, Scotts, Upper Lake, and Bachelor valleys on the western edges of Clear Lake[1] since the early 1840s. The Vallejos' *mayordomo* and *vaqueros* had built a log cabin and corral in Big Valley near present-day Kelseyville.

In 1847 Charles Stone and Andrew Kelsey had purchased the Vallejos' cattle. They employed Native Americans to construct an adobe for them. In retaliation for the cruel treatment they received while laboring, the American Indians killed Stone and Kelsey in 1849. In 1850 U.S. soldiers killed close to 100 Native Americans in retaliation for these murders, but the victims were not the individuals responsible for the Stone-Kelsey killings. The massacre took place on an island near present-day Upper Lake. The island came to be known as Bloody Island and today is a hill surrounded by dry land as the result of a reclamation project.

Settlers would not begin arriving in Lake County until 1854. They pursued such activities as farming, grinding grain for food, and sawing lumber for houses. The many streams of Lake County provided power for various types of mills. A number

There are no 1850 Sites to Visit in Lake County

Lakeport Chamber of Commerce,
P. O. Box 295, Lakeport, CA 95453
707.263.5092

of mineral springs led to the establishment of resorts. Small quantities of a great variety of minerals resulted in the establishment of small mining operations.

There are no 1850 Sites to Visit in Mendocino County

Greater Ukiah Chamber of Commerce, 200 S. School St., Ukiah, CA 95482 707.462.4705

AREA WITHIN PRESENT-DAY MENDOCINO COUNTY

In 1850 there were no established towns within the current boundaries of Mendocino County. Until 1859, Sonoma County officials administered the government for Mendocino County. Non-Native Americans did not even discover the existence of Mendocino County's vast coast redwood forests until 1851. The following year, Harry Meiggs of San Francisco established the California Lumber Company at the mouth of Big River in the town of Mendocino.

Only two ranchos were granted in Mendocino County and neither was developed in 1850. *Don* Fernando Felix would not move his family here from Marin County until 1853, and Captain Cayetano Juárez never lived on his, residing instead in Napa County. Two *rancheros* from Marin County applied for grants, but neither was ever confirmed. *Don* Rafael García was grazing cattle in the Point Arena area; William Antonio Richardson[2] applied for a grant near present-day Albion.

The famous Vichy mineral springs had been discovered by Frank Marble in 1848. Vichy Springs Resort—so named because it resembles the famed Grand Grille Springs of Vichy, France—would be established by William Day several years later and today is one of the few continuously operating mineral springs resorts in California.

Mendocino County has many well-preserved later 19th-century buildings and houses, but no structures had been built by 1850. Among the earliest structures still standing are the Silas W. Coombs House built in 1853, which houses the modernized Little River Inn today, and the Ford House built in 1854 in the town of Mendocino, which houses a visitors' center. Lumber and agriculture would spur the eventual development of Mendocino County.

LAKE COUNTY RANCHOS

NAME OF RANCHO	GRANTEE AND/OR 1850 OWNER	1850 AND/OR CURRENT SITES
Rancho Collayomi	Robert T. Ridley	Middletown
Rancho Guenoc	George Rock (Roch)	East of Middletown
Rancho Lupyomi	Salvador and Juan Antonio Vallejo	Kelseyville

MENDOCINO COUNTY RANCHOS

NAME OF RANCHO	GRANTEE AND/OR 1850 OWNER	1850 AND/OR CURRENT SITES
Rancho de Sanel	Fernando Felix	Hopland
Rancho Yokaya	Cayetano Juárez	Ukiah

1

Clear Lake is the largest natural body of fresh water lying wholly within the state of California.

2

See Richardson sidebar on page 163.

The Eliza Ship for California.

Camping Out.

Washing Gold in a Cradle.

Arrival at Sᵗ F. A Monte Bank.

A View of The

One of the few that return.

1850s Letter Sheet

1850 Counties

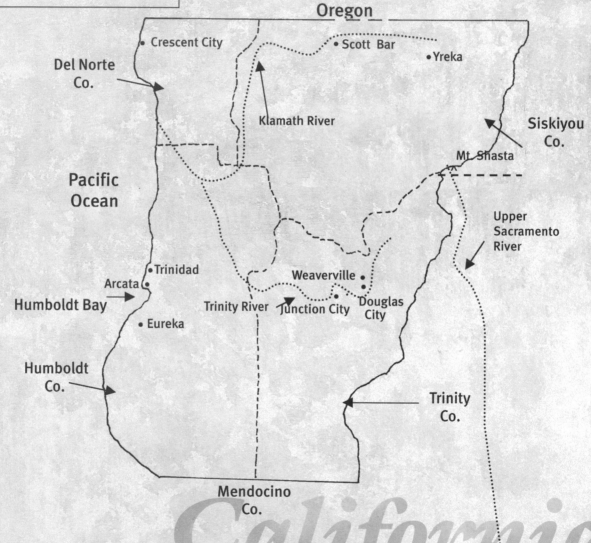

~1850~
❧ TRINITY ❧
COUNTY

Oregon

• Crescent City

• Scott Bar

• Yreka

Del Norte Co.

Klamath River

Siskiyou Co.

Mt. Shasta

Pacific Ocean

Upper Sacramento River

• Trinidad

Weaverville •

Arcata •

Humboldt Bay

Trinity River • Junction City

Douglas City

• Eureka

Humboldt Co.

Trinity Co.

Mendocino Co.

California
1850

Present-day boundary variations indicated by

— — — — —

Settlements/cities of 1850 include: Trinidad, Uniontown (Arcata), Eureka

TRINITY COUNTY 1850

The geographical area of 1850-Trinity County included all of present-day Humboldt, Trinity, and Del Norte counties, as well as two-thirds of present-day Siskiyou County. Its 1,635 residents counted in the 1850 U.S. Census were primarily Americans and Europeans. The uncounted Native American population included members of the Sinkyone, Wailaki, Lassik, Nongatl, Mattole, Wiyot, Hupa, Chilula, Yurok, Karuk, Shasta, and Tolowa tribes.

AREA WITHIN PRESENT-DAY HUMBOLDT COUNTY

Humboldt County[1] would be established in 1853. After Klamath County was established in 1851, and until 1875, the northern one-third of the present-day county was a part of Klamath County.

A sea otter party had entered Humboldt Bay in 1806, but the bay, which is very difficult to see from the ocean, was not rediscovered until 1849 by a land expedition led by Dr. Josiah Gregg, which was seeking an overland route to the Pacific Ocean. In 1850 sailors from the ship *Laura Virginia* named the bay Humboldt in honor of the German naturalist and world explorer, Baron Alexander von Humboldt. The sailors formed the Laura Virginia Association and began the development of the area. By the end of 1850, five newly-formed towns existed—Trinidad, Uniontown, Humboldt City, Bucksport, and Eureka.

The latter three towns were founded on Humboldt Bay. This bay, the only deep-water port between San Francisco and Coos Bay, Oregon—a 600-mile stretch—would become a major North Coast lumber port and shipbuilding center. Eureka eventually absorbed Humboldt City and Bucksport and within four years there were seven mills processing lumber in Eureka. Uniontown was founded on Arcata Bay by a group from San Francisco led by L. K. Wood; it was renamed Arcata in 1860.

Trinidad, the oldest town on the northern California coast, was founded in April 1850 on Trinidad Bay. Robert Parker of Marin County and several others from San Francisco laid out the town. Trinidad would become a vital supply link for miners working inland up the Trinity and Klamath Rivers. During the summer of 1850, miners discovered gold in the black sands of the ocean beach at Trinidad. Shiploads of men immediately began arriving from San Francisco, but the process of separating the fine particles of gold from the sand was not cost-effective. Most of the miners soon departed for the gold camps along the Trinity and Klamath rivers.

The rugged coastal mountains of Humboldt County extend 150 miles inland from the ocean and follow a general southeasterly to northwesterly direction. The

There are no 1850 Sites to Visit in Humboldt County

Greater Eureka Chamber of Commerce, 2112 Broadway, Eureka, CA 95501 707.442.3738

county was difficult to reach by both land and water in 1850. It would be 1914 before the first major land route was established between San Francisco and Eureka with the opening of the Northwestern Pacific Railroad. The coastal mountain ranges contain oak, maple, madrone, and pepperwood trees, as well as the magnificent stands of coastal redwoods that the whole northern coast of California is known for—the same redwoods that have been the battleground for the lumber industry and preservationists for more than a hundred years. Cape Mendocino, the western-most point of California, had been a landmark for mariners along the Pacific Coast since the 16th century.

AREA WITHIN PRESENT-DAY DEL NORTE COUNTY

There are no 1850 Sites to Visit in Del Norte County

Crescent City-Del Norte Chamber, 1001 Front St., Crescent City, CA 95531 707.464.3174

Del Norte County[2] would be established in 1857 from a portion of the Klamath County established in 1851, but which was disestablished in 1876. It occupies the northwestern-most corner of California.

Although gold had been discovered on the Klamath River in 1849 and several vessels had anchored in Crescent Bay as early as 1850, it would be 1852 before any settlement was made north of the mouth of the Klamath River. The hills surrounding Crescent Bay would briefly be scattered with mining camps in the 1850s and 60s, and Crescent City, founded in 1853, became the chief port of entry and supply center for the gold miners of southern Oregon and northern California.

The county's several rivers have a history of misidentifications. The Klamath River empties into the Pacific Ocean near present-day Requa near the southern border of the county, but this final ocean entry point was not discovered until late in 1850. British and American trappers had been trapping for beaver on the Upper Klamath and its tributaries since 1827, but none had ever followed the river to its mouth. When Major Pierson B. Reading,[3] a *ranchero* in Shasta County, discovered gold on the Trinity River in 1848, this river became a popular destination for the miners. The rich gravel beds extended both up and down the river and within a short time many hundreds of men were at work with pans and rockers in such places as Coffee Creek, Swift Creek, Rush Creek, and Deadwood Creek. When the miners sought a more direct route to this river than the Sacramento Valley and explored access by sea, they mistakenly identified the Klamath River as the Trinity River. The Klamath was also mistaken for the Salmon River.

Like its neighbor to the south, Del Norte County is blessed with coastal forestlands. The world's tallest tree is located in Redwood National Park.

AREA WITHIN PRESENT-DAY SISKIYOU COUNTY

Two-thirds of present-day Siskiyou County lay within the county lines of 1850-Trinity County; the other one-third was part of 1850-Shasta County. In 1852 Siskiyou County would be created from a portion of what had become Klamath County in 1851, as well as the Shasta County one-third. After Klamath County was disestablished in 1876, Siskiyou County's border was extended further to the west.[4]

In 1829 Hudson Bay Company trappers had traveled through the valley where McCloud[5] stands today. The California-Oregon Trail passed around the western base of Mount Shasta[6] and had first been used by a settler bound for Oregon in 1834. A wagon party crossed the Siskiyou Mountains from Oregon into California in 1849, but turned around when they reached Shasta Valley, fearing the Native Americans and being concerned about the remoteness of the area. It would be 1854 before the first wagon team from the Sacramento Valley successfully entered the county.

Mining began in Siskiyou County in June 1850 in the Salmon Mountains. A camp of several hundred men formed at the mouth of the North Fork of the Salmon River. From here some miners led by John W. Scott spread out into Scott Valley. They discovered gold at a point on Scott River they named Scott Bar[7] after their leader.

Another large party of miners was panning for gold at every bar along the Klamath River, from its mouth in present-day Del Norte County to the Shasta River in Siskiyou County. Towards the end of the year, many of the miners headed for the settlements of the Sacramento Valley for the winter. In January 1851, however, gold was discovered at the site of present-day Yreka, on the "flats" near a ravine called Black Gulch. Abraham Thompson's mules pulled gold flecks up on the roots of the grass they were eating. Soon prospecting parties were spread over the entire region and camps would spring up at every bar, creek, and gulch along the county's rivers and creeks in early 1851.

Yreka was founded in March of that year and laid out in May. It was originally called Shasta Butte City, but to avoid confusion with Shasta in Shasta County, its name was changed to Yreka. Yreka quickly became the commercial and transportation hub for the surrounding communities and mining camps. Its tents and shanties were gradually replaced with permanent structures, some of which remain today with *circa* dates from 1853 on.[8]

The California Stage Company would begin operations in 1856 and the Southern Pacific Railroad finally made its way to Siskiyou County in 1887-88.

Sites to Visit in Siskiyou County

Siskiyou County Courthouse, 311 Fourth St., Yreka (Gold Exhibit) 530.842.8084

Siskiyou County Museum, 910 South Main St., Yreka 530.842.3836

Yreka Chamber of Commerce, 117 W. Miner St., Yreka, CA 96097 530.842.1649

Mt. Shasta, an inactive volcano, dominates the surrounding landscape.

Sites to Visit in Trinity County

J. J. "Jake" Jackson Memorial
Museum, History Center, and
Trinity County Historical Park, 508
Main St., Weaverville
530.623.5211

Trinity County Chamber of
Commerce, 211 Trinity Lakes Blvd.,
P. O. Box 517, Weaverville, CA
96093   1.800.487.4648

AREA WITHIN PRESENT-DAY TRINITY COUNTY

In 1850 the area within present-day Trinity County consisted of the county seat, Weaverville, and numerous river bar camps set up on the Klamath and Trinity rivers. The mining town of Weaverville was established in 1850, named for John Weaver, a gold prospector who had arrived in the area in 1849 and built the town's first cabin. Devastating fires in 1853 and 1855 would destroy the town's first buildings, but today several buildings built after 1855 are still in use in downtown Weaverville.

In July 1848, Pierson B. Reading had discovered gold on the Trinity River below the bridge at present-day Douglas City. After working six weeks with a crew of about 60 Native Americans, he left the stream and returned to his home in Shasta County.

A Frenchman named Gross may have been the first settler in Trinity County in 1849. He built a cabin on the Trinity River at Evans' Bar. During 1850 many gold miners entered the county, either across the mountains from Shasta County, or up the Klamath and Trinity rivers from Trinidad Bay. There would soon be river bar camps along the rivers with more people then living within the borders of Trinity County than have ever lived here since.

During the summer and fall of 1850, sixty miners constructed the Arkansas Dam across Trinity River, above present-day Junction City. The water was diverted from the bed of the river into a canal, allowing the miners to work the gravels of the riverbed. The dam was subsequently washed away in the first rain of the season. A trading post and a gristmill were established at Sturdevant's Place, where Junction City is located today.[9]

In 1850 Weaver and Company was mining at Big Bar below present-day Helena. Mad River, which runs through the southern part of the county, had been given its name in 1849 when a party of surveyors reached the waters after two months of near starvation.

The inaccessibility of the area within Trinity County's boundaries greatly handicapped the miners on the Trinity River. To reach these diggings in 1850 required a trek across the high Trinity Mountains from the upper Sacramento Valley, down from Oregon across the Siskiyou Range, or across the coastal mountains from Uniontown (Arcata today). Any miners unprepared to wait for improved conditions on trails due to inclement weather ran the risk of starving to death. Beginning sometime in 1850, Sacramento River barges were able to reach present-day Red Bluff, and freight wagons could then go as far as Shasta. From Shasta, the Trinity Mines were reachable by a rough mule trail.

Approximately 77 percent of Trinity County is located within Trinity National Forest. Other parts of the county lie within parts of Shasta National Forest and Six Rivers National Forest. The Clair Engle Lake would inundate Trinity Meadows in the 1960s when the Trinity, Lewiston, and Whiskeytown dams were completed.

1

Humboldt County would become a significant area of conflict between the Native Americans and the newly-arriving Euro-American settlers between 1850 and 1865. Fort Humboldt was established in 1853 and approximately ten military posts were set up throughout the region in the early 1860s.

2

The famous trapper and explorer, Jedediah Strong Smith, and his exploration party had blazed trails through the steep and rugged mountains of Del Norte County in 1828, when they were establishing a northwest trail from the Sacramento Valley into Oregon that generally coincided with present SR 36, the Red Bluff-Eureka Highway. Smith was the first non-Native American to make the journey up the California coast to Oregon.

3

See Reading sidebar on page 206.

4

All of the area in present-day Siskiyou County is covered in this section.

5

One of the Hudson Bay Company trappers was Alexander McLeod, thus the derivation of McCloud's name.

6

The summit of Mount Shasta rises 14,162 feet, dominating the landscape for a hundred miles, and may be seen from nearly 200 miles to the south on a clear day. No one would record an ascent of the mountain until 1854.

7

The Scott Bar of 1850 was located across the river from present-day Scott Bar.

8

Holding on to a tradition of the 1850s, Yreka would be the site of the last lynching in California in 1935, as chronicled in the book *Just a Little Lynching Now and Then...* by Alan McMurry.

9

Today huge mounds of gravel left as tailing, primarily from the hydraulic and "bucket line dredge" mining done in the late 1800s and early 1900s, can be seen in the vicinity of Junction City.

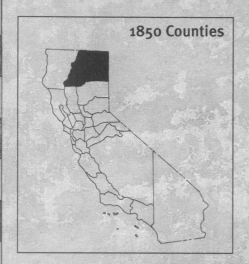

1850 Counties

☙ 1 8 5 0 ❧
⤙ SHASTA ⤚
COUNTY

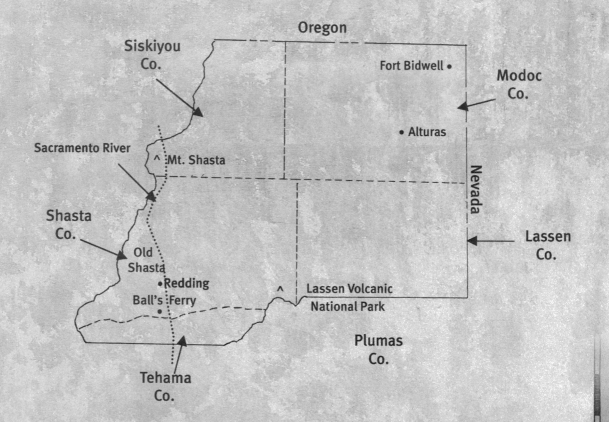

Oregon

Siskiyou Co.

Fort Bidwell •

Modoc Co.

Sacramento River

• Alturas

^ Mt. Shasta

Nevada

Shasta Co.

Old Shasta

Lassen Co.

• Redding

Ball's Ferry •

^ Lassen Volcanic National Park

Plumas Co.

Tehama Co.

California
1850

Present-day boundary variations indicated by
- - - - -

Settlements/cities of 1850 include: Shasta (Old Shasta)

SHASTA COUNTY 1850

In 1850 Shasta County covered 20,000 square miles, extending from Butte County to the Oregon border and from the summit of the coastal range to Nevada. The county would subsequently be whittled down to less than 4,000 square miles when first Siskiyou County was established in 1852, then Tehama County in 1856, and finally Lassen County in 1864. (Siskiyou and Tehama counties are discussed in other chapters.)

Shasta County's 378 residents counted in the 1850 U.S. Census were primarily Americans and Europeans. The uncounted Native American inhabitants included members of the Shasta, Modoc, Wintu, Achumawi, Atsugewi, and Yana tribes.

AREA WITHIN PRESENT-DAY MODOC COUNTY

In 1874 Modoc County would be formed from the eastern portion of the Siskiyou County that was earlier created in 1852. Many had passed through the area on either the Applegate Trail, which headed north into Oregon, or the Lassen Trail, which turned south down the Pit River toward the Central Valley. In the late 1820s, these travelers included Hudson Bay Company trappers, and in the 1840s and 50s, the travelers included John C. Frémont[1] and his expedition party, Peter Lassen,[2] Peter Burnett,[3] and thousands of other emigrants headed for either Oregon or the gold fields of California. However, it would not be until the 1860s that any settlers built log cabins, began cattle ranching, and established roots in the county. Many wars between the Modoc Indians and Euro-American settlers took place here in the latter half of the 19th century.

AREA WITHIN PRESENT-DAY SHASTA COUNTY

In 1850 the area within present-day Shasta County consisted of the county seat at Reading's Ranch, the only Shasta County rancho; and the towns of Reading's Springs, Reading's Bar, Whiskeytown, and Morrowville.

Reading's Springs was founded in 1849 and renamed Shasta in June 1850. Shasta would become the metropolis for northern California during the 1850s with supplies for the mines of the Trinity, Scott, and Salmon rivers passing through this town. Beyond this point the trails west and north were rough and poorly marked. Thus, merchandise had to be unloaded, warehoused, and eventually transported by mules into the mountains.

There are no 1850 Sites to Visit In Modoc County

Modoc County Chamber of Commerce, 522 S. Main St., Alturas, CA 96101   530.233.4434

Sites to Visit in Shasta County

Shasta State Historic Park, Hwy 299 west of Redding, Shasta 530.243.8194

Redding Greater Chamber of Commerce, 747 Auditorium Dr., Redding, CA 96001 530.225.4433

An ample supply of wood and pure water made Shasta a desirable campsite. A log cabin, the first permanent structure, had been built late in 1849. In the spring of 1850 a whip-saw mill began operation nearby and wood frame buildings were constructed adjacent to the canvas structures along Main Street. Isaac N. Roop, a widower from Ohio, was operating a mercantile business. Shasta became the county seat in 1851 and remained so until 1888 when this honor was transferred to present-day Redding.[4] The entire business section of Shasta was destroyed by fire in 1853, but today several half-ruined brick buildings and three restored buildings constructed following the fire make up the Shasta State Historic Park. The former 1855 Shasta County Courthouse, restored to its 1861 appearance, serves as a museum.

Reading's Bar, where Pierson Barton Reading and his Native American laborers discovered the first gold in Shasta County in 1848, came to be known as Clear Creek Diggings and later as Horse Town. Hotels, stores, a Catholic church, and numerous saloons would serve its one thousand residents before the town was destroyed by fire in 1868.

Whiskeytown, first called Whiskey Creek because a barrel of whiskey fell off a pack mule into the stream, had been settled by gold miners in 1849. Since 1963, the area has been inundated by Whiskeytown Reservoir, which is part of the Whiskeytown-Shasta-Trinity National Recreation Area. Nearby Shasta Lake and Shasta Dam would be constructed between 1938 and 1944.

The town of Morrowville had been founded in 1849 by French miners where French Gulch is located today. It would become one of the state's richest gold producing areas—over $20 million. Several Gold Rush-era buildings remain today.

The Ogburn family had settled in the Shingletown area of today in 1848. The Ogburn Ranch is still in operation.

Several emigrant trails ran through Shasta County, including the California-Oregon Trail, which I-5 and the Shasta Route of the Southern Pacific Railroad follow today. In 1850 "Doc" Baker established a tent hotel east of present-day Anderson for emigrants traveling on the Lassen Trail.

Rancho San Buenaventura

Only one rancho was granted in Shasta County—*Rancho San Buenaventura*, known in 1850 as Reading's Ranch. It extended for 18 miles along the west bank of the Sacramento River between Cottonwood Creek in the south to Salt Creek in the north in the vicinity of present-day Redding. Major Pierson B. Reading owned the rancho and lived in his 1847 adobe along the river just south of present-day Ball's Ferry. Reading's Ranch would serve as the county seat until it was moved to Shasta 25 miles away in February 1851.

The 10,457-foot Lassen Peak and half of the area of Lassen Volcanic National Park lie within Shasta County. Peter Lassen had explored this region in the 1840s.

Pierson Barton Reading (1816-1868)

- Arrived at Sutter's Fort from New Jersey with the Chiles-Walker party in 1843
- Major in California Battalion during Mexican-American War
- Signer of Capitulation of Cahuenga in 1847
- Discovered the first gold in Shasta County in March 1848 on Clear Creek
- Discovered gold on Trinity River later in 1848
- U.S. Special Indian Agent known for his kindness
- After marrying in 1855, he became known for his hospitality

AREA WITHIN PRESENT-DAY LASSEN COUNTY

There are no 1850 Sites to Visit in Lassen County

Lassen County Chamber of Commerce, 84 N. Lassen St., P. O. Box 338, Susanville, CA 96130   530.257.4323

In 1864 Lassen County would be organized from parts of Plumas and Shasta counties. However, in 1850 about two-thirds of the land located within its current boundaries was located in Shasta County and the other one-third was located in Butte County.

Fur trappers and explorers had passed through this county in the 1820s and 1840s, but it would be 1854 before the first Anglo settler, Isaac N. Roop, settled in present-day Lassen County—in the Honey Lake Valley where Susanville was eventually established. Peter Lassen arrived in the area in the early 1850s after he lost his rancho in Tehama County. (Although Lassen was financially unsuccessful, his peers respected him enough to use his name in several place names in the area.)

A portion of the Lassen Trail traversed through present-day Lassen County over which covered wagons and gold seekers en route to California passed during 1848-1853. From the north, the trail passed what is now Bogard Ranger Station on Hwy 44, southward to Big Springs and Big Meadows (now Lake Almanor) in Plumas County, westward to Deer Creek and on to Vina in Tehama County and the Sacramento Valley.

The eastern portion of Lassen Volcanic National Park is located in Lassen County, but Lassen Peak is located in Shasta County. Directly to the east, Eagle Lake is the second largest natural lake located entirely within California—second only to Clear Lake in Lake County.

Notes ⌒ SHASTA COUNTY

1

See Frémont sidebar on page 253.

2

See Lassen sidebar on page 192.

3

See Burnett sidebar on page 137.

4

Redding was named for a railroad executive, B. B. Redding, not Pierson B. Reading as might be surmised.

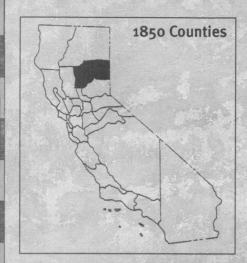

1850 Counties

~ 1850 ~
⊰ BUTTE ⊱
COUNTY

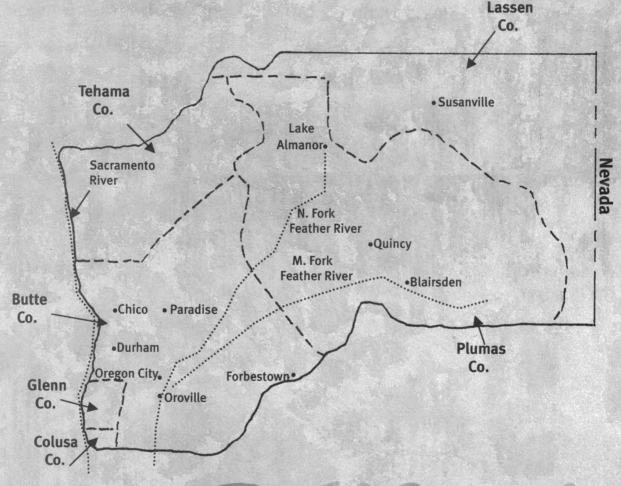

Lassen Co.

Tehama Co.

• Susanville

Sacramento River

Lake Almanor•

N. Fork Feather River

Nevada

• Quincy

M. Fork Feather River

•Blairsden

Butte Co.

• Chico   • Paradise

• Durham

Oregon City•

•Oroville

Forbestown•

Plumas Co.

Glenn Co.

Colusa Co.

California
1850

Present-day boundary variations indicated by
— — —

Settlements/cities of 1850 include: Oregon City, Ophir (Oroville), Forbestown

BUTTE COUNTY 1850

The geographical area of 1850-Butte County included the areas that today make up Plumas County, the eastern portion of Tehama County, and the southern portion of Lassen County. (Tehama and Lassen counties are discussed in other chapters.) Its 3,574 residents counted in the 1850 U.S. Census included people from all over the world. The uncounted Native American inhabitants included members of the Nisenan, Konkow, Yana, Maidu, and Atsugewi tribes.

AREA WITHIN PRESENT-DAY PLUMAS COUNTY

Plumas County was organized in 1854. In 1850 the area within its current boundaries consisted of a favorite stopping point for emigrants traveling the Lassen Emigrant Trail, as well as several mining camps where gold had only very recently been discovered. The stopping place for food and water was Big Meadows where Lake Almanor[1] is located today. The mining camps established within Plumas County were located along the tributary streams of the Upper Feather River canyon.

The original influx of miners came as a result of J. R. Stoddard's assertion that he had stumbled upon a lake that had shores covered with chunks of gold. His famed "Gold Lake" was never found, but the miners were not disappointed by what they discovered in the tributary streams. One of the richest discoveries was made in July 1850 on the east branch of the North Fork of the Feather River, which came to be known as Rich Bar. In August 1850, one thousand men were mining on North Fork claims, but most of the claims were deserted by the time winter arrived. However, the following spring these claims would be revisited and a town site established here. Camps on other river bars on this part of the Feather River were established in the early 1850s.

Two Mexicans set up a camp in the Meadow Valley area west of present-day Quincy in July 1850. Their camp came to be known as Spanish Ranch along Spanish Creek. The two raised cattle, sold meat to the miners working in the area, and took care of the miners' horses and pack mules. Horace Bucklin and Francis Walker set up a ranch in the fall of 1850 in an area southwest of Quincy that has been inundated by Buck's Lake, since a dam was constructed in 1925-27.

Finally, the mining camp of Rabbit Creek or Rabbit Town was established where La Porte stands today. It actually was part of Yuba County until 1852 and became heavily populated when hydraulic mining was in vogue, but would dwindle in size when this type of mining was outlawed in 1884.

Sites to Visit in Plumas County

Plumas County Museum, 500 Jackson St., Quincy 530.283.6320

Plumas-Eureka State Park, 310 Johnsville Rd., Blairsden 530.836.2380

Plumas County Visitors Bureau, P. O. Box 4120, Hwy 70, Quincy 95971 1.800.326.2247

Mining would begin on the east slope of Eureka Peak in the summer of 1851, and ultimately honeycombed the mountain with miles of mine shafts. Today the Plumas-Eureka State Park commemorates the fascinating history of this area through the first half of the 20th century. The Western Pacific Railroad was constructed up the Feather River Canyon in 1909.

AREA WITHIN PRESENT-DAY BUTTE COUNTY

Sites to Visit in Butte County

Bidwell Mansion State Historic Park, 525 The Esplanade, Chico 530.895.6144

Butte County Pioneer Memorial Museum, 2332 Montgomery St., Oroville 530.538.2529

Colman Memorial Community Museum, 13518 Centerville Rd., Chico 530.342.9124

Gold Nugget Museum, 502 Pearson Rd., Paradise 530.872.8722

Lake Oroville Visitor Center, 917 Kelly Ridge Rd., Oroville 530.538.2219

Yuba-Feather Museum & Gold Trader Flat, 19096 New York Flat Rd., Forbestown 530.675.1025

Chico Chamber of Commerce & Visitor Bureau, 300 Salem St., Chico, CA 95928 1.800.852.8570

In 1850 the area within present-day Butte County consisted of the county seat of Hamilton, hundreds of mining camps, and nine ranchos. Hamilton was located on the Feather River in the southern part of the county. Miners had been active in the area since 1848. However, as Hamilton's diggings were exhausted, the population moved further up the river, taking the county seat designation with it—first to Bidwell's Bar in 1853, and then to Ophir City in 1856. Nothing but a monument marking the site of the first county seat remains of Hamilton today.

There were more than 200 mining camps located in southeastern Butte County along the Feather River by the end of 1850. Bidwell's Bar, which lies beneath Lake Oroville today[2], had sprung up when John Bidwell discovered gold there in July 1848. In 1850 a new owner was operating the store Bidwell had established. Charles Fayette Lott arrived in 1849 and soon established a law practice .

Nearby, Stringtown had been established in 1849. It derived its name from the manner in which the buildings were strung out in the settlement. In 1850, 200 men were working at nearby Wyandotte. In September, Benjamin Franklin Forbes founded Forbestown on the South Fork of the Feather River. Forbes opened a trading post and his brother, James D., joined him later that fall. Forbestown would remain a mining community for 30 or 40 years and is a small rural community today. The Yuba-Feather Museum and Gold Trader Flat are located here.

Ophir City, renamed Oroville in 1856, was set up as a mining camp in 1850. James Watt was operating a ferry between Ophir and Hamilton. Long's Bar, above Ophir, had been founded in 1849 when the Long brothers, Southey, James, and William from Missouri, established a store. The Longs earned so much money by March 1850, that they sold their store to James Burt and moved to Solano County where they became prosperous farmers. Two gentlemen by the names of Cross and Foster began operating a ferry at Long's Bar in July 1850.

BUTTE COUNTY RANCHOS

NAME OF RANCHO	GRANTEE AND/OR 1850 OWNER	1850 AND/OR CURRENT SITES
Rancho del Arroyo Chico	John Bidwell	Chico
Rancho de Farwell	Edward A. Farwell, Thomas Fallon, John Potter	Chico
Rancho Llano Seco	Sebastian Kayser	Southwest of Durham
Rancho Aguas Frias	Salvador Osio	Durham, extended into Glenn County
Rancho Esquon	Samuel Neal and John A. Sutter	South of Chico, Durham
Rancho Fernandez	Dionisio and Maceimo Fernandez	West of Oroville, Biggs
Rancho Boga	Charles W. Flügge	Gridley, Live Oak in Sutter County

Oregon emigrants led by Peter Burnett,[3] later the first governor of the State of California, established Oregon City in 1848-49. The placer mines of the district were very rich and the mining population was quite large in 1850. Finally, Pentz and Dogtown were located along the West Branch of the Feather River. Dogtown was accorded its name because the Bassett family living here raised and sold dogs to the miners for companionship. Dogtown would be renamed Magalia in later years.

Gold had been discovered in Butte Creek in 1848 at Rich Bar, located about two miles upstream from the 1894 Honey Run covered bridge that remains today. The settlement of Diamondville was established on the acre of land owned by James Diamond in 1849, and Helltown, seven miles above Diamondville, was founded the following year.

In 1845 Charles Roether, from Germany, had settled on the north side of Honcut Creek, which forms the border between Butte and Yuba counties. The miners who later came to this area wrote home that there were many grizzly bears in the area.

Butte County Ranchos

Of the nine ranchos granted in Butte County, John Bidwell's was the most significant. Bidwell was living in a cabin he had built on his *Rancho del Arroyo Chico* and growing wheat.[4] County Judge Moses Bean called his court into session on this rancho in July 1850, but quickly moved it to Bidwell's Bar when court business did not materialize.

Edward A. Farwell and Thomas Fallon had settled briefly on the Farwell Grant or *Rancho de Farwell* along the Sacramento River. But John Potter was the one to establish the first permanent settlement in Butte County in 1845 when he obtained a portion of the Farwell Grant and built an adobe on Chico Creek in present-day downtown Chico.

John Bidwell (1819-1900)

- Leader of first overland company of Americans to come to California, the Bidwell-Bartleson party

- Employed by John A. Sutter at Sutter's Fort and Sutter's Hock Farm

- Participant in Bear Flag Revolt, served under Frémont in U.S. forces, general of California Militia

- Carried news of gold discovery to San Francisco and made the first set of scales and weights to weigh the first gold

- Humanitarian and advocate for education; donated much of his rancho for public schools, churches, and the Northern Branch State Normal School—present-day California State University, Chico

- Congressman, state senator, general in Civil War, candidate for Governor three times, and Presidential candidate on Prohibition Party's ticket

- Pioneer agriculturist and horticulturist

- Mrs. Bidwell donated the land for Bidwell Park   the second largest city park in California

Notes ∽ BUTTE COUNTY

1

Lake Almanor was created when a dam was constructed at the eastern end of Big Meadows in 1910-1914.

2

The Oroville Dam was completed in 1968—the tallest and one of the largest earthfill dams in the country. Before construction of the dam began, the 1856 Bidwell Bar suspension bridge, the first of its type west of the Mississippi, was relocated to the south end of Lake Oroville in Bidwell Canyon downstream from its original location.

3

See Burnett sidebar on page 137.

4

In 1860 Bidwell founded the town of Chico and later built his mansion that stands today in the Bidwell Mansion State Historic Park. Although this house was not built until 1865-68, it is included in the sites to visit because much can be learned about this significant California pioneer and 1850 life on this rancho.

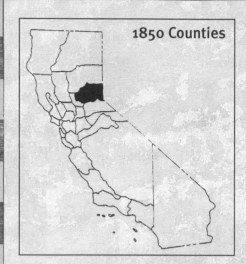

1850 Counties

1850 YUBA COUNTY

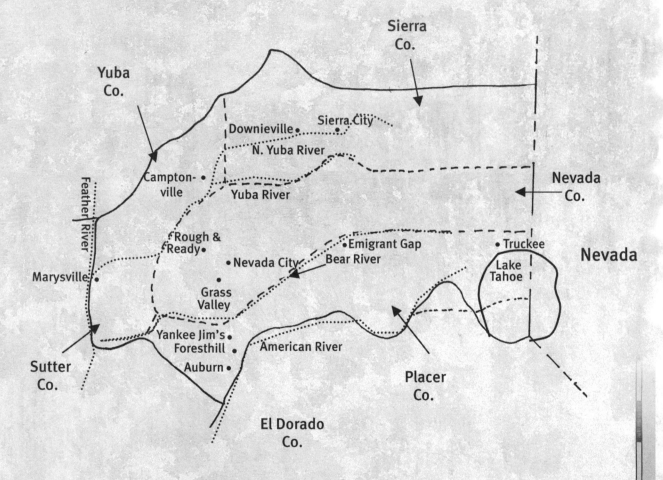

Sierra Co.

Yuba Co.

Downieville • • Sierra City

N. Yuba River

Campton-ville •

Yuba River

Nevada Co.

Feather River

Rough & Ready •

• Emigrant Gap

• Nevada City   Bear River

• Truckee

Nevada

Marysville •

Grass Valley

Lake Tahoe

Yankee Jim's Foresthill •

American River

Auburn •

Placer Co.

Sutter Co.

El Dorado Co.

California
1850

Present-day boundary variations indicated by
— — — —

Not settled in 1850: Truckee, Camptonville, Sierra City, Emigrant Gap

YUBA COUNTY 1850

The geographical area of 1850-Yuba County included the areas that today make up Sierra and Nevada counties, as well as most of Placer county. Its 9,673 population, the third largest in the state according to the 1850 U.S. Census, included people from all over the world. The uncounted Native American inhabitants included members of the Maidu, Konkow, Nisenan, and Washo tribes.

AREA WITHIN PRESENT-DAY SIERRA COUNTY

Sierra County would be organized in 1852. In 1850 the area within its current boundaries consisted of several recently settled mining camps. No permanent structures other than rustic log cabins would be built until 1852. The extensive mining opportunities in Sierra County drew thousands of miners to the area and the county's population peaked at 11,387 in 1860. Mining continued through the early first half of the 20th century. One community, Alleghany, is one of the few gold camps remaining in California today where most of the citizens are still involved in the gold mining industry in some way—many of them employed at the Sixteen to One Mine.

Andrew and Miles Goodyear and two partners had settled Goodyear's Bar in the summer of 1849 along the North Fork of the Yuba River. They were soon joined by a number of other miners and all had to endure great hardships during the severe winter of 1849-50. Prosperity returned in the spring, however, and would continue through the 1850s.

Major William Downie, a Scotsman, and 13 other men[1] had settled "The Forks" in late 1849 just above the present-day site of Downieville. They wintered there in a few log cabins that they built and were joined by thousands of miners in the spring of 1850. A cloth tent and clapboard shantytown arose; a Mrs. Galloway operated an eating-house in a large log cabin; and Ned Barker operated the Pioneer Meat Market. As the population of the area grew, Downieville served as a trading center for the Northern Mines. Mining also was quite lucrative in the area. The miners built a flume along the entire Yuba River between Downieville and Goodyear's Bar, only to have it swept away in the winter floods of 1850-51. A fire in 1852 would completely destroy the town of Downieville, but several buildings built soon after the fire remain standing today, including the 1852 store and gambling house built by Chinese immigrants that today houses the Downieville Museum.[2]

Other mining camps were operating at such places as Gold Bluff above Downieville and Kanaka Creek in the Alleghany area where Hawaiian prospectors

Sites to Visit in Sierra County

Downieville Museum, Main St., Downieville 530.289.3507

Kentucky Mine Historic Park & Museum, Hwy 49 east of Sierra City 530.862.1310

Sierra County Chamber of Commerce, P. O. Box 436, Sierra City, CA 96125 1.800.200.4949

were at work, thus the name of the creek. Philo A. Haven and Joseph Zumwalt founded Sierra City high up on the slopes of the Sierra Buttes in the spring of 1850, originally to develop a trading center. However, gold was soon discovered nearby and by the end of the year, a small mining town was thriving. (The town would have to be relocated to the lower elevation of present-day Sierra City along the North Fork of the Yuba River, however, after an avalanche of snow in the winter of 1852-53 crushed many of the buildings.)

The jagged granite peaks north of Sierra City—originally called the Yuba Buttes, but today called the Sierra Buttes—would become one of the greatest producing areas of gold in all of California, following a Mr. Murphy's discovery of a quartz ledge in 1850. The Kentucky Mine, one of the earliest quartz mines to develop after the opening of the Sierra Buttes, would be built east of Sierra City in the early 1850s. A mill later built on this site is the only tourable and operable gold ore stamp mill in its original condition in California today.

Several miners were settled along the Gold Ridge route that ran from present-day Camptonville in Yuba County to Downieville. Peter Yore had built a house in 1849 that would be added-on to in later years and become a two-story hotel. Also in 1849, a "black man" had put up a tent-cabin on a site that came to be called "Nigger Tent."

In the spring of 1850, an old sea captain named Sears discovered gold along the ridge between the North Fork of the Yuba River and the South Fork of the Feather River in a very remote area even today. Many other operations would begin in the vicinity of Sears' Diggings and become very productive.

The 5,000-foot-high Sierra Valley on the eastern side of Sierra County, which extends north into Plumas County, would not be discovered until 1851 by James Beckwourth, the well-known African American mountain man, explorer, and trader. By the 1860s, it was one of the finest agricultural regions in California. The Beckwourth Pass was the lowest and easiest pass across the Sierra Nevada; Beckwourth would later build a road from the pass through the American Valley (now Quincy) to Marysville.

Sites to Visit in Yuba County

Mary Aaron Memorial Museum, 704 D St., Marysville 530.743.1004 (Closed for renovation until late 2000)

Yuba-Sutter Chamber of Commerce, P. O. Box 1429, Marysville, CA 95901 530.743.6501

AREA WITHIN PRESENT-DAY YUBA COUNTY

In 1850 the area within present-day Yuba County consisted of numerous mining camps along the Yuba River, the settlements of Linda, Barker's Ranch, Dobbins' Ranch, and Camptonville; the county seat, Marysville;[3] and three ranchos.

Gold had been discovered in the Yuba River in 1848, first by Jonas Spect at a spot later known as Rose's Bar, and then by Michael Nye and William Foster on Dry Creek near its junction with the Yuba. Gold bar settlements soon sprang up along the river every mile or two. The floods late in 1850 drove the miners away from the sand bars to higher ground, where more gold was uncovered.

John Rose and William J. Reynolds were operating a store at Rose's Bar, where 2,000 men were at work. They supplied the miners with goods from Sacramento and fresh beef and farm products from their ranch south of Marysville.

The richest of all the Yuba River diggings was Parks' Bar located several miles west of Rose's Bar. This bar was named for David Parks because in 1848 he had arrived with his wife and children. Families were few and far between in the early mining camps, so the fact that his family accompanied him gained him notoriety.

The longest Yuba River bar in terms of physical length and length of time to be successful was Long Bar located above Marysville. It was first occupied in October 1848 and received its first organized group of miners from outside California the next month.

Many other mining camps were established on other bars along the Yuba River in the vicinity of Marysville. By 1857, however, hydraulic mining taking place to the northeast began destroying the river bars and their camps. The settlements were eventually buried under 70 feet of debris that was washed down from the diggings in the Sierras.

The settlement of Linda was established on the south bank of the Yuba River above Marysville in 1850 when the stern-wheel steamer *Linda* arrived. In 1851 the *Linda* would be converted to a dredge—possibly the first in California's mining history. Today the site of Linda is buried beneath the silt-laden tailings washed down from the hydraulic mines in the hills.[4]

Three of the other towns in existence in 1850 were located in the northeastern portion of the county and would be joined by many other towns later in the decade. Barker's Ranch was settled in 1850 by Charles Barker. It would come to be known as Woodville, now Woodleaf, just south of the present-day Yuba/Butte County line.

Dobbins' Ranch was located in the foothill valley of Dobbins' Creek. William M. and Mark D. Dobbins had settled it in 1849. By 1850 it was the terminus for an express transportation company. Langton's Pioneer Express transported supplies by stage to Dobbins' Ranch and then the supplies were loaded on the backs of mules for transport over the mountains to Downieville. The small community of Dobbins is located here today.

In later years a significant amount of mining would take place in an area that in 1969 was inundated by Bullard's Bar Reservoir. William M. Foster, a survivor of the Donner party tragedy, had established a store along the river in the vicinity in 1849. The town later named Camptonville arose after a hotel was built in 1850 on the main road from Marysville and Nevada City to Downieville. The town's namesake, the blacksmith Robert Campton, did not arrive until 1852, the same year that gold was discovered on Gold Ridge to the east.

Yuba County Ranchos

Three ranchos had been granted in Yuba County. Theodore Cordua, a Prussian, owned Honcut Rancho, which slightly crossed the Yuba/Butte County line. Honcut Creek traversed the rancho at its upper edge.

John A. Sutter[5] owned *Rancho Nueva Helvetia*. When he originally received his grant in 1841, his property covered an area that exceeded the limits of Mexican law. Consequently, Sutter sublet parts of his rancho to other settlers—a few parts of which lay within the boundaries of Sutter County. (Part of this rancho also was located in Sacramento County.)

Before Cordua purchased Honcut Rancho in 1850, he had been leasing from Sutter the land where Marysville stands today. He later purchased the land and built an adobe home, including a trading room and outbuildings. Charles Covillaud, from

France, purchased the property from Cordua in 1849. Late in 1849, José Manuel Ramírez, John Sampson, and Theodore Sicard purchased all but one-fourth of the property from Covillaud. All six of the one-time owners—Sutter, Cordua, Covillaud, Ramírez, Sampson, and Sicard, and, in addition, Stephen J. Field—laid out the town of Marysville in 1850. It was named for Mary Murphy Covillaud, the wife of Charles, and herself a Donner party survivor.

Because of its location on the California-Oregon Trail through the Sacramento Valley, Marysville became a primary trading center for the Northern Mines, serving the traffic of men and goods from the Central Valley to the diggings in current Yuba, Nevada, Butte, and Placer counties. Cargoes from the riverboats were transported by pack mule trains to the gold fields, not far away. Freight and passenger boats landed next to the plaza, which was located where High Street between D and E streets lies today. The river can no longer be seen from this spot, however, because levees had to be constructed after tailings from the hydraulic mining raised the bed of the river over 70 feet.

William Johnson and Sebastian Kayser owned what came to be known as Johnson's Rancho, located on the Bear River. They had purchased it at auction for $150 following the original grantee's death in 1844. Their adobe house was the first settlement reached in California by emigrant wagon trains using the Donner Trail that traveled down the mountains to the Bear River. Emigrants would rest here and obtain supplies.[6]

A government reserve, Camp Far West, had been set aside in 1849 on part of Johnson's Rancho to protect American settlers in the Yuba region. Two companies of soldiers were stationed here under the command of Captain Hannibal Day.

In 1844 the Stephens-Townsend-Murphy party had been the first group of emigrants to cross the Sierra Nevada mountains with covered wagons. Between 1844 and 1860, over 200,000 emigrants used this trail through Donner Pass, many proceeding down the mountains to Johnson's Rancho. Today rocks near Big Bend Ranger Station along I-80 still bear the marks of wagon wheels.

Yuba County would add another 4,000 people to its census count by 1860—bringing the population to 13,668. Towns that still exist today such as Browns Valley, Smartville, Timbuctoo, and Strawberry Valley were established; many of the towns included clusters of saloons, stores, and hotels. Later, stamp mills and sawmills were erected. In subsequent census years Yuba County's population declined and then leveled off to around 10,000 until 1940, when it experienced growth again, primarily as a result of the expansion of the agricultural industry in the county.

YUBA COUNTY RANCHOS

NAME OF RANCHO	GRANTEE AND/OR 1850 OWNER	1850 AND/OR CURRENT SITES
Honcut Rancho	Theodore Cordua	North of Marysville, Honcut in Butte County
Rancho Nueva Helvetia (New Switzerland)	John A. Sutter, Charles Covillaud, José Manuel Ramírez, John Sampson, and Theodore Sicard	Marysville, Olivehurst, extended into Sutter County and a separate portion was located in Sacramento County
Johnson's Rancho	William Johnson and Sebastian Kayser	Camp Far West Reservoir

Area Within Present-Day Nevada County

Nevada County would be organized in 1851 from a portion of Yuba County. In 1850 the area within its current boundaries consisted of the mining towns of Nevada City, Boston Ravine, Rough and Ready, and numerous mining camps along Deer Creek and the Yuba River.

In 1849 Captain John Pennington and two partners had built the first cabin above Deer Creek in the area that came to be known as Deer Creek Dry Diggings or Caldwell's Upper Store, until the name was changed to Nevada ("Snow-covered") and finally, Nevada City, in December 1850. Dr. A. B. Caldwell had been operating a store since 1849 in a log cabin located on the slope of Aristocracy Hill. He had previously owned a store seven miles below, thus the name Caldwell's Upper Store.

In 1850 more than 10,000 miners were at work on Deer Creek and in the gravel ranges on the various hills in the area. The ravines were wall-to-wall with miners; brush houses, canvas tents, and log cabins covered the hills that had names such as American, Lost, Piety, Aristocracy, Bourbon, and Oregon hills.

William Elwell introduced the method of ground-sluicing in early 1850, and along with this innovation came the development of an elaborate system of ditches and sluice boxes.[7] Another method of mining called "coyoteing"[8] whereby small tunnels were dug also began in 1850 in the gravel banks on Lost Hill northeast of Nevada City. A settlement existed here for several years called Coyoteville. The South Yuba Canal Water Company built its first ditch to supply water for hydraulic mining in 1850, but the building of the reservoirs and flumes used in hydraulic mining would not begin north of Nevada City on the San Juan Ridge until the early 1850s.

The Stamps family was the first family to settle in Nevada City, establishing a home in a ravine behind present-day Coyote Street. Mr. Stamp was serving as the *alcalde*. A Madam Penn partook in mining activities when she first arrived in Nevada City, but in the spring of 1850 she built a boarding house. A theater was situated on Main Street and there were more than 200 other structures—frame houses, canvas tents, and log cabins. Numerous stores, boardinghouses, hotels, and saloons were built during the 1850s, but the disastrous fires of 1856 and 1863 destroyed many of them. The fires convinced the townspeople to use more brick when rebuilding and so today Nevada City's business district has one of the largest collections of Gold Rush-era structures.

Nevada City's unusual street layout can be explained by the fact that most of the mining activity took place near the plaza at Deer Creek. At the end of the day, a miner would return to his cabin located on one of the hills via a trail originating at the plaza. Some of these same trails would be widened to become wagon roads and eventually paved streets.

In 1850 the area within present-day Grass Valley consisted of two settlements—a colony of 20 settlers clustered around a cabin built in 1849 on Badger Hill, and a settlement of emigrants from Boston led by the Rev. H. H. Cummings. Known as Boston Ravine, it was the chief settlement of the area, with a store operating out of a cabin on the south side of the ravine and the Rhode Island Company operating out of the Providence Store near the top of present-day Main Street. Some farming was taking place and a lumber mill had been built in 1849 to provide lumber to build trading posts, stores, and homes.

Sites to Visit in Nevada County

Donner Memorial State Park & Emigrant Trail Museum, Donner Pass Rd., Truckee 530.582.7892

Empire Mine State Historic Park, 10791 E. Empire St., Grass Valley 530.273.8522

Grass Valley Museum, 410 S. Church St., Grass Valley 530.272.4407

Malakoff Diggins State Historic Park, 12 miles n. on Hwy 49 from Nevada City; right on Tyler-Foote Rd.; right on Derbec Rd. 530.265.2740

Nevada County Historical Society Museum, Firehouse No. 1, 214 Main St., Nevada City 530.265.5468

Grass Valley & Nevada County Chamber of Commerce, 248 Mill St., Grass Valley, CA 95945 530.273.4667

Nevada City Chamber of Commerce, 132 Main St., Nevada City, CA 95959 530.265.2692 (downtown guide)

Several families were settled here in 1850. Mr. and Mrs. Scott built a cabin on Main Street and the John R. Rush and Peter Mason families were settled along Wolf Creek. A post office would be established in 1851 under the name of Centreville; this name was changed to Grass Valley the next year. A disastrous fire in 1855 completely destroyed the 300 wooden buildings of the original town, but many brick buildings from the rebuilt town remain today.

Quartz mining began following the discovery of gold-bearing quartz on Gold Hill by George Knight in October 1850. In a matter of days practically every inch of Gold Hill was staked out and claimed. George D. Roberts discovered gold in a quartz outcropping on Ophir Hill before the year was over. Roberts would sell his claim to the company that established the Empire Mine—one of the world's major gold mines. Today the Empire Mine State Historic Park showcases the gold mining history that continued in this region through the 1950s, with a three-year hiatus during World War II. The first Cornish miners—expert "hard rock" miners who lent so much to the rich history of Grass Valley—did not arrive until the early 1850s.

The first commissioned Methodist minister in California preached his first sermon in California beneath an oak tree in Grass Valley in 1849, but it would be 1852 before a church was organized here. Grass Valley became the home of two famous female singers and dancers of the Gold Rush period—Lola Montez and Lotta Crabtree. The latter performer became the first female millionaire in the U.S.

Rough and Ready, west of Grass Valley, was one of the first mining towns in Nevada County—established in 1849 by a group of men from Wisconsin who called themselves the "Rough and Ready Mining Company," after the hero of the Mexican-American War, General Zachary Taylor. By the fall of 1850 almost every foot of ground for miles around was staked out. Hundreds of men were working the ravines and flats in the area and it was difficult to even find a place to pitch a tent.

In protest over the Foreign Miners' Tax and the general lawlessness in the area which local authorities would not address, the town seceded from the U.S. in April 1850, drafted its own Constitution, and elected Colonel E. F. Brundage its first President. A committee to preserve law and order was meeting on a regular basis, a Christian Association was holding services in a shanty, and the Masons and the Odd Fellows formed a joint benevolent association. Secession lasted only a few months, however, because the Great Republic of Rough and Ready did not want to miss out on upcoming Fourth of July celebrations. A disastrous fire in June did not prevent the town from continuing to grow and become the site of more than 300 frame buildings in several years. Later fires destroyed all but 24 houses and the town declined almost as quickly as it had developed, but several structures built in the 1850s remain today.

Miners had been working the Deer Creek and Yuba River surface diggings since the late summer and fall of 1849. River bar camps were established along the running streams—Rice's Crossing, Frenchman's Bar, Condemned Bar, and Jones' Bar.

In 1849 John Rose, for whom Rose's Bar in Yuba County was named, had built a small adobe and cattle corral in Pleasant Valley west of present-day Bridgeport. His original intention was to trade with the American Indians, but once the miners began arriving in the area he turned his small operation into a trading post, first known as Nyes Landing and later Bridgeport. Similarly, a Frenchman had built a corral for his mules along the San Juan Ridge in 1849. Once the area was found to be rich in placer gold, a town—French Corral—grew up on the site of his corral.

Gold was also being mined in the gulches where Graniteville lies today along the northeastern border of the county. A town called Eureka South would arise here, but the name was changed to Graniteville when a post office was established in 1867.

It was through Yuba County that the California Trail passed, used by the earliest overland parties of emigrants—the Stephens-Townsend-Murphy party in 1844, John C. Frémont[9] and his company in 1845, and the ill-fated Donner party in 1846-47. The Donner party's experience is memorialized in the Donner Memorial State Park and the Emigrant Trail Museum in Truckee. The route through present-day Truckee had been a favorite for the original emigrants due to the kindness displayed by an American Indian tribal chief who came to be known as Trokae. The Overland Emigrant Trail roughly coincided with present-day Hwy 49 between Grass Valley and Auburn in Placer County. Emigrants crossing the Sierra Nevada had used this trail extensively in 1849 to reach the gold fields.

AREA WITHIN PRESENT-DAY PLACER COUNTY

Placer County would be organized in 1851 from portions of Yuba and Sutter counties. In 1850 the area within its current boundaries consisted of the mining towns of Illinoistown, Michigan City, Yankee Jim's, Foresthill, and Auburn; numerous river bar camps along the Bear and American rivers, and one rancho.

Illinoistown, originally called Alder Grove, had been settled in 1849 and immediately became the distribution point for supplies to neighboring camps. Goods brought by wagons were then loaded on pack mules and transported to remote camps over steep mountain trails. Today the town of Colfax is located here.

Michigan City was established on a narrow shelf of the Foresthill Divide above several gorges of the American River and El Dorado Canyon. It became Michigan Bluff in 1859 on a slightly different location higher up the steep slope of the mountainside. Charles Tuttle, a lawyer from New York, was selling food and supplies to miners from a store he established in 1850. Although his store was not formally a law office, he accepted his first case in 1850 and embarked on a prominent legal and political career during the 1850s—professions that his descendants followed throughout the 20th century.[10]

The diggings adjacent to Michigan City were attracting hundreds of miners from the crowded gold mining towns in El Dorado County just to the south across the county line. The cabins built in 1850 would begin to settle and slip down the mountainside in 1858, precipitating the move the following year. This area became a site of hydraulic mining in 1858, the scars of which are still evident today.

Yankee Jim, a man of questionable character, who was a Yankee, Irishman, or Australian—there is disagreement among historians, discovered gold sometime prior to 1850 where the town of Yankee Jim's is located today. By 1850 word had gotten out and the entire ridge country was covered with miners. The town named for him became a highly prosperous mining center.

Sites to Visit in Placer County

Bernhard Museum Complex (1851 and later), 291 Auburn-Folsom Rd., Auburn 530.889.6500

Emigrant Gap Monument, at viewpoint west of Emigrant Gap turnoff on westbound side of I-80

Forest Hill Divide Museum, 24601 Harrison St., Leroy Botts Memorial Park, Foresthill 530.367.3988

Gold Country Museum, County Fairgrounds, 1273 High St., Auburn 530.889.6500

Placer County Museum, Placer County Courthouse (1894), 101 Maple St., Auburn 530.889.6500

Placer County Visitor Information Center, 13460-A Lincoln Way, Auburn, CA 95603
530.887.2111

Rich diggings were found in a canyon near Foresthill (originally Forest Hill) in the spring of 1850 and miners descended upon the area from all directions. Todd's Store was operating as a trading center out of a brush shanty located where the Forest House, a hotel, stands today. By the middle of the summer at least 1,500 men were working with rockers and pans along the banks and bars of the American River from the junction of the Middle and North forks to the river's source. After a fire, parts of the community, including the general store, were rebuilt using "fireproof" brick. Some of these structures still stand on the historic main street of Foresthill.

An agreement was reached between five companies[11] to consolidate their efforts in building a flume covering more than a mile of the American River. This was no small task, especially since there were not any sawmills. A bizarre method of sawing the wood was devised using horses to supply the "horsepower." A few thousand feet of lumber were sawed by this method, but eventually the horses were too debilitated to perform effectively so a new design for the flume had to be created.

The end product was a flume entirely lined with canvas, with the framework of the last portion constructed by splitting puncheon (wooden posts) from the sugar pine and forming a puncheon flooring. Sailors and anyone else skilled with their hands earned a half-ounce of gold per day in wages for sewing the canvas flume lining. The structure was completed in September 1850, but several days later a tremendous rainstorm hit the area and swept the entire flume far downstream. The flume did not break up for several miles and would supply miners along the way with canvas for several years thereafter.

The Frenchman Claude Chana had discovered gold in Auburn Ravine in May of 1848, and in early 1849 one of the earliest mining camps in California was established. The camp began at the bottom of the ravine where gold was first discovered and consisted of tent-type buildings made from brush, wood, and canvas. The camp took on the name of Woods Dry Diggings because John S. Wood built one of the first cabins and also because there was no water in the ravine. The name was changed to Auburn in late 1849, probably by miners who had come to California in 1846 with Stevenson's Regiment of Volunteers from Auburn, New York.

Auburn, with more than 1,300 residents, served as the county seat of Sutter County from the spring of 1850 until 1851 when Placer County was organized and Auburn became a part of it.

A fire in 1855 destroyed the original town, but the lessons of hindsight caused the replacement buildings to be built of solid brick, so a number of later 1850s and 60s buildings remain today on a location slightly up the hill from the original campsite. A volunteer fire department was organized in 1852; the department was challenged by major fires in 1855, 1859, and 1863.

In 1850 it took a full day to travel to Sacramento and two to return, due to the uphill climb. It cost $6 going to Sacramento, and $10 on the return. Auburn served as a staging area for travel to other remote gold regions. A "travelers rest" would be built in 1851 to accommodate passersby on their way to the gold fields; it was the two-story portion of the Bernhard Museum that remains today.

The first courthouse was a wood frame structure with a cloth cover. Auburn's first lynching took place on Christmas Day in 1850. The *Placer Herald* would be published for the first time in 1852.

A rich quartz gold discovery was made in 1850 in Spanish Corral, a mining camp that had been founded in 1849. The camp's name was changed to the Biblical land of gold called Ophir soon after the new discovery, and by 1852 Ophir would become the largest town in Placer County. A fire in 1853 destroyed most of the town, but a few private residences from that era remain in this residential/agricultural community today. The Newcastle mining camp was located where the town of the same name would be established in 1864 in connection with the arrival of the railroad.

Many of the sites of the river bar camps along the North Fork of the American River were inundated by Folsom Lake when Folsom Dam was built in 1955. Beal's Bar was the first of these camps to be established, and Horseshoe, Smith's, and Rattlesnake bars followed. Present-day Auburn-Folsom Road parallels the former express trail that led to these camps.

Other camps totaling about 1,500 men were located along the Middle Fork, including Sailor Claim, Buckner's, Rocky Point Slide, Mammoth, Texas, Quail, Brown's, Kennebec, Buckeye, American, Sardine, Yankee, Dutch, African, Drunkard's Horseshoe Number Two, and Stony bars. River bar camps located above the confluence of the North and Middle forks of the American River along the North Fork would be washed away or buried by the debris of hydraulic mining produced in the Iowa Hill and Gold Run regions northeast of Auburn between 1854 and the early 1880s.

Placer County Rancho

One Mexican land grant was made in present-day Placer County on the south bank of the Bear River. Theodore Sicard, the French sailor recipient in 1844, built an adobe house above Johnson's Crossing east of present-day Wheatland in Yuba County. Sicard's Ranch became one of the last stopping places along the Overland Emigrant Trail before reaching Sutter's Fort in Sacramento County. In 1846 Sicard and his fellow countryman, Claude Chana, had planted a few pits of dried peaches brought by an emigrant family and some almonds that Chana had in his possession. The trees that grew from these pits would become the basis of the first commercial orchard of the Sacramento Valley. This whole area was later buried by debris carried by the Bear River from the hydraulic mines to the northeast.

The northwestern portion of Lake Tahoe is located within Placer County. John C. Frémont was the first non-Native American to sight the lake in 1844 while leading the U.S. Army's first official exploratory expedition across the Sierra Nevada into California. He named his discovery Lake Bonpland after his fellow traveler, Aimé Jacques Alexandre Bonpland, a French botanist. In 1853 the state mapmaker would name it Lake Bigler, after John Bigler, the third governor of California. When the first settlers arrived in 1860, the lake was commonly referred to as Lake Tahoe (Big Water), but the name was not legalized by the State Legislature until 1945.

A portion of the Overland Emigrant Trail passed through a low opening in the mountains at the head of the Bear River known today as Emigrant Gap. At this point even after the Gold Rush, covered wagons were lowered by rope over the cliff to the floor of Bear Valley. This was one of the most dangerous parts of the trip. A monument commemorates Emigrant Gap at an I-80 Vista Point.

1

The 13 men with Major William Downie included ten African American sailors, one American Indian, an Irishman named Michael Deverney, and a Kanakan from Hawaii named Jim Crow.

2

Today Downieville is considered the least changed of all the Gold Rush towns in California. The forests on the surrounding hills are second-growth, because by 1880 the hills had been clearcut of trees for fuel and construction.

3

The discussion of Marysville is included in the section on Yuba County's ranchos.

4

There is a small suburb of Marysville called Linda today, but it is in a different location than the original Linda.

5

See Sutter sidebar on page 226.

6

The relief parties that rescued the stranded members of the ill-fated Donner party in 1846-47 had left from Johnson's Ranch. Johnson was the first husband of Mary Murphy of the Donner party, who later married Charles Covillaud and became the namesake for Marysville.

7

Many old mining ditches serve the irrigation needs of orchards and gardens in the hill country of the Sierra Nevada today.

8

In "coyoteing," a shaft was dug about 30 feet deep into the bedrock along the shore of a stream. Then tunnels were dug in all directions to get at the rich veins of paydirt. It is believed that hundreds of miners met their demise entombed by coyote hole cave-ins.

9

See Frémont sidebar on page 253.

10

Another future prominent Californian, Leland J. Stanford, founder of Stanford University and one of the Big Four of the pioneer railroad industry, would operate a store in Michigan City from 1853 through 1855.

11

The five companies that built the flume near Foresthill, consisting of a total of 400 members, were the Vermont, Buckner's Bar, Sailor Claim, Murderer's Bar, and New York Bar companies.

The Sierra Buttes were one of the greatest producing areas of gold in all of California, following the discovery of a quartz ledge in 1850.

Malakoff Diggins was the world's largest hydraulic gold mine before it ceased operation in 1884.

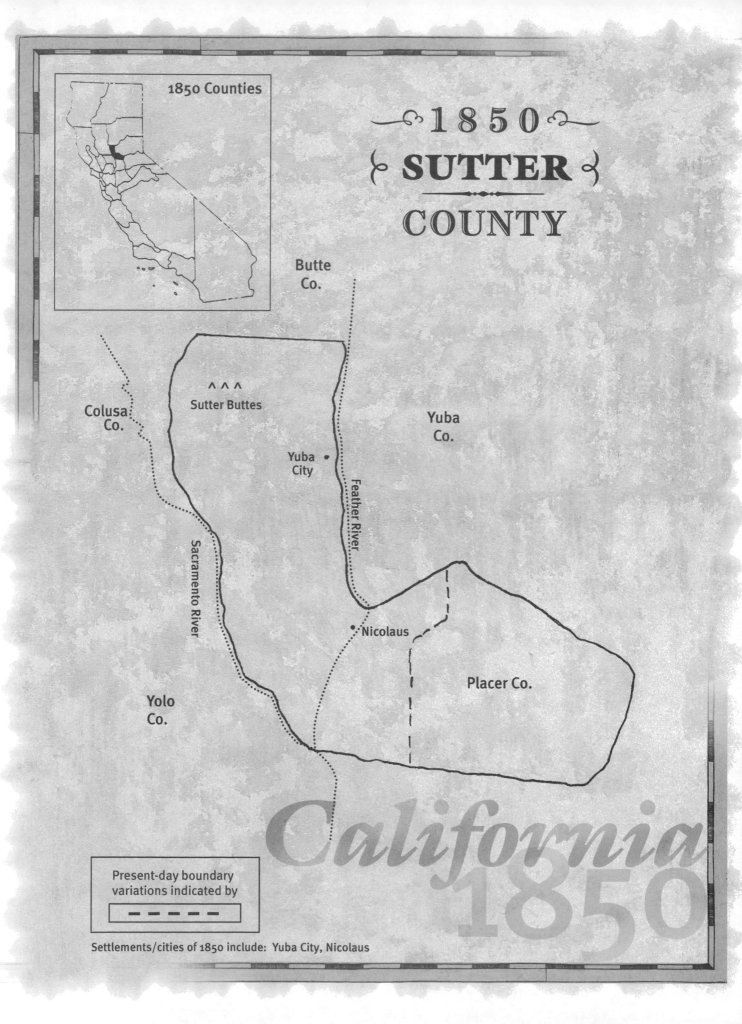

1850 Counties

1850
SUTTER
COUNTY

Butte
Co.

Colusa
Co.

^ ^ ^
Sutter Buttes

Yuba
Co.

Yuba
City

Feather River

Sacramento River

Nicolaus

Placer Co.

Yolo
Co.

California
1850

Present-day boundary
variations indicated by

- - - - -

Settlements/cities of 1850 include: Yuba City, Nicolaus

SUTTER COUNTY
1850

The geographical area of 1850-Sutter County included the southwestern portion of present-day Placer County where Auburn is located. Auburn was the county seat of Sutter County during the latter half of 1850 and until Placer County was organized in 1851. (This portion of Sutter County is described in the Placer County section of the Yuba County chapter.) Sutter County's 3,444 residents counted in the 1850 U.S. Census included people from all over the world. The uncounted Native American inhabitants included members of the Konkow, Patwin, and Nisenan tribes.

In 1850 the area within present-day Sutter County consisted of Yuba City, Sutter's Hock Farm, Oro, Nicolaus, and Vernon, as well as portions of two ranchos covered in other chapters—*Rancho Boga* in Butte County and *Rancho Nueva Helvetia* in Yuba County.

Yuba City was founded in 1849 by Samuel Brannan, Pierson B. Reading,[1] and Henry Cheever on land that they purchased from John A. Sutter. They established a distribution center for the miners and Brannan, as senior partner, had the town site laid out and hired agents to sell lots. Yuba City was overshadowed by its neighbor, Marysville, across the Feather River to the east since it was easier for miners arriving from San Francisco and Sacramento to debark in Marysville and continue on to the gold fields further east.

In 1841 Sutter had established a large agricultural settlement below the future site of Yuba City called the "Hock Farm." Agents had looked after Sutter's cattle until 1849 when he retired here from New Helvetia (Sutter's Fort) and built a mansion near his 1841 adobe house. Sutter had a picture-perfect view of the Sutter Buttes[2] that he shared with the travelers and friends who often visited him. Located on the west side of the Feather River, much of the farm would be covered over by silt deposits from hydraulic mining operations during the flood of 1862.

Oro was a "paper city" created by State Senator Thomas Jefferson Green. He had purchased a tract of land from Sutter where the Bear and Feather rivers meet just north of Nicolaus and convinced the State Legislature to designate it the county seat. However, in the spring of 1850 the county residents voted to transfer this honor to Auburn, so the town of Oro never materialized.

The town of Nicolaus began as a ranch and trading post owned by Nicolaus Allgeier, who had acquired a plot of Sutter's Hock Farm land in 1843 in exchange for construction and ferry services he provided Sutter. Allgeier built a primitive ferry in 1843, which Native Americans operated for him across the Feather River; in 1847

Sites to Visit in Sutter County

Community Memorial Museum of Sutter County, 1333 Butte House Rd., Yuba City   530.822.7141

Yuba-Sutter Chamber of Commerce, P. O. Box 1429, Marysville, CA 95901   530.743.6501

he built an adobe house to replace the hut of mud-covered tules he lived in the first four years; and in 1849 he built a two-story adobe hotel.

In August 1850, land speculators portrayed the site of Nicolaus as "the head of navigation," merely because a small U.S. government sailing boat had arrived at the ferry landing in Nicolaus the year before. As a result of the promotion, 300 lots were sold, and three hotels, a dozen stores, and over 100 houses were built during 1850. Soon, however, everyone realized that when the river was low, boats could only travel as far as Vernon, nine miles downstream. By 1853, many of the houses would be torn down and the town was nearly deserted. Today, Nicolaus is a small farming community protected from the Feather River by a levee.

In 1849 another group of land speculators had purchased a square-mile piece of Sutter's property located where the Feather and Sacramento rivers converge on the southern border of Sutter County. During the dry winter of 1848-49, boats had been forced to unload at this site, called Vernon, which justified a high selling price for these lots. An elaborate hotel built of Chilean mahogany was among the structures built in 1849. However, the heavy rains of 1849-50 raised the level of the Feather River so much that ships were able to travel as far as Marysville, thus negating the lure of Vernon. Nothing remains of Vernon today, but a settlement called Verona would later be established on the site and still exists.

Notes ⟶ SUTTER COUNTY

1

See Brannan and Reading sidebars on pages 127 and 206, respectively.

2

The Sutter Buttes are an unusual range of volcanic promontories that rise abruptly from the level floor of the valley in the northern portion of Sutter County. They are purportedly the "Smallest Mountain Range in the World."

John Augustus Sutter (1803-1880)

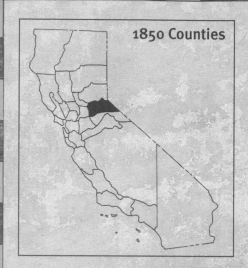

1850 Counties

⚬ 1850 ⚬
❧ EL DORADO ❧
COUNTY

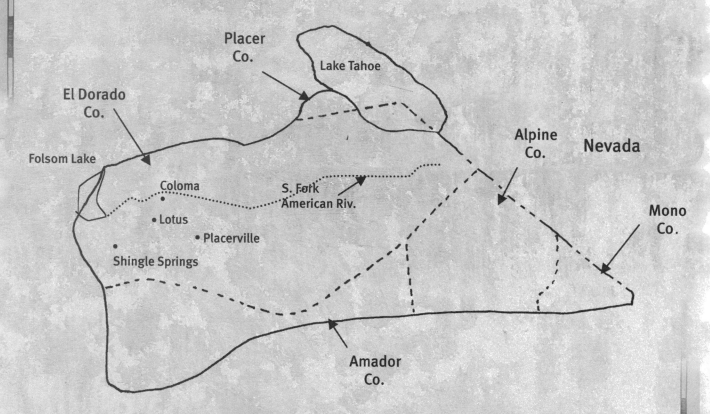

Placer Co.

Lake Tahoe

El Dorado Co.

Folsom Lake

Coloma

S. Fork American Riv.

Lotus

Placerville

Shingle Springs

Alpine Co.

Nevada

Mono Co.

Amador Co.

California
1850

Present-day boundary variations indicated by
- - - - -

Settlements/cities of 1850 include: Growlersburg (Georgetown), Marshall (Lotus), Coloma, Placerville, Shingle Springs

EL DORADO COUNTY
1850

The geographical area of 1850-El Dorado County included portions of present-day Amador, Alpine, Placer, and Mono counties. (Placer and Mono counties are described in other chapters.) With its 20,057 residents counted in the 1850 U.S. Census, El Dorado County qualified as the most populous county in the state. People from all over the world, especially from Germany[1] and France, had immigrated to the area. The Nisenan tribe constituted the uncounted Native American population.

AREA WITHIN PRESENT-DAY EL DORADO COUNTY

In 1850 the area within present-day El Dorado County consisted of about a dozen towns and/or significant mining camps, as well as a multitude of smaller river bar camps. More than 700 mining sites would spring up during the height of the Gold Rush in this county. The Carson Emigrant Trail by way of the Kit Carson Pass was located in the eastern part of the county and was the main route to the Gold Country for the emigrants traveling the overland route from the east. John C. Frémont[2] and Kit Carson had been the first non-Native Americans to cross the Sierra Nevada by a route close to this pass in 1844, as well as the first to cross the length of present-day El Dorado and Amador counties. (Kit Carson never traveled on the actual Carson Emigrant Trail, however.)

In 1849 a party of Oregonians had established itself along Oregon Creek and Hudson's Gulch. First known as Growlersburg because the gold nuggets found in the streams were so big that they "growled" in the gold pans, the camp consisted of tents and shanties on the creek at the foot of what is now Main Street in present-day Georgetown. After a fire totally destroyed the tent city in 1852, Growlersburg was moved up the hill and the name changed to Georgetown. Two buildings, one built in 1852 and the other in 1869, stand today as reminders of Georgetown's earlier era.

The isolated Georgia Flat camp lay two miles northwest of Georgetown. It would come to be known as Georgia Slide after a mountain slide occurred here. A group of miners from Georgia had been working the spot for its placer gold since 1849. Spanish[3] Dry Diggings was located beyond Georgia Flat, near the Middle Fork of the American River. Andrés Pico[4] had discovered a rich ore deposit here in 1848.

John Greenwood, a former trapper and guide, had established a trading post in 1849 in Long Valley west of Georgetown. Other stores opened and in 1850 the town was named Lewisville after the first Anglo child born here. The name would later be changed to its current Greenwood.

Sites to Visit in El Dorado County

El Dorado County Historical Museum, County Fairgrounds, 104 Placerville Dr., Placerville 530.621.5865

Gold Bug Mine, N. Bedford Av., Placerville 530.642.5238

Gold Discovery Museum Visitor Center, 310 Back St., Coloma 530.622.3470

Marshall Gold Discovery State Historic Park, SR 49, Coloma 530.622.3470

James Calvin Sly Museum, Sly Park Recreation Area, (entrance of Miwok Trail), Jenkinson Lake 530.644.2545

El Dorado County Chamber of Commerce, 542 Main St., Placerville, CA 95667 1.800.457.6279

James W. Marshall
(1810-1885)

- Native of New Jersey who worked his way west with a six-year stopover in Missouri where he worked as a farmer and carpenter

- Arrived at Sutter's Fort in July 1845 and was hired by John A. Sutter as a craftsman

- Served in American Army during Mexican-American War

- Made the first discovery of gold in northern California on the American River in Coloma on January 24, 1848, while examining the tailrace of the partially completed mill he was building for Sutter

- Claimed ownership of most of Coloma Valley and became an inactive partner in the sawmill until it was abandoned after 1850

- Prospected on his own and was hired by several prospectors

- Left area, but returned in 1857; purchased 15 acres; built a cabin and worked as vintner and carpenter

- Unsuccessful in most of his business pursuits

- Awarded a $200 a month pension by the State Legislature from 1872 to 1878 as compensation for his discovery of gold

- Died in poverty in Kelsey where he had eked out a living as a blacksmith and operator of two small gold mines

- Monument to him was erected on a hill above Coloma five years following his death at a cost of $9,000

Mining had begun in present-day Pilot Hill in the summer of 1849. Originally called Centerville, the name would be changed to Pilot Hill when a post office was opened in 1854. "Pilot" fires to guide travelers were frequently lit on the promontory rising to the north above the surrounding ravines and hills.

The town of Lotus began in 1849 as Marshall, named after James Marshall, who made the first momentous discovery of gold in northern California on January 24, 1848, a mile and a half downstream. When California was admitted to the Union, Marshall became known as Uniontown. Later in 1881 the name was changed to Lotus.

When Marshall discovered gold at Coloma, he was inspecting the sawmill under construction for John A. Sutter.[5] By summertime, more than 2,000 miners were panning for gold along the American River near the mill and California's first mining town was founded in early 1849 on the site of Marshall's discovery.

In 1850 Coloma was serving as the county seat, over the strong objections of nearby Placerville and Diamond Springs. Most of its 600 to 900 residents lived in tents. A post office had opened in 1849 and Captain William Shannon[6] was serving as *alcalde*. Coloma served a surrounding population of several thousand, and tens of thousands more passed through. It managed to remain fairly peaceful and quiet, however, in comparison to its rowdy neighbors to the south (in Hangtown).

Several businesses were in operation, including Captain Shannon & Cady's general store, S. S. Brook's store, John Little's emporium, and Wright's Store. The latter was the first store, opening in the summer of 1848. It was built of lumber cut at Sutter's mill on the foundation of a cabin planned for Sutter. The rest of the town was built around this store.

Dr. William Taylor had been operating a hospital since 1849 and also managed a drugstore and pharmacy. Adams & Co. Express, an established East Coast company, provided banking and mail services to the miners. The Coloma branch office opened in 1850, taking mail and packages to San Francisco to be loaded on steamers. The first hotel to open was the Winters Hotel in June 1850, soon followed by saloons, gambling houses, restaurants, banks, stables, and blacksmith and gunsmith shops. "Texas Ellen" Wilson was operating a saloon and house of ill-repute.

The Coloma Protestant Church was organized in April 1850; the exact date that the cemetery was founded is unknown. The earliest known graves date from 1849. St. John's Catholic Church, also known as the Coloma Catholic Church, would not be established until 1856.

Peter and Jenny Wimmer and their three children were the first family to live in Coloma. They lived in one side of a double log cabin built by James Marshall and his crew of Mormon mill workers. Marshall and his crew lived in the other side of the cabin. It was Mrs. Wimmer's pot of soft soap into which Marshall dropped his yellow nuggets to see if they would tarnish—one test for true gold.

Peter and Nancy Gooch, Missouri slaves, had come to Coloma in 1849 with their Mormon-pioneer masters. They were granted their freedom when California entered the Union as a free state in 1850; Nancy Gooch earned money doing laundry and other domestic chores for the miners. (Living frugally for 18 years, she was able to save the $700 needed to buy the freedom of her son, Andrew Monroe, who was still a slave in Missouri.)

A replica of Sutter's mill, post-1851 buildings, and a museum make up the Marshall Gold Discovery State Historic Park in Coloma. The original mill was completed in March 1848, but was never used after 1850 due to management problems and legal difficulties.

The Coloma Road was the first pack trail to be marked out in the mining region in 1847-48. It connected Sacramento with Coloma via present-day Folsom, Mormon Island, Green Valley (present-day Rescue), Rose Springs, and Uniontown (present-day Lotus). Thousands of gold miners traveled this road on foot or horseback; Oregonians brought in the first wagons and Mexicans guided pack mules loaded with freight and miners' supplies.

James E. Birch had established California's first stage line along the Coloma Road route in 1849. Crude ferries were assembled out of whatever was available—beds of abandoned emigrant wagons, for instance—to transport the miners back and forth across the American River. The first official ferry began operation at Coloma early in 1849. The Coloma Bridge was first built as a footbridge in 1849 with a 25-cent toll. Subsequently in 1850, it was expanded into a wagon bridge generating $20,000 in three months.

As Coloma became saturated with fortune-seekers, miners were forced to look for new locations to stake claims along the river bars above and below Coloma. Branches of Coloma Road fanned out in all directions, connecting populous river bar camps like Condemned, Negro Hill, Chile Hill, Whiskey, Oregon, and up to 50 others. Thousands of miners were working every part of the Middle and South forks of the American River, as well as the various branches of the Cosumnes River. Many of the sites of these former river bars lie beneath Folsom Lake today, which was created when Folsom Dam was built in 1955.

The Kelsey diggings were located to the east of Coloma. Benjamin Kelsey, brother of Andrew Kelsey who later in 1849 would be murdered by American Indians in Lake County, had discovered gold here in early 1848. A large camp developed here within a year along with several other camps nearby—Spanish Flat, Dutch[7] Creek, Columbia Flat, and Peru, named by a group of miners from Peru, Indiana. A store had been operating in a primitive log cabin in Spanish Flat since 1849.

To the south, Old Dry Diggins was settled following the discovery of gold on Weber Creek in the spring of 1848 by William Daylor, Perry McCoon, and Jared Sheldon. Because the creek was dry during the summer, dirt had to be carried to other sources of water for washing, thus the name. The El Dorado Canal was constructed in 1850 to provide year-round water for mining.

A replica of Sutter's mill, where James Marshall discovered gold in 1848, stands alongside the American River in the Marshall Gold Discovery State Historic Park in Coloma.

The replica of the "Mormon Cabin" built by James Marshall for himself and his Mormon mill workers stands near the reconstructed Sutter's Mill in Coloma.

One to 2,000 miners lived in tents, brush lean-tos, and log cabins on the gulches, ravines, and hillsides surrounding the camp. About 60 buildings were situated along the camp's main thoroughfare, housing stores, saloons, boarding rooms, restaurants, and gambling halls. The post office opened in April 1850 and the *Mountain Democrat* would begin publication in 1851.

The criminal element had established itself early on in Old Dry Diggins. Without any formal government in place, people began taking matters into their own hands and in 1849, the name of the town was changed to Hangtown, because many people were hanged from a tree that stood in Elstner's Hay Yard on present-day Main and Coloma streets. By 1850, Hangtown had become more civilized and the town became known as Placerville due to the numerous placer holes that made the streets almost impassable.

Even today, the streets of downtown Placerville follow the courses of the streams and gulches and contours of the surrounding hills. In 1850 tents were pitched and log cabins built along the pack mule trails leading to the diggings. A fire in 1856 would destroy the town of Placerville, except for a single 1852 brick and greenstone building. A good number of post-1856 and 1860s buildings make up the historical central area today.

Dozens of camps sprang up around Placerville to work the surrounding ravines and depressions of the hills that were tremendously rich in gold. Weberville, located two miles southeast of Placerville, was established after Captain Charles M. Weber,[8] the founder of Stockton, mined along Weber Creek and founded the Weber trading post in the spring of 1848. Weber had returned to Stockton in the fall, but the trading post continued in operation. W. B. Skellinger built the county's first sawmill on Weber Creek in 1850. Timber harvesting would soon become a new and easy way to make money along other streams and rivers. "Green gold" had been discovered.

Diamond Springs was located on the Carson Emigrant Trail. Before a Mr. McPike, the leader of a party of 200 emigrants from Missouri, discovered gold in the nearby ravines in the late summer of 1850, the crystal clear springs were a welcome luxury to weary emigrants passing through. Diamond Springs became one of the richest sites south of Placerville and would grow rapidly as a mining center.

Pleasant Valley, to the east of Diamond Springs, had been named by a group of Mormons who camped here on their way to Salt Lake City in the summer of 1848.[9] They discovered gold during their stay here, but were anxious to complete their journey east. When a few of these Mormons returned to California in 1849, word got out about their previous discovery and miners descended on the area where the Mormons had built two corrals. The camps of Iowaville, Weber Creek, Dogtown, and Newtown sprang up.

Sly Park Meadow, northeast of Pleasant Valley, had been discovered by James Calvin Sly, a member of the group of Mormons moving to Salt Lake City in 1848. The Mormon wagon road, now known as the Mormon Emigrant Trail, became one of the most frequented roads going east, giving rise to a hotel, dairy, and small store in later years. Jenkinson Lake would be created here when a dam was built in 1955.

Mud Springs, later known as El Dorado, was located south of Diamond Springs, and also was an important stop on the Carson Emigrant Trail even before gold was discovered here. Travelers would stop to water their cattle and other stock, muddying the ground around the springs, thus its original name. James Thomas established a trading post and hotel during the winter of 1849-50 called the Mud Springs house. Diggings at Loafer's Hollow, Deadman's Hollow, Slate Creek, Empire Ravine, Dry Creek, and Missouri Flat fanned out from this camp, which became a substantial mining center. Several rich quartz veins would be discovered in this area in 1851.

Shingle Springs, west of El Dorado, was named for several springs in the area and a shingle mill that had been established in 1849. Realizing the potential demand for building materials, Dr. Richard Ormsby, David Scott, William Von Alstiki, and brothers Henry and Edward Bartlett formed the Shingle Mill Company. The horse-powered mill produced 16,000 shingles per day. Clarksville, further to the west, was located on the Clarksville-White Rock Emigrant Road where the Mormon Tavern, established in 1849, was serving customers.

In 1850 a group of Canadians established Frenchtown along French Creek south of Shingle Springs. The Canadians of French extraction were generally regarded as "French," hence the name.

No mining camps of any significance along the Cosumnes River in the southern portion of present-day El Dorado County would be established until 1851. A company of miners were camped at what came to be known as Grizzly Flats in a rugged area between the North and Middle forks of the river in late 1850.

El Dorado County's eastern border lies on the southwestern shore of Lake Tahoe. In 1860, General William Phipps would become one of the first known permanent residents of Lake Tahoe near present-day Sugar Pine Point. The Tahoe Basin was soon heavily logged and the forests completely denuded. Thus the forest that remains today is "young" second or third growth timber.

In 1860-61 the California Division of the Pony Express would travel a route to Sacramento through El Dorado County roughly paralleling present-day U.S. 50 through Placerville. The railroad arrived in Placerville in 1864.

AREA WITHIN PRESENT-DAY AMADOR COUNTY

Amador County would be organized in 1854 from portions of El Dorado and Calaveras counties. Captain Charles M. Weber had discovered the first gold in the county in 1848 along the Mokelumne River. Gold was discovered in several other areas in 1848, but placer mining was never very lucrative in Amador County. Not until quartz veins were discovered in 1851 did any substantial gold mining develop within its boundaries.

In 1850 the settlements in present-day Amador County included Volcano, Fiddletown, Drytown, Amador's Creek, Sutter Creek, Jackson, Butte City, Ione, Buena Vista Ranch, Lancha Plana, and Middle Bar. There were a number of river bar camps along the Cosumnes and Mokelumne rivers and several of the county's creeks.[10] One rancho, *Rancho Arroyo Seco* (Dry Stream), which crossed the present-day Amador/Sacramento County line, had been granted in 1840 to Teodosia Yorba of present-day Orange County, but it is doubtful that he ever set foot on his property. Amador's Creek, Sutter Creek, Jackson, Ione, and Buena Vista Ranch all were located within the boundaries of this rancho.

Sites to Visit in Amador County

Amador County Museum, 225 Church St., Jackson
209.223.6386

Chew Kee Store Museum (early 1850s), Main St., Fiddletown
209.223.4131

Chichizola Store, 1324 Jackson Gate Rd., Jackson

Amador County Chamber of Commerce, 125 Peek St., P. O. Box 596, Jackson, CA 95642
209.223.0350

Volcano had been established in 1848 by members of Stevenson's Regiment of New York Volunteers, who worked in the area known as Soldier's Gulch. It was named Volcano because the area resembled the crater of a huge volcano. Its placer mining was limited; later hydraulic mining operations would almost destroy the town. Frequent fires over the years also did their damage.

A wagon road constructed in 1850 from Volcano across the Sierra Nevada to Carson Valley became one of the main overland routes. Jerome, Hansen & Smith was a general merchandise store in Volcano; on Sundays the owners permitted a minister to conduct religious services in their building. California's first "rental" library was established in Volcano in 1850, where miners could rent novels and other light reading for ten cents a volume. One of the first "little theaters" in California would be founded by the Volcano Thespian Society in 1854. Today Volcano is best known for two tourist attractions nearby—Daffodil Hill and Indian Grinding Rocks State Historic Park.

South of Volcano, mining was taking place in the gulches of Grass Valley Creek. West of Volcano miners were busy along Rancheria Creek.

A party of "fiddling" Missourians had settled Fiddletown in 1849, where gold was discovered in one of its dry creeks in 1848. (The name would be immortalized in Bret Harte's story, *An Episode of Fiddletown*.) During the height of the Gold Rush, Fiddletown had the largest Chinese settlement outside of San Francisco. The rammed-earth adobe still standing on Main Street today—the Chew Kee Store Museum—was built for a Chinese doctor and his family in the early 1850s. Several other 1850s historic buildings remain standing, as well.

Drytown, located south of Fiddletown, began with the discovery of gold along Dry Creek in 1848. Many of the residents of this camp were panning in the surrounding canyons bearing such names as Blood Gulch, Murderer's Gulch, and Rattlesnake Gulch. Drytown is where the soon-to-be very wealthy George Hearst would establish his mine office in the early 1850s. The town was nearly destroyed by fire in 1857; since all of the available gold had been mined by then, the town was never rebuilt, but a few structures dating from the 1850s remain today.

Two miles to the east, mining had begun at Rancheria in 1848. The murder of a number of Americans in 1855 would occur here, the result of a Mexican backlash to the anti-Hispanic sentiments of some Americans.

In 1844 John A. Sutter had sent some of his employees, some with families, to a place he called "Pine Woods," east of present-day Amador City, to whipsaw cedar and sugar pine lumber, produce charcoal, and manufacture goods for use or sale at his fort in New Helvetia. When he decided that it would be more efficient to have a sawmill operating closer to the source of lumber, he opted to build the one at Coloma because it was closer to New Helvetia than Pine Woods (and you know the rest of the story).

Gold had been discovered in Amador's Creek (present-day Amador City) in 1848. *Don* José María Amador mined along Amador's Creek in 1848 and 1849 and established a camp named Amador's Crossing—the crossing that had been used by Sutter's workers to transport logs to his sawmills. He also opened a trading store here, but by 1850 he had returned to his *Rancho San Ramon* in Contra Costa County with thousands of dollars in gold.

George Hearst (1820-1891)

- Astute businessman from Missouri who arrived in the gold fields in 1850

- Invested in California mines, but amassed his fortune from mines in Nevada, South Dakota, Montana, and San Luis in Mexico

- Established his family—wife, Phoebe Apperson Hearst, and son, future newspaper mogul William Randolph Hearst—in a showplace mansion in San Francisco

- Served as U.S. Senator

R. C. Downs (1828-18??)

- Dry goods clerk who arrived in San Francisco from New York City in 1849

- Mined on American River and Amador Creek his first year

- Operated a merchandising business known all over the state with Levi Hanford from 1850 to 1859

- Became owner of several hard rock mines with various partners, including Leland Stanford

- Served in State Assembly from 1879-80

In 1850 Amador's Creek was lined with tents and winter cabins. The Sacramento-based firm of Hanford and Downs was operating a store here. Levi Hanford and R. C. Downs owned this merchandising company that also served Rancheria, Sutter Creek, and Volcano. The miners in Amador's Creek included James T. Wheeler and four partners, as well as a mining company from New York and one from Virginia that also provided goods for sale. It would not be until a rich gold-bearing quartz vein was discovered in 1851 by four Baptist ministers, however, that any profitable mining occurred in this area. Amador City then became one of the richest mining towns in the entire Gold Country. A fire in 1878 destroyed the town's earliest structures, but several later Gold Rush-era buildings remain today.

John A. Sutter had come to present-day Sutter Creek in 1846 and he was the first to mine the area in 1848. In 1850 a small settlement was centered around a tent where the miners met on rainy Sundays when they could not go to Drytown or Jackson. Just like Amador City, placer mining was never very profitable in what was variably called Sutter's Creek, Sutter, Sutterville, and finally Sutter Creek. Rich quartz deposits would be discovered nearby in 1851 and quartz mining continued into the 1940s. Fires from 1862 through 1888 destroyed different portions of the original Sutter Creek. Today a portion of an inn dating back to 1858 is the oldest structure in town.

In 1850 about 500 miners were working at Jackson Gate on the north fork of Jackson Creek, and the first mining ditch in the county was dug here. Today the 1850 Chichizola Store[11] built by Agostino Chichizola remains standing in Jackson Gate, which is located northeast of Jackson.

One branch of the Carson Emigrant Trail passed through Jackson, which originally was known as "Bottileas" (an American corruption of the Spanish word for bottle, *botella*) because of the empty bottles left alongside a year-round spring by travelers on their way to the mountains. In 1849 early miners named it Jackson's Creek or Jackson. The diggings in the town never were very rich, but Jackson would develop into a convenient stopping place for travelers from Sacramento on their way to the Southern Mines. The population in 1850 approximated 1,500 with more than 100 tents, dwellings, and stores in the town. Quartz mining would bring prosperity to Jackson in later years and two of the world's deepest mines opened here—the Argonaut Mine in 1850 and the Kennedy Mine in 1856.

The *Jackson Sentinel* would be first published in February 1852. Virtually all of the town was leveled in a disastrous fire in 1862, so most of Jackson's remaining historic buildings date from the 1862-63 reconstruction period, although a few were built in the mid-1850s.

Butte City sprang up south of Jackson following the discovery of gold in a shallow basin in 1850. It would rival Jackson in size and importance in the early 1850s, but when the gold gave out, the town was abandoned.

In 1848 William Hicks, who came to California with the Chiles-Walker party in 1843, had been the first settler in the Ione Valley, where Ione is situated today. His ranch, with its adobe house and old log house, served as a primitive inn and supply center for travelers passing through. Miners could also board their horses and cattle here. Hicks was the first to prospect the valley, but without much success, so in late 1850 he sold his rancho to David Waldo of Sacramento. First known as Bedbug and later Freezeout, Ione would develop as a supply center rather than a gold town. Several buildings dating from 1856 and later still stand today.

The Buena Vista Ranch, located south of Ione, provided the same services as the Hicks Ranch in 1850. Its owner, William H. Diggs, also operated wagons between his rancho and the towns of Sutter and Sacramento. Sometime in 1850, New Yorkers Charles Stone, Warren Nimms, and Fletcher Baker purchased the ranch.

Sonora Bar was situated where the Mokelumne River left the mountains (before the Pardee Dam was built in 1929). This may have been the location where Weber's men first discovered gold on this river. In 1850 a settlement at this location called Lancha Plana consisted of a cluster of tents and brush shanties, a store operated by a French Canadian, and a ferry service operated by William Winter and a Mr. Kaiser. Their original ferry was merely a raft made of casks tied together.

To the east of Sonora Bar and south of Jackson, Middle Bar was not only a choice mining spot, but also a very important Mokelumne River crossing. Dr. W. L. Martin and a Mr. Peuch were operating a ferry that transported passengers and supplies between the Middle bars located on both sides of the river. Several other ferries were operating at other bar locations, including Big Bar.

AREA WITHIN PRESENT-DAY ALPINE COUNTY

There are no 1850 Sites to Visit in Alpine County

Alpine County Chamber of Commerce, P. O. Box 265, Markleeville, CA 96120
530.694.2475

Alpine County would be formed in 1864 from portions of El Dorado, Amador, and Calaveras counties. Jedediah Strong Smith, Joseph Reddeford Walker, John C. Frémont, and Kit Carson had traveled through this region—the most difficult and rugged part of the journey through the Sierras. The Overland Emigrant Trail also passed through here. On his way to Salt Lake City in 1847, Sam Brannan[12] had left two men to establish an outpost at the present-day site of Woodfords. The valley between the treacherous pass and Woodfords is called Hope Valley because the Mormon party's hope was restored upon viewing it. The outpost was later abandoned, but other settlers arrived and remained. Daniel Woodford arrived in 1849 and built a hotel. This was the earliest Anglo settlement in Alpine County; it would be the late 1850s before silver was discovered in the county. Besides its beautiful rugged mountains that resemble the alpine country of Europe, Alpine County is known for Grover Hot Springs State Park. A pool slightly cools the 140-degree water that bubbles from the earth.

1

Few Germans became miners; they became storeowners, saloon keepers, butchers, bakers, farmers, and ranchers instead, supplying the needs of the mines.

2

See Frémont sidebar on page 253.

3

There were few natives of Spain in the gold mines, but to the Americans, "Spanish" meant Mexicans, Portuguese, South Americans, and any other Spanish-speaking people.

4

See Pico sidebar on page 59.

5

See Sutter sidebar on page 226.

6

William Shannon was a delegate of the State Constitutional Convention.

7

"Dutch" is the English way of pronouncing *Deutsche* (German). In California the word Dutch was used for any group of miners from Germany, Switzerland, Austria, or the Netherlands.

8

See Weber sidebar on page 262.

9

The Mormons passing through Pleasant Valley were members of the Mormon Battalion who had arrived too late to fight in the Mexican-American War and stayed in California to raise funds for the colony of Mormons struggling in Salt Lake Valley in Utah. In an attempt to avoid deep snow and the fate of the Donner party, a scouting party had selected a new route from Pleasant Valley over the summit near Carson Pass. Although Kit Carson would not travel this route until 1853, because of its location near the pass named for him, it has become known as the Carson Pass. The Mormons deserve credit for pioneering this main southern branch of the California trail through the Sierras.

10

Many of the river bars along the Mokelumne River, including Middle and Sonora bars, would be flooded when Pardee Dam was built in 1930. The neighboring Camanche Reservoir was created in 1964.

11

Agostino Chichizola's younger brother, Antonio, who was only twelve years old in 1850, would become the first president of the Bank of Italy in San Francisco, which later became the Bank of America.

12

See Brannan sidebar on page 127.

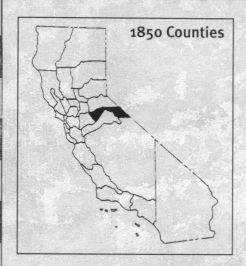

1850 Counties

⌘ 1 8 5 0 ⌘
⌘ CALAVERAS ⌘
COUNTY

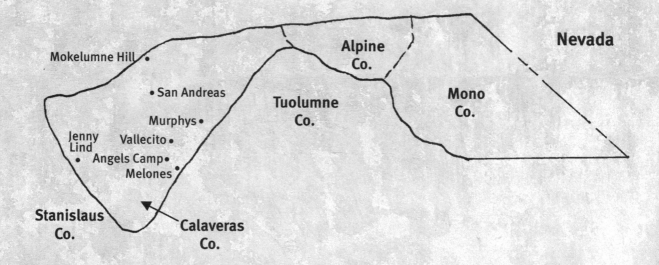

El Dorado
Co.

Nevada

Mokelumne Hill •

Alpine
Co.

• San Andreas

Tuolumne
Co.

Mono
Co.

Murphys •

Jenny   Vallecito •
Lind
• Angels Camp •
Melones

Stanislaus
Co.

Calaveras
Co.

California
1850

Present-day boundary
variations indicated by

– – – – –

Settlements/cities of 1850 include: all shown

CALAVERAS COUNTY
1850

The geographical area of 1850-Calaveras County included portions of Amador, Alpine, and Mono counties, all of which are described in other chapters. The 16,884 residents of Calaveras County counted in the 1850 U.S. Census included people from all over the world. The uncounted Native American inhabitants included members of the Miwok and Paiute tribes.

Bordered by the Mokelumne River on the north and the Stanislaus River on the south and with the Calaveras River coursing through the county in various directions, the area within present-day Calaveras County was a popular location for gold miners. In 1850 Double Springs was the county seat, and a dozen settlements or mining camps were in existence.

Camanche had been established in 1849 by a group of miners from Iowa who named it after their hometown.[1] Oregonians had discovered gold east of Camanche in 1848. Their camp was named Oregon City. After Mexican miners from Sonora, Mexico outnumbered them, the name was changed to Campo Seco (Dry Camp) because there was a lack of water in the area. In 1850 more than 40 different nationalities were working this area. Placer gold would only hold out for a couple of years, but copper was discovered in 1859, luring people back. Fire destroyed Campo Seco in 1854, so any structures remaining today were built after that date.

Dr. John Lind had founded Jenny Lind as a gold mining camp and supply center in 1849, but the area soon developed into the cattle ranching and farming community that it remains today. Double Springs lay east of Jenny Lind, and in 1850 it became the first of four county seats to be designated in Calaveras County. The building that served as the county courthouse during the one year that Double Springs was the county seat was one of a number of camphor wood houses that Sam Brannan[2] imported from China in 1850. This structure still stands on private property.[3]

Placer gold fields had been worked in Paloma since 1849 and quartz gold would be discovered here in 1851. William M. Gwin, a delegate of the State Constitutional Convention and one of the first U.S. Senators from California, established the Gwin Mine here, which operated until 1908.

Mining had begun at Big Bar in 1848, which was located near Mokelumne Hill. In 1850 the Whale Boat Ferry was providing access across the Mokelumne River from here to the northern mining areas.

Mokelumne Hill was settled after gold was discovered at Big Bar. One of the prospectors set up a trading post in a canvas tent from which he earned profits that more than made up for any mining he missed. By 1850, Mokelumne Hill, one of the

Sites to Visit in Calaveras County

Angels Camp Museum,
753 S. Main St., Angels Camp
209.736.2963

Calaveras County Museum,
30 N. Main St., San Andreas
209.754.6579

Old-Timers Museum, 470 Main St.,
Murphys   209.728.1160

Calaveras County Visitors Center,
1211 S. Main St., P.O. Box 637,
Angels Camp, CA 95222
209.736.0049

richest of the digs, also was one of the largest communities in the region.[4] Fights between grizzly bears and bulls were frequently staged here on Sundays. During 1850 the *Calaveras Chronicle* began publication. A fire destroyed the town in 1850, but a few mid-1850s historical structures remain today.

The richest and most-worked gulch in the county was located at Chili Gulch, originally called Chilean Gulch. Three camps of mostly Chilean miners were located along the five-mile gulch. In 1849 the "Chilean War" between Chileans and Americans had occurred. At issue was the Chileans' use of peon labor to work their claims, which upset the anti-slavery American miners.[5] In the end, the Americans won and gained possession of the gulch. Nothing remains of these camps; when the gold gave out, the miners and merchants left the area.

A small group of Mexican miners had arrived in San Andreas in the winter of 1848. By 1850 Americans were working among the 1,000-plus Mexicans and would be followed by a number of French and Chinese miners. A fire in the late 1850s destroyed the original wood and canvas structures. Today the remaining historical buildings in San Andreas, which became the county seat in 1866, date from 1855 and later.

Mexicans had also settled Calaveritas south of San Andreas in 1849. It would be almost completely destroyed by fire in 1858; an 1854 structure is the oldest building remaining today.

Henry P. Angel, from Rhode Island, had established a trading post in Angels Camp following the discovery of gold here in 1848. This camp was the headquarters for over 4,000 miners working the nearby Dry, Greenhorn, and Angels creeks. The streams soon ceased to be profitable, however, and Angels Camp would shrink in size until gold-bearing quartz veins were discovered running practically under the main street of town in 1854. Today the town remains honeycombed with tunnels dug for the many successful hard rock mines. A fire nearly destroyed the town in 1855, but several structures built in the 1850s remain today.[6]

In 1848 Sergeant James H. Carson, a member of Stevenson's Regiment of New York Volunteers, had discovered gold in the vicinity of Carson Hill. Carson's placer discovery in Carson Creek was overshadowed by John William Hance's discovery of a 14-pound lump of gold on the top of Carson Hill in 1850.[7]

Robinson's Ferry, known today as Melones, was located on the south slope of Carson Hill on the Stanislaus River. John W. Robinson and Stephen Mead had established ferry transport across the river for miners, freight, and animals in 1848. They charged 50 cents per person, freight, or animal item. In 1849 they established a trading post as well.[8]

Gold had been discovered along Coyote Creek in 1848 by two brothers, Daniel and John Murphy, members of the large Murphy family of San José. The camp was named Murphys Diggings, but when the brothers became dissatisfied with the yield of gold here, they moved further east and established another Murphys New Diggings, which later came to be known as Murphys Rich Diggings, Murphys Flat, Murphys Camp, and finally just Murphys. The original site then became known as Murphys Old Diggings until some Mexicans located here and renamed it Vallecito (Small Valley). The Mexicans arranged their camp in the typical Spanish manner, with their tents and buildings placed around a central plaza. In 1852 rich deposits of

John Murphy (1825-1892)

- Arrived in San José in 1844 with his family and other members of the Stephens-Townsend-Murphy party

- Arrived in Calaveras County in 1848 with his brother Dan, Henry Angel, and James Carson

- Trading post he and Dan operated did better than many of the claims—sometimes $400 in gold dust per day

- He and Dan used the local Native Americans for labor on their mining claims

- Left Murphys in December 1849 with more gold than any man on the Pacific Coast—between $1.5 and $2 million

- Returned to San José where he held several public offices and later operated a mercantile business

gold would be discovered running through the center of Vallecito. Several structures built in the 1850s remain today.

By 1850 the population in Murphys had reached 1,200. A makeshift post office was in operation, with a carrier appointed to travel to San Francisco once a month for the mail. Sawmills most likely were in operation in the Murphys area by 1850 because visitors wrote about buildings constructed of sawed lumber. Much of the original camp of Murphys would be consumed by fire in 1859, but many historical buildings remain today in the quaint downtown area.

Calaveras County has several remarkable natural phenomena. The Calaveras Big Trees State Park is composed of a stand of the *Sequoia gigantea*, the larger of the two species of California sequoias. A. T. Dowd would discover the grove in the early 1850s and it soon became a destination point for scientists and travelers from all over the world.[9] The California Caverns, underground limestone rock caverns, were discovered in 1850, and the Mercer's Caverns were discovered in 1885.

In the later years of the Gold Rush, Calaveras County became California's second largest producer of wine. The Southern Pacific Railroad arrived in the county in 1871.

Notes ∽ CALAVERAS COUNTY

1
The former Camanche area was inundated by Camanche Reservoir in 1964.

2
See Brannan sidebar on page 127.

3
The Calaveras County Historical Society has been attempting to acquire the camphor wood building for several years, to no avail.

4
It is believed that the first code of mining laws was drawn up in Mokelumne Hill by Colonel Jonathan Stevenson, who, along with about a hundred of his men from the New York Volunteers, were mining here in 1848-49.

5
Because California had chosen to become a free state, American Indian as well as African American slave labor was unacceptable.

6
Angels Camp is the site of the annual jumping frog contest held in May, inspired by Mark Twain's *The Celebrated Jumping Frog of Calaveras County* written in 1864.

7
In 1854 the largest gold nugget in California, a 195-pound mass of gold, would be found at Morgan Mine in Carson Hill.

8
In 1979 the New Melones Dam would be built on the Stanislaus River near Melones.

9
A hotel in Murphys, now known as Murphys Historic Hotel & Lodge (rebuilt in 1861), was built in 1855 to accommodate the many travelers coming to view the giant sequoias. Two hotels each called the Big Trees Hotel were built within the grove, but both burned down, the first in 1864, and the second in 1943.

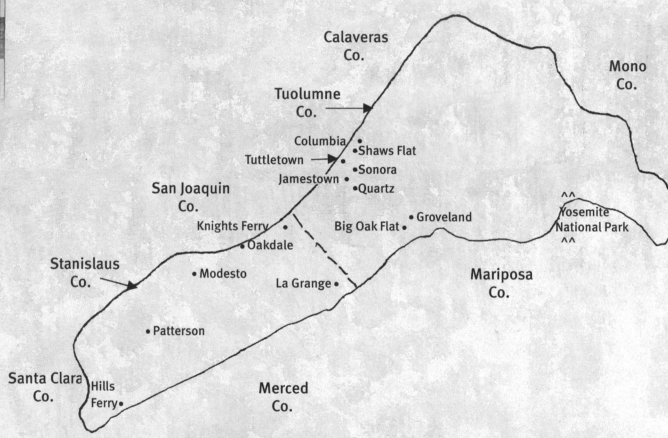

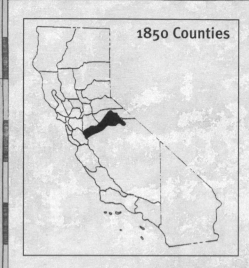

1850 Counties

1850
TUOLUMNE
COUNTY

Alpine
Co.

Calaveras
Co.

Tuolumne
Co.

Mono
Co.

Columbia
• Shaws Flat
Tuttletown
• Sonora
Jamestown
• Quartz

Yosemite
National Park

San Joaquin
Co.

Knights Ferry
Big Oak Flat
• Groveland

• Oakdale

Stanislaus
Co.

• Modesto
La Grange

Mariposa
Co.

• Patterson

Santa Clara
Co.
Hills
Ferry •

Merced
Co.

California
1850

Present-day boundary
variations indicated by
— — — —

Towns not in existence in 1850: Modesto, Patterson, Oakdale

TUOLUMNE COUNTY 1850

The geographical area of 1850-Tuolumne County included most of the area within present-day Stanislaus County. Its 8,351 residents counted in the 1850 U.S. Census came from all over the world. The uncounted Native American inhabitants included members of the Miwok and Paiute tribes.

AREA WITHIN PRESENT-DAY TUOLUMNE COUNTY

In 1850 the area within present-day Tuolumne County consisted of 15 towns or settlements and numerous river bar camps along the Tuolumne and Stanislaus rivers. The first river diggings on the Tuolumne River had been discovered at Hawkins' Bar in early 1849. Several of these former bars lie beneath Don Pedro Reservoir, which was created in 1971.

The waters of Don Pedro also inundated the site of the former town of Jacksonville. In June 1849, Colonel Alden M. Jackson had opened a trading post and established a settlement at the diggings located at the junction of Woods Creek and the Tuolumne River. By 1851, Jacksonville's population would be second in the county to that of Sonora.

Big Oak Flat was originally called Savage Diggings. James D. Savage[1] and his friendly Native American laborers had begun mining the streams and gullies here in 1849 and were soon joined by hundreds of other prospectors. Savage paid his workers in merchandise from his trading post he established.[2] Several Gold Rush-era buildings remain standing in Big Oak Flat today.

Also originally known as Savage Diggings, Garrotte (Strangle), later named for its swift and harsh justice, was located just east of Big Oak Flat. During 1849-50 the adobe Groveland Hotel was built here. It was modeled after the Larkin House in Monterey. The restored hotel, which incorporates the later Queen Anne structure next door, is still in operation in the town that has been called Groveland since 1875. Several other structures built in the 1850s remain today.

Since 1848, a group of Salvadorians had been working the placers at Camp Salvador located on a flat at the top of Shawmut Grade. The following year, 35 Cantonese miners began prospecting here, but when Anglo miners arrived soon thereafter, the Chinese were pushed out to the adjacent Camp Washington, where they were accepted. Other Chinese miners would gravitate to this area and when a post office was established in 1854, the town became known as Chinese Camp.

Sites to Visit in Tuolumne County

Columbia State Historic Park, Columbia 209.532.0150

Groveland Hotel, 18767 Main St., Groveland 209.962.4000

Gunn House Hotel – Josephine's California Trattoria, 286 S. Washington St., Sonora 209.532.3421

Jimtown 1849 Gold Mining Camp, 18170 Main St., Jamestown 209.984.4653

Tuolumne County Museum and History Center, 158 W. Bradford Av., Sonora 209.532.1317

Tuolumne County Visitors Center, 55 W. Stockton Rd., P.O. Box 4020, Sonora, CA 95370 209.533.4420

Montezuma Tent, a trading post operated by Solomon Miller and Peter K. Aurand, was located northwest of Chinese Camp. In June 1850, a group of Mexican miners, upset about the recently enacted Foreign Miners Tax, attacked the tent. Miller escaped, but Aurand was killed during the melee. Little mining took place here until 1852. The small community is called Montezuma today.

In the vicinity of present-day Stent and Quartz, Utterville had been settled by Captain William H. Utter in 1848. The Tuolumne County version of Campo Seco (Dry Creek) was situated a little further north after water was ditched to it in the spring of 1850.

Woods Crossing on Woods Creek was the site where gold was first discovered in

The 1849-50 Groveland Hotel was modeled after the Larkin House in Monterey. The restored hotel is still in operation in Groveland.

Tuolumne County in August 1848. A party of men led by James Woods made this rich discovery where it is said that more gold was taken than from any other stream of comparable size in California.

George F. James, a lawyer from San Francisco, established a settlement at Jimtown after the first discovery of gold on Woods Creek. Not much interested in the physical aspect of mining, he set up a tent and began operating a combination trading post, hotel, and saloon. He also bilked many would-be investors in his proposed mining projects out of huge sums of money through a script scam. He secretly left town and the angry residents changed the name of Jimtown to American Camp. It later was renamed Jamestown.

Jamestown experienced many fires—the most devastating one in 1855. Nevertheless, a number of 1850s brick, stone, and adobe structures line Main Street today, many with the typical Gold Rush-era covered balconies.[3]

Sonora, further up Woods Creek, began as Sonorian Camp when a party of Mexicans settled here in mid-1848. R. S. Ham was elected the camp's first *alcalde* and became known for his unique style of dealing out justice. Sonora became one of the rowdiest Mother Lode camps, with miners brawling and fighting amongst themselves, and pitting bears against horses for entertainment. By the fall of 1849, there were 5,000 people in Sonora, many of them foreigners. Imposition of the Foreign Miners' Tax by the State Legislature touched off a bloodless war in June 1850 and afterwards, half of the population left the area.

Sonora became the county seat when Tuolumne County was organized in February 1850. The *Sonora Herald* was founded in July by John White and John Gage Marvin. It was first printed in the parlor of the two-story adobe house built by Dr. Lewis C. Gunn. Dr. Gunn, the county recorder, also operated the county office in his home. Today this former home comprises a portion of the Gunn House Hotel.

Frequent fires occurred in Sonora, but a remarkable number of buildings erected in the 1850s remain today. The oldest commercial structure in Sonora is the 1852 City Hotel. Originally an adobe structure, it has been extensively remodeled into an 1890s style hotel.

West of Sonora, a company of Mormons had discovered gold along Mormon Creek in the summer of 1848. Soon thereafter, Judge Anson A. H. Tuttle built a log cabin on the future site of Tuttletown. This location was a stopping place for packers carrying miners' supplies from Angels Camp to Sonora. In 1850 it was a prosperous camp of tents and Mexican ramadas (brush houses).

Near Table Mountain, Mandeville Shaw had planted an orchard in 1849 and was operating a store. Gold was discovered in the area at about the same time and by 1850, the settlement of Shaws Flat was established. Mining was a clean and easy operation in Shaws Flat because gold was often found in the roots of grass and the bedrock was only three to four feet below the surface. In 1850 Albert Bullerdieck built the Mississippi House, a two-building complex. The structure stood near collapse until very recently when it was demolished.

In March 1850, John Walker discovered gold in the runoff from a heavy rain at Columbia Gulch, north of Shaws Flat. Walker was a member of a party led by Dr. Thaddeus Hildreth and his brother George. Originally called Hildreth's Diggings, it soon took on the name American Camp, and later became Columbia in 1854. Columbia developed as one of the largest mining camps in California. Although invariably hindered by a lack of water,[4] miners would recover more gold from the gravel here than in any other equally-sized area in the Western Hemisphere, earning it the name "Gem of the Southern Mines."

The streets of Columbia would be laid out in 1851. By 1852, there were more than 150 permanent wooden structures, but a fire in 1854 nearly destroyed the entire town. The reconstructed buildings that make up Columbia State Historic Park today are post-1850.

In April 1850, northwest of Columbia, gold was discovered in the sands of a large spring at Gold Springs. Nearby, Thomas Hill, and a party of prospectors had discovered rich diggings at Yankee Hill in 1849. This camp would develop into a prosperous mining center with saloons and trading posts.

Tuolumne County is the home of several spectacular landscapes contained within the northern portion of Yosemite National Park. These include the Grand Canyon of The Tuolumne, Tuolumne Meadows, and the Hetch Hetchy Valley, which was flooded when the controversial O'Shaughnessy Dam was built in 1923 to provide water for San Francisco. In addition, the South Grove of the Calaveras Big Trees State Park containing the *Sequoia gigantea* crosses the Calaveras/Tuolumne County line and the Tuolumne Grove containing a small number of the same trees lies on the western boundary of Yosemite National Park. John Bidwell[5] had discovered the South Grove of trees in 1841 while scouting for game for the members of his Bidwell-Bartelson party.

It would be 1864 before wagons transporting supplies to the mines east of the Sierra—Aurora[6] and Bodie—traveled over Sonora Pass. The Bidwell-Bartleson party had used a pass ten miles south of Sonora Pass when it entered California in 1841. A wagon road over old Priest's Grade to the floor of the valley was completed in 1874 and the one over Tioga Pass was built in 1883. The Sierra Railroad was established in Jamestown in 1897, at which time this town became an important transportation center for moving equipment and supplies between the mining and logging towns of the area and rail centers in the San Joaquin Valley.

John Gage Marvin (1815-1857)

- Attorney and school teacher from New York City
- Arrived in San Francisco in February 1850
- Moved to Sonora in May 1850
- Served as justice of the peace, Associate Justice of the Court of Sessions, newspaper publisher, and the first State Superintendent of Schools
- Member of the Mariposa Battalion during Mariposa Indian uprisings
- Died in Honolulu while on a trip to restore his health

Sites to Visit in Stanislaus County

U.S. Army Corps of Engineers Information and Visitors' Center, Knights Ferry   209.881.3517 (walking tour map)

La Grange Museum, 30168 Yosemite Blvd., La Grange (Open Sundays only)

Modesto Convention and Visitors Bureau, 1114 J St., P. O. Box 844, Modesto, CA 95353 1.800.266.4282

Area Within Present-Day Stanislaus County

Stanislaus County would be organized in 1854 from the western portion of Tuolumne County. In 1850 a very small southern portion of present-day Stanislaus County was located within the boundaries of Mariposa County. The triangular northeastern portion of the present-day county, which includes Knights Ferry, was annexed from San Joaquin County in 1860.

The western border of Stanislaus County bisects the Coast Range, making travel over the Stanislaus/Santa Clara County line difficult. The Stanislaus River runs along the Stanislaus/San Joaquin County line, and numerous creeks and the San Joaquin and Tuolumne rivers traverse the county—the San Joaquin vertically and the Tuolumne horizontally. These bodies of water created additional transportation barriers to miners on their way to the Mother Lode. More than a dozen astute entrepreneurs benefited from this situation, however, by establishing toll ferry operations and landings for the riverboats that steamed up and down the rivers.

Settlements sprang up at these ferry crossings and boat landings, which typically included a trading post and a hotel.[7] Many of the first ferry boats were whale-boats that had been rowed from the San Francisco Bay. Most of the early ferries were too small to accommodate a wagon, so the wagon would have to be disassembled and taken across in pieces.

By the end of 1850 there were two well-defined and well-traveled roads leading out of Stockton in San Joaquin County that passed through present-day Stanislaus County, en route to the Southern Mines. One of these was the original Mariposa Road, which fairly closely followed the route of the present-day Mariposa Road in a southeasterly direction. The second road, French Camp or "winter route," paralleled Mariposa Road further to the south by way of French Camp in San Joaquin County and crossed the Stanislaus River southwest of present-day Ripon. Sirey and Clark's Ferry was established here in the fall of 1850. These two main arterials attracted professional freighters and stage drivers to the area.

The Stockton-Sonora Road, much of which is still in use today, was another route to the Southern Mines. Stopping places were established along this route, many assuming names of states such as Oregon Ranch, or designations based on their distance from Stockton such as Four Mile House.

In 1850 a small group of Frenchmen settled French Bar, a placer gold mining camp on the south side of the Tuolumne River. Several floods in the early 1850s would wash the town away, but the residents moved a mile east and established the town of La Grange. Two 1850-51 structures remain in La Grange today. One, a former trading post built by John Inman and William Sanders, houses the La Grange Museum.

To the west on the Tuolumne River, A. M. Jackson and Dr. Benjamin D. Horr were operating the Indian Ranche Ferry at what was known as Jackson's Ranche. George W. Claxton and Richard Doss were operating a similar establishment across the river and the two operations formed the partnership of Jackson, Claxton, Horr and Doss until differences of opinion about business practices caused a breakup.

Further to the west, Harvey B. Davis established Davis' Ferry and a roadside tavern in 1850. Davis and his wife had come overland from Texas. They also engaged in farming and corralled some of the wild cattle and horses pasturing in the area.

In 1850 Empire City was established on the Tuolumne River, southeast of present-day Modesto, by E. S. Townsend, Jr. and Edmund P. Hart. The two parted company during the year, however, and John G. Marvin of Sonora took control of the new settlement. He established a ferry, which he sold to W. B. Dameron in October. As a result of Marvin's official duties as quartermaster for the Mariposa Battalion, Empire City became an army depot during the Mariposa War of 1850-51.[8]

In the winter of 1849, Dr. David Adams had founded Adamsville as a Tuolumne River ferry crossing on one of the branches of the Mariposa Road. Dr. Adams built a home here and became the county's first practicing physician. A. B. Anderson and his wife established a hotel.

To the north, just east of where the Tuolumne River joins the San Joaquin River, Paxton McDowell, Major Richard P. Hammond, and Thomas Pyle had established Tuolumne City in 1849, in hopes of equaling or surpassing Stockton as a shipping point to the mines. High-priced lots were staked out and numerous structures were built. Ryer's Ferry, owned by Dr. William M. Ryer, a Stockton physician, was operating in 1850, but the dry winter of 1850-51 would cause cancellations of riverboat schedules and the ultimate demise of Tuolumne City.

This is one of two 1850-51 structures remaining in La Grange today.

A former trading post houses the La Grange Museum in La Grange.

By the fall of 1850, Sirey and Clark's Ferry was operating on the Stanislaus River just east of the San Joaquin River. This ferry was key to the French Camp trail to the Mother Lode. Sirey and Clark had been members of Stevenson's Regiment of New York Volunteers, arriving in California in 1847, too late to see active service in the Mexican-American War.

Stanislaus County Ranchos

The original grantees of the Stanislaus County ranchos used them primarily for grazing cattle rather than as places to live. The eastern boundaries of the three ranchos located in western Stanislaus County lay along the San Joaquin River.

Don Sebastián Núñez owned *Rancho Orestimba y las Garzas*. Since 1849, within the borders of this rancho, a trading post and ferry service had been operating where the San Joaquin River meets the Merced River. Emigrants from Mexico traveling to the mines by way of Pacheco Pass crossed the river at this point. Jesse Hill would be a later owner of the ferry, and the settlement became known as Hills Ferry.

In early 1850, Captain Andrew Jackson Grayson established the ferry settlement of Grayson on the San Joaquin River south of its junction with the Tuolumne River. This site lay within the boundaries of *Rancho El Pescadero*. Grayson and his wife and young son had arrived at Sutter's Fort from Missouri in 1846, and lived for a time in San Francisco and Stockton, where Grayson subsequently formed a general merchandise business with J. F. Stephens in 1849. Grayson and Stephens moved their business to Grayson in March 1850 and established a line of eight-mule teams between the two cities. John Westley Van Benscroten became a partner in the ferry service operation during the summer and operated several other businesses.

Two ranchos lay within the area that was part of San Joaquin County until it was annexed by Stanislaus County in 1860. Alphias Basilio Thompson of Santa Barbara owned Thompson's Rancho. George B. Islip was operating a ferry across the Stanislaus River on a portion of this rancho. His ferry was held in particularly high regard because one of the new express firms was using it to cross the river on the stage road to the Southern Mines.

Also within the boundaries of Thompson's Rancho, Nelson Taylor had established Taylor's Ferry in 1849 where Kerr Park in Oakdale is situated today. Taylor returned to his native New York in early 1850, passing his ferry interests over to Richard W. Heath and Oliver C. Emory. What came to be known as Heath and Emory's Ferry was the most important crossing on the Stanislaus River. In late 1850, Heath and Emory built a pontoon bridge, the first on the Stanislaus.

Dons Francisco Rico and José Antonio Castro owned *Rancheria del Río Estanislao*, which extended east into Tuolumne and Calaveras counties. Several squatters were operating businesses on this rancho. George Washington Keeler was operating a ferry crossing several miles west of Knights Ferry; J. P. Ford was selling pies and other baked goods out of a tent just east of Keeler's Ferry; and Dent, Vantine & Co. was operating several businesses in Knights Ferry.

In 1848, the William Knight for whom Knight's Landing in Yolo County was named, and his partner, Captain James Vantine, had established a trading post and ferry on the Stanislaus River. Knight, however, was gunned down in November 1849. Vantine operated the ferry, trading post, and a hotel on his own for awhile and then formed the Dent, Vantine and Company ferry business with brothers John and Lewis Dent.[9] The company opened a restaurant and boarding house during 1850. The river bars, banks, hills, and gulches in the area were all rich in gold, and a thriving mining town, Knights Ferry, was founded here and served as the county seat for a nine-year period of time after Stanislaus County was organized. Several structures built in the 1850s remain today in Knights Ferry.[10]

STANISLAUS COUNTY RANCHOS

NAME OF RANCHO	GRANTEE AND/OR 1850 OWNER	1850 AND/OR CURRENT SITES
Rancho Orestimba y las Garzas	Sebastián Núñez	Hills Ferry, Pacheco Pass, extended into Merced County
Rancho del Puerto (Port)	Mariana and Pedro Hernandez	Patterson
Rancho El Pescadero (The Fishmonger)	Valentín Higuera and Rafael Félix	Grayson, Westley, extended into San Joaquin County
Thompson's Rancho	Alphias Basilio Thompson	Oakdale, Riverbank
Rancheria del Río Estanislao	Francisco Rico and José Antonio Castro	Knights Ferry, extended into Tuolumne and Calaveras counties

1

See Savage sidebar on page 252.

2

An oak tree, thought to be the largest oak in California, with a 13-foot diameter at its base, stood on the only level part of Big Oak Flat and served as a landmark during the mining era. Miners eventually killed the tree, however, by digging around its roots for gold. A fire in 1863 that destroyed most of the town would leave only scant evidence of the greatness of this oak. Pieces of the giant oak are enclosed in a stone arch along Hwy 120.

3

Jamestown lies at the eastern base of Table Mountain, which is part of a huge mass of lava that filled one of the ancient streambeds. The ancient river channel lying beneath the lava flow of the mountain would later become a phenomenal source of gold. Miners tunneled into the subterranean level of the mountain where millions of dollars in gold are still believed to be awaiting harvest. However, the cost would be prohibitive and the chances of hitting the riverbed in the right place too slim to make it a profitable venture.

4

In fact, in July 1850, the creeks and streams in Columbia dried up completely, forcing the prospectors to move on to other diggings. In anticipation of winter rains, some returned towards the end of the year and were not disappointed. The organization of the Tuolumne County Water Company in 1851, completion of a ditch in 1852, and the construction of a 61-mile aqueduct in 1858 to bring water in from the Stanislaus River would alleviate water shortage problems in the future.

5

See Bidwell sidebar on page 211.

6

Aurora would become the first county seat of Mono County when it was organized in 1861. In 1863, however, it was determined that Aurora actually was within the boundaries of the State of Nevada.

7

Most of the riverside towns in present-day Stanislaus County would decline when traffic to the mines decreased in the mid-1850s. When grain harvesting began in the mid-1860s, many of these towns revived, but declined once again in 1870 when they were bypassed by the railroad that ran through newly established Modesto. The floods of 1851-52 extensively destroyed property along the rivers.

8

The Mariposa War was fought between the Mariposa Battalion and Native Americans who had been on the attack. A treaty was signed in 1851 to bring a quick end to the war.

9

Captain John Dent was a friend and former West Point classmate of Ulysses S. Grant, the 18th President of the U.S. Grant had married the Dent brothers' sister in 1848 and would visit here in 1852. Lewis Dent was a delegate of the Constitutional Convention.

10

The longest wooden covered bridge in the western U.S. was built here in 1863 and remains as a pedestrian bridge today.

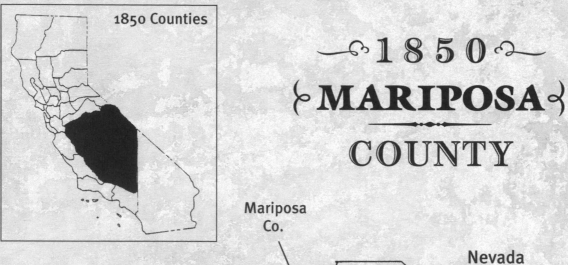

❧ 1850 ❧
⟨ MARIPOSA ⟩
COUNTY

1850 Counties

Mariposa Co.

Nevada

Bodie SHP •

Mono Co.

Merced Co.

• Coulterville

Hornitos• • Bear Valley

Stanislaus Co.

Merced • • Mariposa

• Bishop

Los Banos •

• Oakhurst

Madera Co.

Inyo Co.

Fresno •

San Benito Co.

• Visalia

Tulare Co.

Hanford •

Fresno Co.

Kings Co.

• Bakersfield

San Bernardino Co.

Kern Co.

Los Angeles Co.

California
1850

Present-day boundary variations indicated by

- - - - -

Settlements/cities of 1850 include: Coulterville, Hornitos, Bear Valley, Mariposa, Fresno Flats (Oakhurst)

MARIPOSA COUNTY
1850

With an area of about 30,000 square miles, the 1850-Mariposa County was the largest county in geographical terms, covering one-fifth of the state. Mariposa County included most of present-day Mono and Inyo counties, all of present-day Merced, Madera, Fresno, Kings, Tulare, and Kern counties; and very small portions of present-day San Benito, Los Angeles, and San Bernardino counties. Mariposa has been called the "Mother of Counties." Its 4,379 residents counted in the 1850 U.S. Census came from all over the world. The uncounted Native American inhabitants included members of the Yokuts, Miwok, Paiute, Monache, Tubatulabal, Shoshone, Kawaiisu, Kitanemuk, and Vanyume tribes.

AREA WITHIN PRESENT-DAY MARIPOSA COUNTY

The area within present-day Mariposa County consisted of a half-dozen mining towns and several river bar camps along the Merced River and the various creeks and streams in the county. Only one land grant had been awarded.

George Maxwell, Mexican miners, and others had been at work at Maxwells Creek for some time when George and Margaret Coulter and their infant son arrived in 1850. The Coulters began operating a trading post out of a large tent to serve the miners working the placers at Maxwell, Boneyard, and Black creeks. They displayed a small American flag above the tent, so the settlement came to be known as *Banderita* (Little Flag). A few single story adobe buildings were erected along Main Street. Small wooden frame cottages stood on the streets branching off Main Street. When a post office was opened in 1852, the name of the town would be changed to Maxwell Creek, but later the name was changed to Coulterville. Even after the placers ran out, the town prospered as an important supply center. Merchants delivered goods by pack train to the surrounding mines located in rugged, steep locations. One of the richest quartz veins was discovered here, as well.

Like so many other Mother Lode towns, Coulterville was almost totally destroyed by fire several times. However, a number of ruins and many historic structures remain today, including the 1850 Barrett Blacksmith Shop (a grocery store today), the 1851 Jeffrey Hotel, and the 1851 Sun Sun Wo Company store. The Northern Mariposa County History Center is located in two adjoining early period buildings.

Hornitos was settled near Burns Creek in 1850 by Mexican miners forced out of the neighboring settlement of Quartzburg by anti-Hispanic Americans. There are a number of explanations as to how this town received its name. One version attrib-

Sites to Visit in Mariposa County

California State Mining & Mineral Museum, County Fairgrounds on SR 49, Mariposa 209.742.7625

IOOF Building Museum, Hwy 49, Bear Valley (Inquire @Simpson & Trabucco Store for admission)

Mariposa County Courthouse (1854), 5088 Bullion St., Mariposa 209.966.2924

Mariposa Museum and History Center Inc., 5119 Jessie St., Mariposa 209.966.2924

Northern Mariposa County History Center, Hwy.s 49 & 132, Coulterville 209.878.3015

Coulterville Visitor Center, 5007 Main St., P. O. Box 333, Coulterville, CA 95311 209.878.3074

Mariposa Visitor Center, 5158 Hwy. 140, P.O. Box 425, Mariposa, CA 95338 1.800.208.2434 (Map for historic walking tour)

A grocery store is located in the former Barrett Blacksmith Shop in Coulterville.

utes the name Hornitos, which means "little ovens" in Spanish, to the Mexican graves or tombs built of stone in the shape of little bake ovens and set on top of the ground. Several remain on the hillside just below the Catholic church. Domenico "Domingo" Ghirardelli, the Italian experienced in the confectionery and chocolate trade who had established a base supply store in San Francisco, opened a little store here in 1849. The ruins of his post-1850 store that he operated through 1855, before moving to San Francisco and becoming the world-famous chocolate maker, may still be seen today.

Quartzburg had been founded by Thomas Thorn in 1849. There was lucrative placer mining here for a short time and Quartzburg almost was chosen to be the county seat, but all that remains today is an old cemetery on the hill.

Rancho Las Mariposas

Rancho Las Mariposas, the only land grant in the county, was a so-called "floating grant" for which the acreage was specified but the actual boundaries were left undetermined. Originally the rancho was located within present-day Merced County, but when gold was discovered to the north in 1848, the owner, John C. Frémont, "floated" his rancho up into the hills.

In 1849 Frémont had sent Alexis Godey, Kit Carson, and 28 experienced Sonora miners from Mexico to his property to scout out diggings. After Godey discovered gold on the property, a large number of miners soon settled along the small flat along Mariposa Creek. In the fall, Palmer, Cook & Co., a bank owned by a friend of Frémont's, sent 50 men from San Francisco to work a claim it had leased from Frémont. Mexican miners searching for the source of the rich placers of Mariposa Creek had recently found a huge outcropping. This vein developed into the Mariposa Mine. One of the state's first stamp mills, which had just been brought around the Horn per Frémont's purchase order, was set up on Mariposa Creek.

By the end of 1849, Mariposa's streets were laid out—many of them named for members of the Frémont family. The small mining town grew in size and importance as miners from the surrounding areas gravitated to the rich diggings. Saloons, general stores, restaurants, and hotels were quickly established to cater to the miners. In September 1851, Mariposa would become the county seat. Mariposa partially survived fires in 1858 and 1866. A number of 1850s and 60s structures remain today, including the 1854 Mariposa County Courthouse, which is the oldest courthouse west of the Rockies that is still in use.

Frémont had gold mining operations at several other locations, including Bear Valley, where he built a home in 1858, and Benton Mills. Benton Mills later was known as Bagby and the site now lies beneath Lake McClure, which was formed when the New Exchequer Dam was constructed in 1966.

The placers at Bear Valley, originally called Haydensville after David, Charles, and Willard Hayden, were discovered by Mexican miners in 1850. The Mexican miners were subsequently pushed off by Anglo prospectors. A short boom caused the camp to grow quickly, but the placers gave out within a year. It was not until the 1854 discovery of rich quartz mines that miners returned to the area again. A large portion of the town was destroyed by a fire in 1888, but a few Gold Rush-era buildings and ruins remain in the town today, including the IOOF Building Museum. (Frémont's 1851, two-story Oso (Bear) House hotel, which was built of lumber brought around the Horn, remained in operation until it burnt down in the 1930s.)

The settlement of La Meneta was established in 1850 on the mountain known today as Mount Bullion. The town would later be named Princeton and finally Mount Bullion after U.S. Senator Thomas H. Benton, whose nickname was "Old Bullion" for his campaign to maintain hard currency. Benton was the father-in-law of Frémont.

Mount Ophir was located northwest of Mount Bullion. Mexican miners had discovered gold in this area in 1848. A quartz vein would be discovered here in 1851.

Agua Fria, previously located on the road to Mount Bullion, was where gold was first discovered in Mariposa County. It also was the first county seat from 1850-51. Although an important mining community at one time, nothing remains of it today.

Mormons had settled Mormon Bar on Mariposa Creek in 1849. They moved on after a short time, but other miners quickly took their place. During 1850, James Savage closed his trading post on the South Fork of the Merced River and opened one at the mouth of Agua Fria Creek to the west of Mormon Bar.

Although it is believed that Joseph Reddeford Walker sighted the Yosemite Valley in 1833 while on an expedition through the Sierra Nevada, and that William Penn Abrams and U. N. Reamer, two Gold Rush pioneers, saw the valley in 1849 while in pursuit of a grizzly bear, it was not until March 1851 that the valley was officially discovered and the wonders of it made known to the world. Major James D. Savage, other members of the Mariposa Battalion, and Native American guides entered the valley to capture the Native American inhabitants for transfer to the Fresno Indian Reservation. Bands of Native Americans from Yosemite Valley had recently been attacking Anglos, whom they viewed as trespassers on their territory.

The first tourist group would enter the Yosemite Valley in 1855. Yosemite Valley became a state park in 1864, the area surrounding the valley became a national park in 1890, and Yosemite National Park was established in 1906, when the state ceded the Yosemite Valley and the Mariposa Grove of Big Trees to the federal government.

AREA WITHIN PRESENT-DAY MONO COUNTY

Present-day Mono County would be organized in 1861 from parts of Calaveras and Fresno counties. (Fresno County had been part of Mariposa County in 1850.) The Bidwell-Bartleson overland emigrant party had crossed through Mono County along what came to be known as the Sonora Trail into the San Joaquin Valley, but the first settlement, Monoville, was not established until the late 1850s.

Gold would not be discovered in Bodie until 1859. Today the Bodie State Historic Park preserves the history of this remote post-1850 mining town that was a booming town to as many as 10,000 settlers in 1878.

John Charles Frémont (1813-1890)

- Officer in U.S. Topographical Corp and other branches of the service
- Mapped out California and other parts of the west, fueling the "Manifest Destiny" movement
- Married to Jessie Benton, daughter of U.S. Sen. Thomas Hart Benton
- One of first two California U.S. Senators, but only served three weeks because it was determined that only one Senator was warranted and he drew the losing lottery number
- Spent most of 1850 in Washington, D.C., waiting for California to be admitted to the Union
- Returned to San Francisco in the fall of 1850
- First Republican candidate for President of the U.S. in 1856
- Commanded Army of the West during Civil War, before being removed for misconduct
- Lost his fortune through bad railroad investments
- Wife supported him with her writing, some of it in collaboration with him about his expeditions, until he became territorial Governor of Arizona in 1878
- Died in New York City

There are no 1850 Sites to Visit in Mono County

Bodie State Historic Park (1870s-80s), southeast of Bridgeport off Hwy 270 east of U.S. 395 760.647.6445

Mono Basin National Forest Area Visitor Center, U.S. 395 north of Lee Vining,

Mono County Tourism Commission, P.O. Box 603, Mammoth Lakes, CA 93546 1.800.845.7922

Mono Lake and the Mono Craters are two of the most unique natural features of this county. Mono Lake has no visible outlet, but the steady draining of water from the region by Los Angeles County has caused the surface of the lake to drop, causing great concern to environmentalists. The Mono Basin National Forest Area Visitor Center provides insight into the natural history of the area.

AREA WITHIN PRESENT-DAY INYO COUNTY

There are no 1850 Sites to Visit in Northern Inyo County

Bishop Chamber of Commerce, 690 N. Main St., Bishop, CA 93514 760.873.8405

Inyo County would be organized in 1866 from part of Mono and Tulare counties that had been part of Mariposa County in 1850. The southeastern half of present-day Inyo County, where Death Valley is located, was part of 1850-San Diego County and is covered in that chapter.

Trappers, explorers, and two emigrant parties led by Joseph Reddeford Walker in 1834 and 1843 traveled through Owens Valley in present-day Inyo County, but it would be 1861 before the first Anglo settlers established homes in the area. Gold was discovered in the Inyo Mountains in 1862. Bishop, Independence, and Lone Pine were established in the 1860s. Today the Owens Valley is devoid of its former lush meadows, because the City of Los Angeles acquired land and water rights in 1913, which allow it to pump water out of the valley.

Inyo County is home to several of California's unique natural features. In addition to Death Valley on the eastern border, which is the lowest spot in the Western Hemisphere, 14,494-foot Mount Whitney, the highest peak in the contiguous United States, is situated on the western border of the county. The mountain was named in 1864 in honor of Josiah Dwight Whitney, state geologist and leader of the Geological Survey. John Lucas, A. H. Johnson, and C. D. Begole were the first to climb Mount Whitney in 1873. One other unique topographical feature is the Ancient Bristlecone Pine Forest located within the Inyo National Forest. These trees are able to survive 10,000 feet above sea level.

AREA WITHIN PRESENT-DAY KERN COUNTY

There are no 1850 Sites to Visit in Kern County

Greater Bakersfield Chamber of Commerce, 1725 Eye St., P. O. Box 1947, Bakersfield, CA 93301 661.327.4421

Present-day Kern County, the third largest county today—acreage-wise—would be organized in 1866 from parts of Los Angeles and Tulare counties. (Tulare County had been established in 1852 from Mariposa County.)

Many early California missionaries, explorers, and pioneers had traveled through the passes of the Tehachapi Mountains, which run from east to west. Because wild grapes grew abundantly on the Tejón Pass over the summit, the pass was named *La Cañada de las Uvas* (Canyon of the Grapes) by the Spaniards; it is commonly referred to as the "Grapevine" today. Jedediah Strong Smith had traveled through the region east of present-day Bakersfield in 1827. Joseph Reddeford Walker had discovered the Kern River Valley in 1834 when looking for a southern pass out of the San Joaquin Valley. Edward Kern, a topographer, joined Walker and Captain John C. Frémont on a later expedition, and mapped the upper waters of the Kern River.

Until 1848, most travelers journeying north from Los Angeles to the San Francisco area traveled by way of El Camino Real, stopping at the various coastal missions for food and lodging along the way. There was another inland route, however, which ran along the base of the foothills on the west side of the San Joaquin Valley; it was called El Camino Viejo (The Old Road). For the most part, the road followed former American Indian trails that generally tracked animal trails from water hole to water hole. Travel was usually by foot or horseback, although in later years carts and wagons began using this route. In 1850 the Hudgins party, bound from Los Angeles to Stockton, moved large boulders off the Tejon Trail so they could get their wagons over it.

It would be 1855, when gold was discovered in several areas on the Kern River, before any permanent settlements were established in the county. More gold and silver discoveries were made in 1894, quartz in 1860, and oil in 1864, which created the county's primary industry. The railroad reached Kern County in the 1870s.

Kern County Ranchos

Five land grants were made in Kern County. The southern San Joaquin Valley, especially in the present-day Buena Vista Aquatic Recreation Area, was a prime grazing area for the *rancheros'* wild range cattle. The largest and most significant rancho was *Rancho El Tejón*, which was owned by *Dons* José Antonio Aguirre, a wealthy Spanish Basque trader, and Ignacio del Valle, a Los Angeles County *ranchero* and prominent resident of the city of Los Angeles. The property was home to several American Indian villages and a portion of it would become a government Indian reservation in the early 1850s. Fort Tejón was established in 1854 as the headquarters of the U.S. Army to protect the Native Americans from extermination and to discourage cattle and horse rustling.

Before the arrival of the first Anglo settlers in the area, Mexicans had settled along the Kern River in an area that they called Rio Bravo. They raised vegetables and cattle and were fairly self-sufficient.

General Edward F. Beale would acquire *Rancho El Tejón* in the early 1850s; in the 1860s he consolidated the *La Liebre*, *Los Alamos y Agua Caliente*, and *Castac* ranchos into his *Rancho El Tejón*, which today is part of the Tejon Ranch Co.'s 270,000-acre ranch, one of the nation's largest.

Edward F. Beale (1822-1893)

(Note: Although Beale was not living in California in 1850, he had been previously and returned in 1851.)

- Arrived in California in 1846 and was a hero in the Mexican-American War

- First to reach Washington, D.C. with news and the proof of discovery of gold at Sutter's Mill

- Appointed Superintendent of Indian Affairs for California and Nevada in 1852, Surveyor General of California and Nevada in 1861, and Minister to Austria-Hungary in 1876

- Established the first Indian reservation in California at Tejon and developed Fort Tejon to provide protection for Indians and safer travel through Tejon Pass

- Made several key surveys for transportation projects and conducted an experiment using 25 camels imported from Tunis

- Established Tejon Ranch and made many contributions to the aesthetic and cultural development of Bakersfield, which was founded in 1866

- In later years, he split his time between California and Washington, D.C. where he owned the now-famous Decatur House adjacent to the White House

KERN COUNTY RANCHOS

NAME OF RANCHO	GRANTEE AND/OR 1850 OWNER	1850 AND/OR CURRENT SITES
Rancho La Liebre (Hare)	José Maria Flores	Tehachapi Mountains, Tejón Ranch Co. property; extended into Los Angeles County north of Sandburg
Rancho Los Alamos y Agua Caliente (Poplars and Hot Water)	Francisco López, Luís Jordan, and Vicente Botello	East of Grapevine and Lebec
Rancho Castac (Our Eyes)	José Maria Covarrubias	Castac Lake, Lebec and Grapevine
Rancho El Tejón	José Antonio Aguirre and Ignacio del Valle	Bakersfield, Tejón Ranch Co. property
Rancho San Emigdio	Francisco Domínguez	Southeast of Maricopa

There are no 1850 Sites to Visit in Tulare County

Visalia Convention & Visitors Bureau, 301 E. Acequia St., Visalia, CA 93291   559.738.3435

AREA WITHIN PRESENT-DAY TULARE COUNTY

Tulare County would be created in 1852 from a large southern portion of 1850-Mariposa County, but between 1856 and 1893 it gradually lost acreage to Fresno, Inyo, Kern, and Kings counties.

In 1850 Tulare Lake covered much of the western portion of present-day Tulare County, as well as portions of Kern, Kings, Fresno, and Madera counties. In 1850 the Kings, Kaweah, Tule, and Kern rivers drained into the Tulare Basin, which flooded in the spring from winter rains and the Sierra Nevada snow melt. Huge herds of elk, deer, and antelope roamed the area of tules (bullrushes) surrounding the lake. The lake varied in size from year-to-year. (When it was measured in 1865, it was 35 miles wide and 60 miles long.) After 1852, reclamation districts would be formed and in the early 1870s, water was diverted into irrigation canals. Finally, in 1954 the Pine Flat Dam and Reservoir was constructed in the foothill region above Piedra in Fresno County and today, only in years of very heavy rain and snow melt, does Tulare Lake ever even partially reappear.

Particularly in Tulare County, the shores of Tulare Lake long had been a favorite habitation spot for Native Americans and would continue to be until the 1860s. A number of the characteristic shell mounds, one about 150 yards long and six feet high, were found along the shore of Tulare Lake.

Missionaries in search of new mission sites in the early 1800s, trappers and explorers like Jedediah Strong Smith and Joseph Reddeford Walker in the 1820s and 30s, and John C. Frémont in 1844 had passed through Tulare County, but only a few permanent Anglo settlements existed in 1850. John Wood built a log cabin on the southern bank of the Kaweah River east of present-day Visalia in 1849 or 1850. Loomis St. Johns established a settlement about a half mile away. Fort Visalia would be established in 1852 on the site of present-day Visalia—the oldest town between Stockton and Los Angeles.

In 1856 gold was discovered in Coarse Gold Gulch where the town of White River lies today in the southeastern corner of Tulare County. In 1858 Hale Tharp was the first Anglo to view the giant sequoias of Giant Forest, located within Sequoia National Park. The Southern Pacific Railroad arrived in the county in 1872.

There are no 1850 Sites to Visit in Kings County

Hanford Chamber of Commerce, 200 Santa Fe Av., Hanford, CA 93230   559.582.0483

AREA WITHIN PRESENT-DAY KINGS COUNTY

Most of the land that would become Kings County in 1893 was covered by Tulare Lake in 1850. (See the section on Tulare County for a description of Tulare Lake.) Kings County was formed from a portion of Tulare County, which had been part of Mariposa County until it organized in 1852.

Pedro Fages had passed through the Kings County portion of the San Joaquin Valley in 1772, naming the Kings River, *El Río de los Santos Reyes* (River of the Holy Kings), and Tulare Lake, *Los Tulares* (The Place of Rushes). One land grant had been made in Kings County, *Rancho Laguna de Tache*, a portion of which extended into present-day Fresno County. It was owned by Manuel de Jesús Castro.

It would be the mid-1850s before any settlement of the county began and this was primarily in the form of stage stations and ferry crossings. El Camino Viejo, the inland route that ran along the base of the foothills on the west side of the San Joaquin Valley, passed through Kings County. The county seat of Hanford and Lemoore were established when the branch railroad came through in 1877.

AREA WITHIN PRESENT-DAY FRESNO COUNTY

There are no 1850 Sites to Visit in Fresno County

Fresno City & County Convention & Visitors Bureau, 808 "M" St., Fresno, CA 93721   1.800.788.0836

Fresno County would be created in 1856 from parts of Merced, Tulare, and Mariposa counties. Subsequently, the county's boundaries were changed several times, losing territory to Inyo, Mono, Madera, and San Benito counties.

In 1850 there were no Anglo settlements in Fresno County, but a number of Spanish-Mexican agricultural communities were settled along El Camino Viejo, including *Posa* (Pool) *de Chiné*, *La Libertad* (Freedom), and *Pueblo de las Juntas* (Junction or Meeting Place). They lived in tule-thatched houses of brush and mud-brick. A portion of *Rancho Laguna de Tache*, which is covered in the Kings County section, extended into Fresno County.

Camp Barbour (later Fort Miller) was established in 1850 to provide protection to miners traveling through the area from the hostile Native Americans. The Mariposa Indian War Treaty would be signed here in 1851. American and European settlers began arriving shortly thereafter. The first lumber mill was built in the mountains in 1852. The county seat of Fresno was created with development of the railroad through the valley in 1872 and establishment of the other valley towns followed in the later 1870s and early 1880s.

Means of delivering water to the barren desert valley for development of the agriculture industry would begin with the construction of canals in the 1870s and continue through 1955 with the completion of the Central Valley Project, a federal project to build dams for water storage, flood control, and hydroelectric power. Fresno County's oil industry got under way soon after oil was discovered northeast of present-day Coalinga in the 1890s.

Fresno County's mountains include the Kings Canyon National Park, which had been discovered by Gabriel Moraga in 1806 and American trappers in the 1820s. The *Sequoia gigantea* may be found in seven groves throughout the canyon.

The notorious bandits of the 1850s would have their principal hideouts in the hills north of present-day Coalinga. Joaquin Murieta was killed here by a posse of State Rangers in 1853.

AREA WITHIN PRESENT-DAY MADERA COUNTY

Sites to Visit in Madera County

Fresno Flats Historical Park, School Road, (Rd. 427 off Hwy. 41) Oakhurst   559.683.6570

Southern Yosemite Visitors Bureau, 49074 Civic Cir., P. O. Box 1404, Oakhurst, CA 93644 559.683.4636

Madera County would be organized in 1893 from a portion of Fresno County that had been a part of Mariposa County in 1850. Trappers, such as Jedediah Strong Smith and Kit Carson, had traveled along the eastern side of the valley in the 1820s, and John C. Frémont had camped along the San Joaquin River in 1844, but further exploration or settlement of the central and western portion of the county was postponed for many years due to the impenetrable tulares and the many unfordable sloughs in the San Joaquin Valley. The miners who made their way to the gold mines located in the northeastern part of present-day Madera County did so by way of Mariposa County or the Pacheco Pass in Merced County.

As early as 1849, settlements had been established along the San Joaquin and Fresno rivers in Madera County. Five Texans found diggings on what came to be called Coarsegold Creek, because the particles of gold found here were so coarse. The camp was called Texas Flat, but the fast-growing settlement later came to be known as Coarsegold.

Miners fanned out in all directions from Coarsegold and soon other placer-mining camps were established. These included Grub Gulch, Fine Gold, and Fresno Flats. Coarsegold and Fresno Flats (now Oakhurst) remain today, but the other camps disappeared when the gold played out.

A number of quartz mines operated in the county in the 1870s and 80s. When the Central Pacific Railroad arrived in 1870, a demand for lumber from the sugar pine forests of the Sierra Nevada developed and the lumber industry boomed.

Madera County has several remarkable natural phenomena. The Nelder Grove of giant sequoias is located south of the Mariposa Grove, located in Mariposa County. However, the most unusual site is Devils Postpile National Monument, which is a volcanic formation of columnar-jointed basalt that resembles a stack of posts.

AREA WITHIN PRESENT-DAY MERCED COUNTY

There are no 1850 Sites to Visit in Merced County

Merced Conference and Visitors Bureau, 690 W. 16th St., Merced, CA 95340   1.800.446.5353

Merced County would be organized in 1855 from a part of Mariposa County. Gabriel Moraga's 1806 expedition had passed through the county and named the Merced River, *El Río de Nuestra Señora de la Merced* (River of Our Lady of Mercy). Later explorers and trappers passed through the county as well, including Jedediah Strong Smith and John C. Frémont.

The area within present-day Merced County consisted of several small settlements and three ranchos. In 1849 John M. Montgomery and his partner, Colonel Samuel Scott, both Kentuckians, had begun camping along the Merced River west of present-day Snelling. Montgomery would build a permanent home along Bear Creek by 1852. He later became known as the "Land and Cattle King of Merced."

Other settlers were arriving during 1850, establishing homes along county rivers and streams. The fertile soil along the streams was excellent for grazing livestock and growing crops. Many of the homes opened their doors to travelers passing through on their way to the Mother Lode.

The county would not begin to blossom into the rich agricultural region that it is today until Henry Miller and the Miller and Lux cattle empire became established in the 1860s. The Central Pacific Railroad arrived in the county in 1872.

Merced County Ranchos

Three land grants were made in Merced County. The most interesting one, *Rancho San Luís Gonzaga*, which extended into Santa Clara County, was owned by *Don* Juan Pérez Pacheco. A path blazed through this rancho by the Yokut Indians in their trade with coastal tribes was the main trail between the San Joaquin Valley and the Santa Clara Valley for gold miners and cattle drovers; it is known today as the Pacheco Pass.

Pacheco was one of the first *rancheros* to recognize the gold miners' hunger for meat. He changed the focus of the cattle industry from hides and tallow to supplying beef for human consumption.

The Pacheco family (Juan Pérez was the son of Francisco, one of the largest landowners in California) had built two adobes, a one- and a two-story one. The 1868 earthquake would destroy the two-story adobe, but the early 1840s one-story adobe survived, serving various purposes through the years, including a stopover for travelers on their way from the coast to the valley. However, in 1962 *Rancho San Luís Gonzaga* was selected as the site for the San Luis Dam and Reservoir. A direct descendant of the Pacheco family, who had remodeled the adobe in 1948, decided to move the adobe to the western part of the rancho across Pacheco Pass into Santa Clara County. Unfortunately, the building collapsed on the highway in transit and only two walls could be saved.

Before John C. Frémont "floated" his *Rancho Las Mariposas* in 1848 in order to include gold rich diggings to the north, *Rancho Las Mariposas* was located in Merced County. This maneuver is described in the Mariposa County section.

1850s Letter Sheet—"Long Tom"

COURTESY OF THE SACRAMENTO ARCHIVES AND MUSEUM COLLECTION CENTER; THE ELEANOR McCLATCHY COLLECTION

MERCED COUNTY RANCHOS

NAME OF RANCHO	GRANTEE AND/OR 1850 OWNER	1850 AND/OR CURRENT SITES
Rancho San Luis Gonzaga	Francisco Pérez Pacheco	San Luis Reservoir, Pacheco State Park, extended into Santa Clara County
Rancho Panocha de San Juan y Los Carrisalitos	Julian Ursua	Southwest of Los Banos
Rancho Sanjon (Deep Slough) de Santa Rita	Francisco Soberanes	Southwest of Merced, Santa Rita Park

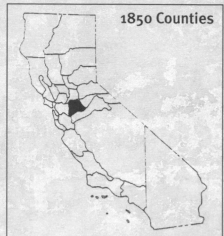

1850
✦ SAN JOAQUIN ✦
COUNTY

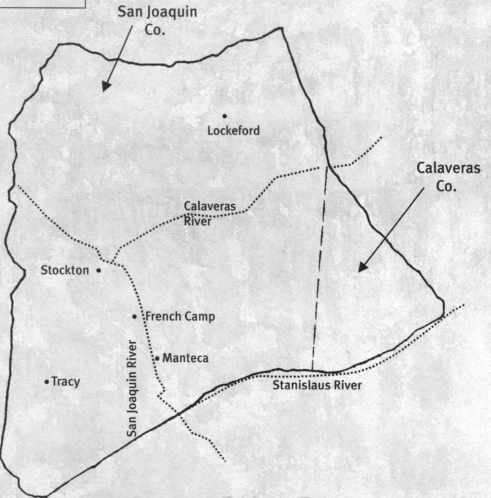

San Joaquin
Co.

Lockeford

Calaveras
Co.

Calaveras
River

Stockton

Tracy

French Camp

Manteca

San Joaquin River

Stanislaus River

California
1850

Present-day boundary
variations indicated by
— — — — —

Settlements/cities of 1850 include: Stockton, French Camp

SAN JOAQUIN COUNTY
1850

The geographical area of 1850-San Joaquin County included the southwestern corner of present-day Calaveras County. Its 3,647 residents counted in the 1850 U.S. Census came from all over the world. The uncounted Native American inhabitants included members of the Miwok and Northern Valley Yokuts tribes.

In 1850 San Joaquin County consisted of its county seat of Stockton, San Joaquin City, French Camp, Chalmer's Ranch, and several ranchos. The San Joaquin Delta—a labyrinth of waterways formed by the Sacramento, Mokelumne, and San Joaquin rivers that eventually empty into the San Francisco Bay—courses much of the county and has contributed significantly to its history.

San Joaquin City, an agricultural settlement that had been established in 1849, was located on the west side of the San Joaquin River near the San Joaquin/Stanislaus County border. Several one-story houses and a number of tents made up the town that, in the 1850s, served as a terminal for boats traveling on the San Joaquin River departing from Stockton. The first steamer to navigate the river in 1850 was the *Georgiana*, which continued on down to Grayson and Tuolumne City in Stanislaus County. Titus and Manly were operating a ferry service here in 1850, as well.[1]

San Joaquin County Ranchos

Two land grants were made in San Joaquin County; portions of three other ranchos crossed the county lines on the north, east, and south. *Rancho El Campo de los Franceses* included both French Camp and Stockton and was owned by Charles M. Weber. He and his San José business partner, William Gulnac, had organized a company in 1843 to form a colony at French Camp.[2] The company established a settlement here in 1845, building corrals and shelters on the peninsula in the Stockton Channel, known today as Weber Point. Emigrants were offered free land as an inducement to settle, but the Mexican-American War, hostile American Indians in the area, plague, and limited food supplies discouraged settlers from wanting to locate here. Disappointed, Gulnac sold his property to Weber for $60. Weber ended up giving away the major portion of the rancho. In 1847 he laid out the town variously known as Tuleburg, Weberville, and Weber's Embarcadero before it was officially named in honor of Commodore Robert Stockton in 1849.[3]

Once gold was discovered in 1848, Weber opened a supply business, and built the first frame building in Stockton—a kitchen and store. A variety of businesses soon sprang up as several businessmen took advantage of the miners' needs in quickly assembled tule tents along the south side of the Channel.

Sites to Visit in San Joaquin County

Haggin Museum, 1201 North Pershing Avenue, Stockton 209.462.4116

San Joaquin County Historical Museum, 11793 N. Micke Grove Rd., Lodi 209.331.2055

Stockton Greater Chamber of Commerce, 445 W. Weber Av., Stockton, CA 95203 209.547.2770

Charles M. Weber (1814-1881)

- Emigrated to America in 1836 from Germany
- Arrived in California with Bidwell-Bartleson party in 1841
- Established business ventures in San José
- Established city of Stockton
- Organized the Stockton Mining and Trading Company, which operated on Weber Creek in El Dorado County, but soon dissolved it to concentrate on building his city
- Sold real estate to settlers, set aside property for city and county government use, and donated land for church buildings
- Funded planting of hundreds of trees, street improvements, and drainage ditches in Stockton

In 1850-51 Weber built a large two-story redwood and adobe house on Weber Point, surrounded by extensive gardens. He and his wife, Helen Murphy from the Murphy family of Santa Clara County, raised their three children here.

With the opening of the Southern Mines, Stockton grew rapidly in importance and size. At the end of 1849 it had a population of approximately 1,000, largely transient residents. The miners came via the Livermore Pass from San José or up the San Joaquin River by boat. The latter travelers crossed the river at Doak and Bonsell's Ferry. As business increased, many steamers were transferred from Sacramento. Gallant Duncan Dickenson, who had built California's first brick house in Monterey in 1847, was operating a hotel to accommodate the miners. (He also served as *alcalde*.) Stockton's First Presbyterian Church had been established in 1849.

By the end of 1850, there were two well-defined and well-traveled roads leading out of Stockton bound for the Southern Mines through present-day Stanislaus County. One of these was the original Mariposa Road that fairly closely followed the route of the present-day Mariposa Road. This road was established as a military road in 1850, as well, when Dr. L. R. Chalmers persuaded the government teams en route to Fort Miller in Fresno County to pass by his ranch. A settlement would develop at Chalmer's Ranch where present-day Collegeville is located.

The French Camp Road, with its sandy loam base, was the only choice of roads during the winter months because the Mariposa Road's adobe base made it impassable. This road headed south from Stockton by way of French Camp and present-day Manteca, crossing the Stanislaus River southwest of present-day Ripon. French Camp became an important staging and freighting center. Boats landed at the end of French Camp Slough to unload their goods bound for the Southern Mines. In the summer of 1850, Major Richard P. Hammond established the town of Castoria. The sale of lots in the new town was handled by Colonel P. W. Noble and A. Stevinson, who built a two-story adobe that served as a hotel and trading post.

Two other roads branched out from Stockton to the Southern Mines in an easterly direction. The Sonora Road left Stockton to the southeast, along the approximate route of present-day Highway 4. Along this road George Theyer and David Wells had built a tule house on the "Oregon Ranch" in 1848. When miners started using this route, Theyer and Wells opened the "Oregon Tent," where Farmington is located today. Less than a mile west of Oregon Tent, James Wasley built the Wisconsin House in 1850.

The Mokelumne Road departed from Stockton to the northeast, approximating State Route 26. Seventeen public houses within 24 miles of Stockton were operating along this road in 1850. One, the Fifteen Mile House, was located where present-day Linden is located.

SAN JOAQUIN COUNTY RANCHOS

NAME OF RANCHO	GRANTEE AND/OR 1850 OWNER	1850 AND/OR CURRENT SITES
Rancho El Pescadero (Fishing Place)	Antonio María Pico	Tracy
Rancho El Campo de los Franceses (French Camp)	Charles M. Weber	Stockton, French Camp

The Sutter's Fort-San José Trail also passed through San Joaquin County. It entered the county along present-day Patterson Pass Road and crossed the San Joaquin River at present-day Mossdale. John Doak and Jacob Bonsell had been operating the first San Joaquin River ferry since 1848. They began their service with a small yawl, but a burgeoning business prompted them to acquire a larger ferryboat. Doak traveled to Corte Madera in Marin County to build one. Upon his return with the new boat, the business flourished even more.

Continuing north, the Sutter's Fort-San José Trail crossed the Mokelumne River west of present-day Lockeford[4] via Staple's Ferry. In the fall of 1850, Staples, Nichols and Company built a toll bridge just west of the ferry. Several other ferries were operating in the vicinity, including C. L. Benedict's and John A. Benson's.

The Sutter's Fort-San José Trail proceeded northwest across Dry Creek and the San Joaquin/Sacramento County line. A Mr. Davis had been operating a crossing here since 1849. A log cabin stood here that had been built in 1846 by Turner Elder, one of the first settlers in the county.

Finally, the Corral Hollow Trail in southwestern San Joaquin County provided passage to the Southern Mines to prospectors arriving through Santa Clara County and present-day Alameda County. This had formerly been a Spanish trail and then a cattle drive trail used by Mexican *vaqueros*. Today it parallels Corral Hollow Road.[5]

Notes ⌒ SAN JOAQUIN COUNTY

1

The Titus-Manly ferry would later be owned by Durham and Fisk and be called the Durham Ferry, thus the name of the Durham Ferry State Recreation Area located here.

2

French-Canadian hunters employed by the Hudson's Bay Company had occupied a rustic camp where French Camp was formed from spring until fall each year between 1832 and 1845, but abandoned it in the spring of 1845.

3

Commodore Stockton, the U.S. Naval Commander in the Mexican-American War, had promised Weber assistance in securing supplies for his settlement after the Mexican-American War—a promise he never kept, however. Stockton became the first city in California to receive an American name.

4

Dr. Dean J. Locke came to California from New Hampshire as a Harvard-educated physician in 1849 and, with his brother, purchased land along the Mokelumne River in December 1850. Within the next few years, the city of Lockeford was established and became a shipping point on the Mokelumne River. Many of the town's original buildings can still be seen today.

5

A tavern called the "Zink House" would be built along the Corral Hollow Trail in the 1850s that was visited by James Capen Adams, popularly known as "Grizzly" Adams in a biographical narrative and television program. Coal would be discovered here in 1856, and manganese in 1863.

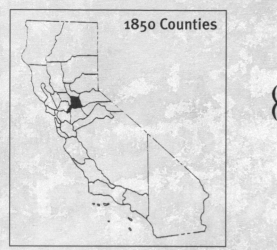

1850 Counties

❦ 1 8 5 0 ❧
❧ SACRAMENTO ❦
COUNTY

Placer Co.

Sutter Co.

Folsom Lake

Mormon Bar

American River

Negro Bar

Yolo Co.

Sacramento River

• Sacramento

Sutter's Fort

Sutterville

El Dorado Co.

Sloughhouse •

Cosumnes River

Galt

Mokelumne River

California
1850

Present-day boundary
variations indicated by

— — — —

Settlements/cities of 1850 include: Mormon Bar, Negro Bar (Folsom), Sacramento, Sutter's Fort,
Sutterville, Sloughhouse, Liberty (Galt)

SACRAMENTO COUNTY
1850

The geographical area of 1850-Sacramento County was identical to what it is today, with the exception of minor boundary variances created by the shifting streambeds of the Mokelumne and Sacramento rivers. In 1850 the county consisted of Sutter's Fort, Sutterville, Sacramento City, several mining camps on the American and Cosumnes rivers, and seven ranchos. Its 9,087 residents counted in the 1850 U.S. Census came from all over the world. The uncounted Native American inhabitants included members of the Patwin, Nisenan, and Miwok tribes.

Sutter's Fort

Native Americans had dwelled in the Sacramento area long before Captain John A. Sutter[1] arrived in 1839 with a few Americans and Hawaiian natives (Kanakas) to establish his frontier outpost. Sutter's dream had been to establish a colony called *Nueva Helvetia* (New Switzerland). Sutter soon became a citizen of Alta California and, in 1841, he acquired 44,000 acres of land from the Mexican government to establish his settlement. He purchased livestock and equipment from the Russians who were abandoning their post on the coast at Fort Ross, in present-day Sonoma County, and began the construction of his fort. After completion in 1844, Sutter's Fort became the commercial and political center of the valley, serving as a trading post and way station.

Sutter employed 100 to 500 men, the larger number at harvest time, which enabled the fort to be entirely self-sufficient. However, the discovery of gold at the construction site of his lumber mill in Coloma in January 1848 signaled doom for his kingdom. The Gold Rush caused his workers to desert him and soon thereafter, squatters began camping in his fields, seizing his property, stealing his livestock, and eliminating his authority. Broke and disillusioned, in 1849 Sutter sold the fort for $40,000 and retired to his Hock Farm in present-day Sutter County.

Sutter's Fort was the focal point of all travelers on the overland trails, whether they intended to cross the Sierra, use the central and southern routes, or enter by way of Oregon. Once they arrived at the fort–when Sutter was still living there–they were sheltered, fed, clothed, and given instructions about what to expect in their new surroundings. After Sutter departed, the personal touch disappeared. Samuel Kyburz was renting the central building of the fort to operate a hotel, and every shanty within or near the fort was a store, a warehouse, or a hotel. For example, Sam Brannan[2] was operating a provision store and warehouse just outside the walls of the fort. This

Sites to Visit in Sacramento County

California Military Museum, 1119 2nd St., Old Sacramento 916.442.2883

California State Capitol Museum, 10th St. between L and N, Sacramento 916.324-0333

California State Indian Museum, 2618 K St., Sacramento 916.324.0971

Discovery Museum History Center, 101 "I" St., Old Sacramento 916.264.7057

Folsom History Museum, 823 Sutter St., Folsom 916.985.2707

Golden State Museum, 1020 O St., Sacramento 916.653.7524

Historic City Cemetery, 1000 Broadway, Sacramento 916.448-0811

Huntington & Hopkins, Hardware, 105 "I" St., Old Sacramento 916.323.7234

Old Eagle Theatre, 925 Front St., Old Sacramento 916.445.6645

Old Sacramento Visitor Center 1101 2nd St., Sacramento 916.442.7644

Sutter's Fort State Historic Park, 2701 L St., Sacramento 916.445.4422

Wells Fargo History Museum, 1000 2nd St., Old Sacramento 916.440.4263

Wells Fargo Bank History Museum, 400 Capitol Mall, Sacramento

Sacramento Convention and Visitors Bureau, 1421 K St., Sacramento 95814 916.264.7777

business was called C. C. Smith & Co. to distinguish it from his Brannan & Co. store in San Francisco. By mid-1850, however, all of the storekeepers had departed for Sacramento City. (See below.)

The restored main building of the fort is the only original structure in the present complex of Sutter's Fort State Historic Park. The walls and other features of the fort were all reconstructed by the State of California in 1891-93.[3] The fort's appearance and the Living History Day activities provided throughout the year are representative of the year 1846.[4]

Sutterville

In 1839 Sutter had built a wharf–the embarcadero–on the Sacramento River[5] just south of its junction with the American River. He received supplies where Front and I streets intersect today to restock his fort located two and a half miles away. A sandbar that was difficult to navigate except in high water was located where the I Street Bridge is located today.

In 1844 Sutter laid out the town of Suttersville (later Sutterville) further south (across from the present-day Sacramento Zoo in William Land Park). The site was chosen because it was on higher ground than the embarcadero and thus was safe from the annual flooding of the Sacramento River. Sutterville once was popular as a

Sutter's Fort was the commercial and political center of the Sacramento Valley.

trade depot and a number of buildings were built there, including one of the first brick structures built in California–a hotel built by George Zins in 1847 out of bricks he manufactured himself.

However, after the discovery of gold in 1848, the embarcadero became a more desirable commercial center because of its proximity to the fort and the route to the mines. Sutterville would continue as a significant settlement and be incorporated into the city of Sacramento in 1950, but today it is preserved in name only–the Sutterville Bend in the Sacramento River and Sutterville Road.

Sacramento City

Sutter's grown son, John A. Sutter, Jr., had arrived from Switzerland in September 1848. Sutter, Sr., deeply in debt, turned over his affairs to his son, who proceeded to contract with Captain William A. Warner and Lieutenant William Tecumseh Sherman to survey the new city of Sacramento City.[6] Sutter, Jr. also contracted with Samuel Brannan and Peter H. Burnett[7] to sell lots to pay off his father's debts. The lots near the waterfront sold for $500 each; the lots further removed sold for $250.

By July 1849, more than 100 structures, mostly frame or canvas, stood in the twelve-block area along the embarcadero.[8] Enterprising merchants hastily constructed shops, hotels, theaters, and saloons to take advantage of the crowds of miners passing through. Today this section of town is called "Old Sacramento" and is preserved as a state historic park. The 40 historic buildings–*circa* 1852-75–located here were restored or rebuilt in the 1960s and 70s.[9]

Among the reconstructed buildings is the Eagle Theatre, which, for three short months between October 1849 and January 1850, featured Mrs. Henry Ray, a celebrated female tragedian from New Zealand. The Eagle Theatre was the first building specifically constructed as a theater in California and accommodated 400. The original wood frame and canvas structure with a tin roof cost $30,000; unfortunately, it was destroyed in the January 1850 flood. In 1974, a replica of the original building was reconstructed on this site where performances occasionally take place.

In March 1850, a structure similar to the Eagle Theatre was built on a different site and opened as The Tehama. Tragedian James Stark performed some of Shakespeare's works. Several other venues attracted large numbers of spectators, including an opera house, a ballet in which Italian dancer Signora Fanny Manten performed, and a circus. The European pianist Henri Herz performed at Sacramento's first concert in April 1850. Despite the rough-and-tumble image characteristic of the "Argonauts," there was a thirst for cultural performances, especially those featuring a woman, since women were so rare in California at the time.

The reconstructed Eagle Theatre stands in Old Sacramento today. When it was built in 1849, it was the first building specifically constructed as a theater in California.

Hubbard and Brown ran the Round Tent Saloon next door to the site of the Eagle Theatre. Other saloon/gaming emporiums were scattered throughout the city, including The Stinking Tent, the Gem, the Humboldt, the Mansion, the Empire, and the El Dorado. Gamblers typically engaged in $100-ante games.

John Forshee, L. A. Booth, and Job Dye, importers and wholesale grocers, established Forshee, Booth & Co. on Front Street in the spring of 1850. Other provision merchants included Hensley & Reading, Orland McKnight, Powers & Perkins, Henley & Birdsall, Earl McIntosh & Co., Moran & Clark, Samuel Gregg, S. C. Bruce, Montgomery & Co., Barton Lee, Burnett Ferguson & Co., H. E. Robinson, Priest, Lee & Co., and Huntington & Hopkins, Hardware.

Sam Brannan owned several stores and hotels, including the three-story City Hotel on Front Street. This hotel had been the site of the first grand ball to be held in Sacramento on July 4, 1849. It was largely constructed of lumber from Sutter's unfinished flour mill at Natoma. Margaret Frink and her husband opened a hotel on K Street—a two-story house that had been shipped around the Horn in pieces. They offered free, fresh milk, which was of great interest to men who had not tasted milk for one or two years. Other hotels included the Elephant House, the Sutter Hotel, the Crescent City, and the Missouri. There were not always enough rooms for rent in Sacramento in 1850, however, so some men slept out in the open.

Pharmacies, law firms, and other enterprises were catering to the miners passing through. Darius Ogden Mills had started the first banking house on the Pacific Coast in 1849 in a small one-story frame building with a stone front. His later 1852 two-story D.O. Mills Bank Building built after a fire in 1852 remains today. In 1850 a respected banking house, Barton Lee, failed. Two other institutions suffered the same misfortune, which created doubt in the minds of many investors, but this was short-lived and confidence in the banks was ultimately restored.

Darius Ogden (D. O.) Mills (1825-1910)

- Arrived in California in 1848 following a successful banking career in New York State
- Opened the first banking house on the Pacific Coast in 1849
- Became the first president of the Bank of California in San Francisco in 1864
- Contributed financially to educational and philanthropic movements
- Served as a Regent of the University of California
- Returned to New York in 1878 where he became prominent in banking and establishing housing facilities for the poor
- Donated the marble Columbus and Isabella statue standing in the rotunda of the California State Capitol today

John Rivett and William P. Fuller started a carpet and upholstery business in 1850. Fuller would later establish the W.P. Fuller Paint Company, while Rivett started Rivett's Carpet Cleaning Works. Peter Kadell, from Germany, established the Sacramento Brewery in 1850 to quench the miners' voracious thirst for beer.

The California Steam Engine Works of Stow & Carpenter was located on Front Street near the mouth of the American River. The molds and machinery needed to operate their business for the mines arrived from Chicago in April 1850. The Eureka Flour Mill was operating just to the east.

Unlike the other major cities of California in 1850, namely San Francisco and Los Angeles, Sacramento had a vast canopy of trees that remain a trademark today. The original oaks and sycamores would be destroyed by fire or stripped by later settlers, but subsequent tree planting made Sacramento a place that once again causes visitors to take note.[10] Another current Sacramento characteristic–"friendly and hospitable"– had its origins in 1850. Many travelers passing through on their way to the mines made note of this in their writings.

Sacramento, with its location at the confluence of two major rivers and its central location in the Sacramento Valley, was the natural supply and transportation center to the Northern Mines. By the end of 1850, there were 28 steamers and over 60 other types of vessels on the Sacramento River, including a steam ferry providing transportation between Sacramento and Yolo counties. The average fare for travel between San Francisco and Sacramento, including a cabin, was $10. Meals and liquor were an additional charge, and freight charges were $8 a ton.[11] The steamers also traveled to Yuba City and Marysville. Unfortunately, shipwrecks, explosions, and mishaps were a common occurrence, often due to reckless operators attempting to outmaneuver competitors and set new records for travel time.

Eventually many of these vessels, deserted by crews seeking their fortune in the mines, became stores, warehouses, or hotels, thus lessening problems caused by the shortage of buildings on land.[12] However, the boats were often lined up two or three-deep on either side of the Sacramento River, thus blocking the dock facilities.

The lack of storage facilities for goods resulted in merchandise being scattered along the banks of the Sacramento River. Some merchants set up makeshift displays for their wares or stored their goods in tents or under old sails. Ships arriving weekly brought a wide assortment of items, often second-hand, which the East Coast no longer desired. Waterfront auctions often took place in which merchants fought for the chance to buy provisions–sometimes sight unseen–still packed in boxes.

The daily stages that left Sacramento to carry passengers to Marysville, Coloma, Nevada City, Placerville, Auburn, Stockton, Drytown, and Jackson also helped earn Sacramento its status as a major transportation terminal. Later in 1855, the first train west of the Rockies would begin running, linking mining camps in the area of present-day Folsom with riverboats in Sacramento. The construction of the transcontinental railroad over the Sierra Nevada was begun in 1863, ultimately connecting Sacramento with the mid-West. Today the California State Railroad Museum located in Old Sacramento commemorates the birthplace of railroading in California.[13]

A post office was located in Robinson's store on J Street between Front and Second streets. The first courthouse would be built in 1851. A city government had been established in 1849 when a second city charter was adopted. (Voters had rejected the first charter because it imposed controls on gambling.) However, the first city hall would not be built until 1854. Today the reconstructed City Hall and Waterworks Building[14] houses the Sacramento History Museum.

The Common Council set flat monthly tax fees on different types of establishments ranging from $5 for those that provided public entertainment to $50 for wholesale or retail trade establishments. Because the canvas and clapboard structures of Sacramento were particularly vulnerable to fire, the Mutual Hook and Ladder Company No. 1 was established in February 1850. The first volunteer fire-fighting unit was put to the test during the destructive fires in April and November.

Sacramento County was renting the bark *Strafford* in 1850 and later in the year, the *Stirling* and *La Grange*, to use as jail facilities. A mob of 2,500 citizens took the law into their own hands during 1850 when it overtook the sheriff deputies guarding the jail and lynched a gambler who had murdered a local merchant.

Many settlers had arrived in Sacramento during 1849, expecting to acquire homesteads as they did in Oregon and the mid-West. They had no appreciation for the fact that Sutter had previously been granted this property by the Mexican government and began claiming the right to at least one free city lot each. Those who had been purchasing lots from Sutter, Jr., however, contested these claims, which resulted in the Squatters' Riot of 1850. A gunfight erupted at Fourth and J streets on August 14th in which four or five squatters, the city assessor, and the sheriff were killed. Unrest continued for several days. Mayor Hardin Bigelow also was seriously wounded and later died from his wounds complicated by his contraction of cholera.

A natural disaster would take other lives in Sacramento in 1850. Heavy rains in November and December 1849 saturated the city's soil and more heavy rain in early January 1850 caused both the Sacramento and the American rivers to surge over their banks, submerging what is now downtown Sacramento in a four-foot deep lake that reached a mile east of the normal bank of the Sacramento River. Large quantities of merchandise floated out of the stores never to be seen again, the adobe buildings dissolved, and all traffic had to move in whaleboats or any other type of vessel that could be crafted from available lumber. Most people, dogs, and cattle were successful in reaching higher ground near Sutter's Fort and a few other sites, but others lost their lives. Another flood struck in March 1850 causing similar results.

After the second flood, the town's businessmen realized that they needed to either move back from the river's edge or build a levee to protect their waterfront location. The residents voted (543 to 15) to approve a $250,000 bond to build a three- to five-foot high earthen dike along the Sacramento River that stretched from Sutterville to the mouth of the American River.[15]

Another calamity struck Sacramento in 1850 that ultimately killed hundreds of people–perhaps as many as 800, including 17 doctors. A cholera epidemic occurred in the weeks between October 20th and mid-November 1850. The germ had been brought by a traveler passing through and the epidemic was exacerbated by the lack of proper sewage facilities. Bon fires burned day and night fueled by discarded clothes, bedding, and furniture believed to be contaminated with the deadly germ. Such fraternal organizations as the I.O.O.F. and the Masons provided aid and nursing to the afflicted during the cholera plague. Many of the residents fled the city in fear and did not return until they were sure that the threat of contracting the disease had subsided.

Joseph Augustine Benton (1815-1892)

- Graduate of Yale who arrived in Sacramento in 1849

- Founded the First Congregational Church and became a leading California preacher, hymnologist, and missionary

- Taught in one of Sacramento's first schools and at the Pacific Theological Seminary in Oakland (today the Pacific School of Religion in Berkeley)

- Co-founded the College of California in Oakland in 1850 (forerunner of the University of California, Berkeley)

Fortunately, Sacramento had 50 or so doctors practicing in 1850, as well as several private hospitals. The Masons and Odd Fellows Hospital was set up in one corner of Sutter's Fort. During 1850 the first medical organization in California, the Medico-Chirurgical Association, was formed by Dr. J. B. D. Stillman and 31 other pioneer physicians for "the cultivation of science, honor, and dignity."

A temperance society was formed in Sacramento in 1850 and a number of churches had been established the year before. The Pioneer Memorial Congregational Church was Sacramento's first church. Its first building was built on Sixth Street in 1850, but would be destroyed by fire in 1854. Today the church is located across from Sutter's Fort.

The first Roman Catholic parish to be established in Sacramento was St. Rose of Lima Church. Mass was said at various locations during 1850 and in the early 1850s, the church would be built where St. Rose of Lima Park is located today at Seventh and K streets.

The Reverend Joseph A. Benton had founded the First Church of Christ (Congregational) in 1849. This dynamic preacher often left his parish for several weeks at a time to do missionary work in outlying areas, where he caught the attention of the Christian and non-Christian alike.

The Methodist Church of Colored People of Sacramento City, first known as Bethel and later St. Andrews, was organized in 1850. It was the first church on the Pacific Coast to be associated with an African American religious congregation. The First Baptist Church also was organized in 1850 by Reverend O. C. Wheeler.

Finally, the Methodist Episcopal Church was organized by the Reverend Isaac Owen and had been meeting in a prefabricated building on Seventh Street. The building was shipped around the Horn from Baltimore in 1849 and would later become the first congregationally-owned Jewish Synagogue on the Pacific Coast in 1852. The first religious gathering of Jewish immigrants in Sacramento had taken place in 1849 in the Front Street home of clothing merchant Moses Hyman and a chapter of the Hebrew Benevolent Association was organized in 1850. The Jewish community was active in serving the needy and sick.

In 1850 California's first Jewish cemetery was established at Chevra Kaddisha (Home of Peace Cemetery) at 33rd and K streets. In 1849 John Sutter had established Sacramento's first cemetery–New Helvetia Cemetery, which stood on present-day Alhambra Boulevard between I and J streets where Sutter Middle School is located. When the bodies buried here were exhumed and moved in 1955-56, city officials expected to find 1,500 bodies, but were shocked when remains of 5,235 people were found–some in mass graves. It is surmised that the mass burials took place during the cholera epidemics of 1850 and 1852.

In 1849 Sutter and H. A. Schoolcraft had donated a total of 28 acres for the establishment of another cemetery–the Sacramento City Cemetery. Today the Historic City Cemetery, located on Broadway, remains the final resting place for such Sacramento pioneers as John A. Sutter, Jr., the first mayor, Hardin Bigelow; Judge and Mrs. Edwin Bryant Crocker, founders of the Crocker Art Gallery; Mark Hopkins, co-builder of the Central Pacific Railroad; Reverend O. C. Wheeler, organizer of the First Baptist Church; and the third governor of California, John Bigler.

Sacramento's first newspaper, *The Placer Times*, was first printed at Sutter's Fort in April 1849. Several other newspapers were being published in 1850, including the *Sacramento Transcript*, the *Settlers & Miners Tribune*, and the *Index*, Sacramento's first afternoon paper. *The Sacramento Union* would begin publication in March 1851 (and continue through January 14, 1994). Sacramento's current daily newspaper, *The Sacramento Bee*, was started in 1857 as *The Daily Bee*, joining the 50 to 60 other publications available at the time.

C. T. H. Palmer had established the first private school at the corner of Third and I streets in 1849, but he closed it after one month. There would be no public school in Sacramento until 1854.

Mining Camps

Mormon Bar had been the site of the second major gold strike made less than two months after James Marshall's discovery at Coloma in late January 1848. Gold was discovered by two members of the Mormon Battalion employed by Sutter to build a flourmill. Sam Brannan, as a Mormon leader, took advantage of the discovery by demanding a royalty of one-third on all the gold taken out at Mormon Bar and he immediately established a store here. (It was nuggets from this site rather than from Coloma that Brannan held high as he walked across Portsmouth Square in San Francisco exclaiming, "Gold, gold, gold, from the American River.")

Several anti Mormon Missouri pioneers soon arrived and Mormon Bar was divided between the two groups. The Missouri pioneers included Nicholas Carriger, Joseph Wardlow, Elias Graham, and Henry Thornton. Miners excavated a canal across the bar, forming an island–Mormon Island. A fire in 1856 would destroy most of the island that had a population of 2,500 at one time; it never was rebuilt. Situated on the South Fork of the American River, Mormon Island was inundated by Folsom Lake in 1955.

Negro Bar had been mined by African Americans in 1849.[17] It would become the town of Folsom in 1855–named after its founder, Joseph L. Folsom. As noted previously, the eastern terminus of the Sacramento Valley Railroad, the first train west of the Rockies, arrived in 1855, linking mining camps with riverboats in Sacramento.

Numerous other mining camps were located further down the American River towards Sacramento. Between 1849 and 1854 mail was delivered between mining camps along the American River by Pioneer Express riders.

Two men from Michigan founded Michigan Bar in 1849 along the Cosumnes River. The introduction of hydraulic mining would destroy most of the original town site where 1,500 lived in the early 1850s. A number of other short-lived towns developed near Michigan Bar, including Cook's Bar, which was founded in 1849 by Dennis Cook.

Sacramento County Ranchos

Of the seven ranchos granted in Sacramento County, *Rancho Omochumnes* was the most interesting. A partnership formed by Jared Sheldon and William Daylor acquired this rancho in 1844. They erected a gristmill in 1846-47 on the Cosumnes River where they milled wheat for Sutter. Jared Sheldon built a house in 1850 that he called "Slough House." It was located near Deer Creek, which was called a slough at the time, and became an inn and roadside stagecoach stop on the way to the hills. The original hotel burned in 1890, but it was reconstructed that same year and is a restaurant today called the Sloughhouse Inn.

Sheldon got along well with the many Native Americans still residing in the area, but he would become involved in a serious confrontation with miners in 1851 when the dam he built to provide water for his mill flooded their claims. He and two others lost their lives in the ensuing battle. (Sheldon's dam was washed away in the floods of 1851-52.)

James Hall opened the Old Elk Grove Hotel in 1850 on the site of present-day Elk Grove. It was named for the Missouri town where he had lived before leaving for California. The hotel would burn down in 1857.

Chism Cooper Fuggitt founded the town of Liberty in 1850 on the edge of *Rancho Zanjon de los Moquelumnes*. Located seven miles east of New Hope Landing on the Mokelumne River, it had been a perfect stopover place for teamsters on their way to the gold fields. Liberty would be absorbed when Galt was founded nearby in 1869.

Other Facts About Early Sacramento County

The numerous Delta islands that lie within Sacramento County today did not exist as such in 1850; high tides regularly flooded them. The first levees were built on Grand Island in 1850, which soon became a profitable potato and cabbage field for Armstead Runyon, Reuben Kercehval, and James Collins.

The state capital would be established at Sacramento in 1854. The current capitol building was not built until 1861-74, and was completely renovated between 1975 and 1982 to reflect how it appeared at the turn-of-the-century.

Between 1860 and 1861 (for 18 months), the Pony Express would terminate its runs from Missouri in present-day Old Sacramento. However, when the first transcontinental telegraph was received in 1861, there no longer was a need for the Pony Express.[18]

The widow of Judge Edwin Bryant Crocker, Margaret Rhodes Crocker, would deed the Crocker art collection to the city of Sacramento in 1885. The Crocker Art Museum became the first art gallery west of the Mississippi. Sacramento gained the distinction of being called the "Camellia Capital of the World" when the first shipment of camellias arrived from the East Coast in 1852.

SACRAMENTO COUNTY RANCHOS

NAME OF RANCHO	GRANTEE AND/OR 1850 OWNER	1850 AND/OR CURRENT SITES
Rancho Zanjon de los Moquelumnes (Deep Slough of the Mokelumne)	Anastacio Chabolla family	Elk Grove
Rancho Cosumnes	Heleno	Wilton, Cosumnes
Rancho Omochumnes	William Daylor, Jared Sheldon	Sheldon, Sloughhouse
Rancho Río de los Americanos (River of the Americans)	Captain Joseph L. Folsom	Folsom, Gold River, Rancho Cordova
Rancho San Juan	Joel P. Dedmond	Antelope, Citrus Heights, Fair Oaks, Orangevale, Carmichael
Rancho del Paso (Of the Ford or Passage)	Samuel Norris	Rio Linda, Del Paso Heights, Gibson Ranch County Park, Sacramento, Cal Expo
Rancho Nueva Helvetia (New Switzlerland)	John A. Sutter	Sacramento; larger portion was located in Sutter and Yuba counties

Notes ⟋ SACRAMENTO COUNTY

1

See Sutter sidebar on page 226.

2

See Brannan sidebar on page 127.

3

The California State Indian Museum is also located on the grounds of the Sutter's Fort State Historic Park. This museum offers one of the most complete collections of California Indian relics and greatly enhances one's appreciation of California's earliest social and cultural history.

4

Many of California's major events of the 1840s occurred at Sutter's Fort. The Mexican leader General Mariano Vallejo was imprisoned here during the Bear Flag Revolt; Captain John C. Frémont and his troops stayed here for awhile; survivors of the Donner party straggled in here after their tragic ordeal in the Sierra snows; and James Marshall brought Sutter the news of his discovery of gold at Sutter's sawmill in Coloma.

5

Lieutenant Gabriel Moraga had discovered the Sacramento River on an expedition from Mission San José in 1808. He named the river and surrounding area Sacramento in honor of the Holy Sacrament or "Lord's Supper." Several later expeditions explored the river area in the early 1800s, including Jedediah Strong Smith's in 1828. Smith had blazed the Sacramento Trail for trade and immigration north up the Sacramento River, eventually reaching Fort Vancouver in Canada.

6

In 1851 the State Legislature would vote to drop "City" from Sacramento's name.

7

See Burnett sidebar on page 137.

8

George V. Cooper was one of the first to illustrate the Sacramento embarcadero in 1849. More than 100 years later, his lithograph would serve as the basis for some of the restoration work for the Old Sacramento State Historic Park. Today one of the copies of the lithograph hangs in the Wells Fargo History Museum in Old Sacramento.

9

Fires in April and November 1850 and the Great Fire of November 2, 1852 that left 90 percent of the city in ashes are the reasons for the lack of any pre-1852 structures. As the business center of town moved closer to the Capitol at 10th and L streets, the original town site became a slum. When the State decided to build a freeway through the old district in the 1960s, historians were successful at forging a compromise to save as many of the historically important buildings as possible. Old Sacramento was dedicated as a National Historic Landmark in 1965.

10

In 1976 Sacramento was the only city in California to win an award in the first annual Tree City USA contest sponsored by the National Arbor Day Foundation. Sacramento has since won other similar awards.

11

The Sacramento riverfront began to decline in the 1870s, primarily because the railroad replaced the need for river travel. Also, silt from the hydraulic mining upstream substantially decreased the river's depth, thus preventing the big steamboats from being able to navigate the waters between Sacramento and San Francisco Bay.

12

George McDougal, the brother of John McDougal, the second governor of California, was the first to convert a ship into a store.

13

Charles Crocker, one of Sacramento's pioneers, had arrived in California in 1850, but he would not leave the mines to settle in Sacramento and open a store until 1852. He later developed a strong business relationship with Mark Hopkins, Collis P. Huntington, and Leland Stanford, who together came to be known as "The Big Four" for the part they played in the rapid economic development of the state. The Central Pacific Railroad they built began in Sacramento and crossed the Sierra Nevada mountains in order to join the Union Pacific from Nebraska in Promontory, Utah. The first transcontinental railroad was completed in 1869.

14

Sacramento was the first California public entity to erect an edifice and machinery for supplying the fire department and residents with water. Before this, William E. Henry had been pumping water from the river and selling it in buckets, which he delivered door-to-door. Another man sold buckets filled with water he pumped from the Sutter Slough. William Henry became the city's first waterworks superintendent.

15

Even after building the first levee along the Sacramento River and rebuilding and raising it in 1854 following the floods of 1852 and 1853, the threat of flooding and all its disastrous results would prompt Sacramentans to undertake the task of elevating the entire city by filling in the streets with dirt and converting the second floors of two-story buildings into the ground levels of the buildings. The phenomenal engineering task was completed in the 1870s and cobblestones were quarried from the Folsom area to pave the new streets. Old Sacramento businesses located in basements today, as well as sunken alleys, attest to the original location of the streets five to twelve feet below what they are today. The high wooden sidewalks were another step taken to adapt to annual flooding conditions.

16

See Frémont sidebar on page 253.

17

Giant dredges were used on the west side of Folsom as late as 1962 and created some of the most extensive rock tailings anywhere in California.

18

The California State Telegraph Co. had been transmitting messages between Marysville, Sacramento, Stockton, and the San Francisco Bay Area since 1853.

The state capital would be established at Sacramento in 1854. The current State Capitol was not built until 1861-74, and was completely renovated between 1975 and 1982 to reflect its appearance at the turn-of-the-century.

JANICE MARSCHNER
THE AUTHOR

Janice Marschner is a California native and has lived in various parts of northern California throughout her life. She has criss-crossed California in her travels, enjoying the backroads and marveling at the state's natural beauty and variety of landscapes.

Janice is a graduate of the University of California, Davis with a degree in International Relations and the California State University, Sacramento with a Masters in Public Policy and Administration. She has spent the past eleven years working in California state government, first as an administrative assistant to a state senator and more recently as an analyst for the California Trade and Commerce Agency and the Employment Development Department.

Janice lives in the Sacramento area with her husband Jeff, enjoying the empty nest after raising two children.

For additional purchases of:

California 1850 - A Snapshot in Time

See Internet page: www.CAL1850.com or contact

Coleman Ranch Press: 1-877-7OLDCAL (toll free)

P.O. Box 1496, Sacramento, CA 95812-1496